THE RED BERET

First published in Great Britain by Michael Joseph Ltd. in 1950
First Four Square edition 1961
Reprinted 1965
Reissued in this NEL edition 1968

*

NEW EDITION DECEMBER 1971
Reprinted April 1973
Reissued in this New Edition May 1975

*

NEL Books are published by New English Library Limited from Barnard's Inn, Holborn, London, EC1. Made and printed in Great Britain by Love & Malcomson Ltd., Redhill, Surrey.

45002717 1

The Red Beret

HILARY ST. GEORGE SAUNDERS

NEW ENGLISH LIBRARY
TIMES MIRROR

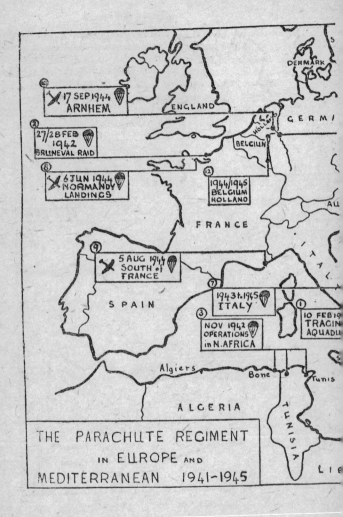

THE PARACHUTE REGIMENT
in EUROPE and
MEDITERRANEAN 1941-1945

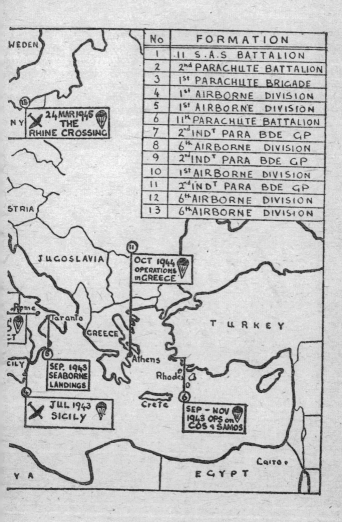

No	FORMATION
1	11 S.A.S BATTALION
2	2nd PARACHUTE BATTALION
3	1st PARACHUTE BRIGADE
4	1st AIRBORNE DIVISION
5	1st AIRBORNE DIVISION
6	11th PARACHUTE BATTALION
7	2nd INDt PARA BDE GP
8	6th AIRBORNE DIVISION
9	2nd INDt PARA BDE GP
10	1st AIRBORNE DIVISION
11	2nd INDt PARA BDE GP
12	6th AIRBORNE DIVISION
13	6th AIRBORNE DIVISION

WEDEN

NY

24 MAR 1945
THE
RHINE CROSSING

STRIA

JUGOSLAVIA

OCT 1944
OPERATIONS
in GREECE

Rome

Taranto

GREECE

TURKEY

SEP. 1943
SEABORNE
LANDINGS

Athens

CILY

Rhodes

JUL 1943
SICILY

Crete

SEP - NOV
1943 OPS on
COS & SAMOS

Cairo

YA

EGYPT

This record of the exploits of the
Parachute Regiment has been set down
'to encourage all valorous hearts and
to show them honourable examples'

Author's Preface

THIS is the story of the Parachute Regiment, of the officers, non-commissioned officers and men, drawn from almost every unit of the British Army, who volunteered to reach the field of battle by a novel and unique method. They were the first to wear the Red Beret, and to earn for themselves the name of the 'Red Devils', bestowed upon them in North Africa by an enemy who had good cause to fear their prowess. They were not, however, the only members of the British Army to wear this distinguished headgear. Those who dropped with them belonging to the Royal Engineers, the Royal Artillery, the Royal Corps of Signals, the Royal Army Service Corps and the Royal Army Medical Corps and those who went to battle in gliders also wore it and added lustre to its fame. Their story will, I hope, one day be told, when the facts have been collected and are available.

This story which, as I have said, concerns only the Parachute Regiment, does not pretend to be complete, for it does not record every single deed performed by the units and individual members of the regiment. As one of its officers said to me when I was writing it, 'I hope your record will show what sort of people we were'. I have tried to do so, and in this honourable task I have been greatly aided by Lieutenant-General Sir Richard N. Gale, K.B.E., C.B., D.S.O., M.C., Major-Generals E. E. Down, C.B., C.B.E., G. W. Lathbury, C.B., D.S.O., M.B.E., R. E. Urquhart, C.B., D.S.O., Brigadiers S. J. L. Hill, D.S.O., M.C., J. H. N. Poett, D.S.O., E. W. C. Flavell, D.S.O., M.C., C. H. V. Pritchard, D.S.O., Colonels J. W. Hackett, D.S.O., M.B.E., M.C., K. T. Darling, D.S.O., O.B.E., Lieutenant-Colonels P. J. Luard, D.S.O., O.B.E., A. S. Pearson, D.S.O., M.C., N. Crookenden, D.S.O., D. R. Hunter, M.C., T. B. H. Otway, D.S.O., J. D. Frost, D.S.O., M.C., Majors E. J. Warren, D.S.O., B. W. Briggs, M.C., J. R. D. Mayne, C. G. Lea, the late Captain J. A. Young, and the late Major R. A. Keene, M.C., and Corporal F. Newhouse who typed much of the material upon which the narrative is based. My thanks in equal measure

7

are due to Group Captain M. A. Newnham, O.B.E., D.F.C., for permission to quote from his book, *Prelude to Glory*.

I must also thank His Majesty's Stationery Office for permission to make use of the official publication *By Air to Battle* of which I am the author, and Sidgwick and Jackson for giving me permission to quote from the *Collected Poems of Richard Spender*.

Finally, I should like to thank my friend Geoffrey Throckmorton, C.B., for his indefatigable labours.

HILARY ST. GEORGE SAUNDERS

'These Terrible Men'

ON 15th February 1941 passengers and staff in the railway station of Naples were given the opportunity to observe a small column of men dressed in bedraggled, dun-coloured uniforms of an unfamiliar pattern. They were marching one behind the other and each was connected with his neighbour by a length of rusty chain to which a heavy iron cannon ball was attached. Under Fascist rule such a sight was by no means uncommon; but these prisoners wore their chains with a difference. They clanked them ostentatiously, and as they did so they laughed aloud. What men were these who jested thus with gyves upon their wrists? The word went swiftly from mouth to mouth: 'British parachutists just captured. Where? In Apulia they say. It is swarming with them.' So, according to bystanders interrogated long afterwards, the rumour spread, fostered by that tendency to exaggerate bad news which afflicts all people at war and the Italians more than most, and by the sinister report, soon proved true, that the number of parachutes picked up exceeded the number of prisoners by about forty.

Some of 'these terrible men' were still at large then, roaming the countryside seeking, like the lion of Scripture, whom they might devour. Many days went by before it was borne in on the Italian authorities that in an operation involving parachute troops stores and weapons were dropped as well as men and that not every parachute, therefore, supported a soldier.

The men who tramped that day, manacled, through the echoing railway station towards an irksome captivity belonged to the 11th Special Air Service Battalion and the adventure which had brought them to this pass had begun a month before.

The officers and other ranks composing the battalion had by then been training for more than six months, mostly at Ringway near Manchester, and they were showing signs of boredom. All were volunteers, all had seen active service for the most part during the disastrous campaign which had ended in the withdrawal from Dunkirk, all had jumped many times; and still action tarried and the more impatient among them had grown

9

tired of waiting. 'In driblets,' records Lieutenant-Colonel Cleasby-Thompson, the historian of those early days, 'men began to ask for return to unit.' They were tired of shewing off before generals and cabinet ministers in exercises in which the risk of possible injury and therefore of being excluded from battle was very real. There was fighting in the stony wastes west of the Egyptian border and their regiments were in the thick of it. They wished to march to the sound of the guns. Small parties of them, good men every one, began to slip away ; nor could their commanding officer say them nay. Patience is not a notable virtue of the young warrior, and it needed both patience and imagination in the dreary winter of 1941 to foresee the day when a whole division would fall upon the foe from the sky as dawn came up behind Ranville and flooded with light the green meadows of Normandy.

Then one day in January a sudden whisper or 'buzz' went round the camp. Something was about to happen. Men awaiting return to their regiments applied to remain with the Parachute Wing and 'a long queue of parachute soldiers formed outside the orderly room each man ready with some ingenious reason to prove that he at least was indispensable' to the success of whatever was in the wind. The commanding officer, Lieutenant-Colonel C. I. A. Jackson, Royal Tank Regiment, paraded the battalion and informed them that an operation which might involve very deep penetration into enemy territory was being planned. He added that it was unlikely that any arrangements would be made for the 'extraction' of what he tersely described as the 'survivors' and that it was by no means certain that, though they would be wearing uniform, the enemy would not regard them as spies and treat them as such. He ended by calling for volunteers. Every officer and man of the five hundred on parade stepped forward.

Operation 'Colossus' was to be the destruction of an aqueduct in Southern Italy. It crossed a small stream, the Tragino, at a point some thirty miles east-north-east of the little town of Salverno in the province of Campania which forms part of the ankle of Italy. The aqueduct carries the main water supply for the province of Apulia, inhabited by some two million Italians who live for the most part in Taranto, Brindisi, Bari, and other towns. To deprive them for a month at least of their regular water supply and compel them to fall back on what was available in the local reservoirs would, it was hoped, create alarm and despondency, and it was thought that this might even have an effect on the two main theatres of war in which the Italian forces were then fighting, North Africa and Albania.

Such, at least, were the alleged reasons for the proposed attack. They were somewhat specious, but provided an adequate excuse for what, in fact, was to be an experiment. Were British parachute troops below, up to, or above the standard of their continental rivals? Was their equipment satisfactory? And their weapons? Could the Royal Air Force take them to the right spot and arrive at the right time? These were some of the questions to which, it was hoped, the raid would supply the answers.

The numbers finally detailed to form 'X' Troop, into which those chosen for the operation were formed, were small, seven officers and thirty-one other ranks. Three interpreters were included. One was an R.A.F. officer, Squadron Leader Lucky, M.C., another Private Nastri of the Rifle Brigade, and the third an Italian from the Savoy Hotel, London, called Fortunato Picchi. 'X' Troop was commanded by Major T. A. G. Pritchard,[1] Royal Welch Fusiliers, and included a party of sappers under Captain G. F. K. Daly, Royal Engineers.

For six weeks they trained while six Whitleys of Bomber Command, under the command of Wing Commander J. B. Tate, were prepared for the operation. One fatal accident took place during this period, Lance-Sergeant Dennis being blown by the wind to fall into an ice-covered pond. Here he stuck fast in the mud and, though a strong swimmer, was not able to free himself and was drowned. On 1st February a full-scale model erected in Tatton Park of that part of the aqueduct to be attacked was assaulted. Once again the wind made conditions difficult and several men 'were blown into high trees where they remained suspended by their parachutes until retrieved by the Knutsford Fire Brigade'. Such mishaps only served as a spur, and 'a more courageous group of men', records Group Captain Newnham, who watched their training, 'and a more determined leader would have been hard to find'.

On 24th January Lieutenant A. J. Deane-Drummond, Royal Corps of Signals, left for Malta in a Sunderland flying boat to organise the arrangements for the raid from what was to be its point of departure.

At dusk on 7th February all was ready. 'X' Troop entered the Whitleys at Mildenhall and, flying through the night, arrived safely at Malta after a flight of nearly one thousand six hundred miles, much of it over occupied France, a notable feat at

[1] Now Lieutenant-Colonel Pritchard, D.S.O., M.B.E.

that stage of the war. The next day the first air photographs of the objective were produced. They had been taken that morning by Flying Officer A. Warburton, D.S.O., D.F.C., a famous member of the Photographic Reconnaissance Unit. The pictures disclosed not one but two aqueducts, situated 'in wild and desolate country'. They were of unequal size and about two hundred yards apart. It was decided to attack the larger of the two.

In the meanwhile, despite Jackson's forebodings, arrangements were being made to bring back the members of 'X' Troop after they had accomplished their task. His Majesty's Submarine *Triumph* was ordered by the Admiralty to be lying off the mouth of the River Sele on the night of 15th-16th February. Since the operation was due to take place on 10th-11th, it was hoped that the parachute troops would have ample time to reach the rendezvous on foot, for, though the country was mountainous, the distance to be traversed was not more than fifty miles.

By the afternoon of 10th February the last preparations had been made, and at dusk eight Whitleys took off from Malta, six freighted with parachute troops and two with bombs. These last were to create a diversion by attacking the railway yards at Foggia, the most important in Southern Italy, and it was confidently—and, as it turned out rightly—hoped that the Italians would believe that these yards were the target for the whole force.

The weather was excellent. The aircraft crossed the Italian coast in a clear sky, and when the target was reached, the aqueduct was easily seen standing out sharply in the bright moonlight. The first Whitley, with Deane-Drummond on board, reached the dropping zone at 21.42 hours some twelve minutes late, a very small margin of error. The drop was made from four hundred feet and he and some of his men landed within two hundred and fifty yards of the objective. The rest of the 'stick' were not much farther away and all at once set about collecting the containers carrying the demolition charges and other material dropped at the same time but more scattered. Four of the following Whitleys arrived according to plan and dropped the covering party and some engineers, though not quite so accurately, one stick landing in a dry river bed and another some three-quarters of a mile away. The sixth Whitley went astray and its pilot spent three-quarters of an hour searching in vain for the aqueduct. It eventually dropped its parachute troops in the next valley, too far away to be of any use. This was unfortunate, for they consisted of Daly and more engineers.

To aid in the collection of the containers Pritchard and his men made use of some dozen farm hands discovered in a house nearby. 'Docile and obedient, these Italian hinds trudged off to their task, one of them remarking that nothing ever happened in that part of the world and that he would now have enough to talk about for the rest of his life.'

Captain C. G. Lea, Lancashire Fusiliers, was in charge of the covering party, which included Sergeants Clements and Lawlay. They took up positions round the aqueduct and in so doing discovered the Genestra, a small tributary to the main stream. This they crossed by a rough wooden bridge, which was at once prepared for demolition.

In the absence of Daly, Pritchard ordered Paterson and such sappers as were available, including Sergeant Drury, Royal Engineers, to carry out the work of demolishing as much of the aqueduct as possible. Two containers had failed, through icing, to leave the aircraft, and the amount of explosive available was therefore smaller than it might have been. More serious, the piers of the aqueduct were found to be made, not of brick as Paterson had been led to expect from the details supplied by the London engineering firm which had suggested the target, but of concrete, a more stubborn substance. He had eight hundred pounds of explosive at his disposal, and, after examining the western-most pier, decided to place six hundred and forty pounds against it and one hundred and sixty against its abutment. At 00.30 hours all was ready and Pritchard fired a warning detonator as a signal for all except the demolition party to withdraw from the neighbourhood of the aqueduct and seek shelter some four hundred yards away behind a small spur. This they did, first shepherding the peasants into farm buildings near the wooden bridge over the Genestra. The Italians were told that to leave the building would mean death, for a sentry with orders to shoot at sight had been posted outside the door. No such order was, in fact, given; but the threat, not unnaturally in the circumstances, sufficed.

'A sixty-second fuse was then lit,' says Pritchard, 'and the demolition party hurriedly joined the main body.

'After waiting for seventy-five seconds, in considerable tenseness, Paterson . . . and myself walked towards the aqueduct to examine the presumably faulty fuse.

'When we had covered one hundred and fifty yards there was

13

what I can only describe as "the Father and Mother" of an explosion, as the one thousand pounds odd of gun cotton charges were in fact detonated with the usual accompaniment of flash, concussion and shower of debris.

'Picking ourselves up again, we ran down to the aqueduct, followed closely by the others. We were all almost inarticulate with a variety of emotions; the dominating fact was that half the aqueduct was down, and from the what seemed colossal square breaches in the concrete water runway a rush of water was pouring down the Tragino Valley, both from the northern end, from which direction water was being pumped, and from the higher southern end, where the breach resulted in the water running back, to spill out and join the northern flow.

'So great was our delight, relief, call it what you will, that what happened thereafter did not really matter very much, as the job was done.'

Almost at the same moment the wooden bridge discovered by Deane-Drummond blew up, pieces of it crashing on to the roofs of the farm buildings and adding to the general depression inside.

It was now time to withdraw. The news that a submarine would be awaiting them at the mouth of the River Sele was broken to the men by their officers who had alone been entrusted with this very secret information. After leaving one man who had broken his ankle on landing in the care of a local farmer, who promised to do his best for him, 'X' Troop formed up into three parties commanded respectively by Pritchard, Lea and Second Lieutenant G. Jowett, Highland Light Infantry, and, abandoning its heavy equipment, began its march to the coast. It was then about 01.00 hours in the morning of 11th February. The three parties had, therefore, four days and nights in which to reach their destination, but the difficulties and perils facing them were many. They were alone in a strange, desolate, mountainous land, two thousand feet above sea-level; their feat, which would certainly be known far and wide before many hours had passed, would rouse the whole country; they were wearing British uniforms, were lightly armed and had very little ammunition. Their best, their only chance, thought Pritchard, was to move by night and to lie up during the day. That first night all went well. Each party was given a different route to the prearranged rendezvous, and separated after moving off from the aqueduct. The story of Pritchard's party, now given, is an account of how that party fared. Lea's party had similar

14

experiences. Jowett's party attempted to shoot its way out of an ambush, but was also baulked by civilians. Under the guidance of their commanding officer they climbed to the snow line on a nearby mountain, skirted it and shortly before dawn reached a small, wooded valley in which Pritchard's party hid themselves for the day. After a time a number of children appeared and began to play there but did not discover the weary men lying behind bushes and in the damp scrub.

That night they set out again, 'following the flank of the mountains', until they came to the River Sele, across which they passed, unseen, by a bridge. The going below the snow line became very bad, as off the tracks and roads the ground was ankle-deep in mud. Walking across-country, therefore, merely resulted in leaving an easy trail for the Italians to follow in the daylight. This, coupled with the incessant barking of watch dogs which are an integral part of Italian country life forced the party to take to roads as often as possible. Now the good fortune which had up till then befriended them began to desert them. Pritchard's intention was to hide in a wood shewn on his map as 'crowning the summit of the Cresta di Gallo—in English the Cock's comb'. Unfortunately the wood had been cut down and the parachutists, pushing higher and higher through the chilly darkness, presently found themselves still walking through mud and snow, with nothing around them by way of cover but rocks and tree-stumps. Behind these and in a small cave they hid as best they could while dawn climbed the sky.

For some time nothing happened. Then a farmer, attracted by the traces of their footsteps clearly visible, appeared and discovered them. He ran to a nearby village and gave the alarm. Pritchard and his men did what they could to prepare a defence ; but their resources were very small and they knew that they would be unable to hold out for long. In the event, they were spared the necessity of fighting, for the Italians were taking no avoidable risks. Surrounded, the parachutists lay in the snow that winter morning and watched the preparations for their capture with growing interest and some bewilderment. In the van of the assault were three hunting dogs, pointers, the forerunners of a motley pack of village curs. After them streamed the village children, hotly pursued by their mothers, 'who cried to them to come back immediately, and behind the mothers were the fathers issuing similar orders to their wives'. Last of all and well in the rear a body of troops advanced with a number of *carabinieri*. To open fire would have placed the women and children in grave danger. 'Pritchard had no choice but to surrender.'

So the adventure ended in farce, or at least broad comedy, which nearly turned to tragedy when some Fascist militia arrived and announced their intention of shooting Pritchard and his men as spies. Fortunately the Italian general officer commanding the district intervened at a later stage and ordered them to be treated as prisoners of war.

Meanwhile Captain Daly and the five men with him, who had landed in the wrong valley, were also seeking the coast. A few minutes after they had touched earth the sound of explosions not very far off told them that their comrades had fulfilled the mission. They set out, and in three nights covered thirty-two of the fifty miles separating them from their goal. By dawn on the 15th they were very short of food and suffering from a grievous lack of sleep. But they could not rest, for the next night the *Triumph*, they believed, awaited them, and they had still eighteen miles to go. These would have, of necessity, to be traversed in daylight, but they began their march, buoyed up with the knowledge that this was the last lap. All went well until about eleven in the morning when they encountered a mixed force of soldiers and police with some civilian hangers-on. Daly, through his interpreter, the brave and resolute Picchi, at once took a high line. They were, he said, German airmen on special duty and it was essential for them to reach Naples by 14.00 hours. Transport must be provided.

For a moment this bluff seemed to be succeeding, for several of the civilians went off to fetch the mayor of the village. He, however, was less amenable and at once demanded papers of identity. Daly had none and had to confess as much. At once the mayor went into action. The parachutists were handcuffed and chained together and in this condition they arrived at Naples, where, as has been recorded, their laughter aroused the wonder and forebodings of the bystanders. Threats of death ensued ; but eventually they suffered the fate of Pritchard and his men and were led off to captivity. All but Picchi. He was handed over to the Fascist militia, briskly tortured, court-martialled and shot. He remained silent to the end.

Even if the various parties had been able to reach the mouth of the Sele, 'disappointment, not a submarine, would have awaited them'. Two of the eight Whitleys which took off from Malta were, it will be remembered, ordered to bomb Foggia. One succeeded, the other developed engine trouble. Its pilot sent out a signal that he was about to make a forced landing. By a coincidence no novelist would dare to use he chose the sandy mouth of the River Sele. He had no idea that a day or two later a British submarine would be lying off that place, for no one except Pritchard and his officers knew of this intention. His signal placed the British High Command in a most difficult position. It had almost certainly been picked up by the listening services of the enemy. That, at least, had to be assumed, and it had been sent in the ordinary code which was relatively easy to decipher. Thus it seemed not only probable but almost certain that Italian police and armed forces would arrive at the mouth of the River Sele about the same time as 'X' Troop and H.M.S. *Triumph*. What was to be done? On the one hand there was a handful of highly trained parachutists to be rescued, on the other a submarine with a highly trained crew which would be gravely endangered. The decision was hard ; but it would have been given in favour of an attempt at rescue had there been the slightest chance of success. A dispassionate weighing of the odds, however, shewed that there was none. No submarine was, therefore, sent.

Operation 'Colossus' had very little effect on the war either in Albania or North Africa. Nor did the dwellers of Apulia suffer much material inconvenience, for the aqueduct was repaired before the local reservoir was dry. The moral effect, however, was great. Alarm and consternation spread even to the North of Italy, and in the area itself the lives of the inhabitants were made a burden to them by the imposition of new and severe regulations which included the most stringent air-raid and anti-parachutist precautions. These were still in force more than two years later when Italy surrendered. The Italian press and other organs of propaganda made light of the raid, but as usual, when so doing, fell into some confusion. Radio Roma went so far as to remark that 'it was impossible to conceal the fact that military circles considered the attempt a complete failure'. Why concealment of this view should have been thought necessary was not explained.

Whatever effect the raid produced on Italy, in Britain it was hailed with sober joy and restrained but unmistakable enthusiasm. That it was but a pin-prick most were well aware ; just as they knew equally well that it was a portent. The British Army possessed parachute troops. They had been in action. They would be in action again, and though the shape of things to come was hardly yet visible, to the eyes of imagination its

17

outline was beginning to appear. How this early promise was in due course fulfilled, how the Parachute Regiment with their comrades, borne in gliders, of the air-landing brigades, became a puissant force exercising decisive influence on great events and issues, must now be told.

The Men and the Means

THE BEGINNING of the airborne forces of Great Britain, and therefore of the Parachute Regiment, can be dated with precision. On 22nd June 1940 General Ismay, head of the Military Wing of the War Cabinet Secretariat, received a brief instruction from the Prime Minister, Mr. Winston Churchill, ordering the formation by the War Office of 'a corps of at least five thousand parachute troops'. The Prime Minister's decision had not been unexpected by the Air Ministry, for early in that month it had called the inevitable conference which had produced a very secret memorandum stating 'it has been decided to establish a parachute training centre'. The place chosen to be its home was Ringway, the civil airport of Manchester, a spot well removed from any centre of operations but not blessed with a very equable climate. Since, however, the parachute troops would have to go into action in all but the worst weather, this was not of the first consequence, though the number of days in the year when flying was impossible was so large that much valuable time was lost. Here, what was at first called 'The Central Landing School' was set up in June and endowed with six 'venerable' Whitley aircraft. It was staffed by the Army and the Royal Air Force working in close co-operation. That, at least, was the theory, but practice lagged behind; the prescience of the Prime Minister did not extend to the higher ranks of the staff either in the War Office or the Air Ministry. The first contented themselves with appointing Major J. F. Rock, Royal Engineers, 'to take charge of the military organization of British airborne forces'. Of what these were to consist, how they were to be trained and what were to be their weapons the War Office appeared to have no notion, for, as Rock recorded in his diary, 'it was impossible to get any information as to policy or task'.

The Air Ministry was obstructive, and considerable opposition to parachute or glider-borne soldiers was not slow to shew itself, one senior officer sadly observing that 'it will be necessary to cover in six months the ground the Germans have covered in six years'. Such a feat was to prove entirely possible ; but at the time, the summer of 1940, when invasion seemed imminent and when the resources of both services were stretched far beyond all normal limits, the task of preparing the delivery of a counter-stroke by new and still experimental means seemed not only uncongenial but a direct contravention of the sound principle, 'first things first'.

About this time the Commandos were also being formed, and this circumstance had a fortunate effect on the development of the Central Landing School. The means by which these new formations were to go into battle were to be varied, and at the time it was strongly held, especially by their commander, Admiral of the Fleet Sir Roger Keyes, that one of them should be aircraft. To make use of the air necessarily involved the training of parachute troops, and it was decided that No. 2 Commando should be composed of these. From this decision, never implemented, for the airborne forces soon outgrew the limits of one Commando, the beginnings of the Parachute Regiment may be said to date.

The creation of the Central Landing Establishment, into which the School was transformed in August, brought to the new enterprise a degree of order and stability not unneeded. Rock had been working with Squadron Leader L. A. Strange. D.S.O., M.C., D.F.C., who was responsible for everything to do with the air side of the problem, and this system of dual control had not proved very happy. The functions and duties of the two men, both of the highest ability and filled with the zeal of pioneers, were now properly defined. Strange was to concern himself with parachute training, Rock with the military require-ments of airborne warfare. The Establishment, belonging as it did to the Royal Air Force, was put under the command of Group Captain L. G. Harvey, with whom were soon associated Wing Commander Sir Nigel Norman, Bart., C.B.E., and Squadron Leader Maurice Newnham,[1] D.F.C., who took over the parachute training side of the Central Landing Establishment in May 1941.

Up till September 1940 the Central Landing Establishment had had a chequered career. On 13th July the first parachute drop

[1] Later Group Captain Newnham, O.B.E., D.F.C.

19

was made by the 'pull off' method in which the jumper crouched on an inadequate platform fashioned by removing half the rear gun turret of a Whitley, pulled the ripcord and was whirled instantly into space. This method was for a time considered by Rock and Strange to be the easiest way of introducing a new-comer to parachute jumping. It was in fact far from being so and was abruptly discontinued when on 25th July the parachute of Driver Evans, Royal Army Service Corps, failed to open and he fell to his death, the first fatal casualty of the Parachute Regiment, then still No. 2 Commando. He was a victim of the phenomenon, always to be dreaded, known as 'a Roman Candle' in which the parachute leaves the bag but fails to fill with air and streams behind the jumper affording him no means of support.

The next mishap occurred when the steel bar above the hole in the fuselage, which provided an alternative exit from the Whitley, gave way and three dummies, whose static lines were attached to the bar, were precipitated into the void with unopened parachutes. The third accident, which also took place about this time, was the fouling of a Whitley's tail-wheel by the canopy of a parachute to which, most fortunately, only a dummy was attached. The pilot, Flight-Sergeant Bruton, made a success-ful landing, with the two-hundred-pound dummy trailing behind the aircraft 'like a big fish on the end of a line'.

These mischances, to give them no worse name, convinced Rock that the Whitley was a totally unsuitable aircraft for para-chute work, and he firmly refused to allow any more soldiers to jump from it unless he received written instructions from the War Office. These took a week to obtain and the reluctance of that Department to issue them was only surpassed by the obduracy of the Air Ministry. It refused to give way and turned a deaf ear to the somewhat plaintive demands of the War Office for Bombay aircraft, which 'would be much more suitable for training parachutists.' Bombays, it averred, were needed for the carriage of troops and stores; moreover, as operational aircraft they were useless for the proposed purpose. It must be Whitleys or nothing. The Prime Minister intervened, and on 14th August training with Whitleys began again. Subsequent experience shewed that the stand taken by the Air Ministry at that time was justified and indeed inevitable. The provision of aircraft with doors depended on the speed of production in America, and at that stage in the war priority could not be given to transport aircraft.

A streamlined spat was fitted over the tail-wheel of the Whitley to fend off any errant canopy, but the death of Trooper Watts, Royal Horse Guards, whose parachute failed to open, shewed that the problems of static lines and the stowage of parachutes had not yet been satisfactorily solved. The Bombay may have been a very slow aircraft, and its use at that time for other purposes may have been very important, but the fact remains that exit from it was by door and not by a hole in the floor, and that when Dakotas, in which the exit was also by a door, became at last available, this method of leaving was found far safer and more practical.

At the time that training first began there was in the archives of the War Office a report from a General Wavell, who had been present when twelve hundred men—headed by a general—a hundred and fifty machine guns and eighteen light field guns had been successfully dropped by the Russian Army during their summer manœuvres. 'If I had not witnessed the descents,' he wrote, 'I could not have believed such an operation possible.' The date of his report was 1936. What notice it had attracted is not known ; of action taken on it there had been none, and the British High Command entered the war unconscious of the existence of airborne troops or indifferent to their potentialities. Now when it was necessary to raise and train them, there was no one to shew how it was to be done. In 1940 Russia was to all appearances the friend of Germany ; the Moscow Pact was still in force and the Union of Socialist Soviet Republics did not become our ally until exactly a year from the day on which Winston Churchill ordered the raising of parachute troops.

Thus in this, as in so many other fields, the inspired amateur was given his head. He did his best, and if men's lives were lost it might be his misfortune ; it was certainly not his fault. He risked his own life time and again jumping to ascertain whether such and such a method of stowing the rigging lines in the packing-bag was foolproof or to discover the right speed and angle at which a Whitley should fly when men were dropping from its belly, to mention but two of the uncounted problems met with and solved by these empirical methods. 'Not enough credit seems to have been given by airborne forces to those men,' dryly records the historian of one of the parachute battalions. If that be so, here is the place to make amends. The early Royal Air Force pioneers very soon earned, and will always keep, the unbounded admiration of their colleagues in khaki. They dared all, not once but as many times as was necessary, often several

21

times a day. They can truly be said to be among the architects of the victories later achieved in Normandy and beyond the Rhine. In the autumn of 1940, however, these were far below the horizon and for many months the time-honoured process of trial and error, of which the English are strangely proud, was the order of each weary day. 'During the first six months of the Parachute School's existence—July to December 1940—some four or five hundred men were initiated and to some extent practised in the art of parachuting,' records Newnham. 'They were not trained parachutists to the standards that were established later because no really scientific technique for parachute flying or landing had been devised.' The fact was that it was not until by the inevitable process of trial and error the parachute itself and the method of using it had been modified that British parachute troops forged ahead. By learning how to jump at night and how to carry weapons and supplies in kit bags, they advanced the art of military parachuting to a point beyond that reached by similar troops in other countries.

Not all those in authority at Ringway began as amateurs. There were from the start a number of Royal Air Force instructors from the Establishment at Henlow where for some years before the war pilots had been put through a course of parachuting 'so that if ever they had to "bale out" in emergency they would know something about it'. On taking charge of the school at Ringway Strange very sensibly called on these men, experienced in the maintenance and behaviour of parachutes, to provide volunteers, and there presently arrived the formidable Flight-Sergeant—afterwards Wing Commander—Brereton and eight fabric workers. They were joined by Regimental Sergeant-Major Mansie, Lance-Sergeant Dawes and a number of non-commissioned officers from the Army Physical Training Corps, also volunteers. These formed the nucleus of what was soon to be a renowned and devoted band of instructors. Brereton was a man of great physical strength and was soon famous as a 'dispatcher', the man who gives the word to the pupil to go. Many owe their lives to him, not the least among them the young soldier who, having pulled the rip-cord, found himself still on the platform of the Whitley enveloped in the silken canopy of his parachute which had blown back on him. 'Brereton sat firmly on his chest until the Whitley made a landing and deposited them, shaken and bruised, but safe, on the airfield.' 'How well the veterans,' records Cleasby-Thompson, 'remember their first launching into space by . . . Brereton. He was six-foot full of sixteen stone and had played rugger for the R.A.F. He exuded confidence. "When I just touch you on the shoulder, step out," he would quietly say. At the precise moment he would take a full arm swing and the frightened and frozen victim would be jet-propelled through the door and nearly clear of the tail plane. Brereton understood parachutists and they liked and admired him.'

The instructors had to learn the art of jumping and this they did with speed and address, soon reaching a high standard of skill. They continued to be drawn both from the Army and Royal Air Force until October 1941, when it was decided that the school should be composed entirely of staff taken from the Physical Training Branch of the Royal Air Force. The instructors were put under the command of Flight-Lieutenant—afterwards Wing Commander—J. C. Kilkenny, O.B.E.; and before the war ended 'schoolmasters, professional footballers and boxers . . . a road cycle champion, a circus acrobat, a "Wall of Death" rider and a male dancer from the ballet had served in their ranks'. All saw active service, and by the end of 1944 had jumped more than sixteen thousand times, the record being held by Flight-Lieutenant Charles Agate, who made above fourteen hundred descents in the four and a half years he served at Ringway, on one occasion jumping sixteen times between dawn and dusk.

How they impressed their pupils is best described by Captain J. M. Carew, M.C., Royal Horse Guards, who joined the Parachute Regiment as a private.

'Presiding and commentating was a flight-lieutenant. . . . It suddenly occurred to me that his tunic was devoid of either wings or decorations. . . . It is a significant fact that R.A.F. parachute instructors wear no insignia to denote their calling and rarely go into areas that qualify for campaign awards. They are totally unsung, and only the men under their instruction really appreciate the patience and cold-blooded courage that is theirs. The flight-lieutenant was thin, fair-haired and slightly effeminate in appearance. He had done a total of sixty-eight jumps. He was severely deprecatory of the dangers of parachute jumping. He unsettled us slightly at the outset by addressing us as "gentlemen".

'He said: "Someone once described parachute jumping as dicing with death in the skies; a frightful phrase, quite apart from being grossly untrue. You simply do exactly the same as you did at Hardwick, the only difference being that you have a

23

parachute and there's a bit farther to fall. I have it on good authority that our parachutes are good ones—they ought to be at sixty quid apiece. I know that tomorrow you'll all jump simply beautifully out of the balloon. The balloon is far worse than a plane, and I personally think its existence is purely bloody-mindedness on the part of the high-ups. That, of course, is just between you and me. Anyhow, it's a piece of cake. One last word of advice. This neighbourhood is rich in pubs, and it's quite easy just by walking the hundred yards to the airport to get very drunk. Do so by all means, but not the night before a jump. That's all—and good jumping tomorrow." '

The Hardwick referred to by the flight-lieutenant was Hardwick Hall, a seat of the Duke of Devonshire, and came into use at the end of 1941. By then what may be described as the empirical stage of parachute training was over. It had been carried out by No. 2 Commando. During the initial period it was this proud band of volunteers who provided the 'vile bodies' for the experiments conducted by the Establishment and by those responsible for training in tactics and the use of weapons. Following commando practice, it was divided into 'A', 'B', 'C' and 'D' Troops, each under a captain. The necessity of secrecy was impressed on all ranks, no special badges were worn and as little as possible said of their activities at the Central Landing Establishment. It was perhaps for this reason that in the early days Rock once received a letter from the War Office addressed to the 'Central Laundry', and Private Crane a letter from his girl-friend sent to the 'Central Sunday School'.

Except for the two-shillings-a-day extra duty money,[1] which was in due course introduced, there was no special inducement to join the ranks of the parachute soldiers, and these, indeed, at first made objection to the additional money on the ground that it 'might encourage undesirable men to join the unit'. From the beginning an inarticulate, but very strong, pride filled their hearts. They had been specially chosen and the interviewing officers had rejected three-quarters of the applicants. Of those who remained all had seen active service, were physically very fit, bore exemplary characters, as the phrase is understood in the Army, and shewed a lively intelligence. Like the instructors at Ringway, they had been drawn from all walks of life and could

---

[1] Initially the extra duty money was four shillings a day for officers and two shillings a day for men. Some time in 1942 it was made two shillings for all ranks, as it was felt that all ranks performed similar duties for the money and therefore should receive the same rate.

claim acquaintance as civilians with a larger number of professions than the average regiment belonging to the Infantry of the Line. A platoon officer was a Bond Street modiste, the second in command of a battalion, conspicuous for his soldierly qualities, had been stage manager at Drury Lane. Others were fishermen, office clerks and shepherds from the Welsh hills. A few were the battalion bad characters.

'Drawn up outside the guardroom,' says one of these, who in 1944 won a Military Cross in the jungles of Burma, 'we tried to imagine that we were the cream of Britain's manhood—an illusion speedily dispelled by the regimental sergeant-major. . . . Next to me stood my life-long friend, Sandy. Sandy was generally considered to be a bit of a card and provoked universal mirth when he was seen crouched over the wheel of the salvage truck in search of errant tins. . . . He had volunteered successively for commandos, ski-troops and midget submarines. . . . Next to him were the two inseparables, Jim and Joe. . . . They were oddly alike, both being fair-haired, but, while Jim's face was a ruddy pink Joe's was invariably chalk-white. The medical orderly attributed it to constipation, adding . . . that parachute jumping should soon fix *that*. . . . At the end of the row was Bert. He only looked like the traditional paratroop of fiction. He was thick-set, bow-legged and vaguely simian in appearance. His hair was black and heavily creamed, his lower lip protruded, he looked frankly evil. In fact, he was, for he had deserted from the Army twice and at the age of fifteen had been committed to Borstal. . . . His crime sheet was just entering its second page. . . .[1] The R.S.M. approached and eyed us with scarcely veiled hostility. . . . "Take those horrible-looking people away," he said to the orderly corporal.'

By 1st August 1940 every officer and man of No. 2 Commando had completed three jumps and was regarded, therefore, as a qualified parachutist. They had leapt either from the rear of a Whitley in the manner described or from a hole in its fuselage. This aircraft 'was vile from the comfort point of view. The dark, noisy, draughty, smelly and crampled bowel of the aircraft was no health resort. There was seldom reluctance to go through the "hole". The Whitley was nicknamed "the Elephant" and the aperture had a very obvious nickname also'. One of its draw-

---

[1] 'Bert' failed to qualify for admission to the Parachute Regiment and in 1944 died gallantly for his country on the windswept ridge of Kohima. The others qualified and fought as parachute soldiers with great success.

backs, inseparable indeed from jumping through a hole rather than from an open door, was that if the jumper were not careful he might strike his face on the other side of the aperture. This came to be known as 'ringing the bell' and was the cause of not a few lost or loosened front teeth.

No. 2 Commando had also occasionally leapt from the old-fashioned Bombay troop carrier, a high-wing monoplane 'with plush seats', but possessing, as has been pointed out, the advantage of a door from which to make the exit.

The first demonstration of what British parachute troops might one day accomplish took place on 18th November 1940 near Shrewton on Salisbury Plain before a number of senior British and allied officers. Fifty officers and men dropped and at once set about seizing their objectives. For this purpose Cleasby-Thompson, commanding 'B' Troop, commandeered a large limousine and in it 'surprised the bridge-guard' at Shrewton. It was not until later in the day that he discovered that the car belonged to one of the more distinguished of the spectators, His Royal Highness, Prince Olaf of Norway.

Christmas brought reorganisation and expansion. The 11th Special Air Service Battalion, as No. 2 Commando had been renamed in November, was to have two wings, a Parachute Wing and a Glider Wing. 'There followed a period of intensive training, experiments and demonstrations, which most of the men rather resented. Roman holidays for spectators were not popular.' Injuries due to dropping had been reduced to five per cent, not a very large figure 'considering the crudeness of the equipment and lack of parachuting experience and technique.' Next, as has been recounted, came the attack on the Tragino aqueduct. While it was in progress the Eleventh Troop of the Parachute Wing was formed and composed entirely of recruits from the Brigade of Guards under Captain P. E. Bromley-Martin, who nearly failed to take up his command. On 4th February 1941, while undergoing his training, he jumped number four after Major H. O. Wright. 'The next recollection I have,' he records, 'is that of Major Wright, with parachute open and canopy fully filled, some hundred and fifty feet directly *above* me. My parachute had at that time not fully opened, and I had then the gravest doubts as to whether it would fully function before it had been repacked. I was unable to devise a method of repacking it within the limited time at my disposal. As I was also unable to think of any satisfactory means of assisting the contraption to perform the functions which I had

26

been led to expect were automatic, in my submission I had no alternative but to fall earthwards at, I believe, the rate of thirty-two feet per second accelerating to the maximum speed of one hundred and seventy-six feet . . . this I did. Having dropped a certain distance, my parachute suddenly opened, and I made a very light landing.'

He was, perhaps, more fortunate than Guardsman Garlick, who, a few months later, quitted a Whitley above the airfield of Drem near Edinburgh. The hook connecting his static line to the strop fouled the canvas bag holding his parachute and he was, therefore, suspended beneath the fuselage. He was the last of the 'stick' to jump and the dispatcher had not the strength to haul him against the full force of the slip-stream back into the aircraft. Informed of what had happened, Edward Cutler, the pilot, decided to land as slowly as he could with the tail of the Whitley as high as possible. This he did. Guardsman Garlick was dragged and bumped over the grass. The bag on his back and the parachute inside it were torn to ribbons and the heels of his boots ripped off. When the Whitley stopped, Garlick 'slowly collected himself and walked unhurt to the N.A.A.F.I.', remarking as he did so that he thought that his landing must be a record. It was.

Of the many exercises carried out by the battalion the most memorable was perhaps that which took place on a bleak Saturday in April 1941 in the presence of the Prime Minister, Mrs. Winston Churchill, Mr. Averell Harriman, Major-General Sir Hastings Ismay, Air Marshal Sir Arthur Barratt and others. Five Whitleys made ready to take the air with their complements of parachute troops. The proceedings were under the control of Norman, and a loudspeaker had been set up so that the distinguished visitors might hear the words of command. 'Hallo, formation leader,' said Norman, 'are you ready to take off? Over to you.'

'No,' came the answer, 'I'm not. Five of the chaps have fainted.' Despite this inauspicious beginning the exercise was successful, though the high winds caused forty of those who dropped to suffer injuries. Mr. Churchill was impressed and himself suggested an improvement in the arrangements of the static lines inside the Whitley. It was adopted and proved most successful. Despite the enthusiastic talk of Harvey, Norman, Strange and Rock, who developed their theories to the full, it needed imagination to believe that they might one day become facts. Fortunately in that attribute Mr. Winston Churchill has never shewn himself deficient. He listened with sympathy and attention, and, though a long time was to pass before the Parachute Regiment became possibly that, of the whole British Army, which was the most dreaded by the enemy, he saw to it that progress, though it might be slow and difficult, was steadily and steadfastly maintained.

Leaping from a balloon had begun at Ringway in April 1941. The first experiments had been carried out by the three instructors, Ward, Elliot and Brereton, who went to Cardington for the purpose and made the preliminary ascent inside a huge hangar which had formerly housed an airship. The balloon, once silver grey, 'but the birds had changed all that', rose slowly to the roof, against which it bumped and bounced to the annoyance of the 'bats and pigeons which had their homes there'. Presently 'Brereton', reports Elliot, 'got to his feet, looked over the side and was sick. Ward raised himself slowly, looked over the side and was sick. I was sick'.

Despite this unpromising beginning, their report on the possibility of using balloons was favourable. There were certain great advantages. The tendency of the pupil to twist in the air or to somersault, 'which he was very liable to do when jumping from a Whitley owing to the impact of the slip-stream on his body', was almost eliminated. The instructor on the ground below could control his movements through a megaphone. On the other hand, the jumper, having no slip-stream to aid him, had to fall a far longer distance before his parachute became fully opened. This was a drawback despite the official description in the Central Landing Establishment's manual, which maintained that 'the delayed opening produces an additional thrill'.

The men of the 1st Parachute Battalion hated this 'foul, loathed sausage' from the moment they were introduced to it. 'The misery of the slow ascent to the heavens,' exclaims Cleasby-Thompson ; 'the cold, the nauseating sway and the deathly silence. The culminating order to jump and the stomach-lifting drop of about a hundred and twenty feet before the 'chute opened.' This dislike so influenced a few that they refused to jump. Courts martial ensued and some men suffered what was for the parachutist, as for the commando soldier, the most dreaded penalty of all—that of being 'returned to unit'. One such court martial of three men of the battalion who had refused to leap from the balloon took place in the presence of representatives of the Press and was fully reported in the Daily Mirror, which briefed King's Counsel to defend them. They were found

28

guilty and given sentences of detention. After serving them, they returned to the battalion, where 'they fought with gallantry and distinction'.

Jumping from a balloon was presently made an integral part of parachute training. The feelings of a novice making his first jump from its swaying basket have been set down by Lieutenant-Colonel R. G. Parker,[1] who commanded the 12th Battalion and went through his period of training in the summer of 1943.

'As C.O.,' he writes, 'I had the privilege of jumping first. We embussed in the early morning, all slightly apprehensive. It wasn't so bad for me, as I knew that I had to set an example. . . . On debussing we had to wait about a bit, as there was too much wind. . . . The wind dropped, and to give us confidence the instructors gave a demonstration jump. It was now our turn. Our first sticks embarked in the balloon baskets and positioned themselves for jumping. The interior of the baskets was exactly similar to the wooden platform which we had used in the gymnasium—a large round hole with a platform round it. The cables were unwound and we rose into the air.

'In practice the instructor had always shouted "go" when we were due to jump, but I was allowed to shout myself out on this occasion. One sits on the edge of the hole with one's hands gripping the rim behind one in a position of attention, and then, when the time comes to jump, thrusts oneself forward, bringing one's hands to one's side, heels down and feet together in a rigid position of attention. You should keep this position until your parachute opens when you reach with your hands for the strings and bend your knees, always keeping your heels down.

'I went out correctly enough, but didn't keep my hands close enough to my sides or my feet properly together which caused me to do a slight somersault. However, I soon righted myself and heard my parachute open and then experienced for the first time that delightful sensation of floating through the air. There was not one of us who did not feel a thrill whenever this happened, and I think even in action the parachutist feels a sense of regret when this phase is over.

'I made up for my bad exit with a good landing. . . . I think that my own experience exemplified that of the average man who made his first jump that day. Some of us made bad exits, others bad landings, but we all, with the exception of a few landing casualties, felt that we were super-men. Our instructors deflated

[1] Later Colonel R. G. Parker, D.S.O.

us later, but most tactfully, so that we still retained our sense of superiority over other men.

'Exit accidents are rare and we were lucky to have none among our men at Ringway, but accidents on landing were not so uncommon. We had been taught how to land among trees, in water and on uneven ground and how to compete with wind. Whenever one lands, no matter how level the ground, poise and quick mental action are essential. One has to position oneself for the correct roll while in the air—knees bent, feet together and parallel to the ground be it up or down hill and elbows bent and drawn into the body. Those of us like myself, who were stocky and short-legged found little difficulty in landing, but most of us, myself included, got bruised before we had complete confidence in ourselves. Those of us who had long legs and bodies suffered most. . . . We had a few broken legs and cases of concussion, but very few really bad casualties. . . . We found that it was much easier to jump from a plane and that the sensation was a much pleasanter one. . . .

'The routine for jumping from a plane never varies. Shortly before it is time to jump, a red light goes on and the parachutists get set for jumping. As soon as a green light appears No. 1 jumps, followed in quick succession by the remaining jumpers. When containers have to be released from under a plane containing a stick of ten, No. 6 has to allow a short interval for this release before leaving the plane.'

The place in which jumping casualties were treated was the Daveyhulme Hospital in Manchester. To its doctors and nurses many airborne soldiers owe a debt, and they look back with warm appreciation to an institution whose staff were, one and all, lavish of their care and skill. Here embryo parachutists, who had in some cases literally fallen by the wayside, found themselves lying beside 'Frenchmen, Poles, Dutchmen and Belgians . . . all fairly secretive about their ambitions and probable future, but, in spite of the damage they had already suffered through landing wrongly or too hard, very enthusiastic over being "airborne" types. . . . One had to listen to the news on the wireless three times a day in five different languages'. These foreigners were some of those gallant men who fought the oppressor of their native lands as saboteurs and agents of the Special Operation Executive. They were not envied but greatly admired by the regular parachute soldiers, who met them at Ringway usually for the first and last time.

Having accomplished his two jumps from the balloon, the

recruit had to make five more from an aircraft before receiving the coveted blue parachute wings. The jumps were made first in 'slow pairs', then in quick, then by fives, and finally in a 'stick' of ten. The emotions aroused when jumping for the first time from an aircraft have been described by Captain Peter Carew.

'"Your stick emplanes in ten minutes," said the sergeant. "Just line up here and I'll check your 'chutes." He walked up the line feeling straps with a sure and practised touch. When he came to the safety box, he placed one hand underneath it and hit it hard. Alistair said it reminded him of a crusader examining the chastity belts of his women folk.

'"Always give your box a knock," counselled the sergeant, "but for God's sake don't get doing it in the kite. There's nothing worse than ten blokes all bashing their boxes at the same time. Besides, it isn't nice, it seems you don't trust your sarge."

'A few minutes later we were marching in file to a Whitley a few hundred yards away. In the days of Superfortresses, Whitleys would appear laughable and almost pathetic. To us they were evil, black monsters of incredibly menacing appearance out of which we were shortly to hurl ourselves.

'On this my first aeroplane jump I was to be number two. I had been told we were to do "slow pairs". The popular opinion seemed to be that on slow pairs numbers one and two were the best off. I wondered a little about this.

'Number one was a Frenchman. He was a small dark man . . . with the saddest eyes I have ever seen . . . he spoke not at all, but gazed straight in front of him. Suddenly I felt scared. For the space of approximately five minutes I was to sit facing this man over the hole. I did not like it. . . . Then I thought, "It's only five minutes and he can't look any worse than Alistair in the balloon."

'Seating accommodation in a Whitley is far from luxurious. The floor is hard and irregular and only the shorter men can stretch their legs at full length. . . . The plane droned on and then . . . the engine gave a little splutter and took on a new, quieter and indescribably sinister note. I defy any parachutist to say that the change in the engine does not cause a faint tightening in the stomach. Did I say "faint"? That applies to jumpers with more experience than two balloon jumps. . . . We were over the dropping zone. The sergeant leant over the hole, placed his thumb to his nose and extended his fingers. Somebody tittered nervously. It was me. . . . Then just above the Frenchman's head I saw the red light and the sergeant became galvanised.

'"Action stations, number one," he yelled and raised his right hand.

'The Frenchman swung his feet into the hole and sat looking up at the sergeant's right hand. He seemed quite disinterested in the proceedings and his eyes never blinked. I felt certain that mine were like organ stops and that is exactly how Alistair described them later.

'With the appearance of the green light, the sergeant dropped his hand and shouted "Go". The Frenchman disappeared neatly through the aperture. "Up the Froggies!" observed the sergeant cheerfully. "Action stations, number two."

'Sitting with my feet in the hole, I wondered if anyone ever got used to it. I was going, yes. In fact I *wanted* to go. I don't think I ever consciously thought of refusing. But why, oh why, must my stomach feel like this? A company sergeant-major whom I met the other day had jumped into Tunisia, Sicily, Normandy and over the Rhine. He was a battered-looking warrior with the D.C.M., four campaign stars and two wound stripes. He had done in all thirty-eight drops. He is still wondering the same thing. "Nerves," he said, "that's all it is". . . .

'Leaving an aeroplane, one knows considerably less about the uncomfortable interim period of hurtling through space than on a balloon jump. This is entirely due to a highly technical-sounding phenomenon known as the slip-stream. The slip-stream takes charge of you thoroughly and completely. It simply, and almost, it seems, apologetically, whisks you away from the plane on to the end of your parachute. Just as easy as that. Then, if you are the right way up, your legs are whipped up so that you seem likely to kick your own nose, and you feel as if your fall has been arrested by a giant hand grabbing your braces. . . .

'I was gratified to notice that I was the right way up but aggrieved to hear a cultured but friendly voice (through a mega-phone), "A somersault, number two, but you're O.K. now." I thought: "What the hell do you mean, *now*?" My exit had been perfect. To this day I don't believe I did a somersault, though another R.A.F. instructor swore I had done two. Apparently the rest of my descent was unremarkable as the voice lost interest in me. . . .'

In June 1941 Lieutenant-Colonel E. E. Down[1] took over from
[1] Later Major-General E. E. Down, C.B., C.B.E.

Jackson the 11th Special Air Service Battalion, which in September became the 1st Parachute Battalion. Down was a man of utmost energy. He purged the small amount of dross which had inevitably collected, and set about raising the standard of his command to even higher levels. He was quite uncompromising in the fulfilment of this intention, and for the first six months was known by the somewhat sinister name of Dracula; but 'as we got to know him, our respect for him changed to extreme loyalty and affection' and the sobriquet became 'Charlie Orange'—C.O. 'Charlie Orange,' records the historian of the battalion, 'was ruthless, and, though sympathetic, he never showed sympathy. There was nothing that the battalion could do that he himself could not do better. March or run, ride or shoot, Eric Down was the superior. He gathered about him a team of officers and men who worked for him and with him to no union hours. Though hated at first by nearly every officer and man in the battalion, there soon came a time when all would have gone to the end of the earth for him—not from fear but from affection.' Such was the man who was afterwards to rise to high command in the airborne forces.

He began by moving the battalion to Bury for weapon training in order to secure the generous and enthusiastic help of the Lancashire Fusiliers, the XXth Foot, whose home it was. After two strenuous months the battalion marched back to Knutsford through Manchester, a gruelling experience over the Lancashire cobbles, which were 'agonising' and caused the feet to feel as though they were 'red hot'. At Knutsford 'ever harder tactical training was the order of the day and balloon jumping the order of the night'. Down would sometimes invite his officers to dine with him at the George. This inn was kept by Mr. Leighton, a Jew, who 'with his family has found a warm place in the heart of many a parachutist' for his generosity and kindness. On one occasion after dinner the party 'adjourned to Tatton Park in their blue patrols to do a balloon jump or three, only deigning to remove their spurs'. The jumping was not always of a strictly orthodox kind. On another, at the word of command four officers 'rose simultaneously and, standing on the sides of the cradle, swallow-dived into space'.

In September 1941 the 1st Parachute Battalion, formerly the 11th Special Air Service Battalion, was ordered to Hardwick near Chesterfield in Derbyshire. Here the 1st Parachute Brigade was forming. It was to consist of the 1st Battalion, the 2nd under Lieutenant-Colonel E. W. C. Flavell, M.C., the 3rd under

33

Lieutenant-Colonel G. W. Lathbury, and the 4th, formed a little later, under Lieutenant-Colonel M. R. J. Hope-Thompson, M.C., M.B.E. The brigadier was R. N. Gale,[1] O.B.E., M.C. Expansion was now more than a rumour; it was becoming slowly but steadily an accomplished fact. The patience, hardihood and steadfastness of those who had joined No. 2 Commando in the early days were to be rewarded—not perhaps in the conventional manner with medals and promotions, but with something more precious—the sight of other men, volunteers like themselves, who, seeing their example, felt the same urge and were eager to face the same risks for the same reward.

The newly formed brigade was part of an airborne division composed of parachute and glider-borne troops which Major-General F. A. M. Browning, D.S.O.,[2] had been ordered to raise in October 1941. To this tall guardsman and fine soldier the Parachute Regiment owes much. From that month he was intimately concerned with its creation and expansion, and later on with its exploits in the field. The spirit of the Brigade of Guards was strong in him, and the Parachute Regiment will always be grateful to him for all that he did to link it with a splendid tradition and thus to assure it a future of promise and fulfilment.

For nearly four years, from February 1942, he, and in consequence the regiment, were to be given strong and unswerving support by Major-General K. N. Crawford, M.C.[3] the Director of Air at the War Office. A man of imagination, he divined the needs of men, conducting a new type of warfare, and did all he could to supply them. Though far from young, he qualified as a parachutist in order the better to be able to understand their problems.

By the autumn of 1941, the pioneers, as the men of No. 2 Commando, of 11th Special Air Service Battalion and of 1st Parachute Battalion could proudly call themselves, had learnt much and survived more. Their hard-won experience was to stand in good stead both themselves and their successors, who, before the war was over, were to pass in their thousands through Hardwick and Ringway. Side by side with the Royal Air Force

[1] Now Lieutenant-General Sir Richard N. Gale, K.B.E., C.B., D.S.O., M.C.
[2] Later Lieutenant-General Sir Frederick Browning, K.B.E., C.B., D.S.O.
[3] Later Lieutenant-General Sir Kenneth Crawford, K.C.B., M.C.

instructors, they had found and solved many problems. The statichute, invented and made by two civilians, Raymond Quilter and Leslie Irvin, had proved its worth and these pioneers had proved it. The airborne forces in particular and the country in general owe much to the ingenuity and patient skill of Quilter and Irvin, who, with the aid of Rock, Strange, Norman, Newnham and others, eventually evolved the standard pattern of jumping parachute and harness which is still in use today. The official publication *By Air to Battle* thus describes it:

'To the parachute harness is attached a bag carried on the back. In it is housed the parachute in an internal bag divided into two compartments. The outside bag remains attached to the harness: the inside is pulled violently from it by a static line, which is a length of webbing, of which one end is attached strongly to the inner bag. At the other end is a metal D-ring, which engages a hook attached to the end of the strop. The strop is also made of webbing and its top end is secured to a "strongpoint" in the aircraft. The length of the static line is twelve feet six inches. The strop has to be long enough to ensure that the parachute will be well below the aircraft before it opens, and short enough so that the 'chute is not caught in the slip-stream and twisted round the rear plane or the tail-wheel. In a Dakota the strop is attached to a steel cable running along the side of the aircraft. The strop attachment is clipped to this cable and moves with the jumpers as they shuffle one by one towards the exit.

'The canopy of the parachute is usually made of nylon, though sometimes of cotton, and has a diameter of twenty-eight feet. In the middle of it is a circular hole, the vent, twenty-two inches in diameter. This vent prevents undue strain on the canopy when it begins to open, and is said to reduce oscillation. The rigging lines attaching the canopy to the harness are twenty-two feet long.'

In the early stages of the training at Ringway the packing of the parachutes in their bags was performed sometimes by a small packing team, sometimes by the men of No. 2 Commando themselves. The drying-room could at first take only a hundred parachutes at a time, and, since they had to hang for forty-eight hours in order to dry through and through, not more than four hundred parachutes a week were available. In 1941, with the advent of winter, came expert packers.

They belonged to the Women's Auxiliary Air Force and they worked under Flight-Sergeant Humphries. By 1945 more than half a million drops had been made at Ringway and only one accident, inevitably fatal, had occurred of which the cause could be traced to faulty packing. Such figures speak louder than words, and it is small wonder that the men of 1st Parachute Battalion and the thousands who followed them along the paths of air had confidence, complete and serene, in the W.A.A.F. parachute packers. Their own view of their duties has been well summed up by one of them, G. D. Martineau, who began to pack parachutes in 1941 and wrote down her feelings in a poem 'which', comments a parachute soldier, 'has been a great comfort while "standing to the door" '. The first and last verses run :

> 'When they posted me here to the section,
> I was free as the pitiless air,
> Unashamed of confessed imperfection.
> Having no sort of burden to bear ;
> I was not an incurable slacker ;
> Neat, not fussy—I fancied of old ;
> But today I'm a parachute packer,
> And my heart takes a turn with each fold.

> 'So is conscience awakened and care born
> In the heart of a negligent maid.
> Fickle Aeolus, fight for the Airborne,
> Whom I strive with frail fingers to aid,
> Give my heroes kind wind and fair weather ;
> Let no parachute sidle or slump.
> For today we go warring together
> And my soul will be there at the jump.'

The expansion of the parachute force presently made necessary a corresponding increase in the numbers of instructors at Ringway. It was then that Newnham shewed his powers of organisation. The School—as has been explained, it was staffed entirely by the Royal Air Force from November 1941—grew with the increase in pupils, and the number of trained parachutists turned out every week soon rose from forty to a hundred, and before the end of the war to many more. The success of Ringway as a training centre was the work of a skilled team at the head of which stood Newnham. His labours were unceasing, his enthusiasm of the kind usually described as infectious, and his shrewdness was equal to all emergencies. The delays, however unintentional, of Whitehall, the differences of opinion between the Air Ministry and the War Office who did not always see eye to eye, the arrival at a moment's notice of half a dozen generals and air-marshals or of parties of mysterious civilian experts, whose demeanour engendered awe or contempt, or of four hundred eager recruits, the problems of oscillation and of twisted rigging lines—even now not entirely solved—the advent of wind, rain, fog and other kinds of unsuitable weather—he faced them all with a genial equanimity, and it was to him and to his instructors that 'the heartfelt thanks and gratitude', to quote the words of Major-General Gale, were given without stint by all who passed through their capable hands.

From the first Newnham was determined that the parachutists should live cheek by jowl with the Royal Air Force, and this happy practice endured throughout the years of war. They were also to live well, for he was no believer in that school of dismal warriors which endures discomfort for discomfort's sake. 'The R.A.F. at Ringway,' notes a parachute soldier who passed through the School in 1942, 'from the station commander to the lowliest aircraftman, extend a welcome to would-be parachutists that is probably unique in the three services. In the surrounding pubs they are fêted. Yet it is not so difficult to understand. The men who go there are under few illusions about the type of war they are going to. The fact that they have chosen one of the most dangerous ways of going to this war explains the willingness of the R.A.F. instructors to make the preparation for this solemn undertaking as pleasant as possible.

'We notice this in a variety of ways, but most forcibly of all in the dining hall. At our first dinner we were confronted not by odoriferous stew and sour-faced army cooks but delectably cooked meals that looked, smelt and tasted excellent, served by young women in white overalls and coquettish chefs' caps. Not all of them were startling beauties (though not a few of them were), but they were delightfully feminine. They smiled with a serenity that was a joy to behold—not the frozen smile with a chorus, but a frank, open-hearted grin as if they thought that custard, potatoes and meat pies were the spice of romance. Furthermore, they dispensed second helpings with a good will that was nothing short of amazing.'

Harvey and Newnham's work and that of the others in charge at Ringway was accomplished little by little, and what can be recorded in a few brief sentences required many months to achieve. The full measure of their success became patent to all the world that sunny March morning in 1945 when armed men, their one-time pupils, dropped in thousands upon sullen fields beyond the Rhine.

As the war progressed further problems arose. How was the parachute soldier to be supplied with weapons and ammunition so that he could fight unaided until reinforced or relieved by the ground forces? 'There is a limit,' to quote once more *By Air to Battle*, 'to what can be carried by a man descending by parachute. How great it was had to be discovered. A container was designed, a rifle and "a bag of shot" loaded into it and it was then dropped from a height of eight hundred feet. "The thing worked in principle," Rock records in his war diary, "but the rifle and shot came through the bottom of the container. We sent it back with remarks." After a time bigger and better containers were designed and constructed, so that it eventually became possible to drop Bren guns, two-inch mortars and ammunition quite safely by these means.' In 1942 Major J. Lander, who was killed in action the next year, 'devised a method of dropping with as much as a hundred pounds weight of extra supplies attached to the parachutist. The ammunition or machine gun was put in a bag attached to one end of twenty feet of rope, the other end being secured to the jumper's waist. After leaving the aircraft, the bag was allowed to fall the full length of the rope. . . . The bag, being below the jumper, was the first to strike the ground; its weight was thus neutralised, the speed of descent of the parachutist was checked, and he could land safely'. This kit-bag method presently replaced to a large extent the use of containers which were 'often hard to find, especially in close country'.

As with dropping devices so with aircraft. Dakotas, as has been said, gradually took the place of Whitleys, and before the war was over Stirlings and Halifaxes had been pressed into service. Neither of these four-engined aircraft was very suitable, for it was necessary to leave them through a hole in the floor and not by the door. Their pilots and those of the Dakotas had to be trained in steadily increasing numbers. This was ultimately accomplished to the mutual satisfaction of pilots and passengers, between whom a warm bond of friendship was forged. Both were intensely critical, but of themselves not of each other, and how closely they co-operated wil be evident when the operations which took battalions of the Parachute Regiment to North Africa, Sicily, Normandy, Southern France, Holland and Germany are described.

To fly an aircraft accurately so as to arrive over the dropping zone exactly at the correct height, the correct angle and the correct moment needed much practice. What happened to Sergeant L. J. Carrier, Royal Electrical and Mechanical Engineers, during the period of his training prior to his posting to the 22nd Independent Parachute Company is an excellent illustration of the difficulties encountered. Soon after D-day 'Tiffy' was helping 'the latest intakes to get some jumping practice, and fresh pilots to drop parachutists. . . . Most of the jumps at this time were from Stirling aircraft, and for the first "drop" for a pilot the routine was this. We made up sticks of fifteen or more men and on the first run-in two men went with a four-to-five-second interval between them to simulate five men jumping. . . . On the second run-in four or five men would go at one-second intervals to give the impression of ten men going. On the third run-in the remainder would go, to illustrate twenty men going.

'"Tiffy" was stick commander and was going No. 1 of the last stick out. . . . On the first run-in he saw that they were running-in at least a mile to one side of the D.Z. and was able to tell the pilot in time to stop him from letting the first two men go. . . . On the second run-in, owing to the angle of the run-in, "Tiffy" was unable to give a warning, and the first two men were dropped a mile to one side of the D.Z. Came the third run-in, and "Tiffy" was ready and was able to point out the "T" and the direction of the smoke signal, with the result that the second stick landed half a mile nearer. The pilot was informed of what the stick commander and those remaining in the plane thought of his marksmanship. "Don't worry," he said, "I will drop you O.K. this time," and got the retort that "you'd better, I am going this bloody time". The pilot was as good as his word, for "Tiffy" was dropped within six feet of the smoke canister and was nearly choked before he got out of his harness and clear of the smoke.

'Another time we were intended to drop as a stick of twenty, from a Stirling aircraft, on Bulford Fields, with a Canadian pilot behind the controls. This pilot had never seen a parachutist before, let alone dropped any, and, prior to emplaning, "Tiffy" had arranged for a five-minute warning, and a five-second red before the green was given. A nice take-off, the usual reshuffle and settling down, and "Tiffy" was snoozing lovely. Suddenly he got a dig in the ribs and was told the red was on (and some of the men had not yet hooked up). There was an unearthly scramble as everyone saw to their kit and took up their allotted positions. There need not have been any scramble though, for that damned red was on for five solid minutes. Anyone who has jumped No. 1 can imagine what "Tiffy" went through in those minutes. First getting a stiff neck staring up at the red light over his head, and then a hasty glance down to see if he could see Tidworth, Bulford or that stretch of woods just prior to the D.Z. It was during one of these downward glances that there was a shout of "*Green*, Tiffy, Green", and away went "Tiffy", to learn afterwards that the red had come on again almost at once but too soon for five men to follow him. That gormless pilot had decided to see if the lights were working O.K. without first warning the stick-commander. What he had done was to switch on the red and tell one of his crew to go back, see if it was on, then to link up with the inter-com. and he (the pilot) would try the green. When this member of the crew realised that we were ready to go, he told the pilot, who misunderstood him and switched on the green before switching on the red again.

'Once clear of the kite, "Tiffy" thought that things were all right, but on looking up he was astounded to see the feet of No. 2 just above his head and to one side, and saw that No. 2 was oscillating like merry hell. As he watched, fascinated, the body of No. 2 became gracefully wrapped around "Tiffy's" rigging lines, his canopy sagged and collapsed. Before he could yell out, No. 2 had kicked himself free, and "Tiffy" dropped. The 'chute trailed out like a wet bedsheet that had just been wrung out by hand. Looking down, the earth was coming up like blazes . . . and then, praise the patron saint of jumpers, no sensation of dropping. The 'chute had reopened.' 'Tiffy' landed in a tree from which he was in due course rescued.

The expansion of the Parachute Regiment to the seventeen battalions it eventually comprised was several years away in the future when the 1st Parachute Brigade, first with three, then with four battalions, formed and began to train in November 1941. The preliminary exercises were carried out at the depot at Hardwick under Army instructors. They consisted of seemingly endless physical training to which was added a synthetic variety. This involved jumping through holes in 'mock up' fuselages, swinging from a trapeze and an airsickness test. It took the form of a twenty minutes voyage in a swingboat 'such as one sees at a fair'. The sergeant instructor was wont to inform the waiting pupils that 'if you aren't sick on this lot, you'll never be in a plane. Come on now—who's first? All the fun of the fair and keep your skirts down, girls'.

Hardwick, noted one of the early arrivals, Major J. D. Frost,[1] who before the war was ended was to drop on France, North Africa, Sicily and Holland, was 'a sad collection of red-brick huts surrounded by a high wire fence set in the midst of sloping park land. Many huts were incomplete having scores of workmen with all their paraphernalia draped round them and the grass verges surrounding the huts churned into glutinous mud by the constant passage of wheelbarrows, vehicles and human feet. The roads winding through the camp so narrow that nowhere could two vehicles pass each other without swerving off on to the grass to the accompaniment of blasts on their horns, high revving in low gears, advice and cursings from drivers and passers-by'.

Many of the senior officers who went through the training at Hardwick expressed their disapproval of the methods employed. They were of the opinion that the first thing necessary was that a man should be a good infantry soldier and that only then should he learn to jump from an aircraft. In other words, parachute soldiers were ordinary infantry launched into battle in a new way. More than one officer was of the opinion that the physical training indulged in so vigorously at Hardwick was entirely unsuited to parachuting. None of the instructors were parachutists, and 'we all got muscle-bound. However, we all felt we were suffering in a common cause. . . . I finished the course muscle-bound and with a purple tummy, the result of a fall into a bed of gravel. We all did our work stripped to the waist'.

Another senior officer, no longer young, who nevertheless succeeded in joining the Parachute Regiment, relates how he understood what the Assistant Director of Medical Services meant when he said men over the age of thirty could not support the rigours of the career. Over fifteen per cent of the men in his course who were well under that age were unable to do so and a number of first-rate men were lost through methods of training which were presently seen to be faulty.

'One of the methods of hardening, as it was called, was to make men swing on a trapeze. At the top of the swing they were ordered to let go, which meant descending backwards from a height of fifteen feet. This was to accustom them to a back landing from an oscillating parachute, but it caused so many

[1] Later Lieutenant-Colonel J. D. Frost, D.S.O., M.C.

casualties that it was given up. . . . Of course, in the early stages the standard of medical fitness had to be very high indeed. . . . I think I am right in saying that more than two missing teeth above and below disqualified a man, because it was thought that false teeth would be lost in parachuting. One of the very expensive and quite useless inventions with which we were provided was a special box for the teeth. . . .'

On the other hand, it is an undoubted fact that very many benefited from their time at Hardwick and can testify to the additions to strength and power they there received. It is not possible to generalise. All that can be said with certainty is that by the time the aspiring parachute soldier had passed through Hardwick and Ringway he was a toughened athlete, physically and mentally alert. Hardwick, indeed, became for the parachute soldier 'what Caterham is to the Brigade of Guards, a place of trial but not of error'.

At the end of a fortnight the recruits went to Ringway. Before they left Hardwick they were addressed by the regimental sergeant-major, and his customary oration has been preserved. 'You lot,' he would say, 'are off to Ringway tomorrow. There you will do seven jumps and go on fourteen days' leave with a nice pair of wings on your arms. But remember one thing. Before you get your wings you can pack up when you like. No one can force you to jump and there's no disgrace if you don't. But after that you have to or you'll be for it. Disobeying orders they call it and that usually means fifty-six days' detention. Another thing—you have your wings stripped off in front of the colonel. And for a bloke with a conscience that's bad enough. That's the position, and no one can say it isn't fair. You'll have a good time at Ringway—plenty of grub, plenty of beer, and plenty of fun. You do your seven jumps on a nice park and there's a canteen there. But later you'll jump at a place where there's no canteen. There'll be Jerries or Japs and it'll be them or you. That's what you've been training for here. Because we're going back—that's certain. Some of you were in France. See what I mean?'

The 'synthetic' training on the ground in the hangars at Ringway was more elaborate than that of Hardwick and was the constant care and study of Kilkenny. In due course the original 'gallows', a grim instrument which was designed to check the fall of the parachutist attached to it by means of a weight within a few pounds of his own released at the correct moment, disappeared. The moment, it was found, was seldom correct and 'sprains, twisted ankles and dislocated knees soon shewed that the calculations of its inventor were not entirely accurate'. The practice of leaping from the tailboard of moving lorries was also abandoned, since it was attended by similar consequences. Fuselages of Whitleys, and later on of Dakotas and Halifaxes, were set up in the hangars at Ringway and at Hardwick. Through these the pupil fell or jumped and in so doing learned the correct posture which the body had to assume —knees and feet together, elbows close to the sides. Kilkenny presently installed 'a number of appliances resembling trapezes, swings and those wooden chutes down which the frequenters of fun-fairs delight to slide'. The most ingenious device was known as the 'Fan'. A steel cable, wound round a drum, was attached to the harness of the jumper, who then leapt from a platform twenty-five feet above the mats. As he fell his weight caused the drum to revolve ; but its speed was checked by two vanes or fans, which revolved with it and thus created an air-brake. This allowed him to land with about the same force as if he had jumped by parachute. Such devices were at the disposal of all pupils whenever they were not doing their jumps in the manner already described.

In March 1942 the 1st Parachute Brigade moved to Bulford on Salisbury Plain and came in contact for the first time with other troops of the Army also training for the day when they would avenge Dunkirk and free Europe. This is how the para-chute soldiers appeared to one who afterwards joined their ranks. 'Now,' he records, 'we'll see what they're really like. A large gathering at the Rose and Crown at Bulford, the garrison cinema and all the pubs in Amesbury and Salisbury gave the lie to the theory that they were spartans who denied themselves all the good things of life. Here were men who drank, smoked and swore like any other soldiers—neither more nor less than the average. They wore the headgear of every known regiment of the British Army. There were guardsmen who remained faithful to their service dress and cheese-cutter caps, the peaks of which sat forbiddingly on their noses. Some indeed, as if reluctant to sever all connections with the Brigade, retained their coloured Guards' flashes on their shoulders above the parachute badge. Scots of both the Highland and Lowland variety were legion. One could discern the kilted Black Watch with their distinctive red hackles in their tam-o'-shanters, the tartan of the Gordons, Camerons, Argylls and Seaforths, and the Hodden Grey of the London Scottish. The K.O.S.B.s, Royal Scots and Scots Fusiliers, as if in apology for their lack of kilts, clung with Lowland tenacity to their trews. Then there were the badges of every county regiment in England and the controversial but effective collar flashes of the Royal Welch Fusiliers. At that time there were only four battalions and we soon learnt to distinguish them. The 1st (from which the ill-fated Italy expedition had been drawn) wore a green lanyard, the 2nd yellow, the 3rd red, and the 4th black. . . . Generally speaking, they were admired. Some admired them enviously, some fawningly and some grudgingly. A few . . . admired nothing or anyone. Some of the paratroops [sic] obviously enjoyed this admiration (and why not?). Some seemed supremely indifferent and some even severely deprecatory. There were a few, but only a very few, who had the profoundest contempt for anyone who was not a parachutist.'

The diversity of headgear noted on Salisbury Plain presently gave way to the Red Beret. Browning was determined that the parachute soldier should wear a distinctive head-dress of which he would feel proud. A number of berets in various shades of red, blue and green were placed one by one on the head of an orderly paraded for the purpose before Sir Alan Brooke, Chief of the Imperial General Staff. His choice hovered between a maroon red and a blue. Unable to make up his mind, he asked the opinion of the orderly who replied: 'Well, sir, I really like the red beret, as the blue reminds me of some labour corps'. This settled the matter and the red was chosen. The head-dress was first worn by the regiment when it went into action in North Africa in November 1942. It presently earned for its officers and men the nickname, the 'Red Devils', bestowed upon them by a reluctantly admiring enemy, who from that time onwards had good reason to dread its appearance on the field of battle. At the same time the regimental badge, a parachute crowned and winged, was adopted.

Why had they chosen this calling? For calling it was, something beyond the ordinary expectation of the citizen who joined the armed forces of the Crown in those years of pride and peril. The reasons were varied. 'As a student of Russia, I believed that airborne forces would play a big part in warfare.' 'My unit had been in a static role a long time and parachuting appeared to be more interesting, particularly the good comradeship feature.' 'I was a regular officer commissioned in 1931 . . . and did not like being a G.3.'[1] 'The excitement appealed to me.' 'Revenge for

[1] General Staff Officer, 3rd Grade.

Dunkirk.' 'Disliked being shelled . . . and expected to meet bullets only as a parachutist.' 'I was a trained soldier and who better for the job?' 'The General said, "I will take you providing you pass your parachute course. If you fail, I will take you as my A.D.C." "Sir, no threat could possibly encourage me more".'

'I . . . was wounded near St. Valery. On rejoining I found that most of my mates were either killed or prisoners. . . . I thought I would find people I understood better in the parachute units.' 'The glamour of the Red Beret and, in part, through a feeling of superiority in being in the picked arm of the Service.' 'I was company sergeant-major. Two-thirds of my company volunteered, so I went with them.' 'I wanted to experience the thrill of a parachute descent.' 'I knew I would be scared, but I thought that for my self-respect I must volunteer' (this parachute soldier subsequently rose to a high rank). 'I was married in 1943 and, realising that I was destined to take part in the Second Front, wished a reasonable chance of getting there and of survival.' 'My unit had trained for two years in Iceland.' 'I'm a fairly athletic type, keen on rugger, etc. I felt I should be fairly useful in the Parachute Regiment.' 'I could not swim well and thought there was less likelihood of it being necessary if one invaded by air.' As good a reason as any was that given by a young officer who went to see a demonstration of dropping by parachute early in 1942. 'The dropping zone,' he writes, 'was on one of the higher hills of the Lincolnshire Wolds. Approached by a narrow lane, the watching zone gave a view up hill so that the planes when they came appeared suddenly over the not-too-distant sky-line as though projected from catapults. The afternoon was perfect, the sky cloudless and there was a little ground breeze. As I looked up the hill towards the sound of approaching planes, I experienced a thrill of anticipation, and when they came in sight even the old Whitleys looked formidable and the sun dressed them in strange colours. They came in V-formation. We did not know where to look for the parachutists—underneath or at the tail-end. Suddenly, from tiny holes beneath the fuselages, they came, little tumbling figures turning over and over, and—I could not determine the precise moment—they were floating on flowers. Each suspended from the most glorious coloured canopies—red, orange, green, blue and strangely gay black. The sun shone through them and they were the most wonderful things I ever beheld. I had never seen such a thrilling sight. I can remember it yet and will always.'

The Adventure of Bruneval

'ONE AFTERNOON in the middle of January 1942,' records Lieutenant-Colonel J. D. Frost, D.S.O., M.C., then a major newly seconded to the Parachute Regiment from the Cameronians, 'all company commanders were summoned to battalion headquarters (the 2nd Parachute Battalion) for a conference. It transpired that a company was required to move to Tilshead on Salisbury Plain for special training.'

'C' Company, of which Frost was the commanding officer, was chosen. There was, however, one difficulty. Before he could accompany his men to Tilshead he had to acquire the blue wings of the parachute soldier. That he had not already done so was due to an accident in which he had injured his knee when landing on one leg after his second jump from 'the vile, loathed sausage'. It was almost decided that Major Philip Teichman, a brother officer in command of 'A' Company, should take over 'C' until it had returned from its special training. Frost, however, 'heartily disliked this idea' and prevailed upon his commanding officer to allow him to go immediately to Ringway and complete his course.

To do so in the time available before the company left meant jumping five times from an aircraft in six days. At Ringway Frost reported to Newnham, ready with every kind of argument to persuade him of the urgency of the matter. This proved unnecessary, for 'I was pleasantly surprised to find that he seemed to know all about me, and one or two of the remarks he let slip gave me considerable food for thought. He referred to certain articles of equipment which they had had to procure in a hurry "last time", and I wondered what he meant by "last time".' Newnham was referring darkly to the first operation carried out by parachute troops against the enemy, the attack on the Tragino aqueduct in southern Italy. As will be remembered, it had taken place in February 1941, almost exactly a year before, and it is significant that twelve months had had to elapse between that operation and the descent upon the radiolocation station at Bruneval, which Frost was to lead. Some might maintain that to allow so long a time to pass between operations shewed how uninterested were the authorities on the potentialities of warfare conducted by airborne troops. To do so would be less than just. The work of Nigel Norman, Maurice Newnham, Louis Strange, John Rock and all the others at Ringway, and of Richard Gale and Eric Down and their parachute soldiers at Hardwick and elsewhere, bore not slow but rapid fruit—miraculously rapid indeed, when all the circumstances are considered.

Even in peacetime, with all the resources of a great industrial state at their disposal, eighteen months would have been a very short period in which to create from nothing all the gear required for the complicated business of arriving upon a battle-field by way of the air. And to the gear would have to be added the evolution of the training methods, and the devising of the strategy and tactics involved. But the School at Ringway and the airborne forces at Hardwick or in Scotland had neither time nor material. The country was fighting for its life, and, when in June 1940 the creation of parachute troops was decided, was facing the huge task of re-equipping an army which had left behind at Dunkirk or elsewhere in France and Belgium 7,000 tons of ammunition, 90,000 rifles, 2,300 guns, 120,000 vehicles, 8,000 Bren guns and 400 anti-tank rifles.[1] Not only had these enormous losses to be made good, but also the require-ments of the Royal Navy, the Royal Air Force, the Merchant Navy, and the Home Guard and Civil Defence, and the civilian population in general had somehow to be met. But despite these commitments and the fact that 'a damaged parachute and jumping-helmet captured from the Germans were the only models available, and for aircraft . . . four Whitley Mark IIs which were seldom simultaneously serviceable', those responsible for the creation of the airborne forces put them in a position to shew their mettle within seven months, and to be ready at the end of eighteen to carry out a second operation which, though very little larger, was of far greater importance. When all is said and done, and all the difficulties borne in mind, this achievement must be regarded as remarkable.

Such matters, however, were no concern of Frost, as he addressed himself to the task of becoming a trained parachutist 'in five clear days'. Unfortunately the days were far from clear.

[1] *History of the Second World War*, vol ii. "Their Finest Hour", by Winston S. Churchill, p. 125.

The weather at Ringway, he notes, 'was notoriously fickle. On the slightest provocation a smoky fog would creep across the aerodrome from the direction of Manchester, which was only a few miles away, and a wind strong enough to dispel the fog very often made jumping unsafe'. On the first of the five days 'I was ready (at nine o'clock) just outside the hangar . . . and was still waiting there at past four in the afternoon. . . . The second day was almost a replica of the first', when towards evening the fog suddenly lifted, Frost was able to make two jumps from a Whitley. The next day he was able to do his third jump, and on the day following his last two. He then returned in triumph to Hardwick, and thence brought his company down to Tilshead, 'a miserable sort of place with mud everywhere', arriving towards the end of January.

Here, after an inspection by Major-General Browning, they set about training for an exercise which, Frost was informed, 'would probably take place in the Isle of Wight and the whole of the War Cabinet would be there to see it'. The interest and enthusiasm of 'C' Company was aroused and maintained by the information conveyed by Peter Bromley-Martin, the liaison officer with divisional headquarters, that if the demonstration were convincing enough, the company would be chosen to carry out a real raid on the coast of France later on.

Alton Priors, north of Salisbury Plain, was chosen as a suitable spot to practise moving from the dropping zone to the objective, and from the objective to an imaginary coast where, after completing their task, the parachute troops would embark upon imaginary assault landing craft for the return home. Such was the plan as outlined by Bromley-Martin, but, to Frost's annoyance, he went on to explain that 'as this was such a very special demonstration, the normal company organisation would have to be scrapped, and it would have to be divided into parties of different size. Each party would be given a different task, and therefore . . . would be differently organised, armed and equipped'. Frost argued in vain against such a novel departure from all the then accepted principles of the tactical handling of parachute troops, but Bromley-Martin was adamant, and after much discussion the two men 'parted with veiled hostility on both sides'.

In the meantime Flight-Sergeant E. W. F. Cox, an expert radio engineer, was on his way to the Air Ministry in London. Arrived, he reported to an air-commodore, who at once congratulated him 'on having volunteered for a special and dangerous mission'. Cox had certainly volunteered for a special mission, but this was the first time that he had heard that it was likely to be dangerous. His apprehension and curiosity were still further aroused when he was told to report to Ringway to learn 'all about parachute jumping'. He did so and qualified as a parachutist in about the same time as it had taken Frost to acquire his wings.

While he was doing so 'C' Company were busy with their rehearsals at Alton Priors. Their commanding officer and Bromley-Martin were no longer at loggerheads, for the liaison officer had been allowed to tell the truth: the demonstration before the whole of the Cabinet was a mere cover story. 'Actually,' said Bromley-Martin, 'you will be taking the company over to the coast of France before the end of February.' The news, though 'it flung a heavy cloak of responsibility' upon him, filled Frost with exultation; nor was this damped when he found that 'a very detailed plan' had been made by one of the planning syndicates at Combined Operations headquarters.

This time the objective was not a snow-covered aqueduct in southern Italy, but a snow-covered hole in the ground in northern France. It held a radiolocation apparatus known as a giant Wurzberg. This was a device, one of a chain stretched along the coast of western Europe. These installations were designed to give warning to her German masters of the approach of hostile aircraft or ships. That they were doing so had been known for months, but the precise nature of the apparatus used in these installations was still a matter for the argument and conjecture of experts. Photographed many times, their ultimate secrets were hidden behind thick walls. The capture of one such apparatus would, it was hoped and believed, shew not only the mechanical methods of radio-detection used by the Germans, but equally, if not more important, whether these were in advance or behind those which we ourselves were using. Precisely how accurate the devices of the enemy were was a matter of no small concern to Bomber Command, which night after night went forth to battle. In this, therefore, the second operation of parachute troops, the stakes were much higher than those of the first. They were called upon, not to interfere with the problematic water supply of some Italian peasants, but to seize and bring back an instrument which was playing a very important part in the ceaseless warfare waged between the bombers of the Royal Air Force and the defences of occupied Europe.

The force given this task eventually consisted of one hundred and nineteen all ranks, divided into three parties, to which the code names of three famous sailors—Drake, Nelson and Rodney —were given. Browning chose them out of compliment to the Navy and to emphasise the fact that the projected operation was one in which all three services would play an essential part. The Air Force would take the Army to the objective, and when the Army had done its work it would be removed from France and brought back to England by the Navy. Among the one hundred and nineteen officers and men finally chosen were a small party of Sappers and a few men from 'B' Company. Conspicuous among the non-commissioned officers was Company Sergeant-Major G. Strachan of the Black Watch, 'a man who knew exactly how a company should be run'.

The training was strenuous and everyone worked long hours, for time was short; but at week-ends the admirable rule that there should be complete relaxation for twenty-four hours was strictly kept. As the winter days went by Captain J. G. Ross,[1] a Scotsman from Dundee, and Frost's second-in-command, began to receive an ever-increasing quantity of stores. These arrived at irregular moments, both by day and by night. Soon every man was equipped with the then newly invented Sten gun, something between an automatic rifle and an automatic pistol. At that time it had not been perfected—as the Canadians were to find to their cost some months later at Dieppe—and therefore contained a number of defects absent from the later model. These the parachute troops did their best to discover and remedy, being consoled by the fact that, though the new weapon might not be perfect, it was greatly superior up to a range of fifty yards to the rifle and bayonet with which they had up till then been equipped.

During the training at Alton Priors the embryo raiders made the acquaintance of No. 51 Squadron of the Royal Air Force, flying Whitleys, which was to take them to their destination. It was commanded by Wing Commander P. C. Pickard, D.F.C., who before his death in action two years later in the attack on the gaol at Amiens was to be admitted three times to the Distinguished Service Order. He was an airman of the highest ability, and was well known to the general public, for he had played a leading part in the film *Target for Tonight*, at that time drawing large audiences throughout the country. After talking with the pilots, Frost and his men 'were left in no doubt as to their efficiency, and we felt that if anybody was going to

[1] Later Major J. G. Ross, D.S.O.

put us down in the right place they were the people to do it'.

After some time spent on Salisbury Plain, they travelled to Inveraray on Loch Fyne, removing their parachute wings for obvious reasons of security during the journey, and there made contact with the officers and crews of the assault landing craft, whose duty it would be to take them back to England. The parent ship of these craft was the *Prince Albert*, on board which the parachute troops took up their quarters. This part of the training was found to be very enjoyable, 'although it meant long hours and frequent wettings in the icy Loch'. What was disconcerting, however, was the discovery that the business of embarking in the dark was not so easy as they had imagined. Moreover, the captains of the landing craft did not by any means always discover the whereabouts of the parachute troops as they waited for them on the cold lochside, and this augered ill for their successful retreat on the night of the enterprise. By then few doubted that they would reach their destination, but that they would be able to leave the shores of France after accomplishing their mission seemed less certain.

Having completed their training at Inveraray rather less than more to their satisfaction, the party returned to Tilshead, where they carried out a practice drop from the aircraft belonging to No. 51 Squadron, which had never had parachute troops on board before. 'Although the ground was brick-hard there were no casualties', and it was noted that Sergeant Grieve, Seaforth Highlanders, and his men left their aircraft far more smartly than any of the other sticks.

By then Frost and his men had reached that point in their training, well-known to all who rehearse something which they will subsequently perform in public, when nothing seems to go according to plan. The hardest part of the business would obviously be the embarkation in the dark when the operation was over, and consequently 'nearly every day a small convoy of five troop-carrying vehicles' could be seen 'travelling down to the Dorset coast at a steady forty miles per hour'. The weather was fickle, and more than one of these journeys proved fruitless. The last rehearsal 'could not have been a more dismal failure'. The parachute troops were to leave their lorries at a point near the sea where the ground was flat ; aircraft were to fly over and drop containers carrying their weapons and a mock attack would then be made on a fictitious radiolocation post, after which the raiders would move down to the beach and enter the landing craft. That was the plan. Very little of it was put into practice.

51

The containers were dropped in the wrong place; the landing craft arrived at the wrong beach; the parachute troops lost themselves in a minefield ten miles from the correct spot.

The next morning Frost was faced with something of a crisis. The first available date for the operation was only forty-eight hours away, and the naval authorities, quite rightly, insisted that a further rehearsal was essential. Very fortunately the weather intervened: a postponement of the raid was inevitable, and the night of Sunday, 23rd February was spent on the shores of Southampton Water in a final exercise. This time all went well, save that a miscalculation of the time of the tide caused the landing craft to stick in the mud sixty yards from the shore. 'Though,' says Frost, 'we walked out to heave and shove, hard and fast they remained, and we went home to bed.'

Only four possible nights were now left, the Monday to the Thursday of the week beginning 24th February. A full moon, or a moon nearly so, was essential if the parachute troops were to see and recognise their objective, and the Navy required a rising tide. By then every man had been briefed in detail, new information being given to him as it arrived, which it did 'in almost incredible detail'. Before they set out all knew the exact position of every enemy defence, the strength, the billets, the weapons, the temper of the German garrison, and even some of their names. What the small building containing the radiolocation device looked like and its exact whereabouts were impressed on everyone by means of a scale model of remarkable fidelity. It shewed a section of high white cliff, the abrupt ending of some flat fields traversed by paths, of which one connected a circular hole in the ground holding the radar installation with a fair-sized modern villa of great vulgarity and little charm. It was quite new and approached by a rather more than semi-circular drive.

The task of Frost and 'C' Company was to enable Flight-Sergeant Cox and a section of the 1st Parachute Field Squadron Royal Engineers, under Captain Denis Vernon, to dismantle the radar station, bring back parts of it, and photograph those which could not be moved. The radar experts had, therefore, to be brought to the station, protected while they dismantled it, and then removed with their booty to the boats.

The German defences were far from negligible. Their garrison consisted of three bodies of men: first the signallers and covering troops on duty at the radar post itself and the villa, who numbered about thirty; next those in immediate support, some hundred all told, stationed at La Presbytère, a cluster of farm buildings in a wooded enclosure about three hundred yards to the north of the villa. They served as billets for coast defence troops and for the signallers when off duty. Finally there was the garrison of the village of Bruneval itself, numbering forty, who might be manning the pillboxes and earthworks covering the village and the beach from which the evacuation would have to be made. These pillboxes were situated both on the top of the cliffs and at their foot where they joined the beach.

The three parties into which Frost had divided his force were of unequal strength. The largest, to which Cox, Vernon and the sappers were attached, was called 'Drake', and consisted of fifty men. They were subdivided into two groups, one under Lieutenant Peter Young, whose orders were to assault the radar station itself. The other, under Frost, who would attack the villa. 'Drake' was to drop first and to be followed after a short interval by the second party, known as 'Nelson' and made up of Lieutenant E. C. B. Charteris, King's Own Scottish Borderers, and forty men. The third detachment, 'Rodney', which was to land last after another short interval, was composed of Lieutenant John Timothy, Royal West Kent Regiment, and thirty men. They were to deal with any Germans advancing to counter-attack either the station or the beach, and to act as a general reserve.

In the later stages of planning and rehearsal Frost and his men derived much amusement from trying to imagine what the enemy in the villa in Bruneval were doing or might be doing when they arrived. The village was known to possess 'a fairly well-appointed estaminet', and it was hoped that on the night chosen it would be well patronised. In order to achieve swift and overwhelming surprise every man of Frost's party was to be in his position before the assault began, and after much discussion it was decided that Frost himself should give the signal for the battle to begin by blowing his whistle just as he broke in the door of the villa. What, he wondered, should he do if the door were locked? 'Ring the bell,' suggested one of his men; 'but in the event it proved unnecessary'.

It will be observed that throughout everyone taking part in the raid, regardless of his rank, discussed the plan and was encouraged to make suggestions. This admirable practice—one with which the commando troops who wore the green beret were familiar—was followed whenever possible by those who wore the red. On more than one occasion it provoked timely suggestions which contributed to subsequent success.

One point was of paramount importance: the operation had to be timed very accurately. The force was to remain on the soil of France for just as many minutes as would be required to seize the radar apparatus, dismantle and remove it, and for not one minute longer; and those minutes had to be as few as possible, for—a fact that they did not forget—these hundred and nineteen men were thrusting themselves into the outer defences of an enemy who, with every road at his command, could bring overwhelming strength against them in a short time. Moreover, there was also the Channel tide and its vagaries to be considered. The assault craft must not be left stranded on the rocks as they had been on the mud during the final rehearsal.

The ships which were to take them back to England were under the general command of Commander E. N. Cook, Royal Australian Navy, and consisted of motor gunboats of the 14th Flotilla, assault landing craft and support landing craft. These were under Lieutenant-Commander W. G. Everett, Royal Navy. Two destroyers were detailed to act as escort. The assault landing craft were empty except for their crews; but in the support landing craft were thirty-two officers and men of the Royal Fusiliers and the South Wales Borderers, with orders to provide covering fire while the parachute troops, their task accomplished, were embarking.

By 24th February all was ready. The containers carrying demolition charges, signalling apparatus, additional weapons and other necessary gear had been packed and sent to Thruxton airfield, the last orders had been given, the last adjustments made, and the parachute troops lay down in the afternoon to take a few hours' rest. They were not unnaturally keyed up, for they had been living under a certain strain during the period of preparation. All were young, high-spirited, and possessed of their fair share of the faults and virtues of that time of life. Their behaviour had in it the 'excuse of youth and heat of blood' and had therefore to be carefully watched; for, as Frost noted at the time, 'if the enemy has an inkling of the project we shall be doomed'. Though the many details of the attack were known to all, for all had had a share in working them out, the object and the destination of the force were kept a close secret from everyone except the officers. That the place was Bruneval and the objective the radar station close to it were only divulged at the last moment. Even so, Frost had his moments of anxiety, especially when one evening some of the wilder elements of his command arrived in camp from the public houses of Tilshead marching behind an improvised band playing 'borrowed' instruments, the property of the local branch of the British Legion. 'Thereafter the guardroom door yawned more widely' and the threat that such conduct would mean a swift and ignominious return to Hardwick, and thence to unit, sufficed. Though as noisy as most in their cups, no parachute soldier gave a hint of what was so soon to be in the wind.

At teatime on the 24th a message was received announcing a postponement of twenty-four hours owing to adverse weather conditions. On the next day, the 25th, and the day after, the 26th, it was repeated. 'Each morning we braced ourselves for the venture, and each evening, after a further postponement, we had time to think of all the things that could go wrong.' On Thursday morning, the 27th, the weather seemed no different, and Frost was expecting to be sent on leave with orders to be ready to operate in a month's time when the moon should again be favourable, when a staff officer arrived to say that the period of waiting would be extended by another twenty-four hours. 'Listlessly and without much enthusiasm,' the containers were once more packed and sent to the airfield.

Throughout this trying period, one with which officers and men of the Parachute Regiment became only too familiar before the end of the war, Company Sergeant-Major Strachan alone refused to be depressed. He was quite convinced that Thursday would be the day, and when at teatime, in place of the staff officer, Major-General Browning himself arrived to say that they were to take off that night, he was quietly triumphant. The weather was at last favourable. 'No wind . . . and a bright moon, with a little cloud and a light haze,' reported the naval commander afterwards; and his words were echoed by Wing Commander Pickard, who stated that 'visibility in the area was found to be two to four miles, with excellent definition'.

The men were in high spirits when they arrived at Thruxton airfield. Here they formed up and marched round the perimeter 'like Guardsmen', behind pipers playing the regimental marches of Scotland. There was time for a last cigarette and a mug of tea well laced with rum before the twelve sticks entered the twelve Whitleys, silently waiting. At the last moment Frost was called to the telephone to speak to Nigel Norman in charge of the air side of the operation. France, he reported, was covered with snow, and the light anti-aircraft defences 'seemed to be particularly alert'.

One by one the aircraft took off, Frost flying in that piloted by Pickard. The parachutists, wrapped in sleeping-bags, gave vent to their feelings in song, the favourites being 'Annie Laurie', 'Lulu' and 'Come sit by my side if you love me', the special song of the parachute troops of which only that line is printable. Not to be outdone by the Army, Flight-Sergeant Cox 'obliged' with a solo rendering of 'The Rose of Tralee'. Others in other aircraft played cards—the old army game of pontoon. Among them was Corporal Stewart, an inveterate player, who was carrying a wallet well-filled with former winnings which he had steadfastly refused to leave behind. To these he was now able to add, remarking as he did so, that if he were hit whoever was near him would find himself in luck's way. . . . .

From time to time Pickard sent back messages telling of their progress and whereabouts. An hour went by, and, despite the sleeping-bags, the cold inside the cramped bellies of the Whitleys was beginning to cause great discomfort. Added to this, 'the huge mugs of hot tea we had drunk before taking off soon began to scream to be let out. In that restricted space, and encumbered as we were, there was, alas, no way'. When they had been flying for two hours the coverings over the holes in the floors of the Whitleys, through which they were to jump, were removed, and soon afterwards they could see the coast of France near Le Havre. Their presence did not pass unnoticed by the enemy and anti-aircraft shells began to burst in the silver air about them. A number of aircraft were hit, though no serious damage was caused, but two of the Whitleys, one with Charteris on board, had to take avoiding action and in consequence arrived late and not quite at the right dropping zone.

At the moment planned the red light shone. Frost sat on the edge of the hole, and on the appearance of the green light thrust himself into space. As soon as his parachute opened he could see all the features he had expected 'standing out in the bright moonlight'. There was the forming-up place, a row of trees by a gully. 'That they had arrived at exactly the right spot was,' he was convinced, 'in great part due to the excellent air photography which had been provided.'

On reaching the ground Frost and his stick performed a natural function. This 'was certainly not good drill, as now was the time when a stick of parachutists are most vulnerable . . . but at least it was a gesture of defiance'. 'The first thing that struck me,' said Flight-Sergeant Cox afterwards, 'was how quiet everything was and how lonely I felt, and then I heard some

56

rustling and saw something outlined against the snow. It was a container.'

It took the men composing the 'Drake' contingent ten minutes to collect their weapons and form up in the belt of trees by the gully. They then set off, moving—since they had been dropped inland—towards the coast and the radar station. The only sound was the noise made by the engines of the departing Whitleys, and some distance away a few bursts of machine-gun fire aimed probably at the aircraft. From the bijou villa and the radar station beyond, 'which we could see plainly, there was no sign of alarm'. At a slow run Frost, Young and the men of 'Drake' approached and surrounded them in silence. According to the plan, Frost made for the door of the villa. To his surprise it was open and 'I nearly forgot to blow my whistle before going in. As soon as I blew it explosions, yells and the sound of automatic fire' broke the silence of the quiet night. At the head of four men, Frost, shouting 'Hände hoch!' dashed into the villa, which was found to be unfurnished. Running upstairs, they killed the only German inside, who was leaning from the window of an upper room firing on Young's men now entering the buildings which housed the radar instruments.

Leaving two men in the villa, Frost with the rest made off to join Young. On reaching him he found that the Germans manning the radar post had been killed or captured. One of the prisoners had, in the confusion, leapt over the edge of the cliff, but had landed on a ledge ten feet down and been hauled back. He was immediately interrogated, was found to be a signaller and confirmed the information already known to the raiders, that the number of Germans in the immediate neighbourhood was not more than a hundred. For the moment all seemed well. Denis Vernon with the sappers had arrived, and with him was Flight-Sergeant Cox, who was beginning to inspect and dismantle those parts of the radar set which were to be taken back to England.

It was then that fire from La Presbytère opened. Fortunately it was inaccurate, but one man was killed and two bullets struck the apparatus under Sergeant Cox's hands. Frost and his men were forming a defensive perimeter round the radar set, of which most stood above ground and resembled 'an old-fashioned gramophone loudspeaker', and were soon in position. Twenty minutes passed then three enemy vehicles were observed moving behind the wood of La Presbytère. This was serious, for if they contained mortars and opened fire they would catch the parachute troops in the open and 'it would be difficult to get the equipment away'. The signallers reported that the small wireless sets they carried were not working, and Frost 'began to feel the lack of a proper company headquarters' organisation. We had turned ourselves into an assault group for the attack on the villa, and now when I wanted some signallers, runners and my sergeant-major, they were all dispersed doing other tasks'. Vernon and Cox presently reported that they had dismantled the instruments needed, the party moved towards the beach, and presently came under fire from a pillbox situated on the edge of a cliff. Several men were hit, including Company Sergeant-Major Strachan, who received three bullets in the stomach. He was dragged to cover and given morphia.

By now, however, contact had been made with the 'Rodney' party further inland, though some confusion was caused by a sudden shout, 'The boats are here; it's all right! Come on down!' This news—who cried it in the night whether one of the enemy, or a parachutist excited by this his first time in action is not known—was immediately contradicted by John Ross, the second-in-command. He was near the beach and shouted that the defences had not yet been taken. Obviously something was wrong, and at that moment Frost was told that the Germans had reoccupied the villa and were advancing against him. What had happened was this.

Charteris and the 'Nelson' party had been dropped at the wrong place, for, as will be remembered, some of the Whitleys had had to alter course to avoid anti-aircraft fire. They had, in consequence, landed two and a half miles away from their chosen assembly point, and because of this were late in arriving at the scene of action. Without the 'Nelson' party, Timothy and the 'Rodney' contingent were not strong enough to attack the German pillboxes and other defences covering the beach. On landing, Charteris had at once realised that he was in the wrong valley, though 'it looked very like the right one, but there was no row of trees at the bottom of it as there should have been, and it was not deep enough. I don't mind saying that this was a nasty moment'. Seeing that the aircraft which he had just left had turned and was flying north, he and his men moved in that direction at that Red-Indian lope, between a fast walk and a trot, which was the gait of the trained parachutist. He soon caught sight of the lighthouse at Cap d'Antifer and this gave him his bearing. Almost at once he and his men came into contact with the enemy. Both sides were moving in single file in the moonlight, and one of the Germans attached himself to the men of 'Nelson', under the impression that they belonged to his own patrol. Subsequent explanations resulted in his death. Moving in the traditional manner to the sound of the guns, in this instance the rattle of machine-gun fire, Charteris, after a running fight near the village of Bruneval, fell in with Frost close to the largest pillbox on the beach.

Their relief in meeting was mutual, and Frost immediately ordered Charteris and Timothy to attack and clear the beach. As he did so, he saw Vernon, Cox and the sappers 'slipping and sliding with their heavily laden trolleys' down the frozen path from the site of the radar set towards the shore. They were accompanied by Sergeant-Major Strachan, half-walking, half-carried, calling out, under the influence of morphia, unintelligible orders.

Charteris and his men, shouting their war-cry 'Caber Feigh'[1], supported by Timothy and his, rushed the beach. A house on its outskirts received 'two volleys of hand grenades', while the garrison of a nearby pillbox was speedily despatched. For some moments the enemy resisted violently with machine-gun fire and grenades. A splinter struck Corporal Stewart on the head and laid him low. Mindful of his pontoon winnings, he called out to his nearest comrade, Lance-Corporal Freeman: 'I've had it. Here's my wallet.' Freeman hastened to take it and then examined Stewart, clearly visible in the bright moonlight. 'You've only a scalp wound,' he said, to which Stewart immediately retorted, 'Gie us my bluidy wallet back, then.'

The house, like the villa, was found to be empty, save for a very frightened German orderly engaged in a telephone conversation with a furious company commander some miles inland. It was broken off just as the officer was threatening the German garrison with condign punishment on the following morning for making so much noise and disturbing his rest.

The hour was now about a quarter-past two in the morning; the beach was in our hands and the instruments, dismantled by Vernon and Cox, lying upon it with the wounded. But where was the Navy? Some minutes went by and then the signallers informed Frost that they were unable to make contact with the ships which by then had been many hours at sea, for they had to start long before the parachute troops. Signals by lamp were tried, but 'still we got no reply. There was a light mist out to sea and visibility was no more than half a mile'. As a last

[1] The antlers of the deer.

emergency Frost had arranged to fire a red Very light, first to the north and then to the south of the beach. He now did so more than once; but from the dark and heaving waters there came no sign. 'With a sinking heart', he records, 'I moved off the beach with my officers to rearrange our defences. It looked as though we were going to be left high and dry, and the thought was hard to bear. The prisoners were questioned as to the whereabouts of the enemy's reserves, but they were too frightened to be coherent.' On each side the great cliffs loomed above the little beach and the little force, and seemed to 'dominate us with ever-increasing menace'.

But all was well. The men had hardly taken up their new positions, when a signaller shouted, 'Sir, the boats are coming in; the boats are here. God bless the ruddy Navy, sir!' And 'we saw several dark shapes glide in across the water'. In obedience to their order, the covering party of Royal Fusiliers and South Wales Borderers at once directed a heavy fire upon the cliffs, of which the noise echoing to and fro was deafening. They were with difficulty persuaded to cease; but fortunately none of the parachute troops was hit. All six landing craft came in together, and for some moments a mild confusion reigned. Frost, however, was able to put the wounded and the captured radar equipment into one landing craft, and then the parachutists scrambled on board the others, each man as best he could, as the Germans began 'to lob grenades and motor bombs onto the beach'. The orderly withdrawal which had been planned had gone by the board, and there was no time to make sure that everyone had been taken off. Eight men were in fact left behind; two of them were dead and six had not yet reached the beach. As he stepped on board one of the motor gunboats, her wireless operator informed Frost that he had just picked up a message from two of the six who had lost their way and only arrived at the beach after the landing craft had put out to sea again.

The raiders were taken from the open landing craft into the gunboats, which then made off for England with the landing craft in tow. Below deck, in the warmth and amid the mugs of rum, Frost and his men learned that while the flotilla had been lying offshore awaiting them a German destroyer and two E-boats had passed by less than a mile away, and 'by God's good grace had failed to notice us'. This was the reason why no reply had been sent to the signals of the raiders.

On board one of the gunboats was Doctor R. V. Jones, a radar expert, who informed the parachutists to their delight that

Flight-Sergeant Cox and Lieutenant Vernon had been able to remove almost everything that the scientists desired to examine.

At dawn the flotilla was not more than fifteen miles from the French coast, but it was met by a squadron of Spitfires which gave it cover throughout the passage home. 'We vainly tried,' says Frost, 'to sleep as the gunboats rolled and jerked across the Channel. I went on to the bridge as we approached Portsmouth. There were destroyers now on either side of the flotilla, and when we broke away to head for the *Victory*, they came by and saluted us.' A little later Pickard and his pilots were welcoming their passengers, amid a confused crowd of 'staff officers, photographers and reporters'.

So ended the raid on Bruneval which, at the cost of two killed, six wounded and six missing, fulfilled the exact intention of those who had planned it. Frost and Charteris were awarded the Military Cross; Young was mentioned in Dispatches; Flight-Sergeant Cox received the Military Medal, as did Sergeants Grieve and McKenzie. Company Sergeant-Major Strachan was awarded the Croix de Guerre with Palm; he recovered with great speed from his wounds, and a few weeks later was back with the 2nd Battalion.

The affair of Bruneval has been told in detail so that the hazards and opportunities of this strange and then still novel form of attack may be understood. On the day after the raid a Hurricane was sent in a reconnaissance over Bruneval and La Presbytère. Its pilot saw a number of German officers standing round the circular hole which had housed the radar apparatus and which now gaped wide and empty. He dived and opened fire with his machine-guns. The hole was quickly occupied.

The Red Devils

ON SATURDAY, 4th April 1942, Mr. Harry Hopkins and General Marshall 'took off for London to propose the invasion of the Continent of Europe'.[1] On Sunday, 8th November of the same year, an Anglo-American Army landed

[1] *The White House Papers of Harry L. Hopkins,* by Robert E. Sherwood, Eyre & Spottiswoode, vol ii, p. 523.

at eleven points in French North Africa, from Casablanca in the west to Algiers in the east.

The invasion of North Africa was a compromise, the result of the stalemate reached by the British and American Chiefs of Staff in their discussions on strategy. The first, with the full force of naval opinion on both sides of the Atlantic behind them, were convinced that Operation 'Sledgehammer'—the seizure of the Cotentin Peninsular as a bridgehead—was impracticable with the resources then at the disposal of the Allies; the second were not prepared to press their view too far. Yielding with an excellent grace, Roosevelt was soon proposing Operation 'Gymnast', subsequently known as 'Torch', as a substitute. It was the first considerable operation of war in which British parachute troops took part, and, as will shortly be apparent, except at the outset, they did so, like their comrades, No. 1 and No. 6 Commando, as normal infantry of the Line, though normal is not perhaps the right adjective to apply to men by that time highly trained and grimly eager for battle.

More than eight months had elapsed since the small but singularly successful descent upon Bruneval. During them the 1st Airborne Division came into existence, and its 1st Parachute Brigade, made up of the 1st, 2nd and 3rd Battalions, was got ready and more than ready for action. Through all that summer they trained, the 1st Battalion losing in July, to their momentary dismay, Eric Down, who was appointed to command the 2nd Parachute Brigade then forming. His place was taken by Lieutenant-Colonel S. J. L. Hill, with Major Alastair Pearson as second-in-command. Both were soon to be well known in the ranks of the parachutists. Hill has been described as 'the ideal parachute commander'. Pearson, a Territorial soldier, commanded a battalion at the age of twenty-seven.

Changes also occurred in the 2nd Battalion, whose commanding officer, Flavell, took over the brigade from Gale and handed the battalion to Major Gofton-Salmond, the second-in-command being Major R. G. Pine-Coffin. Gale was appointed to the War Office as Director of Air. These arrangements lasted during the summer, but by the end of October the battalion was being commanded by Frost, since Gofton-Salmond had been found medically unfit for parachute service. Lathbury, who commanded the 3rd Battalion, was transferred to the War Office, his place being taken by Lieutenant-Colonel R. Webb, who at the beginning of the autumn handed over to Pine-Coffin from the 2nd Battalion.

In May the 1st Brigade, as part of the newly formed division, was inspected by the King and Queen, and shortly afterwards by Major-General Browning. More new formations were coming into being, some of them parachute troops, others glider-borne; but the brigade remained together and trained together in and near Bulford on Salisbury Plain. By then, in addition to the blue wings of the parachutists, the Pegasus badge designed by Edward Seago, Camouflage Officer of Southern Command—Bellerophon astride the winged steed, brandishing a spear, his cloak fluttering in the wind—was being worn by all ranks.

The 2nd Parachute Brigade was also forming and before the end of August consisted of the 4th Battalion, the 5th, which was Scottish, and the 6th, which was Welsh. It was commanded by Brigadier E. E. Down. 1st August 1942 is a date of great significance in the history of the Parachute Regiment. It was on that day that the War Office decreed that all parachute infantry units should belong to one regiment, to be known as the Parachute Regiment. The new formation was to be part of the Army Air Corps to which the Glider Pilot Regiment already belonged. A little more than two years had passed since Rock had set out for Ringway to organise the airborne forces of the British Army. An important part of these had now become a regular formation manned by trained men eager to prove that in this new field of warfare, though they had rivals, they had no superiors.

Slowly the tempo increased, and by the middle of the summer more and more Dakota aircraft belonging to the U.S. Army Air Force were replacing the outworn Whitleys to such an extent that battalion 'drops' became increasingly frequent. In the early stages the Dakotas, whose advent had caused much satisfaction, proved to be the proverbial mixed blessing. True, the parachutists could now leave 'like gentlemen', as one of them expressed it, through the door, shuffling along rapidly one behind the other, their static lines clipped to a steel cable running the length of the fuselage; but the lines were too short, and on the first occasion a jump was made the canopies of two parachutes became entangled with the rear wheel, which was not properly protected. The practice of the pilots, before they learned to raise the tail, of flying straight and level when dropping the sticks, added to the danger of fouling the rear wheel. These defects, which caused the deaths of four men, Lieutenant Street and his batman of the 2nd Battalion being among them, were presently remedied. Unlike the early pioneers, the 2nd Battalion was fortunate to receive most valuable aid from the 2nd Battalion of the 502nd

Parachute Infantry, U.S. Army stationed close by at Hungerford. From the first these American parachute troops had used the Dakota, and they were eager to share their knowledge and experience with their British comrades. Lieutenant Timothy, M.C., one of those who had fought at Bruneval, was attached to them as brigade liaison officer.

As the summer days went by, exercises became more numerous. They were carried out by men brought to a high pitch of physical fitness. By the middle of the summer, for example, 'A' Company of the 2nd Battalion had covered eighty miles in three days, and soon afterwards broke this record by marching fifty-four miles in twenty-four hours. This period of training culminated in August with an attack carried out by the 1st Battalion upon pillboxes near Exford under heavy covering fire provided by light machine-guns and mortars firing live ammunition.

When it was over the battalion marched back to Bulford, carrying full equipment and covering a hundred and ten miles in three days and a half. Before this exercise it had been under orders to take part in the raid on Dieppe which was carried out on the 19th August; but a change of plan caused commando troops to be substituted for parachute.

The 3rd Battalion took part in the exercise 'Dryshod', flying from the south of England to the north of Ireland and then to the north of Scotland. They eventually dropped at 22.30 hours. In September hopes of an encounter with the enemy rose sharply when the 1st and 2nd Battalions received orders to take part in an attack upon Ushant. Its object was to kill or capture the German garrison and by so doing to provide the parachute troops with experience in battle and thus to prepare them for great events now brewing. The attack did not take place, however, for the troops taking part in it would have had to remain on shore for forty-eight hours, and the Navy reluctantly came to the conclusion that before this period had elapsed the heavy German garrisons and naval units close at hand in Brest would be fully roused and able to intervene with decisive effect. The task of evacuating the parachute troops would thus have been exceedingly hazardous, if not impossible. Moreover, a preliminary daylight bombing attack carried out by American Fortresses escorted by Spitfires had been a failure. The Americans lost their way and several of their escort, running out of fuel, landed in France. In consequence it was thought impossible to achieve surprise. Back, therefore, went the brigade to the seemingly interminable business of training. Not even the know-ledge that new units were forming, and that the war leaders were obviously determined some time or other to make full use of the as yet almost untried airborne formations, altogether sufficed to still the voice of grumblers. Yet these were few in number, and the historians of all three Battalions make mention of the very high temper of the officers and men at this time.

Even the administrative staff, who were not required to jump, did their utmost to do so. A Sergeant 'Mac', a quartermaster of the 1st Battalion, persuaded one of his officers to allow him to make a practice jump. The officer, Captain R. J. Gammon, M.C., the inventor of the bomb which bears his name, went first, so that he could explain to Sergeant 'Mac', when in the air, the proper position to assume in order to make a safe landing. 'We took off,' he writes, 'and Sergeant "Mac's" boisterous good humour continued, though I thought it to be a trifle forced as the dropping zone approached. I jumped and almost on my neck came Sergeant "Mac" . . . in the air he was a shambles and disorganised. I screamed a screed of instructions, "Keep your feet together", etc., but they were of no avail. Sergeant "Mac" hit the ground like the proverbial sack of potatoes.' He had broken his leg, but to avoid any disciplinary action it was given out 'that he had fallen into an air-raid trench in the black-out when leaving the sergeants' mess'.

The high temper of the brigade continued to swell as the golden October days slipped by, and in the 3rd Battalion reached fever pitch when towards the end of the month 'B' and 'C' Companies, the Mortar Platoon and some of battalion Head-quarters left Bulford for an unknown destination. It turned out to be, first, Netheravon, and then Hurn airfield. These units were the most fortunate of the brigade. The remainder, comprising the 1st and 2nd Battalions, and the rest of the 3rd, were taken about the same time or a little later, not to airfields, but to a seaport, Greenock. They were under sealed orders, and may be left bemoaning the fact that the ships upon which they were embarked were 'dry', winning each other's money at pontoon, and speculating for hours on end as to their destination, while the fortunes of 'B' and 'C' Companies of the 3rd Battalion are considered.

The problems they had to face were many. They had had very little practice in jumping from Dakotas, and their American pilots had only recently transferred from civilian to army life. They had been employed by civilian airlines and had been

C

hastily enrolled in No. 60 Group of the United States Army Air Force. Since each had several thousand flying hours to his credit, they were highly experienced, but they had never flown over hostile territory, or encountered anti-aircraft fire. Moreover, they had not been trained to navigate by compass or the stars, for the aircraft of the U.S.A. airlines were kept on their course by means of radio beams.

The pilots were not the only problem. There was also that of the aircraft themselves: only thirty-three were available, and these had been specially flown from the U.S.A. All the information that Major Marshall, brigade major of the 1st Brigade, could glean about them was that their payload was five thousand pounds. On this meagre datum he had to construct his loading schedules. His first task was to decide with Pine-Coffin, the commanding officer, what men should be carried. Obviously the three-inch Mortar Platoon could not be left behind, but it was impossible to take more than two of the three rifle companies. The choice was made by the three company commanders cutting a pack of cards. Fate decided that 'B' Company, under Major Dobie, and 'C' under Major Hall, should fly; Major Terrell, commanding 'A' Company, was unlucky and had to take his command by sea.

Then came the problem of the equipment and weapons to be carried, and here Marshall suffered a serious setback. On arrival the Dakotas were found to have a payload of not five thousand pounds but only of three thousand because extra petrol tanks would have to be carried owing to the distance which separated Hurn airfield from Gibraltar. The loading schedules, therefore, had to be revised and the problem was tackled by marking out thirty-three rectangles on the floor of a hangar, each rectangle representing one aircraft. The exact weight of every man was then ascertained and marked in each rectangle. Only then was it possible to discover how much equipment could also be carried. Its weight, too, was then noted in the same manner, and if possible the equipment itself was dumped in the rectangle. 'It was,' says Major Marshall, 'a most finicky and brain-tensing business, as allowances had to be made continuously. For instance, if Private Smith, who was down to fly in aircraft No. 28 and who weighed two hundred pounds in his equipment, went sick, and if his place was taken by Private Robinson, any difference in the weight of these two soldiers had to be adjusted by juggling with the loose equipment it was hoped to carry in that aircraft.'

The date was late in 1942; Great Britain had been at war for more than three years, the United States of America for nearly a year, but no more than thirty-three aircraft flown by thinly disguised civilians were available for so important an operation. Marshall and those with him were fortunately too busy to allow this aspect of the situation to weigh upon their minds. The smudged figures on the floor became more numerous, the additions and substractions more complex; but by 5th November, when the companies finally moved to Hurn, all was ready. The next day the Dakotas arrived at the airfield, Pine-Coffin briefed his men, and all awaited the order to take off. It was sent in code by wireless, and its nature depended on the date on which the landings from the sea took place, and on the reception according to the troops who then went ashore. Two days passed, two days of that inevitable strain which was perhaps the most trying element in the life of the parachute soldier. Then on the 8th the success of the initial assault became known; but the elation caused by this news changed into 'great despondency because the whole airfield was shrouded in thick fog'. It would be impossible for the Dakotas, loaded as they were to the last ounce, to take off with safety. During the afternoon the signal to do so was received, but could not be obeyed.

On the next day, the 9th, the fog began to disperse, but it was necessary to wait for darkness before sending the unarmed and slow-flying Dakotas on a long flight during much of which they would be within easy range of shore-based German fighters. Then in the afternoon the weather experts issued a forecast which seemed to dash the last hopes. With the gathering darkness the fog would increase and would be general all over the south of England except possibly in the west of Cornwall. Pine-Coffin and Marshall, Colonel Dorset of the U.S. Army and his pilots, however, were determined not to be defeated by the weather. Urgent messages were sent to the Royal Air Force at St. Eval and to the Southern Railway. In a few hours every man of the airborne party had been driven to the nearest railway station, issued with rations and embarked on a special train. It took them to Newquay station, where Royal Air Force trucks were waiting to take them to the airfield at St. Eval. 'The Army,' says Marshall, 'is always critical of Royal Air Force truck drivers, and there is no doubt that the drivers of these trucks, who had obviously been impressed with the urgency of the journey, certainly alarmed everyone . . . by the breakneck speed with which they rushed the parachutists to the aerodrome. It was just 23.00 hours when they arrived, without incident, let it be said.'

All but two of the Dakotas, detained at Hurn by engine trouble, were awaiting them. This last-minute defection 'called for hectic readjustment, because the two aircraft which had broken down were those destined to carry certain key commanders'. Places were found for them in other aircraft, but their kit had to be left behind. 'The Royal Air Force continued to impress the party by providing a splendid hot meal, so that when the first Dakota took off at 23.30 hours everyone was in very good heart.'

The problem of navigation had also been solved by the Royal Air Force, which had provided at very short notice a navigator for each Dakota.

So they flew through the night to take part in the first operation in which parachute troops would co-operate with ground forces in action against the enemy. Though they did not know it, the position in North Africa was approaching a critical stage, and that only three days after the initial landings. The invasion of French Morocco and Algiers had taken the enemy by surprise. Practised, however, as they are in the art of war, the German counter was swift: while 'B' and 'C' Companies were winging their way towards the Mediterranean, the last German troops were entering their billets on the southern coast of France, which was now entirely occupied. Italian troops were in Nice, and preparations for an immediate riposte to the Allies' stroke in Africa were well under way. The need for haste on the part of the Axis forces could hardly be exaggerated. The strength of the British and American forces landed in Algiers was not accurately known, but they were certainly large; the fact that, with the exception of the Navy, the French armed forces in North Africa had made almost no resistance and were beginning to exchange the orders of Vichy for those of Eisenhower, above all the shattering defeat of Rommel at the beginning of the month at El Alamein, made resolute and speedy action vital if North Africa were not to be lost, with all the grave consequences this would entail.

The Allies had landed some five hundred miles west of Tunis, and Tunis, as the German commander, General von Arnim, saw, was the key to the situation. Whoever held it, held North Africa. Already Lieutenant-General Anderson and the British 1st Army were on the march towards it in streaming rain over rugged and inhospitable hills. Von Arnim set out to oppose them, his army being constantly reinforced as he moved westwards.

Somewhat more than half-way between Algiers and Tunis is situated the port of Bone, with an airfield laid out on the stony ground immediately behind it. This and the port were an obvious and immediate prize, a fact fully appreciated by the Allied and German commanders alike. Both set about their capture. As has often happened in war, it was a race between rival forces for the prize of an important position; but what made this race unique was that the runners were for the first time in history parachute troops. The German parachute formations were among the élite of the German armed forces. They were to prove formidable and worthy opponents.

'B' and 'C' Companies reached Gibraltar safely at dawn and spent the day ostensibly resting, though the garrison and the numerous staff of General Eisenhower, Major-General Charles Haydon among them, were gratified to observe numbers of 'stocky tough-looking parachutists in the street or near the airfield'. Their commanding officer was not so carefree, for, on reporting to military headquarters deep in the bowels of the Rock, he was informed that his force would be required to fly immediately to their target, the airfield at Bone. This meant reloading the Dakotas, a task accomplished only after much hard work and completed in the light of searchlights playing on the airfield. At 04.30 hours on the 11th the first Dakota took off for the large airfield at Maison Blanche near Algiers, which was one of the first objectives taken by the Allies. The rest followed. One Dakota crashed into the sea, and Captain Crichton, the officer who had worked out the loading problems at Netheravon, was drowned rescuing one of the men, all of whom were picked up by an American ship on her way to New York. The parachutists rejoined the 3rd Battalion two months later, having travelled to do so by way of the United States and the United Kingdom. Another Dakota was hit by anti-aircraft fire, for the pilot, in disobedience of his orders, had flown over the harbour of Algiers. One parachute soldier was wounded and the tyre of one of the landing wheels punctured.

By 09.00 hours twenty-nine Dakotas, sufficient for the attack, were assembled on the airfield at Maison Blanche. Pine-Coffin and Major Sir Richard des Voeux, a staff officer, subsequently killed at Arnhem, set out to find Lieutenant-General Anderson and presently discovered him at his headquarters in a ship lying in the harbour. Pine-Coffin and his men were to seize the airfield at Bone, said the general, adding that a battalion of German parachutists were known to be at Tunis and 'would almost certainly be given the same target'. The British parachutists would be relieved by No. 6 Commando, even then on the point of setting out for the port by sea.

Since the American pilots were quite inexperienced in the dropping of parachutists and locating dropping zones in darkness, an attempt to seize the airfield by night was out of the question. It was decided, therefore, to take off at first light on the morning of the 12th, which would mean that the drop would begin about 08.30 hours.

By midday on the 11th the plan of attack was made; the aircraft would fly in line astern following the coast until they reached the harbour at Bone, where the leading Dakota, piloted by Colonel Dorset himself, would turn south-east towards the airfield and prepare to drop its load of parachutists. The pilots of the remaining Dakotas would issue the stand-by order but would not drop their loads until Colonel Dorset, by flying low across the airfield, had made certain that it was not already occupied by the enemy. If it were, the whole force would be dropped a mile away, would form up and at once attack the objective. 'The possibility of a simultaneous parachute descent by both British and German parachutists . . . was one which could not be ignored.'

The briefing was completed by 16.30 hours, its accuracy being enhanced by 'those magnificent R.A.F. models of the airfield at Bone, accurate in every detail'. The briefing by Colonel Dorset of the American pilots took place at 20.00 hours, and was interrupted by the arrival of a German aircraft which dropped a stick of bombs. The Colonel's task was not easy, for the American pilots, never having been called upon to drop parachutists, 'were under the impression that provided they flew over the dropping zone these would choose their own moment for jumping'. The red-and-green light procedure, which they had never heard of, had to be explained to them, together with many other details.

The force took off at the appointed hour. 'The weather was glorious as the string of Dakotas flew along low over the blue waters of the Mediterranean.' To their surprise the parachutists were given a stand-by order at 07.30 hours, an hour earlier than had been planned, but were presently told to stand down. Colonel Dorset in the leading Dakota had mistaken the port of Bougie for that of Bone, but, not seeing an airfield, had realised his mistake and flown on. At exactly 08.30 hours the order to stand by was given once more; this time the number one of each stick standing in the open doorway could see the airfield. The red and then the green light went on, and out tumbled the parachutists. Their fall, unknown to them, was observed by a formation of Ju 52's carrying German parachutists from Tunis. Seeing that the British had won the race, they turned round and were observed to head back east.

The drop was accurate and the two companies with the Mortar Platoon and headquarters contingent landed either on the airfield or close to it. A number of containers fell a mile short. For many the landing was far heavier than any to which they had become accustomed, either because the air in North Africa is less dense than it is in England, or because the parachutists were more heavily laden than usual. Thirteen men were injured, one fatally, and several suffered broken limbs. Among them was an officer, who struck his head so hard against a stone that he was unconscious for four days. He was carried to a house on the edge of the airfield and laid upon 'a fine bed with brass knobs at its four corners. From time to time he was heard to murmur, "I'll have a little more of the turbot, waiter".'

Immediately on landing, the airfield appeared quite deserted, but even before the force had formed up the native Arab population 'descended upon them like locusts and a quantity of arms and ammunition disappeared with startling suddenness'. The silken canopies of the parachutes proved an even greater attraction, and a large number was spirited away. Caught with one of them, an Arab boy observed that they were 'indeed a gift from heaven', for, he calculated, 'not less than five hundred and forty-four sets of silk underclothing could be made from one canopy and sold at a great profit'.

Thus did the three hundred and sixty officers and men of the 3rd Battalion, The Parachute Regiment, strike the first blow in what was to prove as stubborn and hard-fought a campaign as any in the war. That same day the airfield was attacked by dive bombers, but the arrival of No. 6 Commando and a squadron of Spitfires confirmed the 1st Army in the possession of this all-important position seized for it by parachutists. These were brought back to the remainder of the battalion which had disembarked on the evening of the 13th in Algiers harbour, where they had lain for two days under intermittent bombing. On landing, they marched eighteen kilometres east to the village of St. Charles, and there both parts of the battalion were united. The first operation had been successful, and by 15th

November all three battalions were in Africa, had collected their equipment and stored it on the airfield at Maison Blanche. The lack of stevedores and of transport added to the arduous nature of this routine task. None worked harder than the Royal Air Force Parachute-packing Section attached to brigade head-quarters who in a requisitioned cinema laboured in relays round the clock until they had repacked ready for immediate use more than three thousand parachutes. The 1st Parachute Brigade was in Africa eager for battle.

The plans which had brought it there had been drafted to meet three possibilities. If the French had resisted fiercely, the brigade would have been held at Maison Blanche airfield ready to undertake operations against other airfields as and when required. For this purpose loading tables, always a most important part in the planning of any airborne operation, had been prepared and all information available concerning the airfields in North Africa collected. This plan went immediately by the board, for the French offered no real resistance. Under the second plan the brigade would arrive by sea, except for two-thirds of the 3rd Battalion, which would fly to Gibraltar and then be held at the immediate disposal of Anderson and the 1st Army. This, in the event, was the plan adopted at the outset. The third plan was drawn up to meet a situation in which not only did the French offer no resistance but would shew a disposition to collaborate. In that event the parachute troops would be dropped either as a brigade or in battalions, or, if necessary, in company groups, on airfields as far distant as Bizerta and Tunis to help the local French garrisons to deny their use to the enemy.

Before describing the part played by the 1st Parachute Brigade in the campaign its strategic object should be grasped; upon this Eisenhower is very definite: our 'main strategic purpose,' he records, 'was the speedy capture of northern Tunisia. This guided every move we made—military, economic, political. Through success and disappointment, through every incident and accident, through every difficulty that habitually dogs the foot-steps of soldiers in the field, this single objective was constantly held before all eyes'.[1] With this one end in view, Lieutenant-General Anderson, who led the British 1st Army, had been landed, as has been said, east of Algiers, his orders being to capture Bizerta and Tunis, the two main ports available to the

[1] *Crusade in Europe*, by Dwight D. Eisenhower. American edition, Doubleday & Co. Inc., New York, 1948, p. 116.

72

Germans and Italians, as soon as possible. He found himself at once confronted by three difficulties, one of them natural, the other two man-made. The natural, which had a direct and immediate effect on the operation of all arms, and particularly of airborne troops, was the weather. According to Eisenhower 'unseasonable rains soon overtook us'. Were they in fact unseasonable? Those who produced the elaborate plans for the expedition seem to have overlooked or ignored a statement in the *Encyclopædia Britannica*, which no one who took part in the campaign would contradict. 'Heavy rains,' it says, 'prevail from December to March,' and in the winter of 1942 they certainly equalled, if they did not surpass, the general average. Such rains made the airfields unusable, for none of them was provided with runways. Only those at Bizerta and Tunis in the hands of the enemy possessed these indispensable features. Nature was therefore against the Allies, and could reasonably be expected to provide any force seeking to strike swiftly over the barren hills separating it from Tunis with the handicap of rain, mud and presently snow.

The two man-made difficulties were the small size of the 1st Army and the shortage of motor vehicles. Lack of shipping had made it impossible for the Allies to put ashore an overwhelming and therefore decisive number of men. For the same good reason vehicles were scarce ; nor did the single-line railway connecting Algiers with Tunis prove an effective substitute. Nevertheless Anderson, 'a loyal and bold commander', and his men prepared to carry out immediately Eisenhower's 'urgent orders' to move eastwards.

On 15th November, with three brigades of infantry and a brigade of obsolescent tanks, the British commander began his march.

On the next day he made use of his parachute troops, hoping to repeat at Souk el Arba the success achieved at Bone. The 1st Battalion was ordered to seize a road junction at Beja, a key point ninety miles east of Tunis, and the airfield, and to do its utmost to bring the French garrison over to the Allies. If for some reason it could not drop in the Beja-Souk el Arba area, it was to drop as close to it as possible. There was only one map available, a quarter-inch motoring map, and no photographs. Other intelligence was equally scanty. Hill accordingly decided to follow the tactics used successfully at Bone, and fly himself in the leading aircraft, the rest following in line astern. When he had made his choice of a dropping zone he and his stick would jump, and those in the aircraft behind were to follow suit immediately.

At 07.00 hours on 15th November the battalion took off with an escort of American fighters, Lightnings, which disposed of 'two enemy aircraft who were impertinent'; but after flying for an hour and a half through weather which grew worse and worse, had to return to the Maison Blanche airfield. On the following morning they tried again; and then occurred an incident which shewed the stuff of which the Parachute Regiment was made. A number of men had been ordered to stay behind; as the Dakotas taxied slowly round the perimeter of the airfield on their way to the take-off, about twenty men of those ordered to remain on the ground were seen running after the aircraft, borrowed parachutes in one hand, their personal weapons in the other. Their comrades, seeing their determination, helped to drag them aboard. 'It is not every man,' says the historian of the battalion, 'who will disobey orders to parachute into battle.' This time the flight was successful, and Hill, followed by his battalion, dropped on, or near, the airfield at Souk el Arba, many of the men making 'a light landing in soft muddy plough'. One man was throttled in mid-air by a rigging-line which twisted itself round his neck—he was the only fatal casualty; but Major des Voeux, who jumped as liaison officer, broke his leg, and four men were slightly wounded by the accidental discharge of a Sten gun. Major Cleasby-Thompson landed on his water-bottle, which exploded with a loud report. 'For a moment,' records Lance-Corporal C. Coster, who landed beside him, 'he thought it was part of himself which had exploded, and was much relieved to discover that the trickle from his clothes was water, not blood.'

The battalion formed up on the dropping zone and moved towards the village, 'where a multitude of civilians appeared to be assembling'. On reaching the edge of the airfield, they encountered a number of French native troops, 'fierce-looking warriors, perfectly dug in with machine-guns'. They proved, however, very friendly. The second-in-command, Major Alastair Pearson, and a small party, collected the containers and all the parachutes but one, which was seized by a passing Arab who galloped off with it, the silk canopy billowing out behind his horse. The parachutist killed during the drop was buried with military honours and in conformity with French custom, Pearson shook hands with everyone who attended the funeral.

There were some three thousand. The mayor of the village received Hill and his men with flowers, champagne and local wine, and the 1st Battalion felt that they would never make so rewarding an operational jump again. In this opinion they persisted despite the activities of 'a hairy old man wearing a row of ribbons of the last war who kissed us left and right . . . and wept for joy'. A number of French charabancs driven by uncertain charcoal gas were discovered, and Hill decided to move in them to Beja, an important rail and road centre, some forty miles to the north-east. The battalion arrived about six in the evening in drenching rain which rapidly sent the temperature down to a low level. As the weather had been extremely hot in Algiers, the men had left their underclothes behind them, and they had, of course, no blankets. These deficiencies were to be the cause of great discomfort during the next few weeks.

Mindful of the second part of his orders, to bring the French over to the Allied side if possible, Hill interviewed the local commander, who in due course agreed in principle to co-operate. To impress him with the large number of Allied troops which Hill maintained had arrived, he spoke constantly of 'la Grande Armée Britannique avec les chars' and marched the battalion several times in and out of Beja during the day, on each occasion changing their formation and their dress. On the first time they marched with steel helmets; on the second they exchanged these for the red beret, then the headgear of untried troops, but soon with the green, to be the most dreaded object of any on the battlefield. Whether these manœuvres influenced the French is uncertain. They certainly conveyed a false impression to the German commander in Tunis, who received an exaggerated account of the strength of the Allies in Beja from Italians who escaped from the town.

On the next day Major Cleasby-Thompson was sent with two platoons from 'R' Company and a detachment of engineers to the small village of Sidi N'Sir, about twenty miles away on the Beja-Mateur road. His orders were to get into contact with the local French commander who was said to be pro-Ally. The district was said to be frequented by German patrols. It was. 'On arrival, Sidi N'Sir proved,' says Lieutenant A. R. Kellas, to be 'a white house on a hill, and a yellow railway station occupied by a company of Senegalese, silent, child-faced giants, with long bayonets, commanded by cloaked and field-booted Frenchmen. They observed with indifference our little fresh-faced parachutists in their green smocks, round-helmeted, festooned with web-equipment—amateur soldiers by contrast. But by sundown the next day we had made them jealous and respectful'. The French commandant proved most friendly and Cleasby-Thompson decided to push on towards Mateur. When darkness fell he and his men were some fifteen miles short of the little town, 'weary and abominably hungry'. It was decided to lie up for the night 'while a plot was prepared to harass the Hun. Sheep and eggs were bought from local Arabs ; the men feasted ; guards were mounted, and sleep came to them at last'. It was broken at dawn by a short burst of Sten-gun fire from a zealous but not very intelligent sentry who sought by this means to stop the progress of a German column of three armoured and three scout cars. Fortunately it continued on its way unmoved and Cleasby-Thompson and his men waited in hopes that it would return and fall into the ambush which they were preparing.

About 10.00 hours their hopes were realised. The country was ideal for an ambush : 'On one side of the road the hills rose steeply ; on the other the ground was extremely boggy.' The sappers—grand fellows, who were all tragically killed a few days later by an accidental explosion—had mined one end of the ambush and had made arrangements 'to close the door' with mines when the enemy was in the trap. Cleasby-Thompson and most of the men took up their positions on the side of a hill about eighty yards from the road ; the three-inch mortar was mounted upon another hill, and two groups of Bren gunners hidden in the boggy ground opposite. To complete the arrangements made for the reception of the enemy, Lieutenants Philip Mellor and Arthur Kellas crouched in a ditch beside the road with a supply of Gammon bombs.[1] A few minutes before the German armoured column appeared a solitary Arab on a donkey 'tittupped' down the road from Mateur. He passed over the mines safely and saw nothing. 'The sigh of relief,' says Cleasby-Thompson, 'might have been heard in Algiers.'

The enemy column hove into sight, and the parachutists awaited it, every man having been ordered to hold his fire until the leading vehicles struck a mine. It was one of the armoured cars, and it duly did so ; it then rammed the side of the hill, thus blocking the road. The two scout cars behind it received a volley of Gammon bombs and burst into flames ; their occupants, four

[1] The Gammon bomb was a development of the 'sticky' bomb, produced by Major Jefferies in 1940, with the strong encouragement of the Prime Minister. It was made of a substance which caused it to stick to anything against which it was thrown.

in each, 'were killed and cremated'. The crew of the three-inch mortar by skilful lobbing of their bombs caused the remaining German vehicles to close up and move forward into the 'real business end of the ambush'. After two of the crew of the second armoured car had been killed the remainder surrendered, and Cleasby-Thompson accepted the surrender of the occupants of the surviving armoured car and scout car. The action was all over in a few minutes. Company Sergeant-Major Steadman was wounded, and Lieutenant Kellas, who had flung his Gammon bombs at very short range, was badly wounded in an eye. Among the articles captured were the order of battle of the German forces in Tunis, a number of excellent Luger pistols for which American lines-of-communication troops were prepared to pay up to twenty-five pounds in Algiers, some 'first-class Zeiss racing glasses, highly nutritious German sausage and a bottle of Three Star Martell brandy.'

Cleasby-Thompson and his men, the wounded borne in the undamaged captured scout car, returned in triumph to Beja via Sidi N'Sir, where the French commandant, on hearing of the action, became whole-heartedly pro-Ally, being apparently convinced that the parachute troops were armed with a secret anti-tank weapon capable of dealing with heavy armoured cars.

For this small but highly successful action Major Cleasby-Thompson and Lieutenant Philip Mellor were awarded the Military Cross, and Company Sergeant-Major Steadman and Sergeant Ryan the Military Medal.

For the next few days the 1st Battalion remained at Beja, occasionally marching and counter-marching to give the impression of great numbers, but somewhat harassed by German dive-bombers, whose activities caused casualties among the civilian population, and much damage to houses. A second patrol sent out under Captain Michael Stewart on 20th November was a failure: it ran into superior numbers of the enemy at Oued Zarga, and was forced to withdraw, Stewart and one other rank being killed, and a number of others taken prisoner. Among them was a sergeant of 'R' Company, Cooke by name, an old soldier 'well past his fortieth birthday'. Old in years he might be, but not in body or spirit. During a long career of adventure in many parts of the world he had at one time served in the French Foreign Legion. He was one of those who, although ordered to remain behind at Maison Blanche, successfully reached Souk el Arba. After his capture at Oued Zarga he was taken to Italy and shut up in a prisoner-of-war camp. By means unknown he 'acquired a set of overalls, a ladder and a push-bicycle'. Upon this he rode out of the camp, posing as the local electrician, made his way to Rome, and, cycling into the Vatican City, announced that he was a Roman Catholic and an escaped prisoner-of-war. He was in due course exchanged for an Italian prisoner and reached the United Kingdom.

Throughout these early days the battalion had been well in advance of the 1st Army, seeking to move eastwards along the plain which separated the mountains on their right flank from the sea on their left. Anderson and his men were doing their utmost to fulfil Eisenhower's orders; but, hampered as they were by weather and transport, which was quite inadequate, their progress towards Tunis and Bizerta was not fast enough to prevent von Arnim from building up his strength until the inevitable happened and the attackers became the attacked. This development, however, was only beginning when the 1st Battalion reached Beja and dug themselves in.

Here they were glad to find their old friends, the 2nd Battalion, the Lancashire Fusiliers, who during the next few days suffered heavy casualties in carrying out a series of local attacks. James Hill, the fierce and resolute commander of the 1st Battalion, much disliked the period of defensive activity which it now seemed would fall upon him and his men, and when, therefore, a former sailor of the French navy informed him that he knew the whereabouts of an Italian tank harbour about nine miles north-east of Sidi N'Sir, 'the one and only map of the area was brought out, and a plot hatched'.

On the night of 23-24th November it was put into execution. The battalion moved to Sidi N'Sir, picked up the Senegalese troops, who were to carry extra mortar ammunition, 'great ebony warriors, with enormous teeth, and bayonets a yard long', as they appeared to Cleasby-Thompson, and then in broad moonlight advanced silently and in single file down the railway line. Their immediate object was a small hill called Gué, at the foot of which the tank harbour was said to be located. The action was to open with a bombardment by the mortars directed by Major Alastair Pearson. The sappers, under Captain Geary, were to move round the hill and mine the road running to it from the east, so as to hamper the retreat of the garrison or the arrival of reinforcements.

The battalion was approaching the position, when at about 23.15 hours a loud explosion shook the moonlit air. At once Gué hill erupted in a shower of tracer bullets, none of which caused any casualties. The sappers had been carrying their Hawkins anti-tank mines in sandbags ready to lay them; one of these had been accidentally exploded and set off the rest. The party of three officers and twenty-four men were wiped out.

In face of this disaster, which had upset the plan, 'R' and 'S' Companies thought it best to attack at once. They reached the foot of the hill, but found no tank harbour, and streamed up it towards the position from which tracer bullets were still coming. Yelling loudly, in this being equalled and surpassed by the Senegalese, they reached the top of the hill, to find a mixed force of Germans and Italians. The first held on to their machine-gun positions; the second strove to flee. In a very few minutes the position was overrun and strewn with the dead or dying bodies of many of its garrison, of whom twenty-six were captured. Hill discovered the tanks, there were but three of them, and they were Italian light tanks dug into the ground. Hill approached the first, tapped on its turret with the five-foot stick he always carried and demanded the surrender of the crew. They obeyed. He moved to the next tank where he renewed his demand with the same result. The crew of the third tank were Germans; as Hill repeated his order to surrender for the third time, two of them opened the turret and came out with their hands up. Hill accepted their surrender, but a third member of the crew suddenly opened fire with his automatic, putting three bullets into Hill's chest, and two into the neck and face of Captain Miles Whitelock. Both officers fell to the ground, and there followed 'some ugly work with the bayonet'. Hill and his adjutant were placed on an Italian motor-tricycle and driven down the railway line, bumping all the way over the sleepers, to Sidi N'Sir, whence they were rushed to Beja. Here Captain Robb, Royal Army Medical Corps, one of the Parachute Surgical Team, carried out emergency operations and saved their lives.

Meanwhile the battalion had withdrawn with their prisoners, leaving the German wounded to be looked after by their medical orderlies. For this action Hill was admitted to the Distinguished Service Order; his battalion was taken over by Alastair Pearson, and Cleasby-Thompson became second-in-command. On 26th November they became part of Blade Force and moved to a position some ten miles south of Mateur, where they remained until 12th December. During this period patrolling was the main business, and in this certain officers and men shewed themselves particularly active and skilful. The 1st Battalion was perhaps in a better position to carry out patrols than the other two, since it was more isolated, and Alastair Pearson, its commanding officer, was by this fact 'to all intents and purposes his own master'. In the forefront were four of his officers, Philip Mellor, Stanley Wandless, Christopher Perrin-Brown and 'Victor' Coxen.

On one occasion Mellor, after wiping out an enemy outpost, sent his patrol back and entered Mateur alone. He spent some time wandering round the streets pistolling any Germans he encountered, and returned the next day with a bullet hole through his helmet. Wandless, who could speak perfect German, entered an Arab village occupied by the enemy and discovered the billet of some German officers. One of these he stalked, and when the German was sufficiently far away from the house Wandless summoned him in a whisper to surrender. The German thought that one of his friends was playing a practical joke. A knife in the heart may have convinced him that this was not so. Having disposed of the officer, Wandless then crept back to the house and saw the other German officers at dinner. He opened the window and threw a Gammon bomb on to the table 'with one hundred per cent results'. He ended the evening's adventures by rounding up the other Germans in the house and marching them back as prisoners. It was in pursuit of adventures of this kind that Wandless met his death a short time later, when he and the patrol he was leading were ambushed on their way back from a deep penetration of the enemy's lines. He was mortally wounded, and his grave was subsequently found at Mateur. Together with Philip Mellor, he and his patrols had during two brief months they had been in North Africa put out of action above two hundred of the enemy. Wandless 'was brave and cunning, and his troops loved him'.

Perrin-Brown was once sent with half a dozen men to examine a bridge behind the enemy's lines and met some forty Germans marching down the road in the moonlight in column of route. He at once engaged them with sub-machine-guns and grenades. The Germans, believing that they were being attacked by their own side, shouted and screamed at them to stop, but took no further action. Perrin-Brown and his men then slipped away in the darkness, all but two who decided to lie up in cover to see what dawn would bring. It brought another German patrol armed with spades and pick-axes, who buried eighteen corpses. When they had finished their work the two parachutists opened fire with a Sten gun and a rifle from a range of two hundred yards, and then returned to the battalion to report. Some time later the graveyard fell into Allied hands, and twenty-one graves were counted.

'Not only officer patrols had successes,' notes the historian of the battalion dryly, 'but patrols led by non-commissioned officers and even private soldiers produced excellent results. Even greater successes would have been achieved if the battalion had had some snipers' rifles.' Nor were their enemies only Germans and Italians: the local Arabs were for the most part hostile, 'looters and pests', as more than one parachute soldier described them. They were often worse, not hesitating to give away the movement of patrols or the position of a post, being especially prone to do so if its occupants had refused to pay the high price demanded for a chicken or some eggs. Were a wounded man to fall into their hands he was atrociously mutilated. There was but one way, the brigade felt, to deal with these German allies. If caught looting or giving away a position or movement of any of our troops, they were summarily shot.

Among the worst of them was one Eli, soon known as the bandit chief. He was an Arab of some substance who lived in the hills near Beja, and had long earned a comfortable livelihood by raiding and looting the dwellings of French farmers. Edward O'Brien, Irish Guards, was ordered to take a patrol, shoot him and blow up his dwelling. Eli was surprised at home with his wives at dawn, and before shooting him O'Brien unwisely gave him permission to take leave of them. A moment later Eli had 'dived through a back window and "legged" it over the scrub'. O'Brien had to be content with blowing up the house.

About this time a remarkable figure made his appearance at headquarters. Pearson had called for an interpreter, and the station-master of Mateur, one Monsieur Borg, a Maltese—or so he claimed—arrived to fill the post. He certainly spoke Arabic and Italian, but his English was elementary. His credentials, however, were very sound: on their arrival at Mateur, hot foot from Tunis, the Germans had demanded an immediate census of all locomotives and rolling stock. Borg hastened to comply and before long had made up a long train composed of everything on wheels in the station, headed by several locomotives with steam up. As the Germans approached to count them, Borg, who was in the leading locomotive, opened the regulator and the huge train clanked off to Beja. Borg 'was a little man in every respect but in heart. . . . At his request,' says Cleasby-Thompson, 'we dressed him as a parachutist and made him an honorary unpaid acting officer. We also armed him. His normal fighting equipment was rifle with a hundred rounds of ammunition, bayonet, Sten gun and four magazines, pistol with twenty-four rounds, four Mills grenades, two Gammon bombs, and a fighting knife'. The battalion's records state that 'Borg rendered valiant service'. He qualified as a parachutist and dropped in due course on the soil of Sicily.

Apart from patrolling there was a brisk action fought near Coxen's Farm on 1st December and this position was a source of constant trouble—to the Germans. By the middle of the second week in December the 1st Battalion was fighting side by side with their friends and comrades of the 2nd Battalion, the Lancashire Fusiliers. Together they dominated the enemy, and, after more than one German patrol which attempted to penetrate their lines 'had been completely destroyed or captured', were for a time left severely alone. A small but very welcome reinforcement in the shape of a squadron of the 17/21st Lancers with their tanks, presently arrived at the bottom of the hill along the top of which ran the front line. The positions were very well sited, and from them it was possible to see across the plain for five miles. But the enemy was evidently determined not to allow the parachute troops and the tough men of Lancashire to have matters all their own way. On 10th December, just before dawn, he put down a heavy barrage of shell and mortar fire, and as the sun came up a column of enemy motor transport was seen in the direction of Matuer; they had obviously brought up infantry, and, sure enough, a short time later about four hundred German infantry were seen about two miles away approaching in battle formation, a series of purposeful 'blobs' of men. The crest of the hill was at once lined by some one thousand two hundred parachute troops and Fusiliers supported by the six tanks of the 17/21st Lancers, which had crawled up the hill to take part in the battle. The enemy, approaching in perfect formation, were allowed to come to within two hundred yards and then 'the crest of our hill belched fire. Vickers, two-pounders, Brens, rifles, mortars let drive. It was pathetic: the blobs disintegrated or gently subsided to remain in little heaps'; all but one, of which the members were pinned down some seventy yards from the British position in a slight fold of the ground. The second-in-command of the Lancashire Fusiliers possessed 'a beautiful sniper's rifle with a telescopic sight', and the officers took it in turn to pick off the Germans in this fold till all were killed. When the position was examined later, it was found that each of them had received a bullet through his head. To complete the rout of the enemy, the battalion and the Lancashire Fusiliers charged with the bayonet. 'Alastair Pearson leading the Parachute Battalion armed with his usual weapon, a most disgusting pipe. There was no opposition ; it had been a massacre. All ranks were rather disgusted and nauseated'.

After this action the Lancashire Fusiliers and 17/21st Lancers withdrew for a rest to Sidi N'Sir, and the 1st Battalion to Beja and to Souk el Khemis, where it met the gallant remains of the 2nd Battalion, fresh from their fighting retreat from Oudna. At Souk el Khemis, besides clean clothes and extra rations, the battalion received its first mail from England, and spent 'a week of peace, warm bedding, clean clothes and full stomachs'. How the 2nd Battalion had fared must now be told.

This battalion, under Frost, was kept for some time in reserve at Maison Blanche, where they suffered some loss of equipment by a well-aimed enemy bomb which fell upon the hangar in which the containers were stored. On the morning of 28th November Frost was ordered to take them by air to Pont du Fahs and destroy all the enemy aircraft found on the airfield. He was then to move ten miles further on to Depienne and carry out a similar operation which, when it was finished, was to be repeated at Oudna, a further fourteen miles away. The battalion was to rejoin the 1st Army at St. Cyprien about ten miles short of Tunis. It will be noted that these orders would have the effect of placing the battalion well in advance on to the right flank of the 1st Army. They were not, however, to be entirely un- supported: an armoured thrust was to be made at Tunis, and certain elements making it were to maintain what contact they could with Frost.

On 29th November, shortly before the battalion, which had considerable difficulty in loading the containers owing to the mud on the surface of the airfield, entered the waiting aircraft, information came to hand which shewed that the enemy airfields at Pont du Fahs and Depienne had been abandoned. It was, therefore, decided that only the third part of the plan would have to be carried out, and Frost was therefore ordered to drop at Depienne. Protected by Hurricanes, Lightnings and Spitfires, the 2nd Battalion was on its way by 12.30 hours in bad and bumpy weather which caused some air-sickness. It was flying in the Dakotas which had carried the 1st Battalion to Souk el Arba, and Frost was in the leading aircraft. About thirty miles from Depienne the Dakotas, which had been flying high over the mountains, came down to six hundred feet, and on approaching the town Frost chose as a landing zone some plough-land with a watercourse dividing it. He dropped first with the first stick, and the remainder, following the precedents set by the 3rd Battalion at Bone and the 1st Battalion at Souk el Arba, jumped immediately. One man was killed and six injured in the drop, which was otherwise uneventful. The injured were put into the local school house where they were well treated by the French, and 'B' Company set about collecting all the transport available in Depienne. This amounted to no more than a few mule carts. In the early hours of 30th November the battalion moved off towards Oudna, carrying some of its mortars in the carts, but with most of its weapons and ammunition, together with five days' rations, on the backs of the men. 'The march was a gruelling one' over steep, rough tracks which crossed stony hills. At 04.30 hours, having covered twelve miles, they halted and attempted to sleep, but, having no blankets, found the cold too bitter, and were glad to move off again at first light with 'B' Company in the lead. As they went they commandeered any mule carts or pack animals they met with, and this step— inevitable though it was—did not endear them to the local Arabs, who 'could be heard calling from village to village as the column approached'.

By 11.00 hours the battalion had reached a well called Prise de l'Eau, not far from the landing ground—it could scarcely be dignified by the name of airfield—at Oudna. Such French and Arabs as could be induced to talk assured Frost that the enemy was withdrawing on Tunis. In view of the armoured attack which he knew was due to be carried out that day, this seemed not unlikely. After eating a meal, 'A' Company moved forward towards the landing ground, with 'C' Company protecting its left flank, and 'B' Company in reserve. After a brisk skirmish, 'A' Company, skilfully handled by Major Ashford, drove off the enemy, Lieutenant Rendell took his platoon to Oudna railway station, and 'C' Company on the flank advanced round the north of the airfield. Here they came under the fire of four heavy German tanks and lost an officer. They and the rest of the battalion took what cover they could, being attacked at intervals until dusk by low-flying Messerschmitts. The landing ground was found to be deserted.

It seemed to Frost that the battalion had now carried out its orders: the landing ground at Oudna, like those at Pont du Fahs and Depienne, had been evacuated by the enemy before his

84

arrival, and there were, in consequence, no aircraft to be destroyed. Four erections thought to be native tents containing stores turned out to be hayricks. Frost began to plan his withdrawal. The position of the 2nd Battalion should be realised. They had, as it were, been dropped from the blue into the blue, many miles ahead of the land forces. There was nothing but their own resources on which to live, march and fight, save for such transport, mostly mules, on which they had been, or might be, able to lay hands. Their defensive positions on and around the landing ground at Oudna were very insecure; the enemy had had several hours in which to make a full reconnaissance and, therefore, to gauge the numbers against him, and his armoured forces were already moving up in some strength.

What had happened was this. Led astray by wrong information, the commander of the 1st Army had hoped to break into Tunis, using one brigade of the 78th Division and part of the 6th Armoured Division, the advance of this force being aided by the 2nd Battalion, whose task, as has been explained, was to destroy enemy aircraft on the nearby airfields. When, however, the advance began, the enemy was found to be in much greater strength than had been reported, the local Arabs were upon his side and the *Luftwaffe* had been withdrawn. The attack therefore broke down completely, a battalion of the Hampshire Regiment was cut to pieces outside Tebourba, and the 2nd Battalion, the Parachute Regiment, was left surrounded by the enemy fifty miles from the nearest Allied forces. To gain a great prize, a great, but not unjustifiable, risk had been taken. Whether the price would have to be paid in full depended on Frost's ability to extricate his battalion.

After holding off an enemy cautiously advancing by the light of the hayricks which had now been set on fire, he moved back to a stronger position at Prise de l'Eau, which he reached about 22.30 hours. His men, especially those of 'A' and 'C' Companies which had been engaged intermittently with the enemy for twenty-four hours, were exhausted; but the cold was still intense, and sleep, in consequence, almost out of the question. No signals had been received on the wireless sets. Anxiously scanning the sky, Frost saw intermittent bursts of anti-aircraft fire which he rightly concluded was being directed at Allied bombers attacking Bizerta and Tunis, and heard continuous sound of battle from the direction of Tebourba well to the north-west, and therefore a considerable distance behind him. It was his duty, he decided, to remain in the exposed position of Prise de l'Eau, at least until noon on the following day, 1st December, and he prepared to do so.

Dawn broke and with it came a signal at last. It might have caused a man less stout of heart than Frost to quail. The British armoured thrust against Tunis had been postponed. The one chance, therefore, that the 2nd Battalion would be able to join forces that day with the advancing British tanks had disappeared. 'He was almost, if not quite, surrounded.' The enemy were beginning to arrive in strength, and his armoured cars were patrolling every road in the neighbourhood. About 10.00 hours a small German column of tanks, armoured cars, light artillery and infantry carried in lorries was seen approaching from the direction of Oudna. Such an attack had long been expected, and the parachutists were ready. To conserve ammunition, of which the supply was very limited, they were ordered to hold their fire until the oncoming Germans entered the track leading to the position. At one point it ran through a bottleneck between two hedges, and here, in accordance with the standard practice of parachute troops, Frost laid an ambush. Watching the approaching column, which he could then see consisted of two tanks, two armoured cars and two lorries, it seemed at first that all would be well and that they would enter the trap unprepared. This was not to be. One of the armoured cars pushed on ahead and surprised a small party of the battalion filling their water bottles at the well from which the place took its name. The officer commanding the car was killed, but its other occupants succeeded in turning it round and making off. They were thus able to warn the remainder of the column, which immediately deployed. Met, however, by the fire of Frost's three-inch mortars, it presently withdrew, leaving a number of dead.

The first attack had failed. The next, carried out by two armoured cars and a tank, was nearly successful. These vehicles displayed the yellow triangles used by the Allies, and this ruse —a perfectly legitimate one—deceived the non-commissioned officer in charge of the post approached by the cars. He went forward displaying his own triangle and was at once seized and made to walk in front of the armoured car till he reached his section, which was then captured. The Germans sent him with a message to Frost, pointing out that the battalion was surrounded and demanding its surrender. The demand was rejected and an attempt made to attack the German vehicles, which presently withdrew.

The situation of the 2nd Battalion was now very precarious.

As has been said, it was about fifty miles from the leading troops of the 1st Army. With the exception of an anti-tank rifle or two, and some Gammon bombs, it had no other weapons with which to deal with any armour sent against it ; the enemy could shell it from a distance, and it had no means with which to reply. It was also at the mercy of the Luftwaffe, and its movements were watched by hostile Arabs who lost no time in reporting them. To crown all, ammunition was far from plentiful, and there was no means of sending the wounded to the rear. Nevertheless there was no thought of surrender, and in the afternoon in great heart Frost began his retreat, moving first to the northern slopes of a ridge called Sidi bou Hadjeba, where fortunately a well was found. From these low heights a view towards the north could be obtained, and columns of enemy artillery and armour were observed. Two small hills which overlooked the position were held, one by 'C', and one by 'B' Company, with 'A' Company in reserve, and battalion headquarters to the right and to the rear.

The parachute troops were not left unmolested for long. About 15.00 hours a resolute attack was delivered supported by tanks and heavy mortar, artillery and machine-gun fire. The battalion lost Major Cleaver commanding 'B' Company, and Lieutenant the Honourable H. Cecil of 'C' Company, which in two hours almost ceased to exist as a fighting unit. The situation seemed desperate, when help appeared from a most unexpected quarter. Enemy fighters swooped from the skies, but, mistaking the situation, attacked their own men with great accuracy and knocked out a number of the hostile tanks.

Towards evening the attacks died away, and Frost decided that each company should move independently as soon as darkness fell to the village of Massicault, about eight miles nearer to the 1st Army than St. Cyprien. By then casualties were about one hundred and fifty killed and wounded. To leave the wounded to the mercy of the Arabs was unthinkable, and accordingly Lieutenant Playford with what remained of his platoon was left behind to collect and bring them to a small Arab farm where they would be under the care of Lieutenant McGavin, Royal Army Medical Corps. At 18.30 hours Frost gave the signal to retreat on his hunting horn, and the battalion set out down the stony hills to the plain below. The path was very steep and difficult, 'and when at length the level ground was reached the stumbling, weary men encountered wide stretches of plough-land where the going was very heavy'. Part of 'B' Company became detached from the remainder, was surrounded by the enemy in a vineyard and forced to surrender. A few escaped capture, among them being Captain Stark, who was able to lead Lieutenant Crawley, temporarily blinded by a wound, back to the British lines, which they reached in safety, although at one time they found themselves in a German tank laager. Major Ross, with six men from 'C' Company, took another route and eventually rejoined the battalion at Medjez el Bab. He was more fortunate than Major Teichman and Captain Short, the adjutant, who with a small party of men were ambushed, Teichman being killed and Short wounded and taken prisoner.

In addition to the plough-land there were numerous ditches to cross, and the only water found was that in the River Miliane, which 'was brackish and only just drinkable'. So hard was the going and so exhausted the men that they were unable to reach Massicault and stopped at a farm near El Fedja. Here they once more took up a defensive position, lining a cactus hedge which surrounded the farm. There was very little ammunition left, and Frost gave orders that fire was not to be opened until the enemy were within ten yards. The morning passed without incident, except that at noon 'A' Company, which had also been separated in the retreat on the night before, arrived and reinforced the garrison of El Fedja. Some hours before, the battalion had lost Lieutenant Charteris, its intelligence officer, who with two men had set out in an attempt to get through to the 1st Army, elements of which were said to be at Furna, a small village on the main road to Tunis. He and his men were ambushed and killed.

Not only was the battalion to hold its fire ; it was also, ordered Frost, to remain as silent as possible. The enemy, he thought, would in all probability be unable to deliver an attack in force until fairly late in the day, and if, therefore, he and his exhausted but indomitable men could hold out till sunset, there was still a chance of escaping. It would be heightened by silence and immobility.

This indeed proved to be so, for though by 16.30 hours the battalion was entirely surrounded and under mortar fire, it made no attempt to retaliate and 'this silence on our part seemed to mystify the enemy'. About 17.00 hours a small party of Germans, led by two officers, approached to within ten yards of the cactus hedge and were all killed by men of 'A' Company. After this the enemy's fire increased as dusk fell, but much of it went high so that some of the parachutists were led to believe that the Germans were firing at units of the 1st Army which had at last appeared on the scene. One or two even went so far as to maintain that they heard English being shouted. This was a delusion: the battalion was still surrounded, and the 1st Army far away.

One last effort, thought Frost, could be made. There were still some two hundred men at the farm; when he sounded his hunting horn once more these would leave their positions, concentrate at battalion headquarters, charge the enemy's position which barred the way to the hills, and reform on the ridge of Djebel el Mengoub. Before they could put this plan into practice the Germans launched another heavy attack, which was repelled, one section of the attackers being wiped out by Sten-gun fire and the last of the grenades. Frost then blew his horn and such men as were still capable of moving—none of them had more than five rounds of ammunition left—made for the ridge, which they reached successfully. At 04.00 hours in two parties they arrived at a farm owned by a Frenchman 'who warned Frost that an Arab known to be in the pay of the Germans had made off to inform the enemy of their whereabouts'. He provided the parachutists with a meal of eggs and bacon and champagne; when they had eaten it they were able to notice 'the beauty of their host's daughters'.

The weary men, about one hundred and eighty all told, stumbled away again almost at their last gasp, to exchange the friendly shelter of the farm for some barren heights known as Ksar Tyr. With the coming of daylight they saw before them in the middle distance the town of Medjez el Bab, and the main road running across the tumbled plain. Soon afterwards Frost was told by an Arab that Medjez el Bab was in the hands of the Allies. Hope mounted as they slowly set off towards it, passing through a number of orchards, and, since the enemy no longer pressed them, halting beneath the boughs of the trees for a meal. About 13.00 hours they reached the main road and marched along it until the advance guard caught sight of 'an armoured vehicle . . . bumping and rolling across the country. It reached the road at a point ahead of them, turned and made towards them. It was an American reconnaissance car'. That evening at 17.00 hours the 2nd Battalion, the Parachute Regiment, summoned up sufficient strength to march smartly past the French outposts into Medjez el Bab. Their retreat was over; it had cost sixteen officers and two hundred and fifty other ranks.

'Today some silent valley of Tunisia,' wrote Richard Spender,

one of the battalion's officers who was to be killed in action a
few months later,

> 'Shall tremble at their stroke from sky unsheathed,
> And, with the night, perhaps some God looking down
> With dull, cold eyes, by the near stars, will see
> One lonely, grim battalion cut its way
> Through agony and death to fame's high crown,
> And wonderingly watch the friendless strength
> Of little men, who die that the great Truths shall live.'

There followed some days of alarms and excursions, during
which the battalion was more than once called upon at short
notice to take part in the defence of Medjez el Bab. There was
no more fighting, however, and on 13th December, after being
relieved by the Coldstream Guards, it was taken in vehicles to
Souk el Khemis, where officers and men were at last able to
reorganise and rest. Their spirit is best shewn by two stories of
what happened to some of them who were captured by the
enemy during that arduous retreat. A corporal, who was a
medical student in time of peace, was wounded and taken. He
had been hit in the arm, which was placed in a sling, but he
contrived to hide in it his fighting knife. After dark he watched
his opportunity, stabbed the German guard, freed his companions, and they all eventually reached the British lines. A
number of men belonging to 'B' and 'C' Companies were being
taken to bondage in an Italian lorry escorted by Italian
armoured cars. One of them overpowered a member of the
escort, seized his pistol, shot the driver of the lorry, and escaped
with his companions across country, eluding the pursuit of the
armoured cars. They, too, reached safety.

After its initial operation, resulting in the capture of the
airfield at Bone, the 3rd Battalion was perhaps less fortunate
than the others. During the period they spent at St. Charles
many airborne operations were planned, but always came to
nothing. On 6th December it was put into cattle trucks at Bou
Farik and journeyed for five days to Guademau to rejoin the
brigade. During the journey the padre succeeded at one of the
many halts in dropping a large stone on a thin chicken for which
its owner demanded a pound. This the padre considered to be
too high a price, and the matter was settled by the officer commanding the train, who decreed that the Arab should be paid,

but that all officers should contribute towards the cost of what was hoped would prove a welcome addition to that night's dinner. The first course—chicken soup—was enjoyed by all, but when the chicken arrived on the table it was found quite uneatable, for the cook, intentionally or otherwise, had not drawn it.

On reaching its destination the battalion was marched through Beja and halted on the roadside in the middle of the night, which was dark, cold and full of rain. To add to the general discomfort the men were informed that by dawn they must be in a position fourteen miles away in the front line north of Beja. It was then 01.00 hours. The battalion reached the position in time. It was known as Hunt's Gap, and was 'nothing more than a track through very hilly and rocky country . . . this very unpleasant position was situated on top of rocky hills with no cover'. Through sixteen days they held it, though it was impossible to dig trenches, for after a few inches solid rock was encountered. The men had neither blankets nor greatcoats, though the 'weather was as cold and wet as in the hills of Scotland during December'.

Their time was far from wasted, however. On most nights they went out on patrol, and though they suffered casualties they inflicted as many, if not more, upon the enemy. During this period Lieutenant Livesey of the 1st Parachute Squadron, Royal Engineers, with a sergeant and two sappers, made a reconnaissance behind the enemy's line which lasted thirty-six hours, and brought back accurate information concerning the tracks and roads in an area where it was planned to deliver an attack. At one moment the sergeant was compelled to remain motionless for more than two hours, his head resting on his hand and his elbow on a bed of sharp stones. Throughout that period of time a German sentry was but five yards away and the slightest movement would have meant the discovery of the patrol.

From the outset of the campaign the 1st Parachute Brigade had proved of the greatest value. The arrival of British parachute troops some three hundred and fifty miles ahead of the main force and but seventy miles from Tunis may well have saved the 1st Army many miles of heavy fighting, for had they not been dropped in the Beja area, the enemy's outposts might have been established a hundred miles to the west of that town. Moreover, the presence of the brigade had a great influence on the French Army in Tunisia, which, encouraged by its swift advent, began by refusing a passage to the German troops and were soon actively engaged against them. Such were the prizes won by the imaginative and intelligent use of determined men.

Before the 1st Parachute Brigade had been a month in North Africa, all three of its units had been heavily and constantly engaged in exactly that type of fighting for which they had been trained. Now it was that the dreary months at Hardwick and on Salisbury Plain were seen by every officer and man in their true light, as a period of vital preparation for the endurance of great fatigue, much hardship but—and this was what counted—much hand-to-hand fighting against a resolute and well-led foe. Those who had seen action before and those who were confronting the enemies of their country for the first time became veterans, as it seemed, in a trice. To such a pitch had hard discipline, hard living and good comradeship raised them that they were at once able to perform feats of arms of which battle-hardened troops with months of fighting behind them would have been proud. The Arabs called them the 'men with tails', from their habit of wearing the fork-piece of their smocks hanging down behind them. The Germans chose a different term; and presently the word went through von Arnim's host that men had appeared in Africa wearing red berets who were red devils. Evidence that this was the name given to them by the enemy first came into our hands at the end of February 1943; but it had been earned many weeks before. How will now be made clear.

'Waho Mohammed'

ON CHRISTMAS EVE, 1942, Generals Eisenhower and Anderson paid a visit to the headquarters of the British 5th Corps at Souk el Khemis. The commander-in-chief had come by car, for the weather was too bad to fly, and his object was to hold a final conference with Lieutenant-General C. W. Allfrey, the corps commander, whose troops were to launch what Eisenhower later described as 'our final and most ambitious attack'.[1] In this the 1st Parachute Brigade were to have taken part. They were to pass through the 1st Guards Brigade to exploit the initial success which it was hoped this

[1] *Crusade in Europe,* by Dwight D. Eisenhower, p. 124.

formation would achieve after its capture of the now famous 'Longstop Hill'. The conference took place in drenching rain, and the three generals carried out a personal inspection of the ground over which the troops were to advance. While doing so Eisenhower saw four men trying to drag a motor-cycle from the clutches of the mud which stretched in a dreary waste in every direction. Their efforts were fruitless, and when they gave up the attempt the motor-cycle was more firmly embedded than ever. 'It was this incident,' he records, 'which as much as anything else . . . convinced me of the hopelessness of an attack.' Insufficient troops and transport combined with vile weather had prevented Lieutenant-General Anderson from moving further east upon Tunis and Bizerta, and he was to be hard put to it to hold the ground he had been able with such difficulty to gain.

It will be noted that after its initial entry into action in the Dakotas of the 60th and 64th American Groups of the United States Army Air Force, the 1st Parachute Brigade fought as infantry of the Line. This was indeed inevitable in the early stages of the campaign, when they were correctly playing the part designed for parachute troops in a battle. They had been dropped far in advance of Anderson's main forces to seize a number of key points. Then had ensued an intermittent period of which constant patrolling was the chief feature. By Christmas, however, Eisenhower had abandoned his design, or, more properly, had been forced to abandon it, 'pending', as he himself says, 'the arrival of better weather in the spring'.[1] In these circumstances the question what should be the role of the parachute troops, immediately arose. It cannot be too strongly emphasised that such troops were created for a special purpose —to facilitate the general advance of an army by seizing key points to the rear or flank of the enemy's position, thus creating confusion and, to use a text-book phrase, 'alarm and despondency' within and behind his lines at the most critical moment. Despite the grievous shortage of aircraft, the 1st Parachute Brigade had been so used, and their subsequent patrolling operations, though not, perhaps, strictly in accordance with the theory and practice covering the employment of parachute troops, were not very far removed from them. Now, however, with the 1st Army at a standstill, with rain sluicing down the barren hills, alternating with rare periods of 'delightful sunshine', and with frost and snow on the upper levels, parachute troops could not be used in the particular role for which they were trained.

[1] *Crusade in Europe,* by Dwight D. Eisenhower, pp. 124 et seq.

Brigadier Flavell, their brigade commander, urged with all the strength at his command that his brigade should be withdrawn and allowed to re-form, be strengthened by much-needed reinforcements to replace its already considerable losses, and kept in reserve until it could once more be used as an airborne force. That he was, in principle, entirely right in this contention will very probably be the verdict of the military historians of the future. Unfortunately a variety of considerations prevented the Higher Command from following his counsels.

As has been explained, not only were Lieutenant-General Anderson and the 1st Army unable to advance further in the direction of Tunis and Bizerta, they were even hard put to it to maintain the positions which they had won. There were many reasons for this, the chief being lack of troops. The Germans and Italians, reinforced from Sicily and Italy, could build up their strength more quickly than the Allies, at least in the initial stages. They would also, unless Montgomery could catch him, be presently reinforced by Rommel and the remnants of the Afrika Corps. To hold the enemy the Allies had need of every man. For the next few months, therefore, the 1st Parachute Brigade, like the men of the green beret belonging to the 1st and 6th Commandos, also specially trained, were to fight in a ground role.

After Christmas spent in the open, but enlivened with a visit from Major-General Browning and a generous issue of rum, the 3rd Battalion moved up to the Northern Sector on 3rd January 1943 to take part in an attack on Green Hill. The road linking Sedjenane with Mateur was commanded by two high features, of which one was Green Hill on the left looking east, and Commando Hill with the smaller Bald Hill the other, about half a mile to the north-west. These were to be captured and 'A' Company of the 3rd Battalion was to go into action with the Buffs, 'B' with the Royal West Kents, and 'C' to remain in the rear to prevent any infiltration by the enemy.

On 4th January just after dawn the attack on Green Hill was launched, and by 10.00 hours the first crest was in our hands. The second crest, a hundred yards away and fifty feet higher, was heavily defended by an enemy who had had time to build concrete emplacements, set up plentiful festoons of wire and lay many mines and booby-traps. 'A' Company was in a particularly exposed position and under fire from three directions, nor were their general circumstances improved when the British guns, in response to their urgent request, opened a heavy fire. So close was the crest 'A' Company had captured to the crest they were seeking to attack that as many of our own shells fell in 'A' Company's position as on the Germans. Nevertheless, in the evening an attack by 'B' Company captured the second crest, and for a short time they succeeded in holding it. The Germans then launched two counter-attacks, the first made by about one hundred and eighty men, who went forward shoulder to shoulder, chanting war songs and were almost entirely wiped out. In so doing, however, 'B' Company ran short of ammunition and the next German counter-attack forced them off the crest and back to the bottom of the hill.

All three companies were then withdrawn to Souk el Khemis and thence to St. Charles, where for a moment they rested 'in a country of tangerine gardens and pink and red roses, with a background of blue mist, and far beyond the faint gracious outline of high mountains'. Here they met with the rest of the brigade.

On 7th and 8th January the 1st Parachute Brigade, without the 2nd Battalion, were moved by rail to their base in Algiers to prepare for a parachute operation which involved the capture of Sfax in conjunction with American armoured forces. The object was to prevent the junction of Rommel and the Axis forces in Tunisia. This projected operation never materialised, and on 24th January the brigade once again returned by sea to 5th Corps for duty in a ground role.

During this time the 2nd Battalion had been in the Beja area holding among other positions, a lead-mine, and receiving a very welcome reinforcement of some two hundred officers and men to replace those who had been lost on the long retreat from Oudna. On 15th January the battalion had been moved to the Munchar area near Sidi N'Sir, and while in position in the hills there were able to observe the habits of the local Arab population. The most noticeable, perhaps, was the shouting of messages from one village to another across the valleys. It seemed to the parachute troops that every such communication began with the phrase 'Waho Mohammed' and this they presently adopted as their battle-cry. It soon spread to the rest of the brigade, and was presently to be heard on many battlefields.

During this period the enemy were continually feeling for the right flank of the army, and on 3rd February the battalion was moved to this flank. The esteem in which superior authority held the fighting powers of one parachute battalion was such that the battalion commander was warned he might have to face the attack of ten battalions and a hundred tanks of the enemy on the following morning. Fortunately this threatened attack did not materialise, and after some desultory fighting, which cost the lives of Major R. Ashford, M.C., and Captain Moore, the battalion returned on 8th February to the brigade which was by this time in the Bou Arada sector.

The Corps commander had realised that the best way to obviate the danger to his right flank was to start a limited offensive in this sector, and that if he could capture the heights of Djebel Mansour and El Alliliga he would create such a dangerous salient in the enemy's line that the Germans would be forced to deal with this and eliminate it.

Consequently the 1st Battalion, which was in position in the sector confronting these two heights, was ordered to attack, capture and hold Djebel Mansour and El Alliliga on the night of 2nd-3rd February. To assist them in this task they were allotted a company of the French Foreign Legion, many of whom were Saxons and Bavarians, magnificent soldiers, and entirely loyal to France. The battalion were also informed that the 3rd Battalion, Grenadier Guards, would be available to consolidate the positions when they had been captured.

The plan of attack was for 'R' and 'T' Companies to assault Djebel Mansour crossing the start line at 05.00 hours on 3rd February, and on reaching the top of Djebel Mansour, to swing right-handed along the ridge and capture El Alliliga. Meanwhile 'S' Company would follow up and consolidate on Djebel Mansour. The French were to create a diversion against El Alliliga. Before starting, Lieutenant-Colonel Pearson was informed that the battalion of the Grenadier Guards would take over their existing positions as soon as the assault was launched.

To assist 1st Battalion to find the starting line in the dark Captain Coxen was ordered to lay tapes. He did so, but when the advance began they were found to be cut, possibly by an enemy patrol, and in consequence 'S' Company went astray and suffered heavy casualties among booby traps and from machine-guns firing along fixed lines. Captain Philip Mellor lost one of his legs and was also wounded by machine-gun bullets fired at very close range. The last that was seen of him was 'as he crawled towards the machine-gun post firing his pistol. No braver man ever lived'.

The other two companies had better fortune and after a very steep climb swept into the enemy's positions with the bayonet. Although a thousand yards away, the Foreign Legion reported that the shouts of 'Waho Mohammed' which burst from 1st Battalion as they charged could clearly be heard above the rattle of small arms fire and the general din of a hand-to-hand engagement. Within three-quarters of an hour Djebel Mansour was captured, and by 06.30 hours El Alliliga, though there was still at least one machine-gun and several snipers active on the ridge. Casualties had on the whole been few, but 'the German dead littered the ground'. Then occurred a misfortune which might have led to disaster. On debouching on to the plain below, the mules carrying the reserve ammunition were met by very heavy machine-gun fire. The muleteers, all Arabs, fled incontinently, but Major Prioleau, the French officer in charge of them, and Cleasby-Thompson, leaping on horses, each seized a pair of mules and galloped them to the battalion.

As 'R' and 'T' Companies launched their attack on El Alliliga, 'S' Company, somewhat battered, arrived to take over Djebel Mansour. The enemy were quick to react to the attack on El Alliliga and brought up reinforcements. Consequently 'R' and 'T' Companies were unable to consolidate the position there, and Pearson then decided to concentrate on holding Djebel Mansour. He withdrew from El Alliliga in the hope that this objective might be taken by the battalion of Grenadier Guards already mentioned.

The company of the French Foreign Legion was ordered to take over the position known as Point 646 to cover the left flank of 1st Battalion. This point was of vital importance, as it overlooked Djebel Mansour from the left.

Throughout the day the battalion was subjected to heavy shell and mortar fire and some one hundred and five casualties were evacuated together with thirty-five prisoners under a hail of shells and bombs.

From El Alliliga the enemy overlooked the right flank of the battalion and its lines of communication. This made the position difficult, and Pearson and his men were cheered by the news, later in the day, that the Guards Brigade would occupy El Alliliga that night. At 06.30 hours on the 4th the intelligence officer was sent across to get in touch with the Guards, but the only contact he made was with the enemy. Later a company of the Guards were found lower down the hill, having been unable to occupy it. As a result the situation of 1st Battalion on Djebel Mansour had become thoroughly uncomfortable.

'Mortar and shell fire began falling on our positions, but it was no heavier than the previous day and casualties were few and light,' runs the Adjutant's report. 'At 14.30 hours a heavy concentration of high explosive was put down by our guns on El Alliliga preparatory to the Guards assault. The enemy replied to this by heavy shell and mortar fire on our positions. Twelve Stukas came over and dive-bombed the valley behind our positions—presumably expecting to catch reinforcements. No casualties were caused. At 15.30 hours the shelling on El Alliliga lifted and a concentration of smoke was put down under cover of which the Guards attacked.

'Contact with them was immediately lost, as wireless communication broke down. We did not know whether the attack had been successful or not ; at any rate it had not dislodged the machine-gun on the eastern side of El Alliliga, nor had the Guards occupied the feature nearest to us. During the remainder of the day our position was made most uncomfortable by this gun which overlooked us, and repeated messages were sent to the Guards via Brigade to ask them to deal with this side of El Alliliga, but to no avail.

'At about 23.00 hours that night there was some firing east of Djebel Mansour and the intelligence officer was sent to contact the French to find out what it was about. The French did not know.

'At dawn on 5th February heavy firing broke out from the French positions and it was soon obvious that the enemy were counter-attacking. Within half an hour the enemy were in possession of the French positions overlooking our own ; Captain Favreau and his lieutenant had been hit and removed back to the aid post. The company had been left in the hands of the sergeant-major who fixed bayonets and charged the enemy, but could not retake the position. After some time it was found that the French had been driven off the hill altogether and what remained of them had withdrawn. It was now obvious that unless reinforcements arrived to drive the enemy off this high ground the 1st Battalion could not hold their position. There was no possibility of these, and the commanding officer therefore decided to hold on as long as possible. Shelling and mortaring of our positions then began, and so heavy was it that casualties began to mount up. By 09.15 hours our own mortars were out of ammunition and the enemy had placed his mortars down the valley to the south of Djebel Mansour. The forward observation officer tried to get artillery fire to bear on them, but, owing to the height of Mansour and the steepness of the valley to the south, our guns could not reach the targets. A message at 10.00

hours established the fact that "S" Company were completely out of ammunition but were remaining in their positions brandishing grenades. "R" and "T" Companies had about one hundred rounds between them, the greater portion belonging to "T" Company. Major Conron had been killed and no other officers were left in "R" Company when they had run out of ammunition altogether. At this stage Pearson wirelessed for permission to withdraw, but no authority was forthcoming, so a message was sent to companies to stay in their positions at whatever the cost. At 10.30 hours the mortar fire and shelling ceased and it became obvious that the enemy was closing in. Some forty yards from our positions the enemy went to ground and opened fire whilst "S" and "R" Companies sat hugging their grenades and shouting to the enemy to come within range. A quarter of an hour passed and the commanding officer again applied for permission to withdraw. He was told to wait five minutes for an answer, but replied that unless the answer came within two minutes it would be too late. Permission was then given to withdraw.

'Lieutenant Jessop was despatched to tell "S" Company to withdraw, bringing their mortars. Major Bull led "T" Company out, and the intelligence officer got "R" Company on their way.

'The enemy were within forty yards of the crest and so it was not many seconds before a hail of fire began following the battalion down the hill. Orders had been issued to re-form at its foot where the gully, down which it was retreating, turned right.

'As the companies re-formed the adjutant sent them off to make their way back to the French lines. By this time shells and mortar bombs were falling in the gully, casualties were being evacuated by every means available—carriers, mules and stretchers. One or two tanks laid a smoke screen across the very open ground in front of the French positions, and so the battalion struggled back under continuous fire.'

The casualties in this action amounted to thirteen officers killed and wounded and one hundred and sixty-nine other ranks killed, wounded and missing.

After this engagement the brigade, still in the Bou Arada sector, regrouped and 'tidied up their positions with the French troops'.

The 3rd Battalion took up a position on or near a feature known as Argoub. It was overlooked by the enemy, but fortunately his troops were Austrian and Italian Alpini, 'not over-anxious to cause trouble'. Fighting was therefore limited to patrolling, and the area became known as the 'Happy Valley'. The 1st Battalion had received reinforcements, Royal Welch Fusiliers, 'fine men with fine officers'. They came from the 2nd Parachute Brigade now formed in England and there were enough of them to form a company. They held the left of the line where, in digging, they came upon a series of underground chambers which they firmly believed were Carthaginian in origin.

For the next fortnight or more the three battalions remained in relatively quiet and static positions in the same area. Shellfire and dive-bombing caused very few casualties.

It was during this period that Lieutenant G. L. W. Street of the 3rd Battalion, going forward in the half light of dawn to visit his most advanced posts, heard a movement among the thick scrub which covered the hillside. He cried out, calling upon the unseen men to keep quiet since the enemy were near at hand, and was immediately challenged. 'Don't make such a bloody row,' he repeated; 'there may be Germans about.' At that moment a German jabbed him in the stomach with a tommy gun and ordered him to lead the rest of the hostile patrol, whom Street had mistaken for his own men, between the lines of the parachute battalion, so that they might attack its headquarters. Street led them instead to the nearest company strongpoint, where they were received with heavy fire. Fortunately Street was not hit and took cover in a fold of the ground with the German officer in command of the patrol. After a short time he turned to him and said: 'Look out, my chaps are throwing grenades at us.' The German officer turned his head, Street struck him a heavy blow, knocked him out, deprived him of his weapons and made off to our lines. He then led some of his men in a charge which destroyed a platoon of the enemy. For these exploits he was awarded the Military Cross.

On 26th February the enemy decided to attack in force. The complacent Austrians and bored Italian Alpini had been reinforced by German shock troops. The main attack developed against the 3rd Battalion into whose positions some of the Germans had infiltrated during the previous night. This they had been enabled to do owing to the wooded nature of the country. 'A' and 'B' Companies and battalion headquarters fought savagely hand to hand for an hour, until 'the whole area was a mass of individuals trying to kill each other.' The crew of a German machine-gun post were killed by Sergeant Fennell and his section with the bayonet only ten yards from company headquarters. Gradually the superior fighting qualities of the men of 'A' and 'B' Companies enabled them to gain the upper hand, and the enemy withdrew down the hill till they reached a wadi, horseshoe in shape, which ran from the foot of the Argoub position to Djebel Mansour, the highest feature of that area. 'Unfortunately for the enemy the battalion had ranged on every part of that wadi the previous day.' Their foresight was now to bear grim fruit. In the space of ninety minutes some three thousand mortar shells were fired into the wadi with deadly effect, and the forty machine-guns, which 'A' and 'B' Companies had by that time captured in this and other encounters with the enemy, were set up so as to cover the ground on the further side of the wadi. 'It was a pleasing sight,' records the battalion historian, 'to see scores of Germans jumping out of the wadi to avoid the mortars, and jumping back to get away from the machine-gun fire.' The enemy were indeed caught in a trap and suffered over four hundred casualties. Some two hundred surrendered. Large numbers were wounded in the legs, buttocks, and back by pieces of three-inch mortar bombs. When searched, some of them were found to have in their pockets pamphlets giving detailed instructions on the best manner of fighting the 'red devils'. This was the first intimation that men of the 1st Parachute Brigade had received of the name bestowed upon them by the enemy. They accepted it 'as a great honour won in battle'. In this action the 1st Parachute Squadron, Royal Engineers, were especially prominent.

The casualties of the 3rd Battalion were light, two officers and twelve other ranks killed, and between thirty and forty wounded, out of a strength of just under five hundred. The confused nature of the fighting is well illustrated by what happened to the brigade's transport. What there was of it was under Captain J. T. Parker and it was ten miles away at El Aroussa. For a time it fell into the hands of the enemy, from whom it was ultimately freed by a squadron of tanks.

Meanwhile the 2nd Battalion was also engaged and fought from 09.30 hours when 'B' and 'C' Companies were first attacked until 18.00 hours without giving ground. That evening a patrol under Captain Stark rounded up eighty prisoners from an Italian Alpini regiment and two from the German Jägers. Their casualties were even lighter than those of the 3rd, being but one killed and two wounded, though they were intermittently in action for eight and a half hours.

The 1st Battalion fared equally well. When the enemy's shellfire became heavy, they withdrew from their outposts to the main position on the reverse slope of the hill and thus avoided casualties. The wire in front of their trenches, which had been 'dug under the eagle eye of Alastair Pearson', their fire-eating and dearly loved commanding officer, had been most cunningly laid so as to lead the Germans into a series of 'funnels' which were covered by machine-guns. True to their previous tactics, the battalion held their fire till the Germans were within point-blank range. Then they delivered a hail of bullets and the attack withered.

Shortly after this action the brigade was relieved by American troops. The battalions felt an immediate liking for the stout allies, but were somewhat taken aback by their methods. The hand-over of the 1st Battalion was described as a nightmare, the noise being like 'Blackpool beach on a summer Sunday afternoon in Wakes Week'. It also appeared that the Americans did not stand-to at dawn. Some months later these same Americans were met with again; by then they were 'first-class fighting soldiers . . . who had learnt their lessons quickly and well'.

The Bou Arada sector was handed over to the Americans on 5th March, and the brigade moved by motor transport to the Tamera Valley, where it was now to perform its most remarkable feat of the whole campaign.

The enemy's offensive had now failed all along the line, except on this, the northern sector, where he had concentrated a division against a weak British brigade, with a view to breaking through along the coastal road. The 1st and 3rd Battalions took up their positions late on 5th March, but the 2nd Battalion was diverted *en route* to clear the enemy from a prominent feature in the Beja area. This task having been accomplished successfully, the battalion rejoined the brigade on the following day.

Critical days followed. Dawn on 7th March broke on the 1st Parachute Brigade astride the main road on the northern sector with the 1st Battalion on the right and south of the road just outside the village of Tamera. The 3rd Battalion was on their left together with elements of a battalion of the Leicesters and late that evening the 2nd Battalion arrived to take over from a battalion of the Lincolns. The brigade sector was overlooked by a large feature called the Djebel Bel, to the south of the main road, too large and too wooded for the 1st Battalion to occupy. It used to send patrols to the top, but this meant a march of several hours and there was no means of bringing food and water from the main road to a permanent post.

At dawn on 8th March the enemy attacked in two thrusts, one against the 1st Battalion, the other against the 2nd. The 2nd Battalion had only just taken over from the Lincolns in the dark and so were caught slightly off balance and 'A' Company suffered a number of casualties. Its commander, Major Lane, rang up battalion headquarters to say, 'We appear to be completely surrounded now, but I am sure it will be all right.' The enemy had almost reached headquarters and 'A' Company required ammunition urgently. Each time a mule column was formed up it was scattered by mortar fire. Captain Radcliffe, the adjutant, was killed while leading a charge with an escort for an ammunition column trying to reach the Company.

In the meantime the enemy were attempting to move round the right flank of the brigade's position along a ridge to the south; but this move was countered by machine-guns from the 2nd Battalion established in a position known as Cork Wood and by the remnants of a battalion of the York and Lancasters. Major Rotheray of the 2nd Battalion was killed while he was conducting an intense machine-gun duel with the enemy across the valley.

The brigade commander decided that if the enemy continued to thrust between the 1st and 2nd Battalions the road might be cut. He therefore ordered the 3rd Battalion to deal with the situation, and it did so at the cost of a number of casualties. Meanwhile, the 1st Battalion had successfully beaten off all attacks. As it grew dark the position became stable despite the bombing of 'B' Company by Stukas. The brigade was still as firmly in position as it had been when the day began; but the enemy's intention was now obvious. Having been defeated everywhere else, he was determined to break through on this northern sector. The 2nd Battalion Coldstream Guards were brought up from the Medjez el Bab sector so as to reinforce the 1st Parachute Brigade.

The 9th passed quietly, but at first light on the 10th the enemy began a very heavy mortar bombardment of the 1st and 2nd Battalion positions. This was followed by infantry attacks which were pressed home. As a result 'T' Company of the 1st Battalion was overrun, but the position was restored by 'an amazing counter-attack' of the headquarters Company led by Lieutenant-Colonel Pearson himself. There were, however, insufficient troops to man the forward positions and the 1st Battalion were forced to hold a smaller perimeter completely overlooked by the enemy on Djebel Bel. The 2nd Battalion had withstood the attacks on their positions but could not prevent the Germans cutting them off from the 1st Battalion.

This savage clash took place in the most unpleasant conditions, for it was very cold and pouring with rain. At close quarters the Germans proved to be no match for the parachutists, who took two hundred of them prisoner. Throughout, the advanced dressing station of the Parachute Field Ambulance remained very far forward. By so doing they gave great encouragement to the fighting men, who when wounded could have their wounds properly dressed before facing the long and bumpy journey back. 'The Regimental stretcher-bearers had a ghastly time stumbling and sliding down the steep sodden slopes with a constant stream of wounded. All the rear areas were continually mortared.'

A pause ensued on 11th March. During it 'A' Company of the 3rd Battalion, supported by Churchill tanks, attempted to push the enemy out of the positions they were holding in front of the 2nd Battalion. In this they were only partially successful and it was determined to make another attempt the next day, supported by as heavy a mortar barrage as possible. During the night 'C' Company of the 2nd Battalion made a resolute attempt to dislodge the enemy, who had had supplies dropped to them by parachute ; and, although this action proved costly, the threat to the main communications was removed for the time being.

During the next day, the 12th, the Corps commander, Lieutenant-General C. W. Allfrey, C.B., D.S.O., M.C., came up and spoke to several men, expecting to find them completely exhausted. Instead he found them in great heart. 'We are O.K., sir,' they said. 'Tell the Germans to send some more: we haven't killed half enough yet.'

Allfrey was aware that the enemy had thrown the equivalent of a division against the 1st Parachute Brigade but he was unable to reinforce the sector effectively for lack of troops. He did, however, decide that the Djebel Bel must be taken if the parachutists were to continue to hold their positions. It seemed incredible that the 1st Battalion could remain where they were, curled round the base of this great hill with the enemy on the top watching every move. They did so because they had established such a degree of superiority man for man that the German infantry hardly dared to approach their positions by day or by night. The enemy could, however, lob shells and mortar bombs onto the brigade's position all day long. They did

104

so, and by the evening of the 12th there was but one officer a company of the 1st Battalion left in the line.

At this juncture it was decided that the Sherwood Foresters should attempt to take the huge and threatening Djebel Bel. They had very nearly reached the summit when the Germans reacted so vigorously that they recoiled and came back down again to the 1st Battalion's lines, leaving many dead behind them. That evening the 1st Battalion were taken out of the line for a belated and well deserved rest.

14th March opened with another severe bombardment of the 2nd Battalion's positions in Cork Wood, followed by an almost successful attempt to make a wide outflanking movement on the right. 'It was interesting to see, late in the day, a senior German officer arrive in a Fiesler Storch to talk to the German soldiers involved. Our own artillery engaged the plane but without effect.'

During all this time the French Corps Franc D'Afrique had been opposing a regiment of Italian Bersaglieri on the left of the brigade sector. The French were extremely gallant but lacked training and the Italians 'were entirely fed up with the whole war.' The fighting here had come to be known as 'the Second Eleven Match, without meaning any disrespect for our gallant allies. Now, however, the Germans elected to take a hand in this area and the whole picture changed'.

In the evening the enemy made a most determined attempt to rush the 2nd Battalion positions in Cork Wood. They scored a fair measure of success until a squadron of Stukas arrived and bombed their own forward troops almost to extinction. The cheers on our side could almost match the curses on the German side, uttered by men belonging to the 10th Panzer Grenadiers.[1]

The 15th and 16th March passed fairly quietly, with artillery, air, and patrol activity alone being noticeable. The brigade positions were bombed each day and the main axis was subjected to extremely accurate shellfire. Owing to the type of country, one of steep hills and thick woods, there was a good deal of infiltration by the enemy, and on two occasions visiting staff officers were forced to fight lone defensive battles well behind the front line.

On 17th March the Germans came on again. This time the

---

[1] It is now known that the German troops attacking in this sector included the Barenthin Regiment which had a number of Luftwaffe men in their ranks; the Tunisian Regiment made up of German reserves in the Mediterranean theatre; the Witzig Regiment of Parachute Engineers, and the 10th Panzer Grenadier Regiment.

weight of the air attack was against the Sherwood Foresters and the Leicesters in front and the Corps Franc D'Afrique on the left flank. The battle raged all day long. Enemy aircraft made frequent dive-bombing attacks and the area was subject to incessant artillery bombardment. The gallant but inexperienced French troops were commanded by a splendid officer, Colonel Durand, who had done wonders with the men under his command. By the end of the day, however, he was forced to inform Brigadier Flavell that he would not be able to hold his positions for more than an hour or two longer. The brigadier reluctantly gave permission for him to withdraw, and himself withdrew later, having no more men with whom to hold the position.

By then the 2nd Battalion had been holding Cork Wood continuously since the 7th, and during this time they had over one hundred and fifty casualties; but they were most reluctant to leave ground over which they had fought so hard. 'B' Troop of the Parachute Field Squadron, Royal Engineers, cratered the road before they left and stayed long enough to see the leading enemy armoured vehicle plunge down into the river below.

The 1st Battalion withdrew over the hills and the brigade transport 'belted down the main road, being miraculously missed by the enemy shells which sought them'. The 2nd Battalion had a ghastly journey from the Tamera Valley literally through a river, the Oued el Medene. The men swam and waded down the stream, carrying all their weapons with them and being subjected to enemy shellfire the whole way. This most unpleasant episode cost the battalion two killed, eleven wounded and five missing, presumed drowned. By the afternoon, completely soaked and exhausted, the depleted companies took up positions on three bare rocky hills between which the river flowed. These were known as the 'Pimples'. On the next day the 2nd Battalion handed over to the Leicesters and went back to rest. In consequence of this withdrawal the enemy were now able to control the important road junction at Djebel Abiod, and to isolate the Allied troops in the northern sector.

The pimples 'were horrible things to hold'. It was almost impossible to dig trenches in the solid rock; they were very steep to climb. The biggest, which was called 'Bowler Hat', was overlooked by the enemy from two sides, and, worse still, was situated on the enemy's side of the river. It was the key to the whole position. No offensive could begin until it was taken. The enemy appreciated this to the full and the next night the Panzer

Grenadiers attacked in full force and pushed the Leicesters back. They suffered heavily and were relieved by the 3rd Battalion, who were ordered to retake Bowler Hat on the following night. This allowed very little time for reconnaissance, and the attack failed.

It was now to be the 1st Battalion's turn. By this time Lieutenant-Colonel Pearson had had an opportunity to make a well-co-ordinated plan. This included the bridging of the river Oued el Medene by the Parachute Field Squadron and a carefully prepared artillery bombardment. The 1st Battalion went forward 'with the sympathy and prayers of the rest of the brigade', for the task was heavy; but its attack was brilliantly successful at small cost. Fortunately the Panzer Grenadiers had been relieved earlier in the night and the German infantry who had taken their place were not feeling at home. The 3rd Battalion took over again after the 1st Battalion's success and now the 1st and 2nd Battalions prepared for the opening phase of the final offensive of the Allied Armies in Africa.

By this time the 8th Army was about to join hands with a greatly reinforced 1st Army and both had come under the command of General Alexander. Rommel had departed by air to Germany and his famous Afrika Korps was now part of the Axis Army of three hundred thousand men commanded by von Arnim, who had been ordered by Hitler to hold out in Tunisia to the last round and the last man.

The first step towards the elimination of the enemy in Africa would have to be the removal of his threat towards the northern coastal road. This was the task given to the 1st Parachute Brigade, who found themselves shortly engaged with, among other German formations, the crack German Parachute Engineers under their resolute commander Witzig. It was he who had captured the Belgian fortress of Ebenemal in 1940.

Brigadier Flavell was ordered to free the main road axis, and for this he was allotted the whole of the artillery of the 46th Infantry Division and a 'Thabor' of Goums. These were stout irregular soldiers from Morocco commanded by the very best type of young French officers. The 139th Infantry Brigade were to carry out an assault across country on the right flank.

It was decided that the 1st and 2nd Battalions, although they were at half strength, should attack frontally, passing on either side of the 3rd Battalion holding Bowler Hat, while the Goums worked round the left flank. At ten o'clock on the night of 27th

March both battalions crossed their start lines under cover of the whole of the divisional artillery. This was the first time that the brigade had ever witnessed concentrated heavy artillery fire 'and they were most impressed'.

The 1st Battalion's attack went almost completely according to plan, and as a result of it the whole of the Bersaglieri opposing them surrendered, including their colonel, who handed over his sword but insisted on keeping his little dog. The 2nd Battalion, on the other hand, had a difficult passage, and 'B' Company suffered a number of casualties when passing through an undetected minefield. Dawn on 28th March found the battalion concentrated on a false crest short of their objective, and Frost, the commanding officer, ordered 'various manœuvres to extricate his men from their very awkward position'. Almost immediately after the rifle companies had been despatched to join the fray, the Germans came on against the 2nd Battalion's base. The brigadier sent 'C' Company of the 3rd Battalion to strengthen the position. 'From now on it was hammer and tongs in an area under constant fire'. The Germans came through the woods and pressed against the battalion's position from three sides. It seemed that the parachutists could not possibly hold. Yet if this position on the false crest were eliminated by the enemy, then the whole attack of the brigade could not but fail, for the Germans would obtain direct observation of the whole Djebel Aboid area. The German ring drew ever closer and tighter, the streams of bullets from their machine-guns cut the branches of the trees, and the rain of mortar bombs and shells made it impossible to evacuate wounded and prisoners. In this critical situation Frost ordered those with rifles to fix bayonets and all others to get ready to charge. 'Desperate emergencies require desperate remedies and the idea was to catch the enemy off balance just before they made their final assault.' At this juncture a private soldier picked up a box of Italian egg-shaped grenades and went round the sector crying out, 'Cigarettes, chocolates. Come on, help yourselves,' as he passed them round. As the Germans emerged through the trees the fire from the supporting artillery and mortars fell upon them and at the same time both 'B' Company and part of the 1st Battalion attacked their flanks. This was too much and the German attack melted away.

By now the 2nd Battalion could only muster one hundred and fifty all ranks and another company of the 3rd Battalion were sent up to strengthen them. During the night both battalions went forward again without meeting serious opposition, and the next day found the brigade back in their original positions astride the main road near Tamera having collected a most useful amount of enemy weapons, equipment and vehicles.

It was soon discovered that the enemy had pulled back to Green Hill and Bald Hill, from which they had begun their offensive in February. There was little therefore left for the 1st Parachute Brigade to do. This was as well, since it was far too weak in numbers to take any further part in the campaign.

The longed-for end was now in sight. On the night of 14/15th April the 9th American Division relieved the 1st Parachute Brigade, which returned to Bou Farik and rest. By then the average strength of a company in any of its three battalions was not more than sixty ; yet the first feeling among the men was one of disappointment that they, who had fought so stoutly, nearly always against superior forces, should not take part in the final stage and enter Tunis, which fell on 7th May. In a day or two, however, they were better able to appreciate the delights of the rest they had so richly earned. No longer was it necessary for Major Stephen Terrell to write in his diary, 'Could do with a lot of whisky ; appreciate the necessities of life as luxuries' ; or, 'Mud, mud, mud, everywhere . . .' ; or, 'Rain and howling wind—"Sunny Africa"!' Instead he could record that it was 'a beautiful sunny day, the country looking lovely, with daisies and wild flowers ; tortoises are crawling about', and a few days later describe his lunch with the local Caïd, 'Hors d'œuvres, eggs in butter, cous-cous, stuffed roast chicken, caramel cream, iced sponge cake, but nothing but coffee and sour milk to wash it down.'

At one point the railway to Bou Farik runs in a wide curve. Within it was a camp for prisoners of war. As the train, carrying the brigade to rest, wound its slow length along, the Germans behind the wire caught sight of the red berets worn by its passengers. They swarmed from their tents to cheer and cheer again men whose valour had aroused their instinctive admiration.

Presently the brigade learnt with joy that it was to prepare for airborne warfare once more. It began to do so under Brigadier G. W. Lathbury, M.B.E. He had taken over from Brigadier Flavell, whose immediate admission to the Distinguished Service Order had been welcomed with the greatest satisfaction by the men he had commanded in such heavy fighting. The brigade was in the highest spirits, as well it might be, despite the one thousand seven hundred casualties in killed, wounded and missing which the three battalions had suffered since the opening of the campaign. To offset this grim total they had put out of action about five thousand of the enemy killed and wounded, and taken some three thousand six hundred prisoners. The men they had been fighting belonged to such famous enemy units as the Hermann Goering Jäger Regiment, the 10th Panzer Grenadiers, Witzig's parachutists, and the Austrian Mountain Division. In less than four months the 1st Parachute Brigade had been awarded eight admissions to the Distinguished Service Order, fifteen Military Crosses, nine Distinguished Conduct Medals, twenty-two Military Medals, three Croix de Guerre and one Legion of Honour. It was a record never surpassed by any formation of the British Army going, as they had gone, into action for the first time.

The casualties would have been still heavier had it not been for the skill, devotion and courage of the regimental doctors and the 16th Parachute Field Ambulance. They remained continuously with the fighting troops, dropping with them when they went by air into battle, or staying almost on the front line when they were fighting as infantry. The officer commanding one surgical team, Captain C. G. Robb, Royal Army Medical Corps, 'carried out one hundred and sixty-two surgical operations, most of them of a severe nature, and of the men so treated only one died. Robb himself injured his knee in his first drop, but concealed this fact and continued to operate for three weeks, his last operation being on himself'.

Whether troops trained for months for the special purpose of carrying out airborne operations should have been employed for most of the campaign in the role of infantry of the Line may be open to question. The use of them in this manner was certainly extravagant, for it takes time to train a parachute soldier. On the other hand, having regard to the conditions in North Africa, and the fact that the Allies did not until the end of the campaign possess that overwhelming strength which could ensure victory, the part which the 1st Parachute Brigade was called upon to play was probably inevitable.

Of one thing there can be no doubt: they proved themselves again and again, as perhaps must all volunteers, to be troops of the highest order. Implacable in attack, steady in defence, they earned the sobriquet bestowed on them by the enemy, not once, but many times. The monument which they raised to their dead in the Tamera Valley on the spot where they had defeated the stout German parachutists stands today to remind the passer-by of what manner of men were these, who upheld the valour of British arms in the first of those campaigns by which victory, complete and overwhelming, was in due course achieved.

Marston Tonight

ABOUT six miles south of the town of Catania an ugly structure of steel girders carries the main road which encircles the island of Sicily across the River Simeto. On 14th July 1943 the bridge—its name is Primosole—was to be the scene of the next exploit of the 1st Parachute Brigade. Before its three battalions arrived to seize it, however, much preliminary work had to be done. The heavy casualties suffered by the 1st Brigade in North Africa had dislocated the plans for the formation of the 2nd Brigade, and this in turn affected the formation of the 3rd. In consequence the 1st Airborne Division was still much under strength, especially in such necessary auxiliaries as units of the Royal Engineers, Royal Corps of Signals and the Royal Army Medical Corps. By June two of these brigades, the 2nd under Down, the 4th under Brigadier J. W. Hackett, but without the 11th Battalion left in Palestine, had joined the 1st in Africa and all three trained vigorously together in the arid country round Sousse. It is, however, with the fortunes of the 1st Brigade that this chapter is concerned. Those of the other two are recounted later.

To a shortage of trained men was added a shortage of equipment, and the shortage of aircraft seemed to be endemic. No. 38 Wing of the Royal Air Force, whose task it was to carry or tow airborne troops into battle, possessed but half the aircraft necessary, and many of these were Albemarles, an exceedingly unsuitable type rejected by Bomber Command, but capable of carrying ten parachutists. They quitted it, as in the Whitley, the Halifax and the Stirling, by means of a hole in the floor of the fuselage. There were no seats, and as the men shuffled one by one to the cavity, they resembled nothing so much in their heavy equipment as a file of ungainly rabbits. For this reason jumping from an Albemarle became known as bunny-hopping.

For the moment this method of reaching the battlefield was in the future as the three battalions, reinforced by drafts from home, began their training in a lonely valley some sixty miles inland from Oran. Here a number of temporary airstrips had been made, and each battalion was encamped as close as possible to a strip so as to maintain intimate contact with the American pilots who were to take its officers and men to their next battle and who were in future to fly most of the Dakota aircraft used in airborne operations. As the swift Mediterranean spring departed and summer approached, the valley became hotter and hotter, until the brigade was 'sitting in an arid and dusty waste', everyone covered with choking dust, when an aircraft on one or another of the airstrips opened up its engines before taking off. An exercise involving a number of aircraft filled the whole valley with a brown and singularly unpleasant fog.

Realising that his new command were tired after the strenuous North African campaign, Lathbury wisely did not at first demand too much in the way of training. Gradually he set about hardening the parachute troops to fit them for what lay ahead and from the start paid particular attention to the weapon training of those men who had come out as reinforcements and who had not so far been in action. He also made certain that every officer and man knew how to handle the weapons of the enemy. Such knowledge was particularly important for parachute troops, since containers were apt to go astray, and the men could never be sure that they would be able to pick up all their weapons after a drop.

This desolate valley, containing two places called Matmore and Mascara, in which three brigades[1] of the division were training, was rendered even more uncongenial by the attitude of the local Arab population who maintained 'a constant and exhausted indifference to anything except money and material gain', and by the absence of all amenities, even a branch of the N.A.A.F.I. The brigadier did his best and made arrangements to send what were known as recreational parties to some of the French North African towns, notably Mostagenen and to some extent Sidi bel Abbes, the base depot of the Foreign Legion. All this was on the debit side ; on the credit side was the swift friendship which sprang up with the American pilots and crews of the Dakotas who went with them into action. The parachutists had great confidence in their flying abilities, but less in their powers of navigation, which the preliminary exercises shewed were far from perfect. This distrust was soon, unfortunately, to

[1] The 1st and 2nd Parachute Brigades and the 1st Air Landing Brigade.

be more than justified. Neither the crews of the aircraft nor their passengers viewed with any favour the additional long-range petrol tanks which had been placed inside the fuselages of the aircraft and greatly increased the risk of fire.

It did not take the 1st Brigade long to work up to normal pitch. By 30th June, when it left on the first stage of its journey towards the scene of operations, it had to its credit a large share in the total of eight thousand nine hundred and thirteen jumps which had been made by the division. Side by side with the parachute troops the 1st Air Landing Brigade, whose task it was to be to attack the Ponte Grande at Syracuse, trained in Waco gliders which had been erected, for lack of ground staff, by their own pilots. There were also a number of Horsa gliders, which had been towed all the way from England.

Some time before Eisenhower had come to see the 1st Parachute Brigade. Of all the generals who from time to time throughout the war felt it their duty or their pleasure to pay the Parachute Regiment a visit, none was more highly regarded; and rightly, for the general's personality was singularly winning, and there was that about him which shewed him to be a leader of men. On this occasion it was recorded that he made several members of the 3rd Battalion blush by his praise and thanks for what the brigade had accomplished in North Africa. He also urged its commanding officer to be more lavish in his recommendations for awards, and extolled the merits of certain American decorations, including the Purple Heart.

Soon after Eisenhower's visit the airborne troops in general suffered a most grievous loss: to the death of Rock, which had occurred in October 1942 as the result of an accident, there was added the death of Nigel Norman from the same cause. Air-Commodore Sir Nigel Norman, commanding No. 38 Wing, was killed in a Hudson of which the port engine failed just after it was airborne. Norman, standing behind the two pilots, was just able to enter the cabin and shout to those inside it to take up crash positions before the aircraft hit the ground. He himself, however, did not have time to do so and was killed instantly. The others, except for the radio operator, who died later of his injuries, were saved by this prompt warning. Norman was one of those pioneers who could ill be spared: a man of invincible determination and infectious energy, he allowed nothing and nobody, however exalted or lowly, to stand in the way of his purpose, and this purpose was first to create and then to develop airborne forces on such a scale that they should be a great, perhaps a decisive, factor in ultimate victory. At the time of his death he had not as yet succeeded, but he was well set on the path of achievement, and to him, as to Rock, the men who leapt to battle by parachute or sailed and crashed to it by glider owed more than they could ever pay. 'England has been always fortunate in her pioneers, whose genius and determination have so often secured her victory, and whose example, if she is to live must ever inspire her sons.'

The training, which increased in intensity as the days went by, ended with three exercises, Cactus I, II and III, which seemed to the parachutists of the 1st Parachute Brigade to have been very aptly named, for more than one of them landed in those prickly plants. The 2nd Parachute Brigade was engaged in similar exercises. Before June was out the 1st and 2nd Brigades moved to an even grimmer spot, near Sousse, south-east of Tunis, a journey of some six hundred miles accomplished 'by every known method of transportation except sea. Motor transport, rail transport, aircraft and gliders, all contributed to giving the Assistant-Quartermaster-general a headache'. Mascara had been hot, but Sousse was much hotter, and here the parachute soldiers, now in full fighting trim, were tormented by a wind from the desert referred to by the local inhabitants under various names, the Khamsin, the Sirocco or the Harmattan, but soon known to the division as 'a bloody hot wind'. Mercifully it did not blow very often, but when it did the temperature rose to more than 100 degrees in the shade.

Despite this disadvantage Sousse was more popular than Mascara ; perhaps because the men bivouacked in olive yards with the sea but half an hour away. Their spirits were very high ; five weeks arduous training was behind them and for one brigade at least, action of the kind which they had deliberately chosen when they joined the Parachute Regiment, and which but few of them had experienced, was immediately ahead. This time they were not to be called upon to fight as infantry, running across bleak wind-swept hills or through dripping cork woods to meet a sudden thrust against a tenuous line ; they were to seize a bridge vital to the communications of foe and presently of friend. When the models were produced, the maps spread, they perceived that their part in 'Fustian', the big airborne operation which included the seizure of certain objectives by glider-borne troops was to take them in advance of the renowned 8th Army, and place them on either side of the River Simeto with Etna towering behind, crowned with snow and fire.

114

The importance of the task to which the code name 'Marston' was given was obvious enough. It was Alexander's intention to put the 8th Army, under Montgomery, ashore on the south-eastern tip of Sicily, that 'stepping-stone between Africa and Europe', with orders to move up the east coast along the main road, seizing as it went Syracuse, Lentini, Catania and other large and small towns, till it reached Messina at the head of the Straits. If the army could move fast enough and in sufficient strength, it would thus cut off the only line of retreat available to the German garrison in Sicily, thought to number about four divisions. These, attacked by Patton's Americans who were to land further to the west, would be herded into the north-east corner of the island where, if all went well, they would find themselves in the clutches of the 8th Army.

There were two ways by which Montgomery could reach Messina: the shorter, the quicker and by far the easier route lay over the coastal plain from the little baroque town of Pachino in the south to Messina in the north. Through it ran a long section of the chief Sicilian road which, as has been said, runs in a circle round the island. By advancing up this road his Army would have its right flank upon the sea, its left upon the olive and broom-clad slopes of Etna. The other way was more difficult: it lay inland through Misterbianco, Paterno, Adrano, vine-encircled Bronte with its memories of Nelson and Randazzo, little towns the same colour as the rocky soil from which they sprang, which nestled on the south-eastern, eastern and north-eastern slopes of Etna. This volcano would then be on the right flank of the Army, for it would have forsaken the easy coastal plain for the steeper interior, with its ridged hills, its deep valleys, and its twisting roads. The route by the coast was the obvious choice, but if it were to be taken speed was even more necessary than usual in war. The 8th Army would have to move forward like a tempest to prevent the German defences from being consolidated on a line somewhere between Etna and the sea.

In the immediate path of the advance were three all-important bridges, the nearest, Ponte Grande, at the entering-in of Syracuse. This, it was eventually decided, should be captured by a glider-borne attack; the next, north-east of dusty Lentini, the Ponte dei Malati, over the River Leonardo, was assigned to No. 3 Commando; and the third and farthest off was the girder bridge crossing the Primosole on the extreme southern outskirts of Catania—this was to be taken by the 1st Parachute Brigade. If these three bridges could be seized and held, the 8th Army

115

would, it was hoped, be able to capture this, the most important town on the east coast of the island, and thence push north into Messina. It was eventually decided that the bridges should be taken one by one as the situation developed. The original plan had included the capture of Augusta and a bridge nearby, by the 2nd Parachute Brigade ; but these objectives were overrun so quickly that the operation proved unnecessary and was cancelled. This was probably fortunate, as subsequent reconnaissance shewed that the dropping zones chosen were most unsuitable, for they were covered with rocks and stones and cut up by steep gullies.

Operation 'Marston', as the attack on the Primosole Bridge was called, was planned in meticulous detail, which laid down even the type of food the parachutists should eat beforehand. Plenty of sugar was counselled, but very little fat. They should also drink as much as possible immediately before and during the flight, for that would enable them to go for a longer period without drinking after they had dropped. A common password for the use of all troops taking part in the invasion of Sicily was issued. The challenge was 'Desert Rats' ; its answer 'Kill Italians'.

In the Sousse area training was relaxed and the men encouraged to rest and bathe in the sea. The principal events of interest were a visit by General Montgomery, and the explosion of the divisional ammunition dump in which some eight hundred tons, the entire supply for the operation, went up in the brief space of half an hour. This occurred on 5th July, but what was lost was soon replaced.

The invasion of Sicily began in the darkness preceding dawn on the 10th. Before the end of that day it was known at Sousse that the glider attack on the Ponte Grande, though very costly, had been successful, and soon afterwards that the operation which would have taken the 2nd Brigade to the fields and olive-yards near Augusta was cancelled as being unnecessary. 12th July arrived, and the troops set out for their various airstrips, only to receive a message that the weather was unsuitable and that the operation was postponed. The lorries returned to the bivouacs in 'clouds of dust through which came floating the ironical cheers of the disgruntled soldiers'. Eighteen hours elapsed and Lathbury was sitting in the brigade mess-tent, when the brigade-major, David Hunter, 'walked in, full of suppressed excitement, and gave the code word "Marston tonight".' After a last conference with his three commanding officers, Alastair Pearson, commanding the 1st Battalion, 'who won four D.S.O.s and a M.C. in eighteen months', John Frost, D.S.O., M.C. of the 2nd, who led the retreat from Oudna, and E. C. Yeldham, commanding the 3rd Battalion—Lathbury climbed aboard the Albemarle which was to carry him and his brigade headquarters to the scene of action.

The plan was for two platoons of the 1st Battalion, with the 1st Field Squadron of the Royal Engineers led by Major Murray, to drop as close as possible to the bridge and seize it by *coup de main*. Five minutes later two platoons of the 3rd Battalion would arrive and capture the four-gun anti-aircraft battery nearby. The rest of the 1st Battalion would then organise the defences of the bridge, and the rest of the 3rd would establish themselves in a loop of the River Simeto about a thousand yards to the north of Primosole. The 2nd Battalion were ordered to seize the high ground south of the bridge, which was composed of 'three features' known as Johnny I, II and III.

At sunset the brigade took off from six landing strips between Kairouan and Sousse. It was carried in 105 Dakota aircraft belonging to the American Troop Carrier Command, and eleven Albemarles of the Royal Air Force. In addition, Halifaxes and Stirlings towed eight Waco and eleven Horsas carrying the men and anti-tank guns of the Royal Artillery. Only three aircraft with parachutists and three towing gliders failed, for mechanical reasons, to take the air, or had to turn back before they reached Malta.

On taking off, the force flew echeloned in tight V-shaped formation, low over the sea along the first leg of the course, which ended in the island of Malta. Thence they turned north-east towards Syracuse, and Augusta and the dropping zones beyond. At Malta a cone of searchlights pointed towards the heavens, and the American pilots had no difficulty in maintaining their course. In accordance with the plan they then turned north-east and headed for Cape Murro di Porco on the south-eastern corner of Sicily. The dropping zones which were the ultimate destination of the parachutists were four in number: two north of the Primosole bridge beside the sinuous Simeto, and two south on the steep banks of the Gornalunga Canal which joins the Simeto a short distance above the bridge. A fifth landing zone to be used by three gliders was close to the southern end of the bridge itself. It had originally been intended to mark the dropping zones with lights, but the plan was abandoned in favour of a radar device known by the name of 'Eureka'. This instrument sent out a continuous stream of signals which could be picked up by aircraft fitted with the necessary equipment known as 'Rebecca'. The device, later perfected, was then in its infancy and uncertain in operation. Eureka was dropped by the 21st Independent Parachute Company, under the command of Major Lander, half an hour before the arrival of the main force. That day Lander was killed, 'a great misfortune to the airborne troops'. He had been at Ringway in the early days, where he had shewn himself to be the fortunate possessor of a singularly fertile mind, responsible for many inventions and improvements in equipment.

Long before the airborne forces reached the neighbourhood of their zones they were in grievous difficulty. Near the Sicilian coast they flew over our own ships, still engaged in covering the landing of stores and reinforcements. Whether the aircraft were off course at the time or whether a misunderstanding on board the ships occurred is hard to determine. What happened, however, is only too clear. The compact force of Dakota aircraft flying in the clear light provided by a three-quarter moon was subjected to heavy anti-aircraft fire. Upon the pilots, most of whom had never been in action before or known the experience of high velocity shells bursting in the sky about them, such a greeting was as unnerving as it was unexpected. They at once began, almost unconsciously, to take avoiding action. Several Dakotas were hit and went down in flames; others suffered such damage as caused their pilots to make at once for Africa. Moreover, since only the leading aircraft in each V-formation carried a trained navigator, many of the Americans, once their course was thus arbitrarily altered, lost the correct direction and could not regain it. There is this to be said for the gun crews whose action that night caused such heavy casualties and almost wrecked the enterprise: they were in hostile waters and had since sundown been subjected to a series of sporadic and somewhat half-hearted attacks by the Luftwaffe, whose aircraft they had quite rightly and properly engaged. There was haze that night, which added to the general difficulty of recognising friendly air-craft after dark, even though, as most of them did, they fired recognition signals. It is also true that some were a mile or two off course and had strayed into the danger zone, a belt five miles wide running along the coast, on entering which all aircraft were liable to be greeted with fire. Moreover, many of the guns' crews were inexperienced and were in action, like the pilots they shot at, for the first time.

Whether justifiable or understandable, this fire wrought havoc in the sky. Very few Dakotas reached the dropping zones; still fewer arrived at the correct moment. In those in which evasive action had been taken, the parachute soldiers, especially those who belonged to the 3rd Battalion, who were dropping for the first time with kitbags containing their weapons attached to them by cords, were stretched cursing on the floor, having been violently flung there by the sudden movement of the aircraft just as they were getting ready to jump. Others received the signal to jump when they were still over the sea or over the inhospitable hills which form so large a part of the centre of Sicily.

The crew chief of the Dakota in which Captain R. J. Gammon, M.C., of the 1st Battalion, was flying told him that they would be over the dropping zone half an hour earlier than had been planned. This statement did not make for confidence, but Gammon moved to the open doorway and stood ready to jump. He had been there but a few seconds when he saw the bridge 'white in the moonlight, a large replica of the models and photographs we had studied during our briefing, pill-boxes, wire and even a soldier standing in the roadway'. All seemed well, when suddenly the pilot banked the Dakota violently: he was under anti-aircraft fire—this time it came from the enemy—and wished to avoid it. Gammon jumped at once to give the others behind him a chance of leaving the aircraft. As he fell he could 'see crops burning on the ground like some prairie fire. The streak of tracer, the steady hum of planes, the crackle of musketry, the deeper note of high explosive, all vied to complete the atmosphere of airborne battle. I reached the ground, but could only find my batman. There was no sight of the others or of the arms containers. I met a few of them two or three days later on the hospital ship which took us back to Tripoli. Apparently the plane had continued to lose height, so many when they jumped broke their limbs, and others were captured in consequence'. The experience of Captain Gammon, grim though it was, was better than that which befell other parachutists, some of whom were landed not in Sicily at all but in Italy, and others in some lonely mountain valley where their bodies still remain.

Of those who fell somewhere near the bridge Lance-Corporal Coster of the 1st Battalion came down on a haystack beneath which six Italians were lying. On seeing the purposeful figure, Sten-gun in hand above them, 'they ran like hares'.

Most fortunately for the success of the operation, brigade

headquarters, carried in Albemarle aircraft of the Royal Air Force, reached the correct zone at the correct moment. Just as the signal to jump was given, the inside of the fuselage was lit up by a burst of anti-aircraft fire. The brigadier landed, fortunately for him, on a piece of soft plough. What had happened was that the pilot had turned at the last moment and dropped the stick 'on the high ground overlooking Catania plain, some three miles from the right place. His reading of five hundred feet on the altimeter represented only just over two hundred feet above this high ground. It was only just high enough, but I could not have cared less at the time'.

Accompanied only by his batman, Private Lake, the brigadier set off down the hill towards the bridge. 'The going was rough and typical of the terraced rocky hillsides of the Mediterranean countries'. Presently they reached the dropping zone, after helping themselves to rifles and ammunition from a stray container over which they had stumbled, and seeing a Horsa glider a hundred feet above their heads with 'five streams of tracer going straight through the fuselage.'

On the dropping zone Lathbury met David Hunter, his brigade major. Only a very small proportion of his staff had arrived, most of the wireless sets had gone astray, and one had fallen into the river. At that moment he was a brigadier without a brigade. The small party, clearly visible to the enemy, 'in the glare of burning haystacks and corn stooks', made off to a deep dry dyke within five hundred yards of the bridge. Here they halted and sent out two men to bring back information if they could. A few minutes passed, and then Frost, walking very lame, for he had twisted his ankle on landing, appeared at the head of about fifty men of the 2nd Battalion. He was making for the high ground, some one thousand two hundred yards south of the bridge, which he had been ordered to capture. He went on his way, and Lathbury, perceiving by then that he had collected about forty to fifty fighting men, divided them into four sections, of which three were to rush the south end of the bridge and the fourth to provide covering fire.

Among them were Gammon and Lieutenant J. Helingoe, a man very small of stature but large of heart. On their way to the dropping zone after landing they had been 'disturbed by the ghostly sound of rushing wind, as a glider swooped in over our heads to crash-land on the road near the bridge. Then came another which seemed to be making straight for us when it just failed to clear the top of the river bank and with a fearful crash and rending of material broke its back, the rear half subsiding into the river, taking with it a welter of men and equipment. We rushed across and found two pilots badly smashed and cut about lying on the grass where they had been thrown through the perspex windows of the cockpit. The glider had been carrying an anti-tank gun and crew, and some of the survivors crawled out of the wreckage, their faces a deathly white under the nigger-minstrel make-up which they had applied. I thanked God that I went to battle by parachute and not by glider'.

As they drew near the bridge, Lathbury heard the voices of men talking in English. 'A figure approached. He was a parachutist from the other side of the river and said that the 1st Battalion had just captured it (the bridge) from the north bank.' Lathbury and his men at once pushed forward and began to cross the bridge, but halted on seeing in front of them a lorry towing an 88-mm. gun. Lathbury 'assumed that it had been captured, but a few seconds later several grenades were lobbed out and landed at our feet'. One of them wounded the brigadier, who was at once given first aid, which included 'a large tot of whisky'. He was thus enabled to proceed, though somewhat slowly, in the direction of the north end of the bridge where there were sounds of strife and the remains of another lorry which had been demolished by an anti-tank grenade. Here he discovered what had happened.

At 02.15 hours Captain Rann, with some fifty men of the 1st Battalion, had landed close to the north bank of the Simeto and seized the northern end of the bridge with but little opposition. He had shortly afterwards been joined by Alastair Pearson and then by Yeldham. By the time Lathbury reached them about one hundred and twenty men were on or round the bridge, including a number of sappers who had removed the demolition charges and flung them into the river. More men were straggling in, and when day was fully come Lathbury could count on about two hundred and fifty men of the 1st and 3rd Battalions to defend the bridge. Three out of eight anti-tank guns had arrived and were in position, there were two 3-inch mortars and a Vickers machine gun, and a surgical team of the 16th Parachute Field Ambulance were at work near the south end of the bridge where they performed seventy-two operations unmolested by visiting German patrols. There were also about three hundred Italians moving aimlessly about after their surrender.

The brigade commander handed over the defence of the bridge to Pearson who disposed the bulk of his forces at its northern end, facing the airfield of Catania a short distance away. Several parachute soldiers had been dropped there in error and one of these reported that in the darkness he had been approached by a dimly seen figure who had enquired of him, in German, 'whether he had found his Schmeisser'. The Germans had chosen that night to reinforce the garrison of Catania with some of their own parachute troops who had been dropped on the same zone as part of the 1st Brigade.

The captors of the bridge at once began to put themselves in a state of readiness to receive the inevitable counter-attack. Strings of Hawkins grenades were laid across the road, the pill-boxes on or near the bridge manned, and slit trenches dug. Sergeants Anderson, Atkinson and Doig of the 1st Airlanding Anti-tank Battery, Royal Artillery, aided by some glider pilots, took charge of the anti-tank guns which they were to keep most gallantly in action through the day. The temper and spirit of everyone was rising, and rose still more when 'some casks of wine were found in one of the pill-boxes'. More parachutists continued to arrive as the morning wore on, and also more and more Italians, 'keen to be made prisoners, spivved up with suit-cases in hand, their hair reeking with sweet-scented oils, their mouths full of such toadying expressions as "Good old Tommy!"'

The first reaction of the enemy was to send a number of Messerschmitts, which flew over, firing cannon and machine-guns, but did little damage. Then came an attack, not from the north as had been expected, but from the south. It was delivered by a body of German parachutists who had evidently been dropped astray and had fallen on the wrong side of the river. Supported by mortar fire, 'it continued intermittently throughout the day, and was only repulsed with considerable difficulty'. The contentment of those at the bridge was completed when at about 09.30 hours one of the few wireless sets with them suddenly sprang to life and put them in touch with the 8th Army, un-fortunately for a few minutes only; during these, however, Lathbury learned that the 4th Armoured Brigade was pushing along the road as fast as possible against stiff opposition. The hours passed and it did not come. Soon everyone was engaged in repulsing a seemingly endless series of counter-attacks, which increased in severity as the day drew on. Two of them—one delivered just before, and the other just after the normal hour for luncheon—were thrown back only with the greatest difficulty. Obviously it was only a question of time before the bridge was retaken by the enemy, and by 17.00 hours the position was very serious. The defenders of the northern end of the bridge had withdrawn under orders to join those at the southern end of the bridge which was under continuous and steadily increasing fire. 'Casualties were mounting and ammunition was running short. It was reported that the enemy had crossed the river lower down and were attempting to turn our flank.' Among those killed at this time was Sergeant Padureano, M.M., a Spaniard 'who desired above all things to win British nationality'. His devotion to duty was a byword even in a battalion to whose conduct that hackneyed but accurate phrase had so constantly to be applied.

The end came about an hour later when the enemy brought up an 88-mm. gun, and with it destroyed the two pill-boxes on the south side of the bridge on which the defence was based. In one of them on the right-hand side of the road Captain Gammon had established himself. 'I remember,' he records, 'the bead curtain as in a continental barber's shop hanging over the open door-way, and I thought at the time of that good old training tag: "Cover from view but not from fire". I picked up an Italian carbine and started to sharpshoot across the river until Sergeant Baber suggested that I desist before the enemy observed the flash of this puerile weapon. He was right. The others with their good British rifles could do the job better and without revealing our position. Time wore on. At any moment the 8th Army must come. At any moment their armoured cars would sweep down the road and up to the bridge, but time wore on and no 8th Army came. . . . I suddenly noticed that the pill-box on my extreme left, fortunately empty, was taking a bashing. To this day I swear as each round of solid shot struck it it heeled over and bounced up again. Perhaps it was the heat haze or the dust, or my fevered imagination, or perhaps—it was made of rein-forced concrete—it did. I realised that each pill-box in turn was to take its punishment, and that mine was the next. . . . I watched the dusty white bridge, keeping my head well to the side of the embrasure. . . . Suddenly there was a crash, fumes, dust, and something hit me in the chest. I could hardly see. . . . Where's the door? Had it collapsed? A shaft of light and I groped my way out into the blinding sunshine.'

As evening drew on perhaps the most ominous circumstance of all seemed to the dwindling band of defenders to be the silence of Frost and the 2nd Battalion which, it will be recalled, had been ordered to seize the features of Johnny I, II and III in the hills to the south of Primosole. To them or, if they had been

123

overrun, to their position Brigadier Lathbury determined to withdraw. No other course was possible: German tanks were arriving; what remained of the men on the bridge had almost no ammunition. The only chance was to reach the high ground and there attempt a last stand. The necessary orders were issued and the parachute soldiers began to move back in small parties. Captain Gammon wandered back 'rather light-headed . . . somehow my steps led me past the parachute field ambulance where some orderlies, like vultures, swooped upon me and whipped me inside. I was a most unwilling casualty as I was sure that the field ambulance and its patients would be captured—as indeed it was. I remember coming to during the night and finding that my eyes would not open, and pleading to be hidden in the bushes'.

Corporal Stanion was more fortunate. He had fought all day at the northern end of the bridge. 'We went back,' he records, 'and I got hit in the back of the neck. I was knocked out for some length of time. When I came to I saw a couple of German machine-gunners in the ditch where our troops should have been. A shell burst in front of me and under cover of this I ran back to the bridge. The battalions had gone. Some Italians I met with tried to explain that they had gone over to the other side. I could not cross the bridge because it was under fire, so I went into the reeds and there ran into some Jerries and was captured. I sat there for an hour or two while they argued amongst themselves as to who was to take me back. Then apparently our chaps started firing into the reeds. Two Jerries got hit in the head straight away. The others ran back and I crawled along through the reeds, which were smouldering in parts. I got down to a point where they went into the water, into which I slipped and dog-paddled over to the other side, where I lay. I was in full view of both sides and feared that, if I tried to identify myself, I would be shot. It was then about four-thirty in the afternoon. I lay there waiting for darkness to come.'

Meanwhile Lathbury's fears regarding the 2nd Battalion were fortunately not justified. 'A' Company, under its commanding officer, Major R. T. H. Lonsdale, M.C., had landed on the right dropping zone at 22.15 hours, and an hour later had been joined by Frost and battalion headquarters. As with those nearer the bridge, the main trouble they encountered was the dry grass which was burning in many places; but they were not under any 'really effective enemy fire'. By 02.15 hours, when between one hundred and one hundred and twenty men had been collected, preparations were made to attack Johnny I, the first of the three features to be captured. Unknown to Frost and Lonsdale, however, it was in the hands of their battalion, which, with an officer and twenty-five other ranks, had already seized it and captured one hundred and thirty Italians. The message they had sent to announce this had gone astray. By 05.30 hours in the light of dawn this was discovered and a perimeter defence established. It was held by about one hundred and forty men, of whom half belonged to 'A' Company. The battalion was hampered by an entire lack of heavy weapons, and was therefore quite unable to retaliate when it came under heavy and continuous fire from the feature Johnny II, two hundred yards to the south-east, which it had not been able to capture. Italian prisoners, 'appearing from all directions, including Navy and Air Force personnel', soon became and remained a nuisance.

By 08.00 hours, after a patrol sent to deal with some enemy machine-guns had been badly mauled by a number of armoured cars, it was found necessary to withdraw the forward troops. The battalion was now under attack from three sides, and its opponents were the redoubtable German 4th Parachute Regiment. Half an hour later the battalion diary records 'that the situation was rather serious. Casualties were increasing'. Another half-hour passed and then Captain Vere Hodge, R.A., the forward observation officer, was able at last to get into contact with a 6-inch cruiser which brought down 'extremely accurate and effective fire on the advancing enemy'. By noon the situation was easier . . . and a general lessening in tension was noticeable. Then just as dusk fell a Sherman tank, the long-awaited harbinger of the 8th Army, hove in sight, and a quarter of an hour afterwards a battalion of the Durham Light Infantry'.

The night passed quietly, and at first light both the 2nd Battalion and Lathbury, with what remained of the defenders of the bridge, got into touch with the 4th Armoured Brigade, which made ready to attack the bridge which the parachutists had captured and been forced to relinquish. To their dismay they watched the Germans trying to blow it up but soon realised they they were unable to do so, for the charges were in the river and there seemed to be no others available.

The first attack of the 4th Armoured Brigade and the Durham Light Infantry failed, for the German defenders of the bridge put up a most resolute resistance. By then Lathbury, overcome by his wounds, had been taken off to a dressing station. That day, the 15th, passed without further incident and the remnants of the Parachute Brigade held on to Johnny I under intermittent shellfire. During the night the Durham Light Infantry made another attack, this time being guided across the river by Alastair Pearson. At dawn on the 16th they reached the bridge, drove off the German defenders, and held it.

'This operation against the Primosole bridge was,' says Lathbury, 'a disappointing one. Of the brigade group less than one-third arrived at the right place. More than one-third were taken back to North Africa without being dropped, and the remainder were dropped in other parts of Sicily.' Their adventures, except those of Lieutenant-Colonel Peter Young and Captain Victor Dover, M.C., have not been recorded. Young broke his leg on landing, but was looked after by fifty Italian soldiers anxious to surrender to him. Captain Dover and his stick were dropped on the slopes of Mount Etna. All were captured a few days later except Dover and one of the brigade signallers. They managed to subsist on a staple diet of apples for twenty-four days. During this time they raided enemy installations and ambushed three dispatch riders, losing two stone in weight in this private war. Of those like Dover and his men who were dropped widely over the island of Sicily, some fought small battles, many committed acts of sabotage and laid ambushes for unsuspecting foes. Their 'nuisance value' is known to have been very great, and for a time the German Command believed that the number of parachute troops dropped on Sicily was very much larger than it was.

Despite all setbacks, however, the Primosole bridge had been captured, lost and recaptured, and the object of the operation may therefore be said to have been attained. Yet the gallantry of the 1st Parachute Brigade and its sustained efforts were in the end of no avail. Though the three bridges had been captured for the use of the 8th Army, it was not found possible to attack Catania from the coastal plain. The Germans had been able to concentrate their defences there more quickly than Montgomery had been able to build up his attack. He did not press it in this area, but moved instead inland round Etna, where he had to fight a series of severe battles before Messina was reached.

The action at Primosole bridge cost the 1st Parachute Brigade twenty-seven killed, seventy-eight wounded, and many missing. Among the casualties must be included Alastair Pearson, who, though not wounded, fell sick of malignant malaria and had to relinquish his command. He handed over to the second-in-command, Major P. Cleasby-Thompson, but later recovered sufficiently to lead with all his old brilliance the 8th Battalion of the 3rd Parachute Brigade of the 6th Airborne Division.

The Red Devils in Italy

BEFORE the 1st Parachute Brigade added to the glory of British arms in Sicily, other parachute units were forming at home. The 2nd Parachute Brigade, consisting of the 4th, 5th and 6th Battalions, has already been mentioned. The 4th Battalion, under the command of Lieutenant-Colonel M. R. J. Hope-Thompson, M.C., Royal Scots Fusiliers, was formed on 1st January 1942. Though afterwards known as the Wessex Battalion, the men who joined it came from all branches of the army and all parts of the United Kingdom. At the outset it passed through a difficult period, for the number of fatal accidents which occurred when it was at Ringway undergoing preliminary parachute training was unduly high. The battalion wore a black lanyard, and this for many became a symbol of those unhappy days, though in fact it had been adopted some weeks before. The training was highly concentrated, particularly during the spring of 1943, and included the usual airborne and ground exercises, which came to an end in April, when the battalion was inspected by the King. By then the habit had been adopted of painting its equipment black, a practice which was prized by the unit, as it was distinctive and smart, besides being practical. This custom was continued until September 1946, when permission to do so in future was withdrawn, no reason being given.

The 5th Battalion was the only parachute unit to be drawn from the Queen's Own Cameron Highlanders. In May 1942, when it was an infantry battalion of the 45th Division, it received a visit from General Browning, 'who in a stirring address informed it that it was the intention to convert the unit as a whole into a parachute battalion'. Such conversions became more frequent as the war progressed, but it should be understood that in all cases where an infantry became a parachute battalion its individual members were allowed freely to choose whether to continue to serve in this new capacity or to transfer to other battalions of the Line. In other words, no man was ever compelled to become a parachutist; he did so of his own free will. This option was not extended to the regiments forming the Air Landing Brigades. Some serving in their ranks were volunteers; but mostly they were composed of units who went to battle in gliders, 'not from choice, but as the result of orders'. At the time the wisdom of this decision was challenged, but their conduct shews that it was more than justified. Ancient and honourable traditions, begun—many of them—when Marlborough and Wellington were the general officers in command, were sustained and enhanced.

The 5th Battalion of the Parachute Regiment was officially called the Scottish, and, as has been explained, was recruited primarily from the Queen's Own Cameron Highlanders. Since, however, the number of men rejected for physical or other reasons before or during training was always high, men from all other Scottish regiments were recruited. When formed, the battalion was allowed to retain its pipe band and to wear, not the red beret, the universal headgear of airborne troops whether parachutists or passengers in gliders, but the Balmoral bonnet with the Army Air Corps badge upon a Hunting Stuart tartan patch. This they wore until September 1944, when they discarded it for the red beret. Under Lieutenant-Colonel A. Dunlop, Argyll and Sutherland Highlanders, it began its initial training, 'the pipe band at Tatton Park' being used to greet the trainees as they floated down to earth, and by the middle of March 1943 was ready for service. Its colonel, having been injured during training, was replaced by Lieutenant-Colonel C. B. Mackenzie.

The 6th Battalion came into being in much the same manner as the 5th, save that its officers and men were drawn from the Principality of Wales, the nucleus being the 10th Royal Welch Fusiliers. Like the Scotsmen, they responded to the appeal made by Major General Browning, twenty-five out of thirty-one officers volunteering to become parachutists, and five hundred and twenty-seven out of seven hundred and eighty-nine other ranks. Gaps in their ranks from injury or other causes were filled by volunteers from other Welsh regiments. The 6th Battalion was allowed to wear the black flash of the Royal Welch Fusiliers.

Thus constituted, the 2nd Brigade arrived in North Africa in April 1943.

Two other parachute battalions joined the 1st Airborne Division in June as part of the 4th Parachute Brigade. They were the 156th[1] Battalion and the 10th. The first of these, originally

[1] Originally known as 151st Battalion.

under Lieutenant-Colonel H. R. C. Hose, was drawn from British volunteers in the ranks of the twenty-seven British infantry battalions serving in India during the early period of the war. The official date of its formation was 18th October 1941. The battalion was organised in six companies, No. 2 Company being the Depot Company, from which approximately six hundred parachute soldiers were eventually chosen. An air landing school was established at Willingdon Airport, Old Delhi, and staffed by Brereton and Law, fresh from Ringway, and a party of Royal Air Force and Army sergeant instructors. The training was marked at the outset by a very unhappy accident, a brigadier breaking both his legs and his brigade major his back. Only two Vickers-Valencia aircraft could be spared, and these were quite inadequate for the rapid training of the battalions. For a long time only twenty parachutes were available, 'so patched and darned that they looked like bed-spreads'. The dropping zone was a racecourse, and on one occasion one of the company commanders landed on the top tier of the grandstand and 'bumped slowly down to the bottom'.

Shortly before Christmas 1941 two other battalions began to form, the 152nd Indian Parachute Battalion, and the 153rd Gurkha.

In view of the entry of Japan into the war, priority was given to the training of these two battalions. This decision was very far from welcome to the 156th Battalion. Most of its members had volunteered to become parachute soldiers for the altogether admirable reason that they wished to see active service as soon as possible. They were high-spirited and individualistic. As day after day, week after week, month after month passed in a hot, uncomfortable climate, and they moved no further either in their training or towards the battlefield, their sense of frustration increased. At the same time they felt a sense of superiority, for, despite everything, they were still 'the only British parachute unit in India'. Such a state of affairs became so serious that the disbandment of the unit was seriously mooted. It was only prevented by the personal intervention of Field-Marshal Lord Wavell, then Viceroy of India, whose faith in the men and their activities remained unshaken. Though their training as para-chutists might, and did, leave a very great deal to be desired, their training as infantrymen was excellent. They learned to handle 'every conceivable and available British weapon, and were familiar with the more usual types of enemy and Allied weapons. Every officer and man . . . was taught to drive motor vehicles of various types, with the emphasis on foreign makes. A percentage were trained to drive railway locomotives, and others to ride and drive animal transport. All collective training began with an imaginary drop which was carried out from moving motor vehicles in sticks of from ten to fifteen . . . it was no uncommon event for a company to cover a hundred miles during the course of a seventy-two-hour exercise'. There was indeed little wrong with such men, nothing at least that action would not cure.

In due course they moved to Kharakwasla near Poona, where they came under the instruction of the Combined Operations School and learned much about seaborne landings. By then three of their number, all sergeants, had seen active service, having been dropped into Burma behind the Japanese lines with a patrol from the 153rd Gurkha Parachute Battalion. Conditions gradually improved, especially when eight more or less modern aircraft, including three Dakotas, arrived. Unfortunately the fatal casualty rate rose with the increased number of jumps, and all parachute training had to be suspended. Such was the general state of affairs when, in October 1942, the battalion was ordered to move to the Middle East. Every possible precaution was taken to conceal its identity, and it sailed from Bombay on 4th November disguised as the 20th Queen's Regiment. The men were even required to learn something of the regimental history of the unit they were impersonating. Their arms, equipment and general bearing, however, gave them away, and the disguise was transparent. They were presently installed in Egypt, where they resumed parachute training from Hudsons and Dakotas, this time with excellent results. There were no more fatal casualties, and confidence was restored. January and February 1943 passed in exercises, 'very popular amongst all ranks', carried out in Palestine.

The 4th Parachute Brigade, under Brigadier J. W. Hackett, was now in process of formation, and the number of the battalion which up till then had been 151 became 156, a change quite meaningless and much resented at the time. The arrival of a new commanding officer in the person of Lieutenant-Colonel Sir Richard de B. des Voeux, with much operational experience behind him, greatly encouraged the battalion and its soldierly bearing was increased by the efforts of Regimental Sergeant-Major Gay, a Grenadier Guardsman like the new commanding officer. Gay soon established his reputation by taking part in a boxing competition in which he knocked out one after another all who were rash enough to avail themselves of what they imagined was a heaven-sent opportunity 'to take a crack' at the sergeant-major. By then they had been moved to Ramat David in the north of Palestine near Haifa, together with the 10th Battalion, under Lieutenant-Colonel K. B. I. Smyth, which was in much the same state of development as themselves. This battalion, formed in January 1943, of which the nucleus had originally been the volunteers from the 2nd Battalion, the Royal Sussex Regiment, carried out its training in Palestine. It specialised in the handling of Italian Breda anti-tank guns, modified so that they could be dropped in the ordinary container. The parachute school was close to their camp, and in general their months of training were smooth, uneventful and very pleasant. The 10th moved to North Africa at the same time as the 156th, and in due course went with it to Italy.

Training in the valley of Jordan and round the Dead Sea was short but intense, and the Emir Abdullah presented 'C' Company of the 156th Battalion with one of his standards. Thereafter it was carried on all occasions, and one of the officers, Lieutenant Bell, who was in charge of it at Arnhem, wrapped it about his body and, though taken prisoner, concealed it successfully and brought it back to England when the war was over.

A number of officers and men from the 156th Battalion were detailed by the brigadier to form the nucleus of the 11th Battalion, and then in May 1943 the 10th and 156th moved to Tripoli. The contrast between the austerities of North Africa and the fleshpots of Palestine was a shock compensated, as time went on, by the growth of a warm friendship with the American Airborne 504th Combat Team, their next-door neighbours.

The story of the 156th Battalion of the Parachute Regiment is a classical example of the harm that can be wrought by a lack of imagination on the part of those responsible for the destinies of fighting men. It needed someone of the calibre and genius of Lord Wavell to appreciate their situation. Nevertheless when the call for action came, and the battalion was embarked on H.M.S. *Aurora* and the United States cruiser *Boise* for Taranto, it was as ready and eager for action as the rest.

Thus, by June 1943 the whole of the 1st Airborne Division, consisting of three parachute brigades, the 1st, the 2nd, and the 4th and the 1st Air Landing Brigade, was concentrated at Sousse and in its neighbourhood. Of the parachute brigades the 1st fought the action at the Primosole bridge, described in the last chapter, and then returned to Sousse to join the 2nd Brigade, which had waited in vain to attack Augusta.

Summer was now at its height, the 8th British and 5th American Armies were battling their way through the Sicilian hills and the tide of war was obviously turning slowly against the Axis. By 17th August the resistance of the enemy in Sicily ended; but before that date an event occurred which pointed inevitably to the early collapse of one of the Axis partners. On 25th July Mussolini resigned and was arrested. Marshal Badoglio became prime minister, and almost immediately opened secret negotiations with the Allies; but these were unknown and unsuspected in the dusty olive yards near Sousse.

The division had been under the command of Major-General G. F. Hopkinson, O.B.E., M.C. since April, the month in which Browning was appointed 'Major-General Airborne Forces', and at last, early in September, he received his orders. By then the 8th Army was lodged in the toe of Italy, and the invasion in force of that country was obviously imminent. On 6th September the waiting parachute battalions were instructed to undertake a seaborne operation against Italy and to be ready to do so in seven days. The 2nd and 4th Parachute Brigades were to be in the van, the 1st Parachute Brigade in reserve. Since sufficient aircraft were still not available—when, they wondered, would they be?—their means of transport were a minelayer and five cruisers belonging to the Royal Navy, and the American cruiser *Boise*. This, as it turned out, was fortunate; for it was quicker to land the two brigades with their transport and gear from ships than from aircraft. Airborne troops, parachute battalions in particular, are specially suited for the conduct of operations which have to be improvised, their equipment being so much lighter than that of infantry of the Line.

The vanguard of the division sailed from Bizerta, and the first hours at sea were spent in the issuing of orders and maps, and in briefing for the landing, which was to be in the great harbour of Taranto. The enthusiasm of officers and men was very great and the number of stowaways from the reserve left behind in Africa large. When half-way to their destination they received the news of Italy's unconditional surrender. The force arrived safely at the edge of the minefield covering the entrance to the harbour. Here it cast anchor while H.M.S. *Javelin* went in alone and returned two hours later with an Italian pilot on board. This period of waiting was enlivened for the parachutists by the sight of two Italian battleships and many smaller warships 'down on the horizon, stealing away to Malta to give themselves up'.

At 17.00 hours on the 9th, precisely twenty-four hours after the squadron had sailed, it entered the harbour of Taranto, led by H.M.S. *Penelope*, which, with the American cruiser, went alongside and began to unload part of the 4th Brigade, whose intention it was to dash ashore and form a bridgehead to be held against possible operations while the remainder of the force landed from lighters.

It was at this juncture that disaster fell upon part of the 6th (Royal Welch) Battalion, the Parachute Regiment. On board the fast minelayer H.M.S. *Abdiel* was its advance battalion headquarters, 'B' and 'C' Companies, and the mortar and machine-gun platoons. About 23.00 hours they and the other military elements on board made ready to disembark. The troops were mustered on deck, and a large number were standing-to below.

Suddenly at about midnight the noise of the lighters discharging men and stores from other vessels was drowned 'by a deep roaring explosion'. The *Abdiel* shuddered violently, listed to port, and began rapidly to sink. She had struck a mine, probably an acoustic mine, and this had detonated the mines on board her, blowing her in half. Both halves sank in about two minutes. Major J. W. Pearson was dozing in an armchair in the captain's lounge, and gives the following account:

'I cannot remember how I got away from the lounge, for when I had partially recovered my senses I found myself sitting on some part of the ship with cold water lapping around my waist. Subconsciously I had removed my webbing equipment and one boot. Some instinct told me to plunge into the water and swim as hard as I could away from the ship. As I did so, a searchlight swept the water and I caught a fleeting glimpse of two huge hulks slowly disappearing below the water. As the stern portion was sinking I saw flashes and sparks which, although most alarming at the time, I now presume to have been caused by live electric wires making contact with the water. I then became conscious of many distressing calls for help around me, and the nauseating smell of fuel oil.

'With great difficulty I managed to remove my bush jacket, and let it go without so much as a thought for the irreplaceable valuables in the pockets. How far I swam after that I do not know, but my object was to reach the only light I could see, and that seemed miles away. After what seemed an interminable period I swam into a floating drum to which I clung for grim death. I rested for a while, then paddled the drum about, and when a small Italian rowing boat loomed out of the darkness there were about ten of us hanging on to one another around the drum. We had been in the water twenty to thirty minutes, but it seemed like hours.'

His experience was typical of that which befell those who survived. Many of the battalion did not, and among them were the commanding officer, Lieutenant-Colonel Goodwin, who had taken over from Lieutenant-Colonel Pritchard, one major, two captains, three subalterns, and fifty-one other ranks, including the regimental sergeant-major. Four officers and about a hundred and fifty men had to be taken to hospital with injuries. Nevertheless, within six hours the 6th Battalion was ready for action, many of its men being clad in the uniforms of sailors and marines. This timely aid from the Royal Navy was all the more appreciated since it was known that its own casualties had been considerable.

The other two battalions went ashore without difficulty. The 4th moved quickly through the town, meeting everywhere with smiling Italians, and took up positions to the north-west. 'B' Company was the most fortunate, for it captured a prisoner who led them to a dump 'which contained quantities of Martell brandy, Chianti, chocolate, etc.' The 5th Battalion occupied a small village twelve miles east of Taranto, its pipe band remaining in the port and marching up and down one of the main streets playing 'Johnny Cope'. In a very short time Hopkinson had received the surrender of the Italian military governor and set up his headquarters in the Albergo Europa. This had been abandoned by the Germans that morning, and bore evidence of their late occupation 'in the form of bottles, standing orders and extensive murals depicting the strength of the German navy'.

The 1st Battalion had the unhappy task of collecting many of the bodies of those who had been killed and flung in the harbour when the *Abdiel* blew up and sank. They were buried in the divisional cemetery at Taranto. It then found itself forming part of the perimeter defence with the 2nd and 3rd Battalions. A south-easterly thrust by the enemy was considered possible, and the 2nd Battalion was put in position to meet it. In the sector allotted to the 1st a train was found, immobilised by bomb craters in front and behind it. It had on board a very large quantity of comforts for the enemy garrison. These included about twenty thousand bottles of Martell brandy, 3 Star. The find, says the historian, was reported to the brigade 'after certain administrative arrangements had been made by the commanding officer of the 1st Battalion, which thereafter was never short of brandy throughout the period of its service in Italy'.

The advance of the 4th Brigade up two parallel roads was swift enough at first. The inhabitants of every village they reached greeted them, not as invaders, but as liberators. The small town of Massafra was taken, and from here the 156th Battalion had its first taste of war when, 'after a brief respite for breakfast', it moved along the Gioia road and seized Mottala. No anti-tank guns were available, for these had gone down with the *Abdiel*, so the gunners made use of the Italian anti-tank weapons which they had been specially trained to use and were soon in the town. That evening the divisional commander arrived and was accorded a reception, afterwards described by one of his staff as 'rather like the end of a rugger match'. In addition, gifts of flowers and fruit were handed to all who asked for them and many who did not. The next day there was a small, briskly fought action in which Major R. J. L. Pott won a Military Cross, and Private Sowden the Military Medal. The battalion then seized a position overlooking the airfield of Gioia, and spent the next few days in patrolling and in linking up with the 10th Battalion.

This had had much the same tasks as the 156th, and it was when watching this battalion in action against the German garrison of Castellaneta, who were offering stout resistance, that the divisional commander was mortally wounded in the head by a burst of machine-gun fire. Major-General Hopkinson had been associated with the airborne forces from their early days, and his death in the forefront of the battle was a great loss. His place was taken by Major-General Down, C.B.E.

Having seized the town, the 10th, like the 156th, spent the next few days in patrolling. When engaged on one of these patrols a member of the anti-tank platoon who was momentarily alone laid down his rifle on the edge of a tomato field in order to pluck some of the fruit to add to his rations. A guttural voice ordered him to put his hands up. Having no choice, he obeyed and became the prisoner of three German parachutists, who treated him well, but kept a close watch on him. At the end of the third day he found an opportunity to escape their vigilance and did so. Thereafter for the rest of the campaign he 'could not be persuaded to leave his rifle, even for a moment'.

It was the German practice to impose delay by holding on to any ridge or building which seemed suitable as a temporary

135

defensive position. One of these was a large bright-red building north of the village of San Basilio. To attack it proved no easy matter. 'A 149-mm. howitzer, carelessly left lying about by the Italians', was trained on the target more as a last resort than in the hope of achieving a result. However, 'much to everyone's surprise, when fully cocked and with practically no charge, a direct hit was scored. Fortunately for the Italian Public Works Department (the building was an official one) the shell failed to explode'. Three more Italian howitzers were secured, but there were no Italians to fire them, and a number of essential parts were lacking. 'They were intended,' commented the brigade commander, 'to disguise the scarcity of our troops on the ground, to give a little support, and to lend tone to the operation. Their antics may well have caused a little dismay to the enemy's troops. They certainly gave pleasure to our own.'

By 13th September, after the fall of Castellaneta, the division was more than twenty miles from Taranto. It consisted of no more than six thousand six hundred and sixty-eight men with but sixteen 6-pounder guns for artillery, and it was grievously short of transport. Down, however, was determined that the Germans, whom he rightly regarded as tough but tired, should be given no chance to retaliate. Patrols were ordered to be as aggressive as possible, and the 156th and 10th Battalions were sent to attack Gioia. A preliminary bombardment was to be carried out by one of the Italian howitzers, but after the first round had been fired 'the retaining nut came adrift and the piece fell off its carriage.'

The capture of Gioia and its airfield was of an importance which increased hourly, for it could be used as a base for fighters and fighter-bombers, whose presence over the beachhead at Salerno was very necessary. At the same time an attack in force by the whole division, or a large part of it, was out of the question, for a firm hold had at any cost to be kept on Taranto. Very fortunately the enemy, deceived by the number of patrols sent out by Down and the resolution which they displayed, and shaken by a spirited night attack delivered by the 10th Battalion, did not stand to fight, but evacuated the place on the night of 16th-17th September. Within two days six squadrons of the Royal Air Force were operating from its airfield.

At first light, after the night action, a very excited Italian approached Brigadier Hackett, with a pannikin of brandy in his hand. He complained that he had offered brandy to a parachutist, who had not only accepted it, but had taken his wrist-

136

watch. Enquiries revealed that a sergeant had the watch. He explained that, having taken the brandy, he wished to know the time, and had pointed enquiringly at the Italian's wrist-watch, whereupon he had removed it in terror, thrust it upon the sergeant and fled. The situation was explained, the watch returned to its rightful owner, who confirmed the story, 'and all ended in brandy and bonhomie'.

On 19th September the 4th Parachute Brigade returned to Taranto, having been relieved by the 1st Air Landing Brigade, which pursued the enemy into the area of Foggia. 'Nine days of interesting though not heavy fighting' had come to an end. They had cost the 4th Brigade eleven officers and ninety other ranks killed, wounded or missing.

During this period the 1st Parachute Brigade had been in reserve, and then moved first to Castellaneta and then to Altamura, from which it was withdrawn at the end of September. At the beginning of October Captain J. Timothy, an officer of 2nd Battalion, gained a bar to his Military Cross by dropping with seven other ranks in the area north of Pescara. He was ordered to get into contact with escaped Allied prisoners and direct them to our lines, and in so doing achieved a fair measure of success. Five of his men were, however, captured, but he with two others returned, and on rejoining the battalion was able to welcome Lieutenant Buchanan and Sergeant Laughland who had been captured in North Africa and had now escaped.

Up to the middle of October the division hoped to be sent in advance of the 8th or 5th Army which, at that time it was believed by many, would sweep in triumph up the Italian peninsula, at least as far as Rome. They were wrong, and many weary weeks and months of hard fighting were to prove necessary before that goal, in itself not final, was reached. The 1st Airborne Division did not play a major part in this fighting. By November it had been withdrawn and was on the way home to England, all save one brigade, the 2nd Parachute Brigade, composed of the 4th, 5th and 6th Battalions under Brigadier C. H. V. Pritchard. These three battalions were thus from that date onward the sole representatives of the Parachute Regiment in the Mediterranean theatre and of this they were rightly very proud. Under their thirty-seven-year-old brigadier they were to uphold the honour of the regiment throughout the long-drawn, dangerous, tedious campaign of Italy and to help to quell a civil war in Greece. How worthily they did so is told later. Mention must be now made of the attempt of the 11th Battalion, under Lieutenant-Colonel R. M. C. Thomas, to capture the island of Cos.

To prepare for the ultimate invasion of Greece the capture of the island of Rhodes, with its fighter airfields, was essential. In the autumn of 1943, however, the forces available for this purpose were small, too small, and the Germans, alive to the importance of the island, strengthened and reinforced their garrison upon it to such an extent that in three days they were firmly established and could not be dislodged without a major operation. The Allied High Command had, therefore, either to abandon all thought for the moment of action in the Greek archipelago, or to attempt to lay hands on the islands of Cos, Leros and Samos, near to Rhodes, but far less heavily defended. Believing that the successive loss of North Africa, Sicily and part of southern Italy, together with the surrender of the Italians, had shaken the Germans, they risked an attack, though any troops engaged upon it could not be given adequate air support for lack of airfields close enough for the use of fighters. This drawback was accepted with disastrous consequences.

Of the islands in question Cos, with its airfield at Antimachia, was far the most important. To seize it and hold it would ultimately make Rhodes untenable by the enemy. The attack was opened by 'A' Company of the 11th Battalion. Formed at Kabrit and subsequently called the 11th Parachute Brigade in order to deceive the enemy, it had been training first near the Suez Canal, and then in Palestine with the 156th and 10th Battalions. By the end of August 1943 three of its platoons, one from each rifle company, had reached a sufficiently high standard to be capable of operations. They were sent, together with a section of 3-inch mortars and a machine-gun section, to Mafraq in Transjordan, there to undergo intensive training with the object of seizing first Rhodes and then, when this was judged too hard, Cos.

On 13th September the parachutists, now brought to a high pitch, were flown to Cyprus in seven Dakotas, each carrying about 1,500 lbs. more than its designed maximum load. The next night the three platoons dropped on Cos, the dropping zone being marked by a squadron of the Special Boat Service operating from canoes. They found the Italian garrison, which numbered about 4,000, only too ready to welcome them. 'They had even spread straw and hay on the landing ground,' reports

138

Corporal Glover, who jumped that night, and as soon as the parachutists touched the earth ran up to help them off with their harness. The detachment of the 11th Battalion remained on the island from 15th to 25th September. All was well at first. The officers and men were set the congenial task of finding beaches suitable for the landing of reinforcements and of examining the Italian defences. In the course of these duties the Greek hospitality encountered was 'first class and the bathing lovely'. It was, however, soon obvious that with the troops available— they included a detachment of the Durham Light Infantry and the Royal Air Force Regiment—some eighty odd miles of coastline could not even be adequately patrolled, much less defended, but every effort was made to hold the airfield at Antimachia. Butterfly bombs, frequently dropped, were a great trial.

Action was soon joined with the *Luftwaffe*, which rapidly grew from a nuisance to a menace. Its aircraft greatly outnumbered those of the Royal Air Force, which could put no more than four Spitfires in the air at any one moment. After four days even this modest force ceased to operate, for its units had all been destroyed on the ground. Beaufighters, which attempted to take their place, arrived over Cos from Cyprus with just enough petrol to circle the airfield once and then make off. In the circumstances there was but one ending. For the parachute soldiers it came on 25th September, when at 23.30 they took off in their Dakotas after saying farewell to the Durham Light Infantry, 'who were envious of our going'. Since they were about to be killed or made prisoners this is not surprising. To have kept trained parachute detachments, however, on the island would have been folly, and they were rightly withdrawn to prepare for a landing on Leros. This island was even more untenable than Cos. There was but one dropping zone, of doubtful value, in the middle of it, and as the 11th Battalion was making ready to take off for it word came that they had been forestalled by the enemy. 'With a sigh of relief we disappeared on ten days' privilege leave which we felt we had earned.' The success of the Germans at Cos and Leros stopped all further operations in the Aegean for some time.

Normandy—The Sixth Airborne Division Prepares

'THERE were about fifteen of us in a ditch,' said Madame Magnenat, the English wife of the Mayor of Bréville. 'We had more or less formed the habit of going there for the night for some little while before D-day. About midnight I heard a plane and soon afterwards another. Then the cows in the field stampeded. "They've come," I said to my husband, who was doubtful.' The occupants of the ditch made their way across a field to Le Bois des Monts, home of the Magnenats, being fired at on the way from two directions. Arrived, they looked through the large windows of the sitting-room and 'there was the night sky sewn with the little black dots of descending parachutists'. What Monsieur and Madame Magnenat saw that summer night was the arrival of the advanced guard of the 6th Airborne Division which dropped on Normandy some hours before the dawn of D-day. Their deeds must now be told.

While the parachute battalions of the 1st Airborne Division were increasing, in Sicily and Italy, a reputation gained in North Africa, another division, the 6th, was formed in England. On 1st May 1943 this new formation was placed under the command of Gale, who had been promoted to the rank of major-general. A nucleus had already existed in the three battalions composing the 3rd Parachute Brigade, recently handed over to Brigadier S. J. L. Hill, D.S.O., M.C., newly recovered from the wounds he sustained in Africa. His brigade was made up of the 7th (Light Infantry), the 8th (Midland Counties), and the 9th (Home Counties) Battalions. These were much under strength, for recruits, when they had finished their training as parachutists, were many of them sent as reinforcements to the 1st Parachute Brigade whose ranks had been thinned by the hard battles round Mateur and Sedjenane. For this reason, though the three units became parachute battalions in November 1942, it was a very long time before they were up to strength.

At the outset Gale received what he described as 'grand news indeed'. General Sir Bernard Paget, then Commander-in-Chief, Home Forces, informed him that a Canadian parachute battalion was to join the new division. This battalion had arrived from Canada on 28th July 1942, and by March 1943 was almost at full strength. By the end of July of that year, under its commanding officer, Lieutenant-Colonel G. F. P. Bradbrooke, it had reached thirty-one officers and five hundred and forty-eight other ranks. Soon afterwards it arrived at Bulford camp and was attached to Hill's brigade. Training was divided into two phases: in the first, attention was given to the formation of specialists and junior leaders, and much store was set by marksmanship. In the conditions in which they would normally operate, airborne troops, said the Canadians, would certainly not have at their disposal unlimited supplies of ammunition, therefore 'every shot fired must find its target'. A staff-sergeant from Bisley arrived, and the standard rose steadily. This ability to hit what was aimed at was to prove of great use later on in France, and saved many lives. By the early spring of 1944 every officer and man of the battalion had passed through the training school at Ringway, so as to become familiar with the British as distinct from the American type of parachute.

This fine battalion from Canada presently took the place of the 7th (Light Infantry) Battalion in the 3rd Parachute Brigade. The 7th Battalion was transferred to the newly forming 5th Parachute Brigade commanded by Brigadier J. H. N. Poett. It also consisted of the 12th (Yorkshire) and the 13th (Lancashire) Battalions. This brigade began to form in June 1943 and had therefore about eleven months in which to complete its training. The 12th Battalion, since February 1944 under Lieutenant-Colonel A. P. Johnson and composed of Yorkshiremen, was given permission to wear a light-blue lanyard. Johnson had taken over from Lieutenant-Colonel R. G. Parker,[1] who, though over forty, had learnt to jump. The Lancashire battalion, who took as its motto 'Win or die' from the line of the poet 'They win or die who wear the rose of Lancashire', joined the 5th Parachute Brigade at the same time and were presently under the command of Lieutenant-Colonel P. J. Luard. These two new parachute brigades formed two-thirds of the new division, which was completed by an air landing brigade, the 6th, commanded by Brigadier the Honourable Hugh Kindersley, M.C., Scots Guards.

[1] He subsequently became Deputy Commander of the Air Landing Brigade.

Over both the airborne divisions Browning, now a Lieutenant-General, was set. His task to begin with was not easy, even though the men belonging to the new battalions of the Parachute Regiment soon shewed themselves to be of the highest quality, lacking only the spur of action to reach the same level of excellence as their comrades of the 1st Airborne Division. What they lacked was aircraft. It was the old story: men were easier to come by than machines. No. 38 Wing of the Royal Air Force had long been detailed to work with the airborne forces; but it was not until the late summer and autumn of 1943 that many of its crews who had taken part in the African and Sicilian campaigns found themselves back again once more in England.

The air side of Browning's problem might possibly have been solved earlier had the devoted band of Army and Air Force officers who had been associated with parachute and glider-borne troops since the beginning been still in existence. Unhappily too many of them had died in action. Squadron Leader Wilkinson, expert in the towing of gliders, had been killed in the attack on the Ponte Grande. Major Lander, commanding the 21st Independent Parachute Company, had met his end at the Primosole bridge. Wing Commander P. May and Wing Commander W. S. Barton, D.S.O., D.F.C., closely associated with No. 38 Wing, were also dead. To these grievous losses must be added the deaths of Rock, Norman and Hopkinson. When a new arm is being developed it is those intimately associated with its beginning who run the greatest risk and pay the highest penalty. So it was in the early days of flight; so it was again when airborne troops began to play their part in war. Fortunately, ready to take the places of the pioneers were men endowed with the same enthusiasm and very soon the same degree of skill.

Once again in the matter of aircraft, as in the early days, the Americans came to the rescue, and the 9th U.S. Troop Carrier Command soon began to play an important and enthusiastic part in the training of the 6th Airborne Division. A policy of expansion more generous than he had dared to hope could now be followed by Browning. Then in January 1944 two groups of the Royal Air Force, Nos. 38 and 46, under the operational command of Air Vice-Marshal L. N. Hollinghurst, C.B.E., D.F.C., were allotted to the airborne forces. Hollinghurst came to his new command with a high reputation for efficiency, and soon his tanned face with its keen eyes and his rotund figure was to be seen moving round the various airfields on Salisbury Plain, chiding, admonishing, inspiring. By 24th April 1944 such great progress had been made that it was found possible to lift the whole division and carry it for a three-day exercise, with the code name of 'Mush', which was, though they did not know it, the dress rehearsal for the invasion of Europe now near at hand.

Planning proceeded side by side with training. But since their only guides, the 1st Airborne Division, had been used mostly as infantry in the North African campaign and again in the invasion of Italy, the planners did not have a great deal of experience upon which to draw. In their first plan, drafted as early as August 1943, provision had been made for the dropping of two-thirds of an airborne division on Caen immediately ahead of the seaborne invaders consisting of three divisions landing between Grande Campe and the River Orne. The drawback to this design was presently seen to be that the airborne troops, being of necessity far more lightly armed than others, might be destroyed by the enemy's armour before the main forces had set foot ashore. It was therefore decided that the best use to be made of them would be to drop them to right and left of the invading armies, and thus make secure the most vulnerable part of them, their flanks, during the first all-important forty-eight hours. To the 82nd and 101st American Airborne Divisions was allotted the right flank on the Cotentin peninsula, their particular task being to secure the causeways traversing the inundated area behind the assault beaches. The 6th Airborne Division would secure the left flank in the area immediately north-east of the old town of Caen by seizing the ridge connecting the villages of Le Mesnil, Bréville and Le Plein. The division would be reinforced by at least one Commando brigade and once it had seized and secured its objectives would hand them over to the more heavily armed infantry of the Line.

The part of Normandy chosen is undulating country traversed by two valleys through which flow the River Orne and the River Dives. Between them is a stretch of land covered with orchards and woods, of which the largest is the Bois de Bavent. The fields and the valleys are lush, and the rivers bordered by reeds and long grass. The hedges have a thick English quality, but open spaces abound where there is pasture or tillage, for the land is some of the best in France. To look at it is not unlike the landscapes depicted by Sisley and Monet. The villages and small towns with which it is sewn are well built of stone and inhabited by a sturdy farming race, prosperous and hard-working.

The detailed planning was carried out by Gale and his small staff in an insignificant villa, 'pleasantly hidden among the trees near the River Avon'. The precautions to maintain secrecy were elaborate and effective—almost too much so. There was but one key to the one door, and when one day the officer who possessed it was delayed, he found on arrival a throng of eager planners, most of them of field rank, in a state of high indignation, for the door 'was fast locked and entry by any other means was impossible, since all the windows were barred. Outside in the churchyard, which, *absit omen*, stood next to the house, the planners had had "to fleet the time carelessly" for an hour in silence or in talk on more trivial matters, the nature of their occupation making it impossible for them to discuss what was uppermost in their minds.'

In the last few weeks before D-day Gale issued his officers a general instruction which has been quoted before, but which must be quoted again, for in it he sums up the whole duty of the airborne soldier. After emphasising the importance of tactical ability and 'a sound and properly working system of supply and maintenance of equipment', he defined the first duty of every commander, whatever his station. It was to know what was expected of him. 'It is not a question of what he wants to do but what he is wanted to do,' said Gale. The degree of freedom allowed to subordinates in the method of carrying out their task was of the greatest moment. 'You must remember,' urged the general, 'that it is your plan, and it must be your duty to ensure that it is your plan which is being carried out. Your responsibility in this is not one that you can be permitted to shirk. Your natural tendency may be to fight shy of it. You cannot, for ultimately the edifice is yours, and its foundation and corner-stones must be laid by you.' Gale then laid down, or rather reiterated, the principles on which an assault upon an enemy must always be based, and was especially emphatic concerning the manner in which the inevitable counter-attack must be met and defeated. 'At night hold your fire,' he advised, 'and beat your enemy by guile. By day or by night you must lay traps for him. Laugh quietly at him if he falls into your snares, and when you have him kick him in the pants.' How best to do so was contained in a number of suggestions or maxims, and the exhortation ended with a pregnant phrase: 'What you get by stealth and guts you must hold with skill and determination.'

By May 1944 the final plans had been perfected. Of necessity these were detailed, and after the very elaborate briefing which each platoon and company of each battalion and brigade received, every man was fully aware of his particular duty and the special perils and opportunities which awaited him. Briefly it was decided that the 3rd and 5th Parachute Brigades comprising two-thirds of the 6th Airborne Division should precede the Air Landing Brigade. They should drop in the early hours of D-day, seize the area to the north-east of Caen and hold it until the evening, when they would be reinforced by the Air Landing Brigade arriving in gliders, save for one battalion which would travel by sea. By then, too, they would be in touch with the 1st Special Service Brigade on their flank, which, it was hoped, would by the early afternoon have arrived to help them to hold the bridges over the Canal de Caen and the River Orne. The importance of these bridges was very great, for they carried across the Orne and the Canal de Caen the main road running roughly parallel to the coast along which any advance by the enemy against the flank of the Allies or by the Allies towards the mouth of the Seine must be made. The bridges were to be captured by a *coup de main* party arriving in gliders.

The specific tasks allotted to each brigade were: to the 5th Parachute Brigade, to land in the area north of the village of Ranville and there to seize the crossings over the Orne and the Canal de Caen, to secure and hold the area surrounding the villages of Benouville, Ranville and Le Bas de Ranville, and finally to clear and protect landing zones in the area so that the seventy gliders with advanced headquarters and the anti-tank guns could touch down unmolested two hours after the parachute troops had landed and the Air Landing Brigade come in safely on the evening of D-day. To the 3rd Parachute Brigade was given the duty of capturing and destroying an enemy battery of coastal defence guns at Merville, so placed that they could take in flank the beaches on which the 3rd British Infantry Division, part of the seaborne invading force, was to land. The brigade was also to demolish the bridges at Troarn, Bures, Robehomme and Varaville which spanned the River Dives and its various tributaries and thus interfere with the movement of enemy reinforcements. Finally they were to block and hold all roads leading into the area from the south and east, by seizing the high ground running from Troarn to Le Plein. The 3rd Brigade had, it will be perceived, a more roving commission than the 5th. Its battalions were to fulfil, if they could, what was rightly regarded as the whole duty of parachute troops, to harass the enemy, to disrupt his communications and to create conditions of alarm and despondency close behind his main battle front.

The total number of aircraft belonging to the fifteen squadrons comprising No. 38 and 46 Groups of the Royal Air Force was four hundred and twenty-three. All had been fitted with 'Gee', a navigational aid, which had been in use by Bomber Command for some time, and also with 'Rebecca Mark II', a short-range homing device which, it was hoped, by maintaining constant communication with the Eureka beacons set up by the 22nd Independent Parachute Company dropped from path-finders, would bring the aircraft accurately to the three dropping zones. These were: first, 'N', an area north-east of the villages of Ranville and Le Mariquet; second, 'V', west of Varaville; and third 'K', south of Ranville. Zones 'X' and 'Y' were situated between the Canal de Caen and the River Orne, one on each side of the main road, and would be used by the *coup de main* party who were to capture the bridges. Zone 'W', north-west of Ranville, would be used by the Air Landing Brigade on the evening of D-day.

By 5th June 1944 all was ready. Weather conditions, however, were bad, and the further outlook was unsettled. So bad were they in fact that the chief German meteorological officer confidently predicted that neither on 5th nor 6th June could an invasion of the continent take place. His opposite number on the Allied side, Group Captain J. M. Stagg, thought otherwise. Conditions, he said, would be impossible on the 5th, but on the 6th there would come a temporary break in the clouds and rain streaming in from the Atlantic, and weather which, though not ideal, would provide reasonably good conditions. After a post-ponement of twenty-four hours, therefore, Eisenhower from his headquarters near Portsmouth gave the order that the invasion was to begin a few minutes after midnight on Tuesday, 6th June 1944.

On the evening of the 5th Air Chief Marshal Sir Trafford Leigh-Mallory, commanding the air forces of the invasion, paid a visit to every airfield from which the British and American airborne forces were to take off. His mind was filled with fore-boding, for he knew as well as any man the difficulties and dangers likely to be encountered by parachute and glider-borne troops; he could indeed comfort himself with the thought that as far as humanly possible provision had been made to cover all eventualities, that the officers and men of the 82nd and 101st Divisions of the American airborne troops and the 6th British Airborne Division had been carefully rehearsed and briefed, and that the pilots and crews of their aircraft knew precisely what

146

was required of them. This was indeed true ; but many of them, and many of their passengers, though well trained, had never seen action before. Exercise 'Mush', however, which had taken place on 21st April over that part of England lying between the estuary of the Severn and the borders of Wiltshire and Oxfordshire, had shewn that, despite imperfections, all were in general up to the high level of their high task. Those ordered to undertake it had at least no doubts. 'I would describe their demeanour,' recorded Leigh-Mallory in his diary on his return that evening from his inspection, 'as grim and not frightfully gay, but there was no doubt in my mind of their determination to do the job.'

Fifty-seven minutes before midnight Squadron Leader Merrick, D.F.C., with as one of his passengers Air Vice-Marshal Hollinghurst, took off from Harwell in the first of the six Albemarle aircraft carrying the pathfinders of the 22nd Independent Parachute Company to the three dropping zones. At first all went well. The moon shone, the sky was clear. Only when the Albemarles were nearing the zones, which they reached punctually at 00.20 hours, did difficulties begin to appear. Three sticks of pathfinders were to be dropped on each zone, but, despite the fact that three of the six aircraft made two or more runs over the area, only one stick landed correctly on zones 'N', 'V' and 'K'. Worse than that, the radar and visual beacons for zone 'V', upon which the 1st Canadian Parachute Battalion and 9th Battalion were to land, were all lost or damaged, and two sticks of pathfinders for zone 'K' dropped on the edge of zone 'N'. Nevertheless a sufficient number arrived in the correct spot to enable the necessary signals to be made, and the position became easier as missing sticks arrived. The first men of the Independent Parachute Company to touch French soil were Captains Tate and Midwood, and Lieutenant de Latour.

In addition to the pathfinders for zones 'N', 'V' and 'K', a small force of six gliders for zones 'X' and 'Y' carrying the *coup de main* party of the 2nd Battalion of the Oxfordshire and Buckinghamshire Light Infantry, and a detachment of Royal Engineers, all under the command of Major R. J. Howard, landed at the same time. Their task was to seize the two bridges, and this they accomplished with efficiency and despatch. Howard in the leading glider landed only forty-seven yards from the bridge across the Canal de Caen, and the remainder, save one, in the neighbourhood. Both bridges were soon in our hands and the code phrase 'Ham and Jam' was being joyfully broadcast by the portable wireless sets.

Meanwhile the main drop of the two Parachute Brigades, the 5th and the 3rd, was taking place.

The 5th Parachute Brigade in Action

HALF AN HOUR later, according to plan, the 7th (Light Infantry) Battalion, Lieutenant-Colonel R. G. Pine-Coffin, M.C., a veteran of the North African campaign, in command, began to drop. Their briefing had been so thorough that each officer and man had had access to all the photographs and models of the area they were to assault and had been allowed to study them individually for three hours. At 20.00 hours on the 5th the battalion, which had completed all its preparations by the early afternoon, was roused from sleep and a final search made in the pockets and wallets of the officers and men for envelopes, letters or other evidence by which their unit might be identified. This practice was, of course, general throughout the armed forces, and was carried out by all battalions before going into action. The chaplain, the Reverend G. Parry, C.F., a man deeply beloved, conducted a short service, and then the battalion moved off, being conveyed in thirty-three lorries, one for each of the thirty-three Stirling aircraft which were to carry them to France. The men were in a sombre, determined mood. 'There were no hysterical exaggerated high spirits, no wisecracking from lorry to lorry, as was usual in an exercise; but there was a certain amount of singing . . . the atmosphere was one of quiet confidence, not unmixed—let us admit it—with a certain amount of honest funk.'

The final few minutes before entering the aircraft were spent in drinking cups of tea, or smearing the face with camouflage cream or, since when it died it was liable to flake, with soot collected from the bottom of the men's tea kettles. Some of the officers and men of 'B' Company carried kitbags with rubber dinghies in them for crossing rivers and streams. 'C' Company, under Major R. Bartlett, were travelling light in order to reinforce Howard and his men at the bridges as soon as possible.

The drop was made punctually at 00.50 hours, but many men missed the dropping zone, and two Stirlings, hit by flak, were lost with their passengers and crew. The difficulty of finding the dropping zone accurately was due to unexpected low cloud, and also to the fact that some of the beacons had been set up in standing crops and were not visible.

The enemy was alive to the situation, having been roused by the arrival of the pathfinders, and fired bursts of tracer at frequent intervals. 'The sight of this criss-crossing over the ground presented a rather pretty picture to the descending parachutists,' most of whom were in the air no longer than ten seconds. As might have been expected, the difficulties of finding the dropping zone led to a wide scattering of the battalion. 'It was,' says Lieutenant-Colonel Pine-Coffin, 'a most desperate feeling to know that one was close to the dropping zone, but not to know in which direction it lay. Time was slipping by . . . it was impossible to pick up a landmark until a chance flare dropped by one of the aircraft illuminated the church at Ranville.'

This church was easy to recognise because its tower, built in the fourteenth century and fortified against English marauders, is separated by several yards from the main building.

The colonel soon assembled a number of men, being aided by Lieutenant Rogers and his Aldis lamp,[1] and Private Chambers, who sounded the regimental call continuously on his bugle ; but it was not until 02.15 hours that he had succeeded in collecting some 40 per cent of his strength. By now, however, his first preoccupation had disappeared, for Major Howard's success signals put out over his wireless shewed that the bridges had been seized. With sighs of relief the 7th Battalion abandoned their heavy boat equipment, and hurried at the double to reinforce the glider-borne men, light infantrymen like themselves, who had done so well. The bridges were crossed shortly before 03.00 hours, and the planned defensive position taken up, though the number of men available to do so was only half what it might have been.

---

[1] This lamp had been a source of difficulty, for those who supplied it had sent it without batteries. When urgently asked to do so, they replied that the lamp was of the most modern and improved type, and that all that was necessary for its operation was to plug it into the mains and switch on.

Two examples of the problems calling for immediate solution at that juncture may be given: many specialists, mortar men, machine-gunners, signallers and the like, were without their special weapons or equipment, for the containers carrying them, which had been dropped from the bomb racks of the Stirlings, could not be found. They had with them only their pistols and a few Sten-guns. Armed with these, they were formed into a battalion reserve. There were no wireless sets and the commanders of the various positions in the defensive perimeter forming west of the canal bridge had been ordered at the briefing not to withdraw unless told to do so by wireless. They were therefore allowed to use their discretion, though urged to hold on as long as possible. In the event, 'not a single commander gave the order to withdraw'.

Nevertheless, as the night wore away and dawn began to climb the sky, Pine-Coffin's position was not, he felt, enviable. Barely two hundred men, and these included Howard's glider-borne party, were available to hold the two bridges, and they had no 3-inch mortars or medium machine-guns. A number of Piats, however, were available. But if weapons were short, courage was high; 'the very act of arriving on the battlefield by parachute inspires a sense of superiority'. Before long, 'A' Company was established in or near the little village of Benouville, 'B' Company in Le Port with a platoon on the bridge, and 'C' Company in reserve or patrolling the area with a platoon occupying a position north of Le Port on the bank of the canal. Four battle outposts had also been set up, two close to the bank some distance each side of the bridge, and two further west.

About an hour before dawn 'A' Company was attacked from three sides at once, and the sound of small-arms fire and bursting bombs seemed to shew that they were in some difficulty. Led by Lieutenant MacDonald, twenty men from the tiny reserve, with orders to pick up the weapons of casualties to supplement their own, were sent as reinforcements, and presently reached the company, which succeeded in repelling this and all other attacks. Had they had their mortars with them they might well have prevented or neutralised many of them before they started. As it was, having no long-range weapons, the company had to wait and deal with the enemy at close quarters. This they did most successfully.

'B' Company, under Major Neale, also under attack, 'were being pecked at almost all the time by parties of varying size. They saw a great deal of fighting'. Two of its platoons held the escarpment and the few houses at Le Port. The third was round the canal bridge itself 'in a tight semicircle'. The difficulties encountered by this platoon are a good illustration of what an inaccurate drop entailed. It had been carried in two aircraft ; one of these had delivered its passengers under Lieutenant Thomas at the centre of the dropping zone, but the other dropped the remainder twelve miles away, and several days passed before they were able to rejoin the battalion. Thomas's men captured a German 44-mm. electrically fired gun which, after repair, was found to be very useful against snipers, though it was once turned against the château, the mistake being realised when a nurse wheeling a perambulator was seen in its garden.

When day dawned the defenders of the bridge were for a time much hampered by a stream of civilians, women and children for the most part, who, having left the main battle area, wished to cross the bridge. 'The obvious pleasure of these civilians at meeting British soldiers was most noticeable and gratifying', but their presence did not make easier the task of defence.

A patrol of 'C' Company under Lieutenant Atkinson, visiting the grounds of the château, were able to destroy or cripple two German tanks, and then in the half light of dawn made prisoner an individual wearing trousers who was found to be the matron of the maternity home established in the main building, a magnificent mansion with a pillared façade. Atkinson, who addressed this lady, Madame Vion by name, in fluent French, informed her that he and his men were the British Army of Liberation. 'What!' exclaimed Madame Vion. 'All of you?' looking at the lieutenant and the nine dishevelled men with him. Madame Vion soon shewed the stuff of which she was made. Atkinson and his men were in the park of the château with its great trees heavy with June foliage. The Germans were scattered in all directions, a small party manning an anti-tank gun being established some three hundred yards from the château at the bottom of the vegetable garden. During the morning a German officer with a sergeant and a private arrived with a machine-gun and demanded to be taken on the roof. Madame Vion protested, saying that the maternity home was under the protection of the Red Cross. This the German ignored, at which Madame Vion took him and his party up the wrong staircase to an empty room on the third floor. The officer looked out of the window, where-upon the crew of the German anti-tank gun in the garden, thinking him and his men to be British, opened fire. The solid shot they used passed right through the château. The officer

151

withdrew, and Madame Vion went out to have further speech with Atkinson. She offered to lead him and his men against the Germans and was indignant when they expressed astonishment at the proposal. She was, she said, a supporter of General de Gaulle and had been in the Resistance since 1941.

During the small hours Germans who had occupied the buildings in the children's clinic for tuberculous patients were driven out. One fled, leaping in the manner of a hurdler the partitions dividing each individual play pen. He was hotly pursued by one of Atkinson's men, who despatched him with a knife before he had completed the hurdle race. Though the Château de Benouville remained under fire for fifty-one days, the indomitable Madame Vion continued to maintain her clinic. Eighteen children were born in the first eighteen days, some of them beneath the medieval chapel to which all repaired when the shelling became too heavy.

As soon as dawn on 6th June was fully come the brigade awaited with a very special personal interest the opening of the Second Front, for 'the parachutist fights a rather lonely battle . . . he has no real front or rear, and gets the feeling that he is fighting the war all by himself'. H-hour, 07.00, came and went, but nothing could be heard except small-arms fire and the bursting of mortar bombs which everyone had got so used to. They had not, however, long to wait, only the time it took the shells to fly from the muzzles of the guns to their targets. For the naval bombardment had begun. 'The noise when it came far exceeded all expectations, and was quite indescribable both in intensity ,and in duration, but it was music to the battalion and spirits rose with the rumbling of it.' Fatigue vanished, for the men knew that reinforcements were at hand and would arrive in due course to consolidate their victory. So it turned out, but before the 1st Special Service Brigade arrived, many hours of strenuous battle had to be endured. The enemy remained very persistent and the casualties in the battalion began to rise. An increasing number were caused by German snipers established in the church tower of Le Port. 'No sooner had one sniper been silenced in it than another would start from the same place.' Finally Corporal Killeen put a bomb from a Piat into the top of the tower and destroyed it, killing twelve snipers. Later on, when entering the church to see what damage he had caused, he reverently removed his steel helmet.

The casualties were cared for, for the most part, in a little café by the swing bridge kept by Monsieur and Madame Gondrée, who are today the proud possessors of a certificate from the War Office stating that in all probability they and their children were the first French citizens to be liberated by the British Army. To the noise of battle Gondrée presently added a more convivial sound. He uncorked ninety-seven bottles of champagne, carefully hidden for just such a day as this, and with the sparkling wine brought comfort to wounded men.

At about 10.00 hours two figures wearing red berets were seen walking across the canal bridge, 'for all the world like umpires at an exercise'. They were Major-General Gale, commanding the division, and Brigadier Kindersley, commanding the Air Landing Brigade which was due to arrive that evening, and they had come to see the fighting. Hardly had they arrived when they were gratified by a view at close range of a brisk engagement with a vessel on the canal. A Bren gun of Lieutenant Thomas's platoon and a Piat of Major Howard's party opened fire on two boats moving up the canal towards Caen. The bullets of the Bren gun splintered the wheelhouse of the first, and the Piat destroyed her engine. She drifted helplessly to the east bank and her crew, 'all young soldiers very scared except for one who was an arrogant Nazi', surrendered. The second boat turned tail and made off towards the sea.

Slowly the long hot hours passed. Despite their exhilaration the strain was beginning to tell, when about 13.00 hours the sound of pipes was heard in the distance. The Commandos of the 1st Special Service Brigade, under their tried leader, Lord Lovat, were at hand. No answering reply by Private Chambers on his bugle was made, lest by so doing the oncoming troops might think that the enemy had been completely mastered and that there were no snipers left. The Commandos 'came through in grand style', and at 14.00 hours Lord Lovat's piper led the way across the bridge. The link with the seaborne forces had been made and made with men wearing a beret of a different hue but with a reputation for courage and hard fighting which not even the parachutists could surpass. It was a moment of triumph and elation. Bullets were striking the metal girders of the bridge ; the strident voice of mortars was insistent, penetrating ; the enemy, far from cowed, was still offering a fierce resistance ; but when, above the sounds of battle, the lilting wail of the pipes stole upon the ears of tired but indomitable men, all knew that their first and greatest object had been gained. The bridge—it has been called Pegasus Bridge to commemorate the deeds performed that day—seized with much vigour and held with such tenacity, was safe. The airborne assault had succeeded. The 7th Battalion had been reinforced, but the Commandos were well ahead of the main force and it was still necessary to hold on with vigour. During the afternoon a number of unexpected figures made their appearance at the wheels of lorries. One of them, a Yorkshireman, was driving a bulldozer and 'thought that life was very unfair and full of hardships', because it was not so large as that allotted to his mate. These welcome reinforcements produced biscuits, chocolate and self-heating soups, which were much appreciated.

Not until early evening was it possible to reinforce 'A' Company. It was then found that all its officers had been wounded, but that the position was still held. That company fought for seventeen hours, and at one time a German attack, bursting through a gap in the defences, reached the regimental aid post, but was then driven off. In the confused mêlée Chaplain George Parry, a friend of every man in the battalion, was killed.

Evening came and with it a wireless message to say that a seaborne battalion was on its way to relieve them. Almost at the same time what seemed to be a never-ending stream of gliders, 'swaying and rustling' through the evening air, swept over the position to land on the flat ground prepared for them west of Bréville. 'This sight,' said Private Owen of 'B' Company, 'was the happiest I ever saw.' And in this he was voicing the opinion of all his comrades. The seaborne battalion arrived soon after 20.00 hours, and the relief began. During it a Focke-Wulf 190, which by flying low had escaped the attention of the air forces, dropped a 1000-lb, bomb on the canal bridge and scored a direct hit. By the best of good fortune the fuse had been wrongly set: it bounced off into the water and did not explode. Pine-Coffin stood at the bridge to count his men as they streamed across it towards Ranville, where they were to spend the night close to the dropping zone on which they had arrived seventeen hours before. One by one or in small groups 'they came through, tired, dusty, hungry, many of them wounded, but all marching, their heads held high'. Their commanding officer remained there until 01.00 hours on 7th June when the last man filed through. The fight had been long and hard, but victory had been won and 'not a single German, other than prisoners, had set foot on the bridge.'

The task of the 12th Battalion was to capture the village known as Le Bas de Ranville. Like the remainder of the brigade, it was airborne by 23.30 hours on 5th June, and the journey was uneventful. As the Stirlings neared the coast of France the hatches were removed from the holes in readiness for the landing, Captain J. A. N. Sim, York and Lancaster Regiment, who was to jump number one from his aircraft, stood on the edge of the hole looking down. 'Suddenly,' he says, 'the monotonous greyness of the sea broke into parallel white lines. I saw the waves rolling towards the dirty yellow beach, then the cliffs forming a step from the beach to the darker woods beyond. For some minutes I gazed down on a landscape clearly visible in the moonlight. The tracks of lanes, fields and hedgerows etched in various tones of grey and black.' A moment later the red and then the green lights went on and he stepped through the hole. 'There was the sudden stillness, the clean crisp rush of air behind the ears and round the body, the swelling of the chute above as it developed, sensations quickly following one after another, and I found myself floating lazily down, silently and, it seemed, alone . . . at any moment now I would land. As I watched the field beneath see-sawing a wire fence flashed to one side; the ground hit me and I rolled over. I was in Normandy and over Hitler's West Wall.' Thousands that moonlight night had a similar experience, and felt the same joy as he at being in the van, the first to come to grips with the enemy in the greatest campaign of all.

As with the 7th Battalion, an hour and a half passed before the 12th had collected sufficient men at the rendezvous to make it possible for them to set about their task. The commanding officer, Lieutenant-Colonel A. P. Johnson, then led them towards Le Bas de Ranville, which they seized without difficulty, finding there many more of the battalion who had landed outside the dropping zone and, recognizing where they were, had thought it best to repair at once to the objective rather than waste time looking for the quarry which was the battalion rendezvous. A few minutes after the move had begun the battalion had its first encounter with the enemy. A light armoured car, followed by a motor cyclist, came rushing down the road towards them. Fire was opened, and the motor cyclist fell. The car continued on its way until it met with those holding the bridge, whose fire sent it reeling into a ditch. 'Out of it was taken the German officer in command of the bridge defences, two empty wine bottles, a number of dirty plates and a quantity of rouge and face powder. Declaring that he had lost his honour by his failure to maintain the defences of the bridges the officer asked for death.'

After they had seized Le Bas de Ranville the 12th Battalion took up positions covering the village, of which the inhabitants, once they had got over their surprise, shewed themselves to be not only friendly but able to impart much useful intelligence. 'How I wish I had learnt more French while at school,' writes one parachutist, 'but perhaps the strong Yorkshire backchat of the members of my party finally convinced the lady (a middle-aged woman who had opened the door of her house to the parachutists) that we were the "mad dogs", as the Germans called us, and not the Gestapo endeavouring to trick her. Weeping and speaking very good English, she embraced and kissed each of us in turn . . . and was then able to impart useful information.'

Dawn found Captain J. A. N. Sim[1] three hundred yards ahead of 'C' Company's main position with twelve other ranks of No. 4 Platoon and a forward observation officer with a wireless set 'busily engaged in ranging his cruiser's guns in likely targets'. Sim and his men lined the hedge and presently saw a party of men who appeared to be wearing parachute-type steel helmets and camouflage smocks. They were about three hundred yards away when they suddenly turned and advanced against the parachutists, and Sim realised that they were the enemy. The Germans moved slowly but steadily towards the position whose defenders they outnumbered by about twenty to one. Sim waited till, thrusting through long grass, the enemy reached a barbed-wire cattle fence fifty yards away to his front. He then fired a Very light into them and his men opened rapid fire. The Germans dropped flat, but two self-propelled 88-mm. guns, advancing behind them in close support, at once opened on the parachutists whose position had now of necessity been disclosed. For some time the guns remained no more than seventy yards away, 'a sitting target for our six-pounder anti-tank gun, but no gun opened fire. Shortly after a soldier crawled up to me on hands and knees and saluted. He was sorry . . . the breech block had been damaged on landing'.

The position for Sim and his men appeared grave. Casualties in the small force came quickly. The man to his right was killed, and another moving towards him suffered the same fate. The forward observation officer was lying badly wounded in the thigh. Soon the enemy, protected by the fire of the self-propelled guns, were seen to be crawling round Sim's right flank. Then, as so often happens in action, all fire suddenly ceased and

[1] Later Major J. A. N. Sim, M.C.

156

silence reigned for a short while. 'I felt fogged and mentally dulled, and not capable of realising that I was in danger.' Presently, to Sim's amazement, the hatch of one of the self-propelled guns opened and 'a German officer, splendidly arrayed in polished jackboots, stiff cap and Sam Browne, leisurely climbed out and lit a cirgarette. He had two puffs only'. The battle was renewed by German mortar fire which burst in the air along the top of the hedge, and presently only four of the parachutists, Sim, his batman, Sergeant Jones, and Sergeant Millburn were alive and unwounded. The hedge could no longer be held, and they retreated by means of a shallow ditch to the main position, 'the Germans firing wildly at us most of the time'. They had held their own for several hours against very great odds. Later Sim, reinforced, returned to the hedge and held the position. By then the self-propelled guns had been destroyed by the anti-tank guns of 'C' Company. Sim was awarded the Military Cross, and the two sergeants, both of whom were subsequently killed, the Distinguished Conduct Medal.

The action fought by Sim and his men was part of a fierce struggle in which the 12th Battalion was involved for much of that day. The Germans made a most determined effort to regain Le Bas de Ranville and at one moment were able to force their way into the village. To meet a threatening situation the parachutists, who had driven them off, but only with difficulty, were reinforced about 13.00 hours by a Commando unit of the 1st S.S. Brigade. Thereafter the enemy made no further progress.

Meanwhile the 13th Battalion were fulfilling their part of the plan. It was for them to seize and clear Ranville, the next village, an important place, for it covered the approaches to the Orne bridges from the east, and, very important, to clear the obstacles, mostly thick-pointed poles on the high ground, so that the gliders carrying advance divisional headquarters and the indispensable anti-tank guns, when they came, might land in safety.

More fortunate than the other battalions of the brigade, more than half the officers and men of the 13th landed accurately on the dropping zone. Of those who did not many were caught in tall trees, and those who were not killed by the fire of the enemy were hard to rescue for no ladders long enough to reach them could be found. One man was eventually brought down by ropes after he had hung in his parachute harness for twelve hours. Quickly rallying to the hunting horns, they reached the village, and, shouting their war-cry 'Tally Ho', had by 02.30 hours destroyed its garrison, a company of the 711th Infantry

Division. Presently the letter 'L', for Lancashire and Luard (the name of the commanding officer), followed by the call 'Gone way', sounded on the commanding officer's hunting horn, announced that the village was in our hands; and Lieutenant Pollak was trying to explain to the owner of the château, the Comtesse de Rohan-Chabot that he was not a German trying to trap her. With dawn she realised what had happened and 'then was kindness itself to all ranks'. Ranville was the first village in France to be freed by the Army of Liberation and a plaque commemorating this feat of the 13th Battalion has been set up at its cross-roads.

While Ranville was thus being seized, 'A' Company of the 13th Battalion, under Major J. F. Cramphorn, together with a number of sappers, cleared the landing grounds for the gliders. When the last of these arrived on the evening of D-day, the battalion had spent the long summer day in beating off a long series of counter-attacks and had knocked out three German tanks.

So much for the exploits of the 5th Parachute Brigade on that momentous day when the liberation of Europe began.

The 3rd Parachute Brigade on D-day

IT IS time to consider the fortunes of the 8th and 9th Battalions and the 1st Canadian Parachute Battalion, which together formed the 3rd Parachute Brigade. 'Gentlemen,' said its commanding officer, Brigadier James Hill, on the day before they took off for France, 'in spite of your excellent training and orders, do not be daunted if chaos reigns. It undoubtedly will.' He proved to be a true prophet, but his men, as he well knew, could deal successfully with Germans and with chaos. The brigade followed *mutatis mutandis* much the same plan as that adopted by the 5th. An advance party made up of part of brigade headquarters and a small party from each battalion, together with one company of the 1st Canadian Parachute Battalion, had orders to drop in advance in order to clear a part of dropping zone 'V' of posts. The object of this was to be sure that the small force of gliders carrying the elements of the

d the only remaining road for lateral communication left
e Germans in the district. It was for these patrolling
es that Alastair Pearson was presently awarded a third
the Distinguished Service Order.

le the 8th Battalion was thus successfully, albeit with
ty, carrying out its task, the 1st Canadian Parachute
ion was attacking Varaville, in order to destroy its bridge
he Dives and also that at Robehomme, after which it would
to its allotted place at Le Mesnil. The battalion, except
e company which, as has been related, had dropped with
dvance party, was carried in Dakotas, of which three were
g gliders loaded with jeeps, trailers and ammunition. Its
ent from the skies occupied half an hour, 'though flying
itions were good and landmarks clearly visible'. The men
scattered over an area ten times the size of the dropping
, with results that might have been unfortunate. Even so, a
inconsiderable number of its men, dropped in small parties
hey were separated from each other by woods and marshes,
e taken prisoner. Of these, five were lined up and summarily
t by their captors. Four fell dead, but the fifth was only
unded in the leg. He slipped away and was presently
coured by Madame Lapouble of Bréville to whom he was
ught by the mayor, Monsieur Magnenat. After eating 'the
t meal he had had since he left his mother', the Canadian
bbled off to rejoin his unit wearing a pair of 'brand new
pers' and supported on one of the mayor's golf clubs.

Two platoons of 'B' Company were dropped two miles away
m the correct zone near Robehomme, and one stick of 'C'
mpany fell west of the Orne river in the zone through which
1st Special Service Brigade was advancing. Both parties
ained the battalion. Despite this faulty distribution all the
ectives were seized. Varaville was occupied and 'C' Company
troyed the bridge in the town. Then they became involved
 long and costly fight with the garrison of a pillbox, who
tinued to resist stubbornly until 10.30 hours, when the bombs
he Piats rendered further resistance vain. Other elements of
battalion seized Robehomme, where Captain A. J. Jack
al Engineers, enhanced that Corps' reputation for courageous
ntricity by blowing the bridge and then sitting down with
men to cook and eat breakfast. Such behaviour when, as the
l inhabitants were quick to tell him, the enemy might appear
ny moment, did much to impress the French and to increase
already high fighting qualities of his men.

162

brigade and some anti-tank guns would be able to land soon
after the parachute troops had dropped, more than twelve hours
in advance of the Air Landing Brigade. These advance parties
were carried in sixteen Albemarles, not all of which were able to
bring their passengers to the right place. One, having tried seven
times to find the dropping zone, was hit by anti-aircraft fire and
forced to turn back for England. The shell which damaged it
blew Major W. A. C. Collingwood, the brigade major who was
waiting to jump, through the hole. His static line became wound
round his legs, and he remained hanging beneath the aircraft
for half an hour. A sixty-pound kitbag was attached to his other
leg, but his companions were able to drag him back into the
Albemarle, which made a safe landing. Undaunted by this experience, he returned to the brigade that evening, this time in a
glider.

Since most of the Eureka beacons and lights were damaged
during the drop, only two green lights were showing on Zone 'V'
when brigade headquarters, the 9th and the 1st Canadian Parachute Battalions, arrived. The zone was also shrouded in dust
and smoke blown across it by the bombs dropped on the battery
at Merville. Anti-aircraft fire caused pilots to take avoiding
action, with the result that Brigadier Hill and several sticks of
the 9th and 1st Canadian Parachute Battalion fell into, or close
to, the River Dives and suffered heavy casualties from our own
bombing when later in the day they sought to rejoin their main
body. The brigadier himself was wounded but remained in
action. Of the gliders carrying the heavy equipment three parted
from their tugs in cloud when nearing the coast of France, and
the others were released north of the landing zone 'V'. Three
touched down on zone 'N', and others about a mile and a half
away from 'V'. Experiences similar to those of brigade headquarters befell the battalions. The 8th, which had as its commanding officer the redoubtable Lieutenant-Colonel Alastair
Pearson, D.S.O., M.C., now sufficiently recovered from the
malaria he had caught in Sicily to see action again, was to drop
on Zone 'K', between Cuverville and Toufréville, with orders to
destroy the bridges over the Dives at Bures and Troarn. It was
then to withdraw to the great wood of Bavent and hold the
south-east sector of the bridgehead to be established by the 6th
Airborne Division across the River Orne. The battalion was
dropped over a very wide area, and the detachments of the
Royal Engineers who were to blow the bridges were not able to
reach the rendezvous in time. Pearson was hit in the hand almost

159

as soon as he touched ground. Disregarding his wound, he eventually collected about one hundred and eighty men and divided them into two groups which moved on Bures and Troarn. They had with them enough explosive to destroy two of the three bridges which were their objectives. Fortunately, however, a detachment of Royal Engineers had landed on the northern outskirts of the Bois de Bavent. They collected a satisfactory quantity of explosive and demolition equipment from the kitbags and container loads dropped with them, and moved off in two parties, one marching towards Bures, dragging their equipment with them on trolleys, the other making for the more distant Troarn in a jeep.

The first party soon fell in with the reconnaissance party of the 8th Battalion who covered them while, according to plan, they destroyed the two bridges. The sappers in the jeep going to Troarn, Major J. C. A. Roseveare and seven other ranks, travelled at high speed, their Bren and Sten guns at the ready. At a level crossing near the town they ran into a barbed-wire knife-rest and it took them twenty minutes to cut themselves and their vehicles free. Though by that time the German garrison had been thoroughly aroused, the sappers would not be turned from their task. At top speed they rushed through the town firing their Sten guns, Sapper Peachey acting as a rear-gunner and making excellent practice. Immediately beyond Troarn the road falls steeply. Down the hill sped the jeep under a hail of machine-gun bullets, all of them fortunately flicking just above the heads of its occupants. The bridge was reached, and five minutes later a gap twenty feet wide had been blown in it. The jeep was then ditched and the party moved on foot to a rendezvous at Le Mesnil.

Throughout the day many other sappers arrived at that place, having had a number of brisk encounters with the enemy. Some had landed close to Ranville and been made prisoner for a time. But not for long: one of them, Sergeant Jones, snatched a Schmeisser from a German and with it killed eight of his captors. Another, Sapper Thomas, though wounded while still in the air, on landing wiped out with grenades a party of three who had been shooting at him.

By the evening of D-Day the 8th Battalion, established on the outskirts of the Bois de Bavent, was about two hundred and thirty strong. Its redoubtable commander, Alastair Pearson, was determined to create the impression in the minds of the Germans that his battalion was much stronger. He did so by means of

vigorous and frequent patrols. The first took pla[...] of 7th June when he led forty men through the w[...] château of Troarn to the rescue of a number [...] have been wounded when the Dakota carrying [...] The patrol kept in close order with a jeep in th[...] they reached a railway bridge east of Bures. Th[...] those which had been blown up the day before [...] Engineers. Pearson and his men presently [...] collapsible dinghy in a glider which had crashed [...] ferried themselves across the River Dives, leaving a [...] to look after the boat, the remainder of the patrol [...] down the railway embankment which ran high ab[...] fields resonant with the croaking of innumerable fr[...] bright moonlight,' says Lieutenant R. T. Thompson, [...] party, 'and we must have presented quite a good ta[...] apparently did not worry the commanding officer, who [...] on his way as if he were leading a glorified nature ramb[...] the patrol reached a small village, pushed on and the[...] while Pearson and a few men investigated a farmhouse [...] vaguely in the darkness. While he did so the rest 'lay in [...] for what seemed a very long time, our excitement and [...] asm ebbing away with every minute of his absence, until v[...] shaken out of our senses by the most fiendish noise comi[...] the direction of the road'. The general opinion was that [...] two enemy tanks were advancing upon them, and the p[...] soldiers crouched even lower in the ditch, or took cove[...] a thick hedge. So they waited, but presently there app[...] squat rumbling tank with its menacing gun swinging [...] and left from the turret like the nose of an uncouth [...] prey on the prowl, but instead the colonel dragging, [...] to the shafts, a farm-cart in which lay eight woun[...] casualties from the Dakota. These he was encoura[...] many great oaths'. On seeing him, the rest of the patro[...] to join with him, 'for all the world like a lot of drunk [...] from market'. All returned safely with the wounde[...] rescued from a farm at least four miles behind the en[...]

The next night, having had the bullet which had [...] his left hand on the first day's fighting removed, [...] another patrol, which, entering Troarn, fought a [...] and inflicted heavy casualties upon a resolute bu[...] bewildered enemy. Two nights later the indefatig[...] took seventy men to the village of Roucheville and t[...] a detachment of Royal Engineers while they [...]

The chaos which Brigadier Hill had prophesied, and into which, as will be realised, both brigades were thrown, is well illustrated by the adventures of Captain R. M. E. Kerr of 13th Battalion. The first to jump from his aircraft, he landed alone in the middle of the River Dives, climbed out and reached a farm, where he picked up four parachutists. A young French boy undertook to lead them to their destination, Varaville, which they reached about 03.30 in the morning. 'Complete chaos seemed to reign in the village. Against a background of Brens, Spandaus and grenades could be heard the shouts of British and Canadians, Germans and Russians. There was obviously a battle in progress.' The captain and his party determined to make for Le Mesnil, where he knew the brigade was to establish a firm base. An Englishwoman, a cockney from Camberwell, about fifty-five years old, then made her appearance and explained what was wanted to their young French guide. On the way to Le Mesnil they entered a wood and had a brush with a German patrol. One of the enemy threw a stick grenade, which burst on the French boy's head and killed him. The party had now lost their guide, 'their maps were not fit to use, and they had already tramped for two miles through swamps with the water often chest high'.

After a time they fell in with some French farmers, who gave them fresh milk and bread. It was now light, and for all that day the party, swollen to about twenty, moved through the fields and through the thick Bois de Bavent. By four o'clock in the afternoon, after they had crossed a number of canals twenty feet deep and 'were all completely whacked', they saw the gliders carrying the rest of the division coming in to land. 'This exhilarating sight revived their spirits, which soared still higher when they saw some Spitfires . . . bring a couple of Messerschmitts down into the swamp quite close to them. They struggled on, not daring to rest in the swamp for fear of drowning'. By ten in the evening they reached terra firma at last, having taken six hours to cover two miles through the swamp. They had still not reached Le Mesnil, but were eventually put on the right road by 'a very drunken Frenchman'.

A few days later, when positions were more stable, an 'inquest' was held to discover the reason why the drop, particularly of the 3rd Parachute Brigade, had been so scattered. These were found to be three. First, a large number of Eureka sets were so badly damaged in the landings as to be unusable. Secondly, the pathfinder teams were too small and the time allowed them to set up their beacons too short. This risk had had to be accepted, for what had at all costs to be achieved was surprise. The enemy was to be given no breathing space: suddenly in the midst of the night armed men in thousands were to drop upon him unheralded and therefore, it was hoped, unsuspected. The third reason for the scattered drop was that pilots and crews of No. 46 Group of the Royal Air Force had had insufficient time to train for the difficult task of dropping parachute troops by night. Formed only in January 1944, they were less practised than No. 38 Group, so much so that they had been instructed to fly in loose formation and to drop their parachutists on receiving a signal from the leading aircraft. Obviously if that aircraft missed the dropping zone—and owing to the failure of the Eureka beacons many of them did—those following after would be led astray, and the error would increase literally with every second.

What happened in one Dakota aircraft of this group is a good example of the hazards run by the parachute troops even before they were on the ground and in contact with the enemy. Having crossed the greater part of the Channel, the Dakota ran into anti-aircraft fire, not, as it subsequently transpired, from the enemy, but from Allied shipping. Its pilot imagined that he was over the coast of France, and, since he was carrying some bombs, let them go. The gunners in the ships were not unnaturally convinced that the Dakota was hostile and redoubled their fire. To avoid it the pilot took violent evasive action, which flung his unhappy passengers, all heavily laden, to the floor, along which they slid or rolled forwards and backwards according to the motion of the aircraft. To cap all, the green light went on and the first three men who jumped fell into the sea and were never seen again. The remainder eventually jumped but were scattered over a very wide area.

Such mishaps, to give them no stronger word, were inevitable. Nor are the pilots and crews to be held worthy of blame. They did their best and it was not their fault that the result was not what it should have been. Great though the preparations for the liberation of Europe had been, they had inevitably been dominated by the time factor. The minimum number of transport aircraft necessary had not been forthcoming in time to provide a fully adequate period of training. This reduced, but did not destroy, the margin between the success and failure of the airborne operations and inevitably increased their hazards.

The Battery at Merville

TO THE 9th Battalion had fallen the most dangerous mission of all, the destruction of the coastal battery near Merville. The battalion was under the command of Lieutenant-Colonel T. B. H. Otway, Royal Ulster Rifles. Otway received his orders on April 2nd and had therefore only two months to rehearse the operation for which he was allowed *carte blanche*. A spot in England at West Woodhay near Newbury, where conditions were very similar to those subsequently encountered in Normandy, was chosen. It was good agricultural land in full production, but Otway obtained the use of it in forty-eight hours, though to do so permission had to be obtained from no less than seven different ministries in Whitehall, a record which should surely stand to the credit of the Parachute Regiment. Here in a week the sappers built a scale model of the battery, its shape and dimensions being known to them from the air photographs available. Tubular scaffolding took the place of the guns. Not only was the actual objective itself reproduced, so also were the approaches to it. Four mechanical excavators and six large bulldozers, brought on tank transporters from as far away as Liverpool and Plymouth, worked night and day, 'the hours of darkness being illuminated by the headlights of vehicles'.

To keep the projected operation a profound secret was naturally of the highest importance, and very stringent measures were adopted. No one without a special pass signed by the commanding officer himself could make use of any road in the neighbourhood, and a number of attractive girls, specially briefed for the purpose, were introduced into the area with orders to extract all the information they could from the parachute troops. In this they failed utterly, though the whole plan was known to every officer and man, the only piece of knowledge withheld being the actual name and whereabouts of the battery. Such elaborate precautions interfered with the lives of the local inhabitants, most of whom took them in good part. 'But a number, eager to maintain the rights of property, had to be pacified by drinks in the mess.'

Rehearsals by day and night were frequent. Most were conducted with live ammunition, and continued until every one of the thirty-five officers and six hundred other ranks composing the battalion knew exactly what his part was and how to play it. On 31st May the Battalion was moved to Broadwell and briefed. The briefing lasted five days, and every man attending was required to submit to his immediate superior his own sketch, drawn from memory, of the position he was to occupy. In addition to the assault by the 9th Battalion three gliders, carrying volunteers from 9th Battalion and No. 591 Parachute Squadron, Royal Engineers, were to crash-land on the top of the battery, regarding which a large amount of information had been collected. The guns were said to be of 150-mm. calibre mounted in concrete emplacements twelve feet high and five feet deep facing north-west. The concrete itself was six feet six inches thick, and in addition earth twelve feet thick surrounded two of the casemates. Access to them was by means of steel doors. The strength of the garrison was thought to be two hundred all ranks (it was in fact one hundred and thirty). The colonel commanding them was a newcomer, the previous occupant of the post having lost it through his love of the bottle. This had led him to indulge in many excesses of which the final and fatal was a ride on the switch-back merry-go-round at the local fair near Merville. As soon as he was well aboard one of the cars, the local inhabitants bribed the owner of the switch-back to keep it in continuous motion for as long as he could. For upwards of two hours the German colonel, deathly sick, was whirled up and down and round and round. When at last it stopped he was taken to his billet in a state of collapse.

To defend their guns the garrison disposed of several machine-guns and one dual-purpose 20-mm. gun. Some twenty weapon pits were plotted on the air photographs. Nor was this all: the position, which measured approximately four hundred yards by four hundred was surrounded by a cattle fence, and a minefield one hundred yards wide, bounded on its inner side by a concertina fence of barbed wire fifteen feet thick and five feet high. Isolated minefields had been laid across all likely approaches to the battery, and an anti-tank ditch, four hundred yards long, dug on the west and north-west. If ever defenders could claim that they were holding an impregnable position, the garrison of the battery at Merville could surely do so. Around it on every side were open field and orchards, much scarred to the south by bomb craters, for Bomber Command had been very active and had attacked the battery more than once, scoring two direct hits on a casemate, neither of which had penetrated the concrete.

It was essential for the battery to be destroyed half an hour before the first assault craft touched down on the beaches. The nearest suitable dropping zone was two thousand four hundred yards away, and the earliest moment at which the advance party of the parachutists could jump was 00.20 hours. Were the attack to be unsuccessful the battery was to be shelled by the Navy. It was therefore decided that the attack should begin at 04.30 hours, and the naval bombardment at 05.30 hours, thus leaving the battalion one hour to overrun the position and be clear of it.

The plan of attack was elaborate and Otway divided his force into eleven separate parties, each with a definite task. Among them were the organisation party at the rendezvous, the battery reconnaissance party, a taping party of one officer and eight other ranks to shew the way, a breaching company, an assault company, and a reserve company. To these were added the glider assault party of three officers and forty-seven other ranks of the battalion and one officer and seven other ranks of the 591st Parachute Squadron, Royal Engineers. Each man wore a jumping smock with a skull and crossbones marked in luminous paint on the left breast. In addition, there were two sniping parties armed with Bren guns and anti-tank rifles, and a diversion party, two of whom could speak German (these were armed with Piats and Bren guns), a firm base party to organise the spot from which the battalion was to launch the assault, and finally what was known as the glider element, made up of five gliders carrying special heavy equipment which included flame throwers, two six-pounder anti-tank guns and three jeeps loaded with ammunition, scaling ladders, Bangalore torpedoes, and duralumin footbridges.

The plan was as follows. The rendezvous organisation and battery reconnaissance parties, ten strong, were to land from an Albemarle, mark the dropping zone and reconnoitre a route to the battery through its defences. Between 00.30 hours and 00.40 hours a very heavy weight of four-thousand-pound bombs was to be dropped by a hundred Lancasters. During the bombing the glider element carrying the special equipment was to land as close as it could to the battalion rendezvous, and have unloaded their cargo in time for the battalion to make use of it when it dropped. The taping party was also to land and, equipped with Polish mine detectors, to clear three paths through

167

the minefield. The commander of the reconnaissance party was to meet the battalion at a cross-roads north-east of the village of Gonneville and lead it to the firm base which he had previously chosen, and which was to be about three hundred yards outside the perimeter to the south-east. To cover the battalion a company of the Canadian Parachute Battalion was detailed to be in readiness.

The assault itself was to be led by the breaching platoons, three in number, which formed the breaching company. Its task was to blow gaps in the wire, whereupon the reserve and assault companies following the tapes were to dash through and to make straight for the battery, protected by two sniping parties. The main attack was to be delivered from the south-east with a demonstration against the gate facing north. The three gliders which were to crash on top of the battery were to be released at a height of six thousand feet at 04.24 hours, one and a half minutes later a bugle was to sound reveille, whereupon mortars from the firm base would fire star shells to illuminate the target. At 04.28 hours the bugler would sound the 'Fall-in', which would be the signal for all fire to cease. The first glider was to land at 04.30 hours, and the bugler would then blow 'Lights out' to stop the firing of star shells.

Naval bombardment parties in touch with H.M.S. *Arethusa*, ordered to open fire on the battery at 05.30 hours if the assault failed, were to drop with the battalion. As soon as the battery was captured, yellow flares were to be lit, and the battalion would then move off to its firm base, reorganise and set out for the high ground on which stood the village of Le Plein, block the roads leading from Franceville Plage to Le Plein and seize a German headquarters at Salenelles.

Such was the objective and such the plan for seizing it. It was explained yet again to every officer and man at the final briefing by the commanding officer. He was followed by the R.A.F. station commander who, having wished them all good luck, committed himself to the rash statement that his pilots had never missed a dropping zone or been late in reaching one. 'It was lucky for him,' records one who survived to write an account of what happened, 'that there was no chance of any discussion on this point after the operation.'

On the morning of 4th June the Reverend J. Gwinnett, C.F., the battalion's chaplain, conducted a drumhead service, at which a special Pegasus flag, made by the Women's Voluntary Services at Oxford, was dedicated. It was offered by the men of the

Permanent Staff of the Transit Camp who as a result of parachute operations were no longer fit for action. Gwinnett's discourse, which was most moving, was on the theme 'Fear knocked at the door. Faith opened it and there was nothing there.' Gale was blunter. 'The Hun thinks,' he said, 'that only a bloody fool will go there. That's why we're going.'

The glider assault force and the rendezvous and reconnaissance parties took off from Brize Norton and Harwell, the rest of the battalion earlier at 23.10 hours. All went well until four minutes from the dropping zone, when moderate anti-aircraft fire was encountered. This was particularly unfortunate, for many of the pilots, who were already finding it hard to distinguish between the mouths of the Oren and the Dives, began to take evasive action, to the great peril and discomfort of their passengers. A man with an eighty-pound load and a parachute on top of it cannot climb quickly to his feet again if he has been thrown down in the confined space of an aircraft's fuselage; and when the green lights came on the men composing many of the sticks were still rolling on the floor. In the result the battalion, instead of being dropped in a concentrated area, one thousand nine hundred yards by eight hundred, was spread over fifty square miles of Normandy, one stick landing as far away as thirty miles from the battery. On the other hand the battery reconnaissance and rendezvous parties dropped at their correct time and on the right spot. They at once set about laying out their lights and signs, and the reconnaissance party moved in darkness towards the battery, narrowly escaping elimination from the shower of four-thousand-pound bombs dropped by the Lancasters. Not one of them hit the target but a number of cattle in the nearby fields were killed and wounded.

Otway himself, like many of his men, had been flung untimely out of his Dakota as it was taking evasive action. His knowledge of the locality, gained by the study of maps and photographs, enabled him to recognise the spot on which he was about to land: it was a German headquarters. He and two men, of whom one was his batman, fell into the garden beside it, and were at once fired at by the Germans inside who fortunately seem to have been armed with nothing more lethal than pistols. One of the parachutists silenced this fusillade by throwing a brick through the window, which the Germans evidently mistook for a grenade. Otway's batman fell through the glass roof of the greenhouse but was able to rejoin him at the rendezvous.

On reaching it Otway found a condition of affairs which

might well have quelled a stouter heart. To quote from his staccato official report: 'By 02.50 hours the battalion had grown to one hundred and fifty strong with twenty lengths of Bangalore torpedo. Each company was approximately thirty strong. Enough signals to carry on—no three-inch mortars—one machine-gun —one half of one sniping party—no six-pounder guns—no jeeps or trailers or any glider stores—no sappers—no field ambulance, but six unit medical orderlies—no mine detectors—one company commander missing. The commanding officer decided to advance immediately.'

'A' Company was in the van, followed by Otway and such of his battalion headquarters as had arrived. Then came a small number of the diversion party, then thirty men of 'B' Company with some Bangalore torpedoes. They were followed by twenty men of 'C' Company, the battalion medical officer, and the medical orderlies. This small but very resolute force set out along country lanes and tracks bordered by high banks and thick hedges, on the other side of which could be seen the dim forms of apple trees heavily laden. They halted often to make sure by the light of the moon that they were moving in the right direction, and at one moment successfully slipped by a patrol of the enemy.

On the way to the firm base they met, as arranged, the battery reconnaissance party under Major G. Smith. They had cut the outer cattle fence, penetrated the minefield, and lain for half an hour beside the concertina wire, spotting the enemy's posts by listening to the talk and coughing of the sentries. During their approach to the minefield an enemy patrol had passed within two feet of the ditch in which they were crouching. They had in due course been joined by the taping party commanded by Major A. J. Parry. It had no tapes or mine detectors, but had marked the way through the minefield by scratching heel-marks in the dust. These tasks had been accomplished without a single casualty, though the officers and men employed on them had had to crawl forward on their hands and knees feeling for trip wires, of which several were encountered.

At 04.30 hours the battalion reached the firm base where 'B' Company was divided into two breaching teams, and 'A' and 'C' Companies were joined together into one assault force consisting of four parties, each of twelve men, one party for each gun of the battery. So far the enemy had made no sign, but hardly had Otway and his men reached their firm base when six enemy machine-guns, all outside the perimeter, opened fire,

from moving to the Orne. By then they were so thin on the ground that there had to be an interval of ten yards between each man.

It was presently discovered that the garrison of the château and the village were for the most part Russians compelled by the Germans to fight for them on the grounds, which they unfortunately believed, that if they fell into the hands of the Allies they would be shot as traitors. The position was eventually captured on the next day by commando troops.

Such were the deeds performed by the five battalions of the Parachute Regiment, the 22nd Independent Company and the 1st Canadian Parachute Battalion on D-day. The palm must be given to Otway and his gallant 9th, but every objective assigned had been taken by troops, hardly any of whom had been in action before. Unable to uphold a tradition which they did not possess, they could and did create one. Most praiseworthy of all perhaps, they had in twenty-four hours shewn themselves to be of the same stout breed as the men of the 1st Airborne Division.

The Battle of Bréville

THE 6th Airborne Division had made a bloody but very successful entry into Normandy. Could it remain there, was the question which exercised the minds of all in command, from the platoon commanders to General Montgomery. Gale knew that he would be hard put to it to maintain his positions, for though it was true that all objectives had been taken, the division was very thin on the ground, and remained so though men dropped in the wrong place rejoined it in small and sometimes large parties for the next few days.

What happened to the 224th Parachute Field Ambulance is typical of the confusion of that time. Part of it landed not far away from the village of Varaville, which was their destination, though many of them fell into the marshes partially surrounding the place, losing some their equipment, others their lives. The survivors eventually joined the Canadian Parachute Battalion, all save No. 2 Section under the command of Captain R. Marquis who should have been dropped near Troarn, but instead found themselves not only east of the Dives marshes but also east of that river, about fifteen miles from their rendezvous. They set out to reach it, marching westwards, and presently found the marshes, in which the water was discovered to be much deeper than they had been led to suppose. Moving by night and making use of toggle ropes and Mae Wests to cross places where the Dives or its overflow was too deep to wade, they reached a solitary farmhouse in which they found a Canadian. With him they set out for Robehomme; but since by then, as has been related, the bridge across the Dives had been blown, they had to cross the river by a felled tree. Having done so, they came upon about a hundred of the Canadian Parachute Battalion under the command of Captain P. Griffin, 'occupying a strong position on a hill near the village church'. The wireless sets were unusable, but eventually an officer got through and ordered them to make for Le Mesnil. They set out to do so, the parachute ambulance men marching in the rear dragging wounded in a hand-cart borrowed from the French. They duly reached Le Mesnil at 04.00 hours on 10th June and there the ambulance team, though well in the front line, remained. Before twenty-four hours had passed they had performed one hundred and twelve operations.

Major Ian Dyer and Lieutenant 'Jock' Lepper of the 9th Battalion were dropped into flood waters half a mile west of Robehomme, more than three miles as the crow flies from their objective, the battery at Merville. Collecting the rest of their stick, they moved north-west, for a time 'waist deep in water', presently reached a road, dodged a German cyclist patrol and at dawn saw two men dressed in airborne smocks who, when challenged, fled. 'Don't you know the password, you bloody fools?' shouted Dyer. One of the fugitives turned out to be Lieutenant-Colonel R. N. H. C. Bray, the G.S.O.1 of the division. Their next move was to make contact with the Canadians at Le Mesnil, in whose ranks they fought for three days, ambushing a large German patrol and not rejoining their battalion until the 9th.

Lance-Corporal Green and Privates Jepp and Penstone landed near Franceville Plage and, after having been hidden for some days by French civilians, swam up the estuary of the Orne to reach the area occupied by the division and report for duty together with their arms and equipment on 24th June. They served with the 9th Battalion till the end of the war.

Its padre, the Reverend John Gwinnett, marched fifteen hours to rejoin his flock and reached brigade headquarters, where he learned that twenty casualties, part of those wounded in the assault on the battery, were lying in a house close to the captured objective. He drove thither in a jeep and successfully brought them all, including Captain H. Hudson, the desperately wounded adjutant, to the main dressing station at Ranville, thus preventing them from falling into the hands of the enemy.

Captain T. E. A. Robinson, also of the 9th Battalion, was seized by the Germans and marched southwards through Troarn, where, 'the vigilance of his guards being momentarily relaxed', he escaped and was led back to Troarn by an old man. The town was free of Germans and Robinson's progress through it became a triumph, 'Young women embraced him, men wrung his hand, bouquets of flowers and bottles of cognac were thrust upon him and innumerable babies were presented for him to kiss.' The situation was too good to last, the Germans suddenly reappeared and Robinson, hastily bolting some strawberries, jumped over the churchyard wall and went to ground in the crypt of the church, 'where he slept for three hours'. Eventually marching by night on his compass, he reached Major Dyer at Le Mesnil.

Such conduct was typical of the thousand-odd men of the division who had been dropped wide on the night of 6th June and of whom many, though unhappily by no means all, eventually found their way back to their unit.

At dawn on 7th June, twenty-four hours after the landing, the division was holding its planned positions beyond the Orne. Pine-Coffin's 7th Battalion, having captured and held its two bridges, had been relieved by a battalion of the 3rd Division which had crossed by sea, and, as has been said, had moved back to the village of Ranville. At dawn it took up positions east of the village. Next to the 7th was the 12th Battalion at Le Bas de Ranville, and the 13th at Ranville and Le Mariquet. North of these were the Canadian Parachute Battalion, and what remained of the 9th, reinforced by commandos, was near Le Plein and Hauger. The key to the position in this beautiful rolling country with its villages of yellow-grey stone and stucco, bearing such lovely names as Hérouvillette, Longueval, Le Mariquet and Sainte Honorine, was the high ground running south from Le Plein through the wood of the Bois de Bavent to Troarn. If the enemy regained this ground they could overlook the Orne bridges and be able to prepare for that attack in force against the left flank of the British 2nd Army, which it was the precise object of the 6th Airborne Division to prevent.

Gale ordered the 1st Battalion Royal Ulster Rifles and the 2nd Battalion of the Oxfordshire & Buckinghamshire Light Infantry, both belonging to the Air Landing Brigade, the first to occupy Longueval, and the second Hérouvillette, and this they did by 09.00 hours on 7th June. At the other end of the high ground commando troops were also by then in Sallenelles and Franceville Plage. The situation would have been quite satisfactory even though attempts to seize Ste Honorine and Escoville failed, had it not been for one circumstance. The village of Bréville in the centre was still held by a very determined German garrison which therefore lay between the Commando Brigade and the 3rd Parachute Brigade. Moreover, being on high ground, the enemy was able to overlook Ranville.

That day the strength of the division was completed by the arrival of the 12th Battalion of the Devonshire Regiment which had crossed the Channel by sea, and which took over positions from the 12th Battalion near Le Bas de Ranville. The effect of these dispositions was to give Gale a small but much-needed reserve made up of the 7th and 12th Battalions and later on an air landing battalion, the 2nd Oxfordshire & Buckinghamshire Light Infantry.

The first attempt of the Germans to break the ring formed by the airborne forces and the Commando Brigade was made on 8th June in the north against the villages of Hauger and Sallenelles. After desultory fighting, which continued throughout the day, a heavy attack was launched in the evening. The enemy, however, could make no progress against the commandos, though he maintained his pressure, extending his front somewhat and striving again and again to break through. In this he was unsuccessful, though on 10th June he made two determined attacks through the Bréville gap; one north-west against the commandos once more holding Le Plein, and the other south-west against the main landing zone, near Le Mariquet, then held by the 13th Battalion. The northern attack eventually failed with heavy loss, though before it did so much fighting was necessary round the Bois des Monts, the summer bungalow belonging to the Mayor of Bréville and his English wife, and the nearby Château St. Côme whose stables housed, among other thoroughbreds, Lord Derby's Plassey and its son Arcot. It was here that Regimental Sergeant-Major Cunningham shewed the stuff of which he was made, that Company Quarter-

Master-Sergeant Graham won the Military Medal, and that Private Cowley particularly distinguished himself. They were all of the 9th Battalion.

This unit was heavily involved throughout these critical days in fighting which presently developed into the battle of Bréville. After being relieved near Hauger by the 1st Special Service Brigade, it arrived at Le Bois des Monts early on 8th June, having traversed the village of Bréville under the noses of the enemy. This was fortunate, for the noise made by its principle means of transport, a creaking brewer's dray drawn by two greys, was considerable.

On the morning of the 9th the enemy, who had been able because of the thick woods to approach from the north-east to within fifty yards of the battalion's position in the Bois des Monts, 'suffered appalling casualties' in the final charge 'and broke and fled'. The parachutists then had to deal with him in the south and in so doing developed a most successful technique for hand-to-hand combat in wooded country. The edges of the wood to be cleared were covered by Bren guns, and the attacking forces moved into the trees in two waves. The second wave would fling a volley of grenades over the heads of the first, which, as soon as they burst, charged the undergrowth firing Sten guns. Beginning on the 8th, and for three more days and nights, 'enemy counter-attacks were almost continuous'. To repel them guile was mingled with courage, the men of the battalion opening fire only at point-blank range and thus, according to prisoners, never revealing their positions. During one action several Germans, when hit, toppled into a ditch on top of those who had killed them.

The enemy's southern attack on 10th June was equally unsuccessful. It was delivered by a German Grenadier battalion of the 346th Division, well-trained troops who when making their advance took full advantage of the cover from view afforded by the gliders. The 13th Battalion awaited the issue in silence, for their commanding officer, Peter Luard, had issued the order heard so often on the battlefields of Spain in the Peninsular War, 'Don't fire till you see the whites of their eyes.' It was meticulously obeyed, and the German Grenadiers were allowed to come to within fifty yards of two platoons of 'B' Company under Captain R. M. T. Kerr before they opened a devastating fusillade. It blew away the head of the attack, causing very severe casualties, and the rout was completed by an immediate counter-attack carried out by 'C' Company under

Major G. H. D. Ford. Those of the enemy who survived retreated to a small wood, where they were later on in the day counter-attacked. This was the first battle in which the three war-dogs, Alsatians, belonging to the 13th Battalion, took part. These dogs, trained to detect mines, had been dropped on D-day. One was soon missing, the second was wounded, but Bing, the third, remained with the battalion till the end of the war and won a medal. At this period of his career he was particularly useful in the Bois de Bavent.

The light infantrymen of the 7th Battalion had also engaged the Germans earlier in the day with medium machine-guns and mortars, much to the satisfaction of the gunners and their commanding officer. 'It was particularly pleasant,' wrote Pine-Coffin afterwards, 'that the mortars and the medium machine-gunners were able to engage this target at all, because theirs is one of the most thankless of all the parachutist's roles. Their weapons were heavy and complicated, and demanded considerable skill to operate and great physical strength and endurance to carry. Their own weight limits the amount of ammunition available, for both weapons and what they fire have to be carried on the back. It is a point of honour that the heavy-weapon platoons will keep up with the rest of the battalion wherever they go and at whatever speed. The men belonging to them are picked for their size and strength, but have to shew a deal of initiative as well, and it is no uncommon sight to see wheelbarrows or even perambulators being used for carrying their mortars.'

Having on the 8th, 9th and 10th June made very great efforts from the east to regain the whole Bréville ridge from which he had been in part driven, the enemy also attacked the two air landing battalions from the south. But though the Germans penetrated their positions here and there, they could achieve no decision and were eventually thrust back, their discomfiture being assisted by the guns of the 3rd Division, which were magnificently served throughout this day, and indeed every day.

The elements of the Air Landing Brigade which had sustained these fierce attacks most coolly and courageously were in due course relieved in the village of Hérouvillette by the 7th Battalion which, with the aid of tanks, had cleared the woods of Le Mariquet. Pine-Coffin kept 'A' Company in reserve to be used as a striking force when needed. 'C' Company was placed 'in a most imposing-looking mansion with stables, empty, and ample grounds including a training gallop'. It had been used by German engineers who had left much of their gear behind. 'C' Company, however, was more interested in the beer which was discovered in the cellars. Battalion headquarters was set up in a small house whose owner, 'an attractive woman', held her guests enthralled by her description of Rommel's visit to Hérouvillette and its neighbourhood a few weeks before the invasion. 'A red-faced, unhealthy looking man,' he had arrived with a fleet of twelve motor cars 'and numerous heel-clicking staff officers', and was chiefly remembered for the orders he had given for the erection of the poles to obstruct the landing of gliders. They were to be twenty feet high; some were to be crowned with mines, and the spaces between them were to be laced with strands of barbed wire. Both the German troops and the civilian population had found this order very unpalatable, for it had entailed much hard work which had been very far from completed when the 6th Airborne Division arrived. Rommel had also gathered together his officers in a field near Bréville from which a fine view of the plain below with Caen in the distance can be obtained. From this same field two months or more later, when Rommel was no more, Montgomery directed the final attack on Caen.

The 7th Battalion had not been in its new positions twenty-four hours when at 04.00 hours, just before dawn, the Germans sought to launch another attack, preceded by a heavy discharge of mortars and shells. This 'stonking' (a word in universal use in the British armies to denote a concentration of shell or mortar fire) did little harm, 'for everyone was in their slit trenches'. It ceased at dawn, and, though the enemy could be seen moving not far away in front of 'B' Company, no attack materialised. Pine-Coffin decided to stir up the hornet's nest, if nest it was, and at 08.00 hours drenched the wood with mortar and gunfire. This caused very great confusion, and the Germans, 'watched with great interest' by 'B' Company, ran in all directions. The German tanks seemed as undecided as their infantry, for they moved half-heartedly against 'C' Company until driven off by our artillery fire with the loss of two of their number.

It seemed to Pine-Coffin that the moment had now come for a counter-stroke, and for that purpose he decided to use Captain W. E. Parrish and 'A' Company. After 'an irritating period on the wireless' demanding that all artillery fire cease, Pine-Coffin ordered Parrish to clear the wood. He advanced against it, intending to pass in through gaps blown by shellfire in the high

179

wall that surrounded it. The first man to enter it was Lieutenant Ian MacDonald, who was immediately shot and subsequently died of his wounds. Changing his plan, Parrish then attacked across the open. He reached the wall and, running along it, presently climbed it, and with his men moved through the wood, finding no enemy. A few prisoners were captured, among them a company sergeant-major, who said that he was in command, and went on to explain 'that none of his officers had taken part in the attack but had done all the planning. He then volunteered his own personal opinion of his officers'.

The battalion remained several days at Hérouvillette in comparative peace, except for one grim moment when rocket-firing Typhoons of the Royal Air Force, mistaking their target, which was Ste Honorine La Chardonerette, further down the road, deluged them with rocket fire.

By then the tactics of the Germans—they belonged to the 346th and 711th Infantry Divisions and the 21st Panzer Division —were becoming clear to Gale. They were much the same as those which Rommel had successfully used in North Africa. 'The Germans,' says Gale in his book on the campaign,[1] 'believed in the regimental battle group form of attack as opposed to the divisional attack supported by co-ordinated massed artillery fire. Pursuing these tactics, the enemy had already delivered a whole series of attacks against the 6th Airborne Division, but none of them had been of sufficient strength to achieve a decisive result. He made lavish use of mortars and self-propelled guns, but did not appear to have registered any target, not even the bridges or the approaches to them. His policy seemed to be the drenching of a particular area where he believed the invaders had dug themselves in, with mortar fire, or fire from self-propelled guns. But he seemed to do so indiscriminately and in pursuit of no definite plan. Though this method made the Germans less effective, it did not make them less dangerous, and the parachute troops had very constantly to be on their guard.

On 7th June, for example, 'A' Company of the 12th Battalion, posted on high ground south of Le Bas de Ranville, was attacked by German tanks closely followed by about a hundred and fifty infantry. The fire of the tanks put the crew of the only anti-tank gun possessed by the company out of action and destroyed a section of one of the platoons. Private Hall, who had been

[1] *With the 6th Airborne Division in Normandy*, p. 95, by Lieutenant-General R. N. Gale, C.B., D.S.O., O.B.E., M.C., Sampson Low, London, 1948.

an anti-tank gunner before he became a parachutist, ran across the road to where the anti-tank gun was lying, loaded it and fired on the leading German tank. He scored a direct hit. The crew jumped out and were killed by rifle and machine-gun fire. Hall then repeated his action on the second and third tanks, after which the Germans, losing heart, retired. For this Hall was subsequently awarded the Military Medal, and his action undoubtedly saved the development of what would have been a difficult situation. Difficult, yes, but not fatal, for seven tanks and a hundred and fifty infantry, though they could have inflicted damage, could scarcely, even at that early stage within twenty-four hours of the landing, have been a decisive influence.

Such tactics taught the parachute troops one very useful lesson: the necessity of digging in as quickly as possible. They had learnt this in theory during the months of training at home, but a few bombs bursting close to them or against the boughs of trees—a favourite German trick—drove home the lesson with speed and precision.

What it was like to be caught in the open by mortar fire has been described by Captain W. F. Parrish. 'We left the bridge far behind,' he said. 'I was forward with Humble (a company clerk) when we heard the sixfold report of the Moaning Minnie. Six reports and the characteristic blood-chilling moan rising in intensity seemed to fill the sky and beat every sense out of me but the one for self-preservation. There was no doubt in my mind that the bombs were meant for us. I had heard of them, but this was the first time that I had encountered them. I threw myself down behind the cover of a tree with a slim trunk. As practical cover it was useless, but there was nothing else. The moan of the six bombs engulfed everything, even time, and when they landed I was incapable of rational thought. I was not hit then, but before the next salvo I heard, or thought I heard, Humble shouting to me that he was wounded. The next salvo followed, the same sequence, the same feelings, and this time they found me. A tremendous shock which was painless and seemed to be centred in no particular part of me. I blacked out and, it seemed, regained consciousness at once, for I began to run back. I do not know why I ran; I certainly was not governed by reason. . . . I lost my senses several times after that until I woke to hear Bob Keene's (Major Keene) voice . . . he insisted on giving me preference on the stretcher.'

So long as the Germans followed what Gale was convinced were bad tactics he had no real fear of the result, and informed

Lieutenant-General J. Crocker, D.S.O., M.C., commanding the 1st Corps, who visited him on the 9th, that he could hold the bridgehead, always provided that the German tactics did not change. The second reason for his confidence lay in the natural strength of the position in which he had placed his division. To the south he held a 'great crescent, the tips of which were Longueval and Hérouvillette'; in the centre was Ranville, apparently weak but defended by troops with 'long uninterrupted fields of fire' before them. If German infantry attacked here they would be subjected to fire from the east, west and north. Between Hérouvillette and Le Mariquet were wide enemy mine-fields which any attacking force would hesitate to negotiate. Much of the area of Troarn and Le Mesnil was covered with the Bois de Bavent, a thick and almost impenetrable wood, the home, among other game, of imported Japanese deer, by then only a dappled memory. Then came the ridge joining Le Mesnil to Le Plein. This, too, was heavily wooded, but—and here was the weak spot—there was the gap between the 3rd Parachute Brigade and the 1st Special Service Brigade, and in the midst of that gap, as has already been explained, stood Bréville, firmly in the hands of the enemy. Its mayor, Monsieur Magnenat, clearly bears a charmed life, for he was used by both sides to tell them the whereabouts of the other. The information he supplied to the Germans was 'grotesque, not accurate'.

Gale's third reason for confidence lay in the overwhelming superiority of the Allied Air Force. Leigh-Mallory's aircraft were here, there, and everywhere, their pilots scrutinising every yard of the battlefield, and those of the photographic reconnaissance unit taking picture after picture. These proved invaluable. 'I had . . .' says Gale, 'the most excellent photographs, always up to date, of the German defences on my front. From these we were able to mark out all his new works and his gun positions.'

On the night of 10th-11th June Gale received as reinforcements three battalions from the 5th Division. One, the 1st Battalion, the Black Watch, he immediately attached to Hill's brigade. The obvious place for it was in the gap at Bréville between the Commando Brigade and the 9th Battalion, and it was there that it was sent. On the next day, the 11th, it delivered an attack, with artillery support, on the ridge towards Bréville, but to no purpose. The Scotsmen lost heavily, failed to capture the village, and the survivors joined with the 9th Battalion and dug in. On the next day, the 12th, the Black Watch advanced again, were again severely mauled, and the enemy's counter-attack almost succeeded. The tanks by which it was supported were driven off at the last moment by Regimental Sergeant-Major Cunningham and Company Sergeant-Major Beckwith, who brought an anti-tank gun into close action. By now the situation was grave. 'I had very few troops,' said Otway, commanding the 9th Battalion, afterwards, 'and the Germans were attacking me on all sides. All my reserves, such as they were, were committed, and I had nothing for a counter-attack. I sent an S O S to James Hill, who arrived personally, leading a company of Canadians, and put things right. Just before he arrived, my "A" Company was engaged in hand-to-hand fighting with the Germans in our own slit trenches—a close call, but we saw them off. We were also shelled heavily, and our regimental aid post was completely overflowing with wounded of all sorts. In fact the place was a shambles.'

The arrival of the Canadian parachutists under the brigadier just sufficed to restore the situation; but it remained very dangerous.

Hand-to-hand fighting had been the order of the day for four days and neither side would give way. It was during this period that on 10th June Captain the Honourable C. P. Greenway stood on a bank in full view of the enemy and directed through a wire-less chain the six-inch guns of H.M.S. *Arethusa* on to the Château St. Côme only four hundred yards distant. A German battalion commander captured that day bemoaned the fearful losses inflicted upon his and other units by the 3rd Parachute Brigade. His own battalion had been wiped out and two more decimated in their counter-attack on Ranville. Private Millward remained in action against a German tank and its escort of infantry after all round him had been killed. Sergeant Frith and his section competed against all comers in shooting down Germans. By the 12th June their score was forty, 'each confirmed by a corpse'. Nor was the lighter side absent. Lance-Corporal Wilson served tea 'complete on tray with teapot and cups' to Brigadier Hill in the midst of heavy shelling. 'It was a real soldier's battle.'

It did not take Gale long to realise that his whole front depended on dealing successfully with the Bréville gap to which the enemy were so obstinately clinging.

To do so his only reserve was the 12th Battalion, The Para-chute Regiment, 'sadly under strength, but a gallant, hard-fighting unit'. To these he added a company of 12th Devons, and a squadron of Sherman tanks belonging to the 13th/18th Hussars.

Four field regiments of the Royal Artillery and one medium regiment provided covering fire, and fifty men of the 22nd Independent Parachute Company stood by to repel any enemy counter-stroke. Looked at dispassionately, the task for this small force—the 12th Battalion numbered no more than three hundred men—seemed too formidable. They would be doomed to failure with heavy losses, for they would certainly not abandon the enterprise lightly. One factor, however, clearly perceived by Gale, was in their favour. The Germans had now been fighting very hard indeed for rather more than three days, and this particular part of the front was held by the 346th German Infantry Division, which, far from up to strength before the invasion, had by now suffered severely. True, they still had the initiative, but even this advantage might be turned against them. Having fought hard all day and gained what was, for the moment at least, the upper hand, they would not, Gale considered, expect to be attacked in strength late in the evening. Rather would the British reaction come in the orthodox manner at first light on the following morning. Gale decided that the best chance of victory was to attack them while they were still exhausted by the actions they had fought during the previous twelve hours. The parachute soldiers were also tired, but could be relied upon to make this final effort.

It was 18.00 hours on 12th June when Gale reached his decision, and an hour later he issued orders that the attack was to be launched at 22.00 hours. Up to then all attempts to capture Bréville had been made from the south. 'This attack was to go in from the west, the start line being the outer edge of Amfréville.' Colonel R. G. Parker, Deputy Brigade Commander of the 6th Air Landing Brigade, came up to watch the assault by the 12th Battalion he had once commanded. Joining its commanding officer, Lieutenant-Colonel A. P. Johnson, he discussed the general situation and listened to the orders given. In brief, these were that 'C' Company of the 12th Battalion was to seize the first objective, the cross-roads at Bréville. 'D' Company of the 12th Devons were to follow in their footsteps and swing left after reaching the village. 'A' Company were to pass through 'C' Company and secure the south-eastern part of Bréville, and 'B' Company would by that time have halted to form the reserve. The start line of the attack was a hedge forming the south-east boundary of Amfréville. Between this and the outskirts of Bréville was about four hundred yards of open country. To cover the infantry one troop of tanks was to move down the right flank and destroy, or put out of action, an enemy strong point, established in what was known as the 'White House' some two hundred yards from the village. The remainder of the tanks were to move on the left flank.

Having heard these orders, Parker left battalion headquarters and moved a little up the road towards Bréville, 'so that I could cheer the lads on as they went up to the start line'. The men themselves had been concentrated in the Baroque church of Amfréville, 'a large solid building standing in the midst of the village', says Captain Sim. 'The men sat in the pews talking in subdued whispers and sucking sweets, and gazing at the gaily painted effigies of saints—St. Martin and St. Sebastian—and the elaborate gilded cross on the altar.' The order to advance arrived in due course and the men quitted the church, to find the Reverend J. O. Jenkins, C.F., their chaplain, standing on its steps with copies of the divisional paper called *Pegasus Goes To It*, which were welcome. Parker had been warned that it was the German custom to shell Amfréville and the neighbourhood about this time of the evening. True enough, at 21.45 hours, a quarter of an hour before the attack was due to begin, a very heavy weight of shells began to fall on the village. This at first did not astonish Parker until he realised that it was our own guns putting down a preliminary barrage but—hideous thought —in the wrong place.

Almost at once Parker was hit in the hand and also felt a thump on his chest. On his way to battalion headquarters he slipped into a first-aid post belonging to No. 4 Commando, 'and asked an officer to put a field dressing on my hand, as I could not reach my own. He did so very quickly. I asked him to put his hand inside my open smock and see if there was any blood. When he found none I was delighted, and dashed off across country to the start line'.

Those few minutes at the dressing station not only saved Colonel Parker's life but were indirectly the cause of victory. Had he gone immediately to battalion headquarters he would in all probability have been killed or badly wounded ; for when he eventually reached them he found Lieutenant-Colonel Johnson dead (he had been awarded an immediate admission to the Distinguished Service Order only the day before), together with Major J. B. Bampfylde, commanding the company of the 12th Devons, and Brigadier H. K. M. Kindersley and Lord Lovat seriously wounded. These and other casualties had been caused by our own guns. Such errors are inevitable in warfare, but on this occasion they were particularly expensive. Parachute troops could ill afford to lose a man like Johnson, and the same was true of the Air Landing Brigade, now deprived of its brigadier, and the 1st Special Service Brigade, who had lost the indomitable Lovat.

Parker saw at once what he must do. He ran forward and took command once more of his old battalion. 'The light was failing now,' runs his account, 'and our tanks were moving forward and firing with all their weapons, making a barrier of fire in front of us. I had on two occasions to signal to the men to stop in order to keep them back from it. I felt sure that some of our men must have reached the village and prayed that they might survive.' They had, and they did. By now night had fallen, but the battlefield was lit by the burning houses of Bréville, only slightly brighter than the fires that burned in Amfréville and Le Plein close by. In flame and fire the 12th Battalion moved forward. 'C' Company, as Parker had feared, had suffered very grievously. So had 'D' Company of the 12th Devons. Only small isolated bodies of men from these two companies had reached the village, there to kill numbers of the garrison. They were, however, too few to capture it.

Parker advanced behind the leading tank searching for any survivors of 'B' and 'C' Companies. At first he found no one except a forward observation officer whom he ordered to bring defensive fire down on the east side of Bréville so as to prevent a German counter-attack from materialising. While giving these orders Parker moved to a large house with a walled garden, and as he passed through its gates shells began to fall all round him. 'I sheltered,' says he, 'against the garden wall, with one eye on my watch and the other on the tank by the garden gate. It was a fascinating sight ; as our shells burst near it, it seemed to recoil, shake itself, and then recover its equilibrium.' Pushing still further forward, Parker came across 'B' Company, 'somewhat shaken, but unscathed.' He told them to remain where they were for the moment. He then went back to battalion headquarters to find that Major Rogers, commanding 'B' Company, had been killed. Parker then moved to the church, which was burning fiercely, and had time to see 'in the ruddy glow of the flames a party of screaming women and children rushing in frenzy towards Ranville, their hair streaming in the wind'.

The shells which fell in and near the walled garden had been fired partly by our own guns and partly by those of the Germans. Major E. J. Warren, the officer commanding the

Support Company of the Devons, which had not been committed to the action, happened to be on the scene. Having helped 'a couple of the wounded who needed their morphia tablets', he reached the fatal hedge near which he found the bodies of Johnson, Bampfylde and others. Warren at once collected about a dozen of 'D' Company of the Devons and set off in the failing light towards Bréville. 'Boches were surrendering as we went forward,' he records, 'and now and again a dim figure got up and ran away into the gathering dusk. . . . It was soon quite dark except for the weird light given by the burning houses and the church.' He presently arrived at the square in the middle of the village, where he found 'a sergeant and about forty men of "B" Company, 12th Battalion'. With these he began to organise the defence of the captured position, when once more our own guns deluged Bréville with fire and caused further casualties. Warren and the others spent the rest of the night 'in digging furiously and patrolling'.

Meanwhile 'A' Company, under Captain P. C. Bernhard, had gone into action. Their commander remembered afterwards 'noticing what a pretty pattern the enemy machine-gun tracer bullets made as they passed overhead'. Bernhard was himself soon wounded, but called upon Sergeant Warcup of 'C' Company to help him forward, for he was determined to remain with his men until the objective was taken. Warcup's method of assisting Bernhard was 'to sling me over his back in a fireman's lift and start running forward. After about twenty-five yards of this I asked him to put me down as it was difficult to appreciate the situation in my present position'. Warcup did so and went back to take charge of 'C' Company, which by then had lost all its officers. Bernhard eventually arrived at the château of Bréville, which was his company's objective. They were just short of it and were about to clear it of the enemy when two white Very lights soared into the night. Bernhard was delighted to see them, for they were the success signal and shewed that Bréville was in our hands. Unfortunately they were also a German signal for mortar fire. This at once fell heavily. Bernhard was again hit ; he was put into a ditch by Corporal Rhind, who happened to be standing next to him and who 'at once did all the necessary first-aid, cheerfully remarking that it was a good job he was a butcher in private life'.

Bernhard was then taken back to the regimental aid post, meeting Parker and Company Sergeant-Major McWhinnie on the way. 'The arrival of our old commanding officer,' he noted, 'heartened us all. He always turned up when he was most needed.' Parker organised the defence of what was now the major part of the village, and there remained until he 'was quite convinced that the Germans were not going to counter-attack before dawn'. They were indeed in no position to do so. Their stubborn defence was the last bolt in their quiver. It had failed, and what was left of them withdrew or surrendered, save for a few snipers, who as usual sold their lives dearly. One of them was discovered by a mopping-up party lying dead in bed, with above his head a notice written in English pinned to the wall with his knife: 'Even if we fight alone England must fall.'

The attack at Bréville, though made at high cost, was a complete success. The 12th Battalion lost eight officers and one hundred and thirty-three other ranks, nearly half its remaining strength. 'D' Company, 12th Devons, besides losing their company commander, lost some thirty-five killed or wounded. But the Bréville gap had been closed, and the enemy never made any attempt to reopen it. The battle in that small battered village achieved results 'of the greatest importance to the whole Normandy campaign'.

By now the 6th Airborne Division had been in close continuous action for six days and nights. Like their comrades of the green beret, they were assault troops trained for the performance of special tasks. They had little or no transport, no heavy weapons and not much divisional artillery of their own. Generally speaking, neither parachute nor commando troops should be kept in action for more than forty-eight hours before the arrival of the main forces, for that period is the maximum time during which the ammunition they carry with them may be expected to last. True they had joined hands with the main invasion forces within twelve hours. But they had still to remain in action. For the division there was no relief. Here in the pleasant fields of Normandy 'with their interminable cider apple orchards', their well-found farms, whose owners were ready at all times to provide the comfort of Calvados, their lofty woods and rich meadows, it was to stay until 17th August, when the pursuit of the enemy began.

Throughout that period, and during the next when they were following hard on the heels of a morose and defeated foe, a number—sometimes all—of their units were in action. In not being withdrawn and being prepared for future airborne landings they had the same experience as the 1st Parachute Brigade in North Africa. At the end of 1942 and the beginning of 1943, to keep specially trained troops for weeks and months fighting as infantry of the Line was probably inevitable, for at that time trained men were few, and every rifle and bayonet had to be used as often as possible. Eighteen months later, when Operation 'Bolero' had brought thousands upon thousands of American troops to Britain, North Africa and Italy, all of them lavishly equipped, it was still necessary for the Parachute Regiment, the air landing battalions and the commandos to hold the line for many critical days. They made no complaint. Indeed the voice of protest would have been heard only had they been withdrawn back into the world of waiting and training from which they had escaped. Now at last they were at close grips with the enemy and they had not the least desire to be in any other position. Moreover, they were as proud of their ability to wage war in the same manner as their comrades in the infantry as they were of the qualifications which enabled them to fight with equal skill and assurance a less conventional type of battle.

The parachute troops stayed in Normandy, solving their own problems of administration, resting when they could 'in a few meadows near the bridges they had captured'. True to the motto Gale gave them, they continued at all times, both by night and by day, to 'Go to it'.

Static Warfare

FROM 14th June until 16th August 1944 the 6th Airborne Division spent their days consolidating and conducting what the Army calls static warfare. The term means that the troops do not move their positions except to patrol or to make local counter-attacks. The 6th Airborne, together with the 1st and 4th Special Service Brigades composed of commando troops, were confined to the left flank of the bridgehead from the area round Sallenelles and Bréville to about three miles north-west of Troarn. They formed a vital part of the pivot upon which the Allied armies were presently to turn and the Americans, far out on the right flank, to make that sweep into France which was utterly to overthrow the enemy, and drive him back ultimately almost to the borders of his own country. This, however, was still in the future, and indeed the very role of the division was hidden from it in those wet June days when heavy rain clouds rolled over the bridgehead and rare patches of blue sky shewed the Allied air forces serene and triumphant, for ever on the wing above it.

Static, though no doubt the correct military term, is hardly the word to use when describing the activities of the division during the next two months. They can be summed up in a single word: patrolling. It was by this means that that aggressive spirit, that determination to inflict the greatest possible hurt on the enemy, was best displayed. As the days went by the skill acquired grew greater and greater.

The arrival in due course of the 51st Highland Division as a reinforcement, not as a relief, was welcome. The Parachute Regiment was also reinforced by some hundred officers and men who, welcome though they were, were found to have had no parachute training. They proved, however, very stout-hearted, and in due course four-fifths of them volunteered for parachute duties and remained with the regiment for the rest of the war.

Once the battle of Bréville was over and the area occupied by the division more or less defined, all units at once resumed the task of patrolling begun as soon as they had landed. It was most frequent and most difficult in that thick forest, the Bois de Bavent. 'It was,' says Major R. A. Keene, 'a most unpleasant place and might well have been confused with a mild type of jungle,' for there was a dense profusion of undergrowth and it was impossible to see more than a few yards in any direction, except down a ride; this impression is amply confirmed by the evidence of many other witnesses who passed their nights, and not a few of their days, probing its silent and far from friendly depths. Here, amid the loud hum of mosquitoes, occurred many encounters with an enemy engaged in similar pursuits. In the task of patrolling the 7th Battalion was greatly assisted by a local poacher, one Barrière by name, who knew the utmost intricacies of the wood. 'This gaining of patrol ascendancy,' runs the battalion's history, 'was an interesting game, and was tackled systematically with great enthusiasm by all concerned. The intelligence section under the indefatigable Lieutenant H. H. Mills worked literally day and night, and prepared a large-scale map of the whole battalion area. The poacher Barrière was found very useful in this task. Known features were given code names for easy reference; many of them were unprintable.' To assist in the preparation of this all-important map the earlier patrols were ordered to bring back all the topographical informa-

or two may be mentioned: there was the raid carried out by seven members of the 22nd Independent Parachute Company under the command of Lieutenant de Latour in which, aided by smoke, they penetrated deeply into the German positions in the Bois de Bavent and seized prisoners without finding it necessary to fire a shot. On the way back, however, fire was opened and de Latour mortally wounded. With his death the 22nd Independent Parachute Company lost its last surviving officer.

There was the second attack by 'B' Company of the 7th Battalion on Bob's Farm, which took place on 10th July in the early afternoon and was not altogether successful. The withdrawal was hard to carry out because of heavy mortaring and fire from several German machine-gunners. They were dealt with by Sergeant Lucas, who climbed up the bank of the gully leading to the position and engaged them with a Bren gun. While he was doing so the company slipped away. For this Lucas received a bar to the Military Medal he had won on D-day. The battalion was disappointed at the results of this operation, but not so the divisional commander. Thanks to this raid, he said, he was now certain that the enemy intended to hold on to this area for as long and as tightly as he could.

Corporal Wilson and Private Butterwood of 'C' Company of the 7th Battalion invariably went out together on expeditions into the Bois de Bavent of which the object was, if possible, to capture a German. One day Butterwood was not available and Corporal Wilson went alone. 'C' Company and the foremost German formation were but a hundred yards apart, and the enemy had felled a large and leafy tree so that it lay across the lane leading to their position, and this gave them cover from observation. To pass it, Wilson slung his Sten gun across his back, and had just slipped over it recumbent trunk, when two German soldiers appeared moving along the lane towards him. Wilson, as he said at the time, was much taken aback. So, too, were the Germans, for they had also slung their weapons, a Schmeisser machine-carbine and a rifle, across their backs. To unsling a weapon, cock and fire it, takes time, and neither side felt quite certain that they would be able to perform this evolution faster than the other. Accordingly 'each side indulged in a dumb charade', Wilson beckoning the Germans to come and surrender, the Germans shaking their heads and beckoning to Wilson to come and do likewise. This wordless argument ended by one of the enemy bolting. 'This broke the tension and the meeting dispersed hurriedly.'

in the art of
other occupations of that nature. O
hit by anti-aircraft fire fell upon two of its hoa
them and killed twenty-two of the occupants.

After a certain time a divisional cemetery was established close to the church at Ranville whose high detached tower was a landmark 'rising above the hubbub of battle'. The division engineers designed and made a fine simple cross, and here w buried many of those who had fallen on D-day and i

supply a daily
food, ammuniti
Fortunately the
a certain quantit

When not aiding, the parachute troops remained in their lines and soon evolved a daily routine which was kept as simple as possible. 'Stand to' was at first light, and during it the officers made a tour of the positions. Then came breakfast, and during the next two hours every man of every battalion was required to shave and to clean himself and his weapons. At midday, after a meal, all, save the sentries, slept. Tea was between five and six, and the men were able to relax somewhat and even move about, provided they did not go far, and that the proper number of sentries had been posted and alert. At the close of day a hot drink and biscuits or chocolate were issued, and with last light came 'Stand to' again with another inspection by the officers.

Such was life in the line, but as soon as it was realised that the division was likely to remain in the area for some time, Gale organised a rest centre to which battalions could be sent a few days at a time. It was as far away from the enemy as it could be, but that was not very far, and was situated close to the Orne bridges, which, since they were the objects of attention by night from the Luftwaffe, made it 'a bit too noisy especially at night, to be really restful. . . . No one did very much beyond changing their clothes and lazing about, perhaps writing a few letters; but in a few days all feeling of fatigue had worn off'. At the end of July the rest centre was shifted to the sea front just outside Ouistreham. Here ten officers and about a hundred men could relax from their labours for four or five days in a row 'of small seaside detached houses facing the beach . . . unharmed, dry and comfortable'. In these dwellings some of those resting received the visits of Mr. Basil Dean of E.N.S.A. and others of a Russian Admiral and his staff. Here, too, was the divisional school for keeping officers and non-commissioned officers up to the mark in the art of leading a patrol, detecting booby traps, sniping and of that nature. One night a German bomber houses, demolished the war. When the first invaders had arrived not a few of its inhabitants were inclined to treat them with reserve and even suspicion. The main reason for so doing, as was soon discovered, was that the French had been told by the Germans that the Allies, if they got ashore, would assuredly be swept back into the sea within a week, after which all who had attempted to help them would pay the inevitable penalty. Until, therefore, it became clear to the farmers in their stout dwellings ringed with apple trees, and to the burghers of Bayeux, Isigny and the other little towns, that these men in khaki were there to stay, relations were not particularly cordial. Such an attitude—it changed the moment it became obvious that when they moved they would go forward and not back—was not unnatural; nor should it be forgotten that the people of Normandy had been occupied for four long years, and were well aware from bitter experience of the extensive activities of the Gestapo. Once their confidence was won, they proved most friendly and eager to help, even grand-mère, the old lady who lived in a house in Hérouvillette and utterly refused to seek shelter in the slit trench in the garden, though the Germans frequently brought mortar fire down upon her house. One night, however, the best part of the roof was removed by a shell. Major Keene, who was in the house with his batman, hastened to quit it. 'To do so we had to pass through grandmère's apartment, and to his complete horror my batman, Private Butler, found the old bird in his arms dressed in her night-dress, 1918 model, and yelling blue murder.' Nor did his opinion of the situation improve when he was ordered to take her to shelter in the garden.

Throughout this stay of the division of more than two months in Normandy one problem was ever at the elbow of its commander. Like the commandos fighting side by side the parachute troops had little administrative se two or 'jettison drop'. This was a scheme whereby the tug aircraft flying in the gliders on the evening of D-day were also to carry containers loaded with stores and drop them. The scheme was fairly successful, and by the end of D-day the Royal Army Service Corps of the 6th Airborne Division had established a dump with the contents of what had been collected.

So life continued in the bridgehead beyond the Orne until every battalion of the Parachute Regiment had occupied each sector of the front at least once, and most of them several times. If the Bois de Bavent was the most mysterious and exciting part of the line, the sector near Hauger was the least attractive. Here was another wood to which the Germans used to crawl through the long grass and then fling hand grenades until the inevitable retaliation gave them pause. Worse than the Germans were the mosquitoes, of which there were enormous numbers, so many in fact that it was 'impossible to eat or talk without swallowing several of them'.

But whatever the situation of whatever battalion, whether it was in slit trenches round the ruined Château St. Côme with its dead and stinking thoroughbreds, or on patrol in the park of the Château of Benouville where Madame Vion dispensed glasses of vintage port to thirsty and appreciative officers, whether in the sinister Bois de Bavent, or the shattered village of Bréville, the effect on officers and men was the same. With every day that passed they knew themselves to be better soldiers. For they had exchanged training in the art of warfare for the practice of it and were daily able to realise how necessary it had been to acquire the first in order to become expert in the second.

Now after more than two months they were about to have their reward.

subsequent fighting. The i re keeping the graves bright wit It took them some time t troops. Normandy, save for

G

and Mechanical Engineers, who scrutinised with care all vehicles and instruments. It was obvious that something was in the wind. These visits gave rise to the usual crop of rumours, of which the most popular and least accurate was that the division was going home; in fact it was about to pursue the tenacious enemy with which it had been at grips for more than two months. By 7th August Gale had received instructions from the 1st Corps to plan the advance of his division in the event of a German withdrawal. The corps commander did not expect the division to pursue the enemy very hotly, for he was well aware that its transport was woefully inadequate, that it lacked artillery, and, above all, bridging materials, both indispensable for a rapid pursuit. Gale however, had other views, and was determined to exploit to the full 'that wealth of pent-up energy' which he knew existed in his command as the result of more than two months' defensive fighting. This, thanks in great part to the fine marching qualities of the Parachute Regiment, he was able to do.

The plan was for the 1st Canadian Army to burst from the bridgehead, march south-east upon Falaise, and then swing eastwards towards the Seine. To maintain unceasing pressure on the enemy's right flank was to be the task of the 6th Airborne Division. Such pressure would, it was hoped, increase the speed of the Canadians' advance, and were the division to reach the Seine quickly large numbers of Germans would be cut off and captured. In addition to the 6th Airborne Division, Gale now had with him the 1st and 4th Special Service Brigades, a brigade of Belgians and one of Dutch troops. He was determined to play his part as fully as he could.

The main difficulty of the advance to the Seine, apart from shortage of transport and the opposition that the enemy might put up, lay in the nature of the ground to be covered. It was traversed by at least three rivers, each of them flooded, and since they were near their journey's end, wide, deep and sometimes tidal. There were two main roads running to the Seine, one inland through Troarn, Dozulé, Pont l'Evêque, Beuzeville and Pont Audemer; the other following the sea coast through Cabourg, Trouville and Honfleur. Both traversed a rolling land, its many hills covered with woods, between which lay fields of pasture divided each from each by thick hedges. The rivers were the Dives, bordered by marshes, the derelict Dives Canal running beside it, with, in the background, a range of hills overlooking the whole waterlogged plain; the River Touques and the River Risle, both of which flowed through deep-cut valleys. The distance from Troarn to the Seine was thirty-five miles as the crow flies, and forty-five by road. Every yard of the country could easily be defended, and was ideal for fighting a series of delaying actions. These were certainly to be expected, at least at the outset, from an enemy who, though heavily defeated, was still fighting vigorously, and might well continue to do so to the end. Whether he would or not, Gale very rightly assumed that opposition would be stubborn.

Of the two possible ways to the Seine, he chose to take the bulk of his forces along the inland road through Troarn to Pont Audemer, though this would entail crossing a valley about 8,000 yards wide full of streams and swamps, with a main water obstacle, a double river, the Dives and its Canal, running at right angles across the path of the advance. His chief concern was artillery support, or rather its lack. 'I had,' he records, 'a most fantastic assortment of stuff.' This was made up of the Light Regiment belonging to the 6th Airborne Division carried originally to action in gliders, two field regiments, a battery of medium guns, and a heavy anti-aircraft regiment transformed for the moment into field artillery. The Belgian Brigade possessed one battery of twenty-five-pounders. For engineers Gale had the two parachute squadrons, the 3rd and the 591st.

The first position which the enemy would certainly hold was the high ground north and south of the village of Dozulé. Gale decided that the 3rd Parachute Brigade should lead the advance, seize Bures, cross the Dives, and establish itself in the island beyond formed by the ground between the Dives and the Canal, and then pursue the enemy as far as the Canal west of Dozulé. The 5th Parachute Brigade was to move into the island in immediate support.

At 03.00 hours on 17th August Hill's 3rd Parachute Brigade began to move forward, and by dawn the whole division was in motion towards a country which 'seemed to be covered with rivers, and all of these ran across the line of the advance'. In the circumstances the code name for the operation 'Paddle' seemed peculiarly appropriate. By 07.00 hours the 8th and 9th Battalions had occupied Bures, finding no opposition, and an hour later the 1st Canadian Parachute Battalion began to sweep through the Bois de Bavent. Here, too, the enemy had withdrawn, but he had been careful to leave behind him much evidence of his presence in the form of mines and booby traps and these cost the battalion ten casualties.

The bridge at Bures, it will be remembered, had been blown up on D-day, and the Germans had not been able to repair it.

It was not, therefore, till late in the afternoon that the 3rd Parachute Squadron, Royal Engineers, had finished constructing a passable route. At nightfall the brigade was across the Dives and pushing ahead till it halted at 21.00 hours. By then the 1st Canadian Parachute Battalion, following the railway line north-east from Bures, was in contact with the enemy at Plain-Lugan. The 8th Battalion was in front of Goustranville which it secured only after heavy fighting, and the 9th Battalion in reserve at brigade headquarters.

On the next day the most serious opposition was met with beyond Goustranville on the Dives canal and railway bridges and at the Dozulé Railway Station.

The attack began at 22.00 hours, the leading troops being the 1st Canadian Parachute Battalion, with orders to seize the four bridges across the canal, of which the most northerly was the railway bridge. In thirty-five minutes 'C' Company had seized that bridge, while the southernmost fell into the hands of 'A' Company, who renamed it Canada bridge. By midnight the other two bridges were also in the hands of the Canadians who had by then taken one hundred and fifty prisoners, and 'successfully liquidated two enemy companies in well-fortified positions'. The 9th Battalion then moved through the Canadians *en route* for Dozulé Railway Station. They presently reached a blown bridge. The canal was found, however, to be not more than four feet deep, and the battalion waded across. For some of them, such as their commanding officer, Lieutenant-Colonel N. Crookenden, who had relieved Terence Otway, and 'an excellent sergeant named Murphy', both of whom were short of stature, the river proved a substantial obstacle. In parts it was deeper than four feet, and at one moment all that could be seen of Sergeant Murphy was the top of his helmet and 'a series of bubbles'. Immediately in front of him another series, but without a steel helmet beside it, shewed that the commanding officer too was totally submerged.

By 01.00 hours on the 19th, at the cost of one casualty, Sergeant Frith, shot through the head as he led the advance, the battalion had reached the outskirts of the village, and, having consolidated, 'awaited the dawn and the sun to dry us'. With their welcome arrival came an unwelcome shower of enemy shells which, not considered serious at first, soon, as they increased in number and ferocity, began to cause casualties. The battalion had had no time to dig in, and the Germans, being on the high ground near Dozulé, were able to give the 9th no peace.

By 11.00 hours fifty-four men had been killed or wounded, and the regimental aid post, set up in a barn a few fields in the rear of the position, had been repeatedly hit. 'Any movement near it . . . brought down a shower of shells.' It was here that 'Lulu' Bell, described as 'a very excellent Irish soldier', and one of the only two jeep drivers in the battalion, distinguished himself. Despite the shelling, he brought up food and ammunition, and continued to do so even after a large hole had been pierced in his jeep, and a piece of the steering wheel carried away, together with a large slice from his hand. Binding up his wound with a handkerchief 'which he had obviously used to wipe the oil from his sump dip-stick, he set about issuing the haversack rations he had brought forward'.

Meanwhile, at 04.00 hours Poett had taken his brigade across the canal by the Canada bridge to the railway line, and then forward against the village of Putot-en-Auge. The 13th Battalion was to advance on the left of 12th and the 7th to pass through the 13th. The operations were of the greatest difficulty and danger, for the enemy were well-posted and obviously prepared to give a good account of themselves. 'In theory the brigade was tackling the impossible, and nothing but muddle could possibly result. In practice, however, no one even considered failure and the ghastly possibilities of muddles in the night with battalions shooting each other up.'

Muddles, or, more accurately, unforeseen difficulties, certainly occurred. The 13th Battalion, for example, when they reached the broken railway bridge over the Dives Canal, found that the level of the water had risen and that what had been passable by the 9th Battalion some hours before was no longer practicable. They had, therefore, to be switched to another bridge. The 7th Battalion found the advance constantly held up by 'impenetrable hedges' which made detours necessary. The enemy was very much on the '*qui vive*', and flares constantly drenched with light the country over which the parachute troops were moving. The Germans also put frequent bursts of machine-gun fire, directed on fixed lines, at all the most likely places through or over which an attacker would be likely to pass. 'They made, however, their usual mistake, and used tracer ammunition so that the line of the gun could easily be seen and the area avoided.' These obstacles so delayed the 7th Battalion that it was an hour late in crossing its start line, the railway.

Dawn was in the sky when it began to move, its commanding officer much troubled by the map, which was here 'completely at fault and shewed a track leading from the station in exactly the direction required'. The track turned out to be no track at all but a hedge, and 'B' Company, under Captain Braithwaite, now recovered from injuries sustained when he dropped on D-day, led the advance up it. As the leading platoon under Lieutenant Thomas, also recovered from wounds, moved forward, a machine-gun opened fire, and Thomas fell once more, seriously wounded. 'B' Company was pinned down with the light growing steadily stronger and stronger, while the rest of the battalion behind were hustling as fast as possible across the railway line, which as soon as full day came 'was likely to become a most unhealthy area'. The effect of the halt and the hustling was to crowd the three rifle companies into a small space where they could ill resist the counter-attack which appeared imminent. Moreover, the 12th Battalion on their right had also encountered the hedgerows and other difficulties, and were only beginning to cross the railway line. At least half an hour would pass before they could attack the village.

What followed next is an admirable illustration of the high qualities of the parachute troops. While 'A' and 'C' Companies remained beside the hedge, 'B' Company sought to find the machine-gun of which the fire was proving so deadly. The section detailed to do so found instead 'a small German detachment with a very business-like dual-purpose gun mounted on wheels', and in a position where its fire could have annihilated any troops moving up the hedge. Fortunately the gun crew were not very alert and did not open fire.

Just at the capture of the gun was reported, all three company commanders informed battalion headquarters almost simultaneously that troops in extended order were advancing across the next field to the left, straight in their direction. Pine-Coffin and his officers assumed that these figures seen dimly in the grey light of dawn belonged to the 13th Battalion, who, it will be remembered, were to pass through at one point and maintain the advance. As the line of men drew nearer, however, it was seen to be made up of Germans. Instantly alert, the 7th Battalion faced round and awaited the enemy. Thus, by one of the chances of war, 'the unfortunate position in which the battalion had found itself was instantly converted . . . into one of unparalleled advantage. The best part of three rifle companies were lining the hedgerow, completely screened from the enemy. The Germans came on steadily like living targets moving up the range, and quite obviously had no idea what was in front of them. It was a dream target almost too good to believe, but at the same time too much like murder to be seized at once'.

Pine-Coffin was determined to capture this body of the enemy if he could. A Bren gun was moved out to a flank to cover them, and Lieutenant Mills, who spoke fluent German, was ordered to wait until the enemy was twenty-five yards from the hedge and then to order them to lay down their arms. 'When he first shouted to them their consternation was amusing to watch. They were taken completely by surprise, and much pointing and gesticulation occurred . . . this absurd situation lasted perhaps thirty seconds. It was ended by one of the Germans who did a very stupid thing. He lay down and opened fire at the hedgerow with a machine-gun.' Inevitably it was returned and 'A' Company opened a devastating fusillade which caused great execution. Within a quarter of an hour the Germans were either dead or busy surrendering. Only three escaped in the morning mist. After this there was no further trouble, and the 7th and 12th Battalions occupied Putot-en-Auge and the ground on the left by 08.45 hours on 19th August and took one hundred and twenty prisoners.

It was now the turn of the 13th Battalion, which had found a way across the canal and was coming up to play its part in the fight. Its objective was a prominent feature known, a trifle ominously perhaps, as Hill 13. It lay just beyond the village. The battalion had waited three hours in the open under direct fire before crossing a thousand yards of bare country. This it did at the double and lost only six men. It then made for the hill. The German garrison remained quiet just beyond its crest. Led by Major R. M. Tarrant, M.C., 'A' and 'B' Companies climbed the hill. On reaching the top they were immediately and most resolutely attacked by Russian troops under German non-commissioned officers at a moment when the men, being out of breath by reason of the steep ascent, were disorganised and incapable of withstanding a vigorous assault. "A' Company held the attack but Tarrant was mortally wounded, and 'C' Company's flanking attack made no progress. Poett therefore broke off the action and ordered the battalion to remain where it was on a line just short of the hill, which was captured by commandos in a night attack of 19th-20th August.

Apart from this setback, the battle of Putot-en-Auge had been very successful. A complicated night attack, carried out by two brigades over a number of formidable obstacles against a well-posted enemy, had driven him from all but one position with a loss of two 75-mm. guns, four 20-mm., six mortars and a very large number of machine-guns. Prisoners numbered one hundred and sixty, of whom a hundred and twenty were unwounded. The parachute troops were still in great heart, despite the fact that they had had no sleep for forty-eight hours.

At 07.00 hours on 21st August the division, with the 3rd Parachute Brigade in the van, resumed the advance through Dozulé. That day the 8th Battalion captured Annebault after a stiff fight, and after dark the 5th Parachute Brigade arrived and passed through the 3rd to reach the River Touques at Pont l'Evêque by midday on 22nd August. Pont l'Evêque is a straggling town built on both banks, and the river which flows through it runs in two channels about two hundred yards apart. Along the eastern channel is a railway carried on an embankment. Poett ordered Luard and the 13th Battalion to secure a bridgehead across both arms of the river, while the 12th Battalion under Lieutenant-Colonel N. G. Stockwell, who had taken the place of Lieutenant-Colonel W. A. B. Harris, M.C., wounded a short while before, were to seize the railway embankment and the dominating spur of St. Julien, south of the town. There were two bridges, one across each channel, and the Germans blew them as the 13th Battalion reached them.

In mid-afternoon, Stockwell led his Yorkshiremen on a one-company front, under cover of thick smoke laid by two regiments of field artillery, towards his objectives. At first all seemed well: protected by the smoke 'A' Company, under Captain J. A. S. Baker, advanced across a thousand yards of open ground towards two fords under the guidance of a Frenchman. Unfortunately they missed the first ford and a direct hit on the wireless set made the sending of messages impossible. Baker and eight men, however, swam the river and drove the enemy from the railway embankment. Here they held on until, with only six rounds of pistol ammunition left, they had to withdraw. 'B' company, coming to their support, was pinned down by machine-gun fire and Lieutenant Bercot killed at the head of his men when very near the river.

From 17.00 hours onwards until dark the battalion went through a very unpleasant time. Two companies were cut off by fire. No more smoke from the artillery was available to help them and so they hung grimly on, mostly up to their waists in water.

It was impossible to bring the wounded, who were also in the water, back. Private Shelly, R.A.M.C., volunteered to cross two hundred yards of open ground to alleviate their sufferings. This he did with great gallantry.

When darkness had fallen 'A' and 'B' Companies were able 'to trickle back, soaking wet and very tired but astoundingly cheerful'. Patrols were sent out to search for the wounded, and seventeen were brought in.

The attempt to cross the river very nearly succeeded and pressed the enemy so hard that instead of withdrawing he had to reinforce his positions. The attack by 'A' and 'B' Companies was carried out with great courage and endurance. It cost one officer and fifteen other ranks killed and about fifty wounded.

To the left the 13th Battalion had, like the 12th, scored an initial success. They had crossed one branch of the Touques, but were held up at the other, the eastern, by an enemy offering the most determined resistance. Gale had secured the aid of a number of tanks, but these, unable to cross the stream, would give no support. The Germans, taking advantage of an east wind, had set fire to the houses, which burned all round the 13th Battalion. Despite the most desperate efforts to advance— Lieutenant J. F. Hodgson, M.C., swam the second branch of the Touques with his batman in an attempt to destroy a troublesome gun—the Lancashire men could do no more. Throughout the night they held on grimly amid the fiercely burning town, and at dawn on the 23rd Captain Skeate and a patrol crossed the eastern branch by the single girder of a broken bridge. He was followed by most of the battalion. Having reached the square in front of the church, they then engaged the numerous machineguns of the enemy, who counter-attacked at noon in force. The battalion was ordered to withdraw into reserve, its place being taken by the 7th Battalion. The withdrawal, a most difficult operation, was made 'in perfect order' under fire, all the wounded being carried back. Among them was a man badly hit who had been laid upon a door. Upon this he was half carried, half ferried across, his passage being covered by Major A. R. Clark, M.C., who stood up to his neck in water 'laughing as he returned the fire of a German machine-gun with his .45 automatic'. He was not hit and the wounded man was conveyed to safety. But that night while Clark was asleep a man stumbled over him and stamped so hard upon his ankle that he was unable to walk and had to be taken to hospital. Such are the fortunes of war.

That night patrols of the 7th Battalion discovered that the enemy was once more withdrawing. Pine-Coffin at once pushed his men across the river on to the high ground beyond, and was soon followed by the 12th and 13th Battalions. The Touques had been crossed.

The next considerable action took place at Beuzeville, where the 3rd Parachute Brigade, which had joined with the 4th Commando Brigade, drove the enemy from this large straggling town. Enemy mortar fire caused casualties in a deep, sunken road. By now the general advance was gathering speed. The 5th Parachute Brigade was in the van, for it had passed through the 3rd at Beuzeville on the 26th and was making for Pont Audemer. The whole brigade was filled with elation and pride. 'Everyone seemed to realise that much was expected of them. The road for the most part was flat and straight . . . an apparently endless stretch, always extending in front, and as the sun got up conditions became uncomfortable.' Cheered on by the frequent presence of the brigadier, and by the shouts and happy tears of the inhabitants of each village through which they passed, all battalions pressed forward. Jugs of milk and fresh fruit were drunk or eaten on the march, and as they drew nearer and nearer to Pont Audemer the 'singers started off again, and so did the whistlers. The whole column became like a runner who has just got his second wind'. So at length the 5th Parachute Brigade entered Pont Audemer where 'we had a warm welcome from the Mademoiselles', reported Private Lawson later, 'and a greengrocer opened his entire shop for us'.

Many snipers were still in the town, but their presence did not deter its citizens from shewing their relief and gratitude to the men who had come so far and fought so hard. 'The citizens rejoiced and the sound of their cheering echoed all over Europe.' There amidst the clanging bells and the shouts of men and women, free after four long years of oppression, the five battalions of the Parachute Regiment, the Canadian Battalion and their comrades in arms of the Air Landing Brigade and the commandos could taste at last the fruits of a victory so stoutly fought for, so richly earned.

The losses of The Parachute Regiment and the Canadian Battalion in Normandy had been high, some forty officers and four hundred and ninety-five other ranks killed, eighty-five officers and one thousand four hundred and seventy other ranks wounded, twenty officers and six hundred and twenty other ranks missing, a total of a hundred and forty-five officers and two thousand five hundred and fifty other ranks. The Regiment could justly maintain that in the short space of eighty-three days all its men had become veterans. They had learned the first and most important lesson of all in the first twenty-four hours: that he who would survive on a modern battlefield must dig and dig again; and that cover from view even when secured by crouching behind a thick Norman hedge or by lying in the long grass of an apple orchard, was not enough when fighting an enemy as skilled as were the Germans in the use of mortars and light machine-guns. It had taken the parachute soldiers but a short while longer to discover that to come first to close quarters and then to deliver sustained bursts of rapid fire were deadly tactics. Nor had they been backward in acquiring the patience of the trained sniper. To these, the tricks of a soldier's trade, they soon added those of the poacher and the gamekeeper; and they learned them in summer nights spent in the dark mysteries of the Bois de Bavent and in grey dawns by the banks of the Dives when the trees were 'hostile wraiths', and the sun a ball of uncertain fire above a country of shapes and shadows where lurked the enemy patrol a yard perhaps, perhaps a mile away. To the usual discomforts of active service were added those caused by a plentiful lack of transport and a system of supply which, despite the prodigious efforts of the quartermasters, was at best no more than adequate. Above all else, close and unbroken contact with a stubborn foe kept them nimble. With every venture into the dark woods, with every notch cut on a rifle butt, with every bomb fired by a Piat masquerading as a mortar, they grew to feel themselves his master. This gave them a pride stronger even than that engendered when the blue wings had first been sewn upon their shoulders. Long before their last march in Normandy down to the sea and the ships waiting to take them back to Southampton they were aware that both as a force and as individuals they dominated the enemy; and this knowledge swelled their hearts and made them look forward to fresh opportunities to prove their worth.

In May they had left Bulford full of resolution; they returned there in September tempered by the fire of achievement. For they had taken part in a great and successful enterprise. Not only were they the liberators of Europe; they were the foremost among them, for had they not been in advance of the van? That was their pride and their reward.

Arnhem : The Plan

THE LIBERATION of Paris on 23rd August, followed by that of Brussels on 3rd September 1944, seemed to many in Britain and America to foreshadow the swift ending of the war in Europe. It was a natural reaction to events of which the significance even trained and experienced commanders did not find easy to interpret correctly. After more than two months of heavy and confined fighting in the beachhead, during which it seemed at times, to the faint-hearted at least, that the stalemate of Anzio would be reproduced on a larger scale in Normandy, the resistance of the enemy had been broken and he had streamed in utter rout across France and Belgium at a speed which made close pursuit the major difficulty. Pressing on from Brussels, the spearheads of the 21st Army Group covered a distance of ninety-five miles in four days. By 5th September the American Third Army, under Patton, had reached Nancy and crossed the Moselle, and a week later the American First Army, under Hodges, was preparing to besiege Aachen. Antwerp was in Montgomery's hands, though until the mouth of the Scheldt was freed it could not be used. The dominant question was, therefore, was the enemy so demoralised that one more heavy blow was all that was needed to knock him out? Field Marshal Montgomery thought that he was and pressed Eisenhower to support his 21st Army Group with all the supplies available and thus enable him to move swiftly straight at Berlin.

The situation was fully discussed at a conference held at Brussels on 10th September, at which the Supreme Commander, as he afterwards set down, gave it as his considered opinion that 'any pencil-like thrust into the heart of Germany, such as he (Montgomery) proposed, would meet nothing but certain destruction'. That was Eisenhower's decision. Future historians with all the facts in front of them may be able to decide whether the Supreme Commander or the Field Marshal was right. Here all that need be recorded is the compromise reached at that meeting. Three bridgeheads were to be seized, one, the furthest off, over the Rhine, thus taking the northern defences of the Siegfried Line in flank, the second over the Waal and the third over the Maas. This operation, to which the code name 'Market Garden' was given, was to be entrusted to three divisions of the 1st Allied Airborne Army, which had just been formed under Lieutenant-General Lewis H. Brereton of the United States Army Air Forces. The date for their triple assault was to be 17th September.

The new airborne army was composed of the 1st and 6th British and the 17th, 82nd and 101st U.S. Airborne Divisions, together with certain engineer and artillery formations. Operation 'Market Garden' was to be carried out under the general direction of General Dempsey's 2nd British Army, now established in small bridgeheads along the Meuse and the Escaut Canal. The scope and daring of the design had been made feasible only by the existence of trained airborne forces. For, apart from the artificial barrier of the Siegfried line, the natural barriers to the north of it were such as to reassure the commander of a defending force. They were indeed truly formidable, being made up in the main of the three great rivers just mentioned: the Meuse, which becomes the Maas when it crosses the Dutch frontier, the Waal, which is the main channel of the Rhine, and is further to the north, and the Neder Rijn or Lower Rhine, most northern of all. The three rivers flow roughly parallel to each other, and all three would have to be crossed by an army seeking to enter Germany round the top of the Siegfried Line, which petered out in the neighbourhood of the Reichswald forest. Joining this forest to the first of the rivers, the Waal, is a ridge of ground which is six hundred and thirty-three feet above sea level at its highest point, and constitutes the only range of hills in Holland. For many years its heavily wooded slopes and its undulating crest, from which observation in all directions over a wide stretch of country is possible, formed the favourite field of manœuvres for the Dutch Army. The position was strengthened still more by the canal connecting the Maas with the Waal flowing along its western side, and by the Waal itself upon its southern. This natural defensive position was in the hands of the enemy, who, after their experiences in North Africa, Sicily and Normandy, rightly feared the advent of airborne troops. They strove to increase its strength by every possible means, even pressing into service twelve-year-old Dutch children, who were forced to take part in constructing two defence lines, the main position running along the Waal to the sea, and a forward line following the Maas. It was this position and the natural defences provided by the three rivers that Montgomery decided should be overrun 'with the utmost rapidity and violence, and without regard to the events on the flanks'.

The obvious and indeed the only line of advance was the main road running from Eindhoven in the south through Grave, where it crossed the Maas, Nijmegen on the Waal, to Arnhem on the Lower Rhine. It was carried over these river obstacles by four bridges, the nine-spanned steel bridge at Grave, a small bridge over the Maas-Waal Canal between Grave and Nijmegen, a great single-spanned steel bridge at Nijmegen, and finally the steel bridge at Arnhem. All these were to be seized by the 1st Airborne Corps, the first three by the American airborne divisions, and the fourth and furthest away by the British 1st Airborne Division, then under the command of Major-General R. E. Urquhart, the 1st Airborne Corps as a whole being commanded by Lieutenant-General Browning.

Since the fighting in Italy, which for the 1st Airborne Division had come to an end in November 1943, the division had been back in England, training. It possessed two parachute brigades, the 1st and 4th, each composed of three battalions and the usual divisional troops. In the 1st Brigade were the 1st, 2nd and 3rd Battalions. The 1st Battalion, under Lieutenant-Colonel P. Cleasby-Thompson, whose place was presently taken by Lieutenant-Colonel D. T. Dobie, was stationed at Grimsthorpe Castle, Bulby Hall and Bourne in Lincolnshire; the 2nd, still under the command of Frost, was in the area of Grantham; and the 3rd, under Lieutenant-Colonel E. C. Yeldham, who through ill health had later to hand over to Lieutenant-Colonel J. A. C. Fitch, in two hutted camps at Spalding. Throughout the winter of 1943 and 1944 training and yet more training, followed by periods of leave and the customary recreations of troops—boxing, athletics and football—were the order of the day and of every day. On the whole it seems to have been a pleasant time. The dwellers in the areas in which the parachute battalions were billeted overwhelmed them with friendly attentions. 'Any man wearing a red beret and the green lanyard of the 1st Battalion,' notes its historian, 'was assured of a welcome anywhere in Bourne. The officers lived in private billets and there was not a man in either "S" or "T" Companies who had not got his "feet under the table" in some house or other. They nearly all had girl friends and the affection in which Bourne was held was reflected in the way in which both companies concerned clamoured to a man for an immediate return to Bourne at the conclusion of each of the many exercises that took place at this time.' The people of Spalding were equally hospitable to the 3rd Battalion, as were those in the villages round Grantham to the 2nd. 'Many homes in Spalding were thrown open to the men of the battalion . . . which was so much thought of by the people that attempts were made to adopt it.'

The 4th Parachute Brigade was composed of the 156th, 10th and 11th Battalions. The 156th, under Lieutenant-Colonel Sir W. R. de B. des Voeux, now recovered from his broken leg, reached England from the Middle East in time for Christmas leave, 1943, and was established first in and around the pleasant Rutland town of Uppingham, and then in Melton Mowbray. Here as elsewhere 'the townspeople made everyone feel at home, and many lasting friendships and not a few marriages were made'. The 10th Battalion, under Lieutenant-Colonel K. B. I. Smyth, disembarked in England from Italy on 10th December 1943, on a typical English winter day, and it too reached Rutlandshire. Battalion headquarters were at Somerby near Oakham, and the companies in the surrounding villages, whose inhabitants treated the troops very well. The 11th Battalion, under Lieutenant-Colonel G. H. Lea, who had succeeded Lieutenant-Colonel M. R. Thomas, joined the brigade and went first to Leicester. Like their comrades of the 156th Battalion, they, too, presently moved to Melton Mowbray, where they received the same cordial welcome.

During this time a large number of officers and men of the 4th Brigade, who had been trained in India and Egypt, passed through a course at Ringway in order that they might become familiar with the methods used by their comrades trained in England since these differed slightly from their own. Rugby football was much played that winter and some battalions made it a practice to send their teams by air to Ringway, the players dropping by parachute straight on to the field of play. By the spring of 1944 the two brigades were busily engaged on a series of exercises, of which the most outstanding was exercise 'Mush', carried out in the lovely country round Lechlade and Fairford. The enemy in this exercise was the 6th Airborne Division, shortly to drop in Normandy. It included the following battalions of the regiment: 8th, 9th, 1st (Canadian), in the 3rd Parachute Brigade, and the 7th, 12th and 13th in the 5th. So the days passed in rigorous training varied by games and sports. All the battalions were now more or less up to strength, and each officer and man was fighting fit in the most literal sense of that term. The two brigade commanders, Lathbury of the 1st, and Hackett of the 4th, were indefatigable in moving round their commands, urging the achievement of perfection.

On 6th June 1944 each battalion of the two brigades paraded under its commanding officer, and were informed that their comrades of the 6th Airborne Division had dropped in Normandy a few hours before. All felt that it would hardly be possible for the 21st Army Group to go to war without the services of the 1st Airborne Division, and confidently expected to be called upon at any moment. This confidence became a certainty when the two brigades were briefed to drop at Evrecy, five days after the landing. Models of the objective were produced, maps issued, all preparations made, and in several battalions, notably the 1st, 'impressive services were held at which hymns with a strong pre-battle flavour were sung'. Then at the last moment came the cancellation. Evrecy had been overrun, and their presence was not therefore necessary. This, all agreed, was unfortunate, but another chance would certainly occur. It did, but not before fifteen weeks had passed, during which fifteen more operations were planned and in turn cancelled, in every instance because the objective had already been reached by the ground forces. The advance of Montgomery's army, after it had broken out of the beachhead, was so rapid that it was impossible to foresee in time what immediate use could be made of airborne forces and therefore to make the necessary plans.

If it is not already apparent, it must be now realised that to put an airborne division into the air and take it to its objective time is necessary. Such an operation cannot be carried through successfully without careful preparation. The very fact that airborne troops arrived at their objective so quickly was, in one sense, a hindrance, for they could only do so by careful and meticulous planning beforehand and this could not be completed in a hurry. Each cancellation, besides depressing the spirits of the troops, threw a great burden on everyone, particularly on those responsible for administration. When a battalion was briefed for an operation it had normally to be concentrated in a special area, where, for obvious reasons of security, it was segregated behind barbed wire. Once there, no one could go in or come out without a pass. A postponement led to shortages of cigarettes, and even of money. Then would come cancellation, and the foreign money issued had to be handed back again.

'Time after time,' says the historian of the 1st Battalion, 'the battalion would go to bed ready for an early reveille prior to an operation somewhere on the continent. But sometime during the night runners would go round announcing that the operation had been postponed or cancelled. Forty-eight hours' leave became frequent, and everything possible was done to make things a little more bearable.' It was too exasperating, and for a time even the most confirmed optimists became almost convinced that the war would end before the division saw further fighting.

Then on 10th September Urquhart received his orders for carrying out his part of 'Market Garden,' called by the code name 'Market'. From his tactical headquarters at Moor Park, that house built by a successful speculator in the South Sea Bubble and decorated, appropriately enough, with many trophies of arms in the style of Verrio, he issued his orders. His own were clear enough: his task was to capture the main bridge at Arnhem, or any other bridge which might still be intact, and, having done so, to establish a bridgehead sufficiently strong to make it possible for the leading formations of XXX Corps of Dempsey's 2nd Army to deploy north of the Lower Rhine. He was enjoined not to make any attempt to forge a link with the 82nd U.S. Airborne Division, which was to seize the bridge at Nijmegen to the south, these instructions being necessary in order to ensure the maintenance of the bomb-line protecting the advancing land forces.

The task seemed simple enough on paper ; but Urquhart found himself at once faced with a major problem. The aircraft available to carry his parachute troops or tow his gliders to the scene of operations were not sufficiently numerous to be able to do so in a single lift. Ten Squadrons of No. 38 Group and six of No. 46 Group were at his disposal for the gliders, the parachute troops being carried by the 9th U.S. Troop Carrier Command. These were all too few, and Urquhart soon realised that three lifts would be necessary. In other words, he would have to accept the great risk of putting down his division many miles behind the lines of the enemy, not in one fell swoop but on three successive days. To borrow more squadrons from the American 9th Troop Carrier Command was impossible, for every one of their remaining aircraft was needed to transport the 82nd and 101st Airborne Divisions to their objectives on the Maas and the Waal. These, being situated nearer to the 2nd Army, had to be seized at all costs if that Army was to advance at all. For this reason a sufficient number of aircraft to carry both the American divisions in one lift was made available.

That the commander of a division entrusted with so important a task as that allotted to the 1st Airborne Division should have been short of aircraft requires explanation. The fault lay, not with the Supreme Commander or the commanders in the field, but far back in America and Britain, where, despite the great efforts made by the many factories engaged on aircraft production, there were not enough transport aircraft to carry the 1st Airborne Division to its destination between sunrise and sunset. In the event, the necessity to carry it piecemeal over three days to its destination was one of the main causes of our failure at Arnhem.

The other can, with certainty, be said to be faulty intelligence. The information with which the division was supplied concerning the enemy and his dispositions was scanty, though, as has been said, it was known that all that part of Holland was being put into a state of defence as fast as possible. 2nd Army headquarters were also aware that the area Arnhem-Zwolle-Ammersfoort had for long been allocated for the training of armoured and motorised units of which some belonged to the Hermann Goering S.S. Division. Yet as late as 13th September, three days after the order to mount the operation had been received, all the information that the intelligence services of the 1st Airborne Division could glean about the enemy was that there was no recent evidence strong enough to enable an estimate of the number and quality of the troops in and about Arnhem to be made. The barracks in that town and in the neighbourhood could hold about ten thousand men, and there were, in addition, all the houses of Arnhem in which troops could be billeted, but whether they were all fully occupied was not known. The general conclusion eventually reached was that on its arrival at Arnhem the division would not encounter any body of troops larger than a brigade group supported by some tanks, in all probably not more than three thousand men at that stage of the war.

With this meagre information Urquhart, Lathbury, Hackett and their men had to be content. Looking into the matter some years later, it seems certain that other and ampler details were available. During the planning of operation 'Market Garden' Dutch underground groups sent in information that there were S.S. troops with a not inconsiderable quantity of tanks just east of the Ijssel and close to Arnhem. One of the intelligence officers deduced from this that the 2nd S.S. Panzer Corps, which had been pulled out of the Normandy bridgehead in time to escape the final rout, was being reorganised in that area. This deduction was correct. His report, however, was received with incredulity at 2nd Army headquarters, which regarded the presence of tanks in or near Arnhem as highly improbable, and asserted that no other source confirmed the information supplied by the Dutch resistance. Moreover, said 2nd Army Intelligence, no tanks were to be seen on any of the reconnaissance photographs.[1] In point of fact the information supplied by the Dutch was entirely accurate; not inconsiderable numbers of both tanks and self-propelled guns were in Arnhem. The unfortunate 1st Airborne Division was therefore dropped or landed in an area through which part of the 2nd S.S. Panzer Corps was moving, and suffered the full consequences. Comment is unnecessary.

The third problem confronting the Divisional commander was the choice of dropping zones and landing grounds. He naturally wished to choose spots on both sides of the river situated as close as possible to the bridge. He was informed, however, that at that particular point the land, being low-lying polder damp, very exposed and cut up by deep drainage, was quite unsuitable for glider landings in force or for the rapid deployment of parachute troops. Four miles north of Arnhem there was some fairly open country composed of rough heath and dunes, and separated from the town by a thick belt of woods. Here parachute troops could be dropped, but not any large number of gliders landed. The ideal spot, the airfield at Deelen, slightly north-west of Arnhem, was out of the question, for it was ringed with anti-aircraft batteries and pill-boxes, and the Allied air commanders were, in the circumstances, not prepared, quite rightly, to accept the heavy casualties these would inflict on troop-carrying and towing aircraft arriving in daylight in large numbers. The only suitable ground appeared to be west-north-west of Arnhem, where large clearings stretched between belts of woodland at a height of 250 feet above the sea level. Such a height is remarkable for Holland, and the land would be firm and free from bog. Here the whole Division could certainly land, and could it have been put down in one operation the fact that these clearings were some eight miles away from its objective would not greatly have mattered. But here again Urquhart was confronted with the inescapable consequences of the triple lift.

On the first day he would have to put down not only enough

[1] This is not surprising. The well-wooded country made the concealment of tanks and self-propelled guns an easy matter.

men to seize the bridge, but also enough to hold the landing zone against the coming of the next part of the division in the second lift, and they in their turn would have to provide a garrison to hold the fields so as to assure the safe arrival of those in the last lift. Were the Germans to remain passive and unconcerned, again the necessity of using part of his force for defences instead of attack would have no grave consequences. But could he rely on the supineness of the enemy? Urquhart was convinced that he could not. He knew that from the outset he would have to fight and that the fight would grow progressively more severe with every hour that passed. He might expect the enemy to be constantly reinforced, and he would have to engage them with a division not at full strength until the third day, and being airborne, short of all heavy weapons save the guns of the Light Regiment under the energetic and capable Loder-Symons, his C.R.A. Since, however, there was no other alternative, he had no choice but to decide on the clearings west-north-west of Arnhem. Of these he eventually chose five, denominated 'Y', 'S', and 'L' north of the railway connecting Arnhem with Utrecht, and 'X' and 'Z' south of it and north of the village of Heelsum. These zones were all within range of anti-aircraft fire. A sixth zone, 'K', close to the bridge south of the river, was chosen at a later stage. Upon it the 1st Polish Parachute Brigade under Major-General Sosabowski were to land on the third day, by which time, it was hoped, the town would be in our hands. In fact when they did land they did so considerably further to the west, at Driel, because the town had not been taken and the anti-aircraft batteries of the enemy had not, therefore, been silenced.

After much thought Urquhart decided that the first lift should carry the 1st Parachute Brigade and the 1st Air Landing Brigade Group. This would require a hundred and sixty-one Dakotas belonging to the squadrons of the U.S. 9th Troop Carrier Command for the carriage of the three parachute battalions, and two hundred and ninety-seven tugs towing the same number of gliders. In the second lift, to arrive twenty-four hours later, a hundred and twenty-six aircraft of the same command should drop the main body of the 4th Parachute Brigade, and three hundred and five tug aircraft of Nos. 38 and 46 Groups of the Royal Air Force bring in three hundred and five gliders carrying the remainder of the Air Landing Brigade. In addition, thirty-five aircraft of No. 38 Group would drop supplies. On the third day a hundred and fourteen American aircraft were to drop the main body of the 1st Polish Parachute Brigade, and a hundred and sixty-three aircraft of the Royal Air Force supplies which by then would certainly be needed. Forty-five tug aircraft with their gliders should bring in the remainder of the Polish Brigade, together with the 878th U.S. Airborne Aviation Engineering Battalion. It will be observed that a high proportion of the transport aircraft belonged to the American Army Air Force, towards whom the 1st Airborne Division had feelings of warm friendship and admiration. Such were the general plan and dispositions.

To come to detail, to the 1st Parachute Brigade was allotted the main task, the seizure of the bridge. They were also to capture the pontoon bridge said to exist a few hundred yards to the west of the main bridge. In fact it did not, for the Germans had removed it some time before. Brigadier Lathbury, the brigade commander, decided that the 1st Airborne Reconnaissance Squadron carried in gliders should attempt to capture the bridge by *coup de main* and should advance to do so from the west and north through the town. In their immediate support would be the 2nd Battalion, which was to move through the village of Heelsum south of the dropping zone along the road following the north bank of the Lower Rhine. On reaching the bridge it was to relieve the reconnaissance squadron and take up a defensive position on both banks. The 3rd Battalion was to take the more northerly road from Heelsum to Arnhem and approach the bridge from the north. On reaching it, it was to form the principal defence of the north-east part of the bridge. The 1st Battalion was to proceed, not to the bridge, but to the high ground immediately north of Arnhem ; but it was not to do so until it was clear that the 2nd and 3rd Battalions were moving towards their objective.

The effect of these dispositions would be that by nightfall a perimeter formed by the 1st Battalion, holding what amounted to a line of outposts, would have been formed, while the main defensive position nearer the bridge would be held by the 2nd and 3rd Battalions. The troops, most of them belonging to the 4th Parachute Brigade, arriving with the second lift on the next day, would construct a larger perimeter enclosing the town and running along the high ground to the west and north-west and across the flat country to the east and north-east. As soon as this had been accomplished the 1st Parachute Brigade, reinforced by the arrival of the Polish Parachute Brigade landing on the other side of the river, would constitute the Division's reserve at Urquhart's disposal for use at any threatened point.

So he planned, well aware of the great risks he ran, but also of the great issue at stake. One thing was beyond doubt or question, the valour of his troops and the high degree of technical skill which they combined with it.

Arnhem : The Execution

AT 09.30 on 17th September, a Sunday, the 1st Battalion left Grimsthorpe Castle in lorries bound for Grantham airfield. Mile after mile went by, and no dispatch riders appeared to cancel the operation. Parachutes had been drawn an hour before—a member of 'T' Company resolutely refusing one marked 'Dummy'—and harness fitted, and the men were in the highest spirits. 'It was a perfect summer day. All the planes were lined up in the bright sunshine . . . the men lay on the ground beside them, resting on their parachutes, eating haversack rations.' With the order to put on parachutes appeared the battalion joker, 'Guv' Beech, the physical training Sergeant, who walked down to the line of men wearing 'his well-known opera hat which he kept taking off à la Winston Churchill', and bowing to left and right.

The 2nd Battalion boarded its aircraft in similar conditions at Saltby, and so did the 3rd Battalion.

The journey was uneventful. 'Once in the air,' writes one who dropped with the 1st Battalion that day, 'one could see an endless line of Dakotas behind. One could catch glimpses of fighters diving about round the convoy.' They came from the 8th U.S. Army Air Force, which provided continuous and most efficient protection, and which, together with the 9th American Army Air Force, attacked anti-aircraft guns which opened up upon the main stream of Dakotas when it reached the Dutch coast. In the van were twelve Stirlings carrying six officers and a hundred and eighty men of the 21st Independent Parachute Company under the command of Major B. A. Wilson. They constituted the pathfinder force, whose duty it was to lay out the various aids and indications on the dropping zone. 'I shall always remember,' says Wilson, a man then in his forties, 'that first

216

flight on that lovely Sunday morning. I sat with the pilot as we flew in over the Dutch coast. Everything looked so peaceful. There were cows feeding quietly in the fields and peasants going about their work. Not a sign of fighting or war. Not a glimpse of the enemy. I had just said to the pilot, "This seems a pretty quiet area. Suppose we get out here", when, before he could answer, a number of shells burst round the aircraft. . . . A few minutes later he wished me good luck as I sailed down to the glorious uncertainty of the welcome I should receive as one of the first parachute troops to enter German-occupied Holland. . . . The ensuing half-hour while we waited for the main force to drop was, to say the least of it, interesting.'

The interest for Wilson and his men lay in accepting the surrender of some fifteen frightened Germans. During the drop two men were hit, one in his ammunition pouches, the other in his haversack. Neither was hurt. Punctually on time came the Dakotas and a moment later the members of the pathfinder force could see 'the blue field of the sky suddenly blossom with the white flowers of parachutes'. The drop of the 1st Brigade and the landing of the gliders with the Air Landing Brigade was more successful than anything which had so far been achieved by the airborne forces of either side in the war, even during an exercise. Nearly 100 per cent arrived at the right time and place. By 15.00 hours the units were ready and prepared to move. All had prospered marvellously, but now came the first check.

The Air Landing Reconnaissance Squadron could not attempt the planned *coup de main* against the bridge, for the few gliders that failed to arrive were unfortunately those carrying the transport. It fell, therefore, to the 2nd Battalion under Frost, that veteran of Bruneval, North Africa and Sicily, to seize the bridge. His simple plan was for 'A' Company in the van to move straight to the main bridge, while 'C' Company following in its rear, was to seize the railway bridge if it was still intact, pass over it and attack the main bridge from the south. To 'B' Company, coming last of all, was allotted the capture of the pontoon bridge, if it existed, and, if it did not, the seizure of some high ground called Den Brink, which controlled the entrance to Arnhem from the west. The battalion had with it a number of anti-tank guns. In the bright sunshine of an early autumn day it moved off, soon quitting the sandy, scrub-covered dropping zone for the shelter of the dark surrounding woods. The advanced guard reached the village of Heelsum without difficulty, having on the way ambushed a number of lorries and a staff car from which fifteen prisoners were taken. The inhabitants of Heelsum, every one of them wearing 'some garment or part of a garment coloured orange, some with favours, and some with orange arm bands', welcomed them with an enthusiasm which, as at Arnhem itself, was to cost them dear. For the most part they confirmed what Frost had learned from intelligence reports concerning the enemy. There was a considerable number of anti-aircraft guns near the railway and the main bridge, but the number of German troops in Arnhem was not, they unfortunately considered, above two thousand, and of these many were recruits under training.

Wasting no time, Frost pushed ahead, determined to cover the six miles separating Heelsum from the bridge at his best speed. Near Heaver Dorp, the next village, 'A' Company, in the lead, came under fire from some high ground and lost one or two men, but their advance continued, until, after another small skirmish at Oosterbeek, they were brought to a halt near the railway line running through the western outskirts of Arnhem. Meanwhile 'C' Company behind them had turned to the right to seize the railway bridge, moving towards it in open order across fields, under cover from their own Bren guns. Lieutenant P. Barry and his platoon, were the first to reach the river bank. They ran down to the bridge and had set foot upon it when the enemy blew one of its spans. 'It seemed,' said Corporal Roberts of the Royal Army Medical Corps, who was with the party, 'to curl back on us'. Barry and two men were wounded. The company halted at the now useless bridge, and then, in accordance with orders, moved against their secondary objective, a building in Arnhem itself said to house the headquarters of part of the German defence. By then they had been joined by some of the 9th Field Squadron, Royal Engineers, under Captain E. Callaghan, M.C.

'A' Company remained near the railway under fire from an armoured car and from machine-guns posted on Den Brink and lost Lieutenant P. H. Cane. Frost had expected such opposition at this point and at once sent, according to his plan, 'B' Company to deal with it. While they were doing so, an anti-tank gun was brought up in readiness to engage the armoured car as soon as it reappeared, and 'A' Company began to move round the backs of the houses towards the bridge. The light was beginning to fade and the enemy's fire to become less accurate. In its advance the company took with it a number of prisoners, who proved to be S.S. Police. One of them was carrying a map which shewed the patrol routes to be followed by a German reconnaissance squadron. A message was sent to 'B' Company to leave Den Brink and follow, but the runner was killed or taken prisoner, and the company continued to push ahead along Den Brink, against opposition which prevented its capture until the early hours of the following morning.

'A' Company pressed on at speed, and with the headquarters company moved through the trim brick-built town, the eyes of those in the lead fixed on the single steel span of the bridge, dark against the September dusk. It was between 20.30 and 21.00 hours that 'A' Company arrived at the northern end of the bridge, its men moving silently, taking what cover they could, and being careful not to interfere with passing traffic, for at that stage Frost did not wish to arouse the Germans more than necessary. He had very few men with him, and he would not risk being overwhelmed now that the objective was partially at least within his grasp.

He was by this time out of touch with 'B' and 'C' Companies, for the wireless sets seemed not to be working, being in all probability masked by the buildings and the many trees of the pleasant city of Arnhem. Major A. D. Tatham-Warter, commanding 'A' Company, proposed that a platoon should be taken across the bridge to secure the southern end. To this Frost agreed, and Lieutenant Grayburn—he was to win death and a Victoria Cross in the next forty-eight hours—with his platoon did all he could to fulfil this order, but was prevented by the steady fire of an anti-aircraft gun and a German armoured car. While he was making this attempt, Frost put the men into various houses close by chosen because their upper stories commanded the approaches to the bridge and the viaduct leading to it. 'We must have presented a curious appearance,' he said, 'for we were wandering round with helmets covered with bracken and camouflage in the midst of a modern town.'

'The atmosphere at this time,' reports an eyewitness, 'can only be described as a trifle crazy. We would knock upon the door of a house and be instantly met by the earnest prayers of its inhabitants not to billet ourselves on them. Seeing our preparations for defence, they would then say most politely, "surely you are not going to fortify this house?" To which I would reply, equally politely. "I'm afraid I am".'

Frost established his headquarters in 'a tall narrow type of house next door to a school, just north-west of the northern end of the bridge'. His men at once set about fortifying it, to the dismay of its inhabitants who 'took a poor view of the curtains being torn up and the knocking of the glass out of the windows'. It was now quite dark, and the sound of heavy footsteps heralded the arrival of more parachute troops. They were the defence platoon of brigade headquarters, and part of headquarters themselves, numbering about sixty officers and other ranks all told, many of them signallers; they were, however, without Brigadier Lathbury.

While the 2nd Battalion were occupying the houses the enemy launched a determined attack, well nourished by mortar fire, against 'A' Company, which had seized the approaches to the bridge. Hardly had it been repulsed, when three lorries carrying German infantry attempted to cross the bridge coming from the south. In the ensuing mêlée the lorries caught fire and their occupants surrendered. The flames, nourished by the fuel in the tanks, so illuminated the southern end of the bridge that any attempt to move towards it drew heavy fire from the farther bank of the river. This was one of the main reasons why it was impossible for the battalion to cross the bridge to the south bank.

During the night an attempt was made to reach it by another route. The defence platoon was sent down the river a little way to the pontoon bridge in the hope that it might be able to cross the Neder Rijn by this means. In this it failed, for the pontoon bridge had been removed. 'B' Company, which had been left on Den Brink, was also ordered to the pontoon bridge. This order got through, but the enemy were too active and it could not be obeyed.

Frost also made every effort to get into touch with the missing 'C' Company, still at the railway, in order to bring them to the main bridge. In this, too, he failed, for 'C' Company was pinned down near the railway station and unable to break out. In the early hours of the morning of 18th September he did, however, receive a welcome reinforcement in the shape of part of 'B' Company, which had at last been able to make their way from Den Brink. They were accompanied by some twenty-five sappers. Shortly before they arrived one and a half platoons belonging to 'C' Company of the 3rd, not the 1st Battalion, also joined the defenders of the bridge.

They had had better fortune than the rest of the 3rd Battalion, whose doings will be recounted in a moment, and had eventually reached a point near the railway station at Arnhem. Thence they had moved through a town deserted except, said Sergeant Mason, 'for two Dutch policemen. . . . We walked down the

220

main street towards the bridge. Just before reaching it a German car was blown up by a Gammon bomb thrown by the leading platoon'. On their arrival the survivors of 'C' Company took up a position in the school next door to Frost's headquarters, and were there joined by the sappers. On his way to the school Private McKinnon entered a butcher's shop and asked for food. The butcher had no meat, but provided him with bread, wine and cheese, and asked if he could bring his daughter, aged twelve, to see the British soldier. She duly appeared and had one sentence of English which she had carefully rehearsed: 'Many happy returns after your long stay away.'

The force at the bridge under Frost's command now amounted to between three and four hundred men. With dawn came German patrols, including a latrine squad. The latrine lorry was knocked out and the others moved 'somewhat aimlessly up and down the road in front of us. Presently the drivers seemed to hesitate. They had seen our ugly eyes looking at them from the windows'. Bombs and machine-gun fire killed them all save two, who were captured badly wounded. Hardly had these bewildered Germans been dealt with when the look-outs on the bridge reported that a German convoy had assembled on the farther end and seemed about to rush Frost's position. There ensued, he said afterwards, 'the most lovely battle you have ever seen. Sixteen half-track vehicles and armoured cars advanced. There they were, these awful Boches, with their pot helmets sticking out. When we dealt with them they smoked and burned in front of us almost to the end of the battle. I believe they belonged to the 9th Reconnaissance Squadron'. They were destroyed by Hawkins grenades, an anti-tank gun and Piats. Some reached the school, where Lieutenant D. R. Simpson, M.C., Royal Engineers, with his sappers provided them with a warm welcome. The school was in shape a square horseshoe, the ends of the two arms being about ten yards from the road. As the German vehicles went by 'Corporal Simpson and Sapper Perry, whose conduct that day was outstanding, stood up and fired straight into the half-tracks with Sten and Bren guns. The range was about twenty yards'. The driver of one half-track, seeing what had happened to those who had preceded him, pulled out to the right along the asphalt path running beneath the windows of the school. 'His vehicle did not get far before it was hit; its crew climbed out and sought the cover of bushes, but were killed before reaching them.'

Much heartened by this small but not insignificant victory,

Frost and his men continued to hold their positions under a shower of light shells and mortar bombs, which grew slowly but steadily heavier and began to cause casualties. They were treated by Captain James Logan, D.S.O., Royal Army Medical Corps, of the 16th Parachute Field Ambulance, whose labours were as skilful as they were indefatigable. This fire came mostly from the north and east, from somewhere, that is, in Arnhem. Frost's main fear at that time was that the Germans would obtain a foothold on the southern end of the bridge, and to prevent this he strengthened the number of light and medium machine-guns established in the upper stories of the houses he had occupied during the night. Their fire was returned by 20-mm. and 40-mm. guns, effective weapons which presently set several buildings on fire and knocked down others. Unfortunately the houses which gave the best field of fire over the bridge were made of wood, and these began to burn.

Nevertheless Frost was still confident. Major D. E. Crawley, M.C., 'a very experienced soldier' commanding 'B' Company, was now with him, and he had a notion that he would soon be reinforced. 'I had reason to be satisfied at this stage, because we had prevented the Germans from covering the bridge with anti-tank guns, whose fire would have stopped the advanced guard of XXX Corps from crossing it.' For hours he had been trying, vainly, to communicate with XXX Corps, whose armour, he had been told, would be advancing up the road from Nijmegen to the relief of the airborne division. About 18.30 hours he did, however, speak briefly with Dobie, commanding the 1st Battalion, and urged him to make all the speed he could. By then sounds of battle to the west had been heard for a considerable time, and Frost decided that he must, if he could, help the 1st and 3rd, obviously in close action in the town, by taking the enemy in the rear. Major Crawley, with a strong force, was ordered to do so. German self-propelled guns, however, and armour were too thick upon the ground, and Frost was informed by his intelligence officer that men belonging to both the 9th and 10th Panzer Divisions were among the prisoners. It was when dusk was falling that he began to feel worried. By then the wooden buildings already mentioned were burning fiercely, and the flames threw the scene into lurid relief. The inevitable snipers were active, but the parachutists were able to give as good as they received and at one point picked off the crew of a German anti-aircraft gun one by one. 'A huge Boche howitzer of elderly pattern', brought into action, fired but one round before a mortar bomb, falling on top of it, killed its crew. The fight was still well-sustained, but ominously the number of wounded grew steadily higher and higher. 'Dusk fell,' says Frost, 'but I was still expecting the rest of the brigade or the leading troops of XXX Corps.' For the moment he may be left with his expectations, while the fortunes of the 1st and 3rd Battalions, seeking eagerly to come to his aid, are considered.

The 1st Battalion, which, thanks to the skill of its American pilots, had made 'a perfect drop, so that sticks had only a couple of hundred yards to go to get to their rendezvous', presently moved off almost at full strength under the leadership of Lieutenant-Colonel Dobie. Behind them was the wide dark clearing upon which they had alighted, littered with parachutes and gliders. 'Jubilant Dutchmen were collecting the parachutes as souvenirs, the more ambitious using hand-carts for the purpose.' The battalion took the Ede to Arnhem road, and were soon heartened by the arrival overhead of aircraft of the 2nd Tactical Air Force, which, in accordance with the plan, attacked German defence positions ahead of them. At this stage of the approach march Dutch women were to be seen waving and cheering, and Dutchmen wearing orange arm-bands. The parachute soldiers pressed on steadily but slowly, hearing from time to time spasmodic bursts of fire on the right flank, from which they rightly concluded that the 2nd and 3rd Battalions were in action. Towards the end of the afternoon German tanks appeared, but at that stage made no attack against them. Their presence, however, made further movement in the direction of the high ground to the north of Arnhem impossible, and when dusk fell the battalion, except for 'R' Company, took up positions on both sides of a narrow tree-lined road. Beyond was a wide expanse of ploughed field. 'R' Company, further away to the right, posted itself in a wood, where it was soon afterwards attacked and suffered heavy casualties.

When it was almost dark a German armoured car arrived and, being fired at by a Piat, made off. Orders were then given to set up a perimeter defence and dig in. This the men did, but hardly had they completed the task when a new order to advance was given. It was now midnight or later and very dark, the darkness being made heavier by the nature of the road along which the battalion had to move. It was a lane bordered by trees in full leaf, their branches overhanging and frequently meeting above the head of the wayfarer. The lane presently gave place to a very dense wood. So hard was it to keep direction in this thick darkness that each man held on to the man in front of him. 'By this time everyone was a bit tired and rather hungry. However, a silent move was made, and first light saw the battalion entering Arnhem itself.'

The time was then 05.30 hours, and Dobie had received a wireless signal from Frost at the bridge saying that reinforcements were urgently needed. He thereupon, and rightly, abandoned the original intention to seize and hold the high ground north of Arnhem—it was indeed impossible to do so, for the enemy were upon it in strength—and turned slightly south-east so as to make straight for the bridge. Casualties were steadily mounting. 'R' Company in the ill-fated wood had lost half its strength, and 'S' Company had had thirty killed and wounded. At 07.00 hours the 1st Battalion met the headquarters company of the 3rd Battalion and took them along.

This they were able to do because the 3rd Battalion had had no better fortune, but, like the 1st, had encountered heavy opposition when trying to reach the bridge along the Utrecht-Arnhem road. At the fall of dusk it was only on the western edge of Oosterbeek. Like the 1st Battalion, it had pushed forward slowly during the night, and during these hours of darkness 'A' Company and battalion headquarters became separated from the remainder who eventually reached a point just west of the St. Elizabeth Hospital. The position therefore at dawn on the 18th was that most of the 3rd Battalion was near the St. Elizabeth Hospital, on the western side of Arnhem, and that the 1st Battalion with the 3rd Battalion headquarters and the missing 'A' Company were to the north, heavily engaged with the enemy in the neighbourhood of the railway station.

Throughout that day the two battalions strove manfully, if vainly, to reach the bridge. The 3rd Battalion was under constant attack throughout the morning, and in the afternoon, having been reinforced by the remnants of 'A' Company who had moved down from the 1st Battalion, attempted once more to push ahead. It could go no further than three hundred yards before being held up by armour and self-propelled guns.

The 1st Battalion was in no better case. After the fight near the railway, which ended inconclusively, an attack was made about 09.00 hours by 'T' Company against a nearby factory, held in strength by the enemy. By fighting throughout the morning and by the eventual use of anti-tank guns against a pill-box in the factory itself, the position was at last cleared of the enemy, who suffered heavy casualties. By then, however,

'T' Company of the 1st Battalion was reduced to twenty-two men. The diary kept by Dobie laconically records the happenings of the next three hours:

'15.00 hours. Reached road junction, came under 88-mm. fire and machine-gun fire from main road. Gained road junction after fight. 16.00 hours. Advanced down main road on south side. Heavy fighting, could not advance past next road junction. Tanks ahead. 17.00 hours. Tried north side of road by backs of houses. Came under heavy mortar fire and sniping. Reached west of hospital. Tried to get vehicles forward. Quite impossible.'

The history of the battalion compiled somewhat later is more explicit. It makes it clear that in addition to the self-propelled guns, armoured cars and tanks, German snipers did grievous harm as soon as they had light enough to see the sights of their rifles. 'With their usual flair for concealment they were extremely difficult to locate, and they inflicted heavy casualties on the battalion.' To deal with them, Major C. Perrin-Brown, M.C., commanding 'T' Company, sought to put some of his men on the roofs of houses, whose inhabitants he had to rouse. 'Two astonished old ladies answered the knocking at their door in the grey light of dawn on that Monday morning.' On being told where it was the parachute soldiers desired to go, 'they were reluctant at first, but soon gave consent with an air of bewilderment. Within a short time the Dutch realised that their houses and gardens were fated to be a battlefield and retired with their families to the cellars. . . . The houses were all very nice—beautifully furnished and spotlessly clean. Some of the people were very demonstrative . . . they would come up and embrace soldiers, who, they said, had come to deliver them from the Germans. When the battle was going against us they wept openly . . . by the afternoon the battalion was still moving forward very slowly . . . through the houses and the gardens. It was necessary to use maximum concealment. The local inhabitants were most helpful. They would point out on the map where German concentrations were likely to be. By this time, twenty-four hours after the drop, everyone was getting very tired and very hungry. Fruit from the trees in gardens was eagerly consumed. Now and then a slice of bread or some other tit-bit would be received from a Dutchman. A twenty-four-hour ration was all that a man carried, and until the division was resupplied there would be no more. As the afternoon went on the firing became more intense . . . snipers were even more active, but they were being located and killed in increasing

225

numbers and their bodies could be seen dangling from their ropes in the trees'.

One thing was painfully obvious: the defences of the enemy had not been hastily prepared; on the contrary, 'their fire plan seemed pretty comprehensive. At any rate, it did not leave any gaps'. So much for 'the Brigade Group and some tanks', which 2nd Army Intelligence had assured them was the whole strength of the enemy.

By the end of the first twenty-four hours' fighting the position was this: Frost, with a mixed force, including the 2nd Battalion, was holding the northern end of the bridge and had successfully repelled all attacks; his casualties, however, were increasing, and he was in urgent need of reinforcements. These the 1st and 3rd Battalions were trying to supply and in so doing had been fought almost to a standstill. The strength of the 1st had fallen to about a hundred men, that of the 3rd was little better. What was happening elsewhere?

The division was momentarily without a commander, and the 1st Parachute Brigade without a brigadier. On landing, Major-General Urquhart had set out to visit units of the 1st Parachute Brigade. On reaching the 3rd Battalion, he met Brigadier Lathbury. By this time the enemy, now thoroughly roused, was subjecting its headquarters to a sustained fire of snipers and mortars. Headquarters were in a small house on the main road joining Heelsum to Arnhem, about half a mile from the suburb of Hartestein, and here Urquhart and Lathbury, being unable to go forward or back, were compelled to remain until 04.00 hours on the morning of the 18th, when they were once more able to set out. For men responsible for the movements of a division and a brigade they were in poor case. Urquhart's jeep had been hit and its driver killed. The wireless was not working, and he was therefore out of touch with all his troops except the 3rd Battalion. Lathbury was in the same unhappy situation. In the circumstances they could do no more than continue to move towards Arnhem in the wake of the 3rd Battalion. This they did, but, the enemy's fire becoming heavier and heavier, they presently found it necessary to take cover in another house. 'Self-propelled guns,' reports the Major-General, 'cruised up and down the street shooting at us and getting very aggressive.' Here they stayed until nearly 17.00 hours, when they decided to try yet again to return, the general to divisional headquarters at Wolfhezen, the brigadier to the bridge, where, though he did not know it, his headquarters had already arrived many hours before.

To cover the exit from the house of the party, which, in addition to the general and the brigadier, was made up of Captain W. A. Taylor and a subaltern, they made use of smoke bombs. 'Would you like to throw a bomb, sir?' enquired the brigadier of the major-general. 'Oh, no,' replied Urquhart, 'you're much better at it than I am.' Screened by the smoke, they made their way through a number of back gardens across the mouth of a street and into the next. Here Lathbury was hit in the back and fell to the ground. Urquhart and Taylor lifted him up and took him into the nearest house, where they laid him in the cellar. While so doing a German looked in at the window. Urquhart shot him dead with his revolver. 'It is seldom in modern war that the commander of a division has an opportunity to fight the enemy at such close quarters.' But this division was airborne, and every man in it, from its commander to the most junior private, was trained to arms and expected to use them at any moment.

Lathbury's wound was seen to be serious, for he was paralysed and unable to walk. At his repeated request they left him and moved to another house, where they remained until the early hours of the 19th hidden in the loft, and prevented from leaving soon after they reached this place by a self-propelled gun which 'came along the road and parked itself in front of our door'. In the darkness which precedes the dawn they slipped out, and for the moment fortune smiled, for they had gone but a short distance when a jeep appeared; Urquhart leapt into it and was soon at divisional headquarters, where he was at last able to resume control of the battle.

Lathbury, in the meantime, had been succoured by some men of the Dutch Red Cross, who conveyed him to the Queen Elizabeth Hospital, where his wound was attended to by a Dutch doctor. Despite its gravity, he prepared to depart for the bridge, where, he now learned, his headquarters were situated. Before he could do so, however, the Germans entered the hospital, and 'I had to slip into bed quickly'.

It was not until the morning of the 18th that the disappearance of General Urquhart became obvious. Brigadier P. H. W. Hicks, D.S.O., M.C., then took command. His one thought was to send as many men to the bridge as possible. The 2nd Battalion of the 1st Parachute Brigade he knew was established there, and the 1st and 3rd Battalions somewhere on their way towards it. They must be reinforced, and the only troops available were 'B' and 'D' Companies of the 2nd Battalion of the South Staffordshire

Regiment, under the command of Lieutenant-Colonel W. D. McCardie, part of the Air Landing Brigade, who had arrived in gliders at the same time as the 1st Parachute Brigade. They started off in its wake, but, like those who had gone before, were presently held up. This was on the morning of the 18th, but by now the second lift was expected and the reinforcements it brought would, it was hoped, avail to secure and hold the position so skilfully won by Frost.

Here a grave defect in the plan which Urquhart had foreseen when he made it, but which, given the circumstances, was quite inevitable, revealed itself. There were already on the dropping zone two fine regiments, the 1st Battalion, the Border Regiment, and the 7th Battalion, the King's Own Scottish Borderers. They had accompanied the 1st Parachute Brigade in gliders, their orders being to hold the landing zones against the enemy, so that the second lift might land unmolested. Like the 1st Parachute Brigade, they had arrived almost intact, and there were thus some fourteen hundred officers and men who, in other circumstances, might have been used for the immediate battle. Instead they played their parts and held the zone, the King's Own Scottish Borderers having to fight a brisk battle, which ended in a bayonet charge, to do so.

The morning of the 18th dawned bright and clear ; the second lift was due at 10.00 hours, and shortly before that hour Major Wilson and his men laid out more markers to make sure that the landing and dropping zones would be recognised. They had been informed that any aircraft seen would be friendly ; but as they were engaged on their work a number of Messerschmitt 109s dived upon them, guns blazing. They leapt for cover and fortunately escaped casualties. 10.00 hours came, then 11.00 hours, then noon, and still there was no sign of the Dakotas, the tugs and the gliders. These were still in England, for, clear though the weather was over Holland, the low cloud and fog so prevalent during the summer and autumn of 1944 persisted over the airfields, and it was not possible to take off.

Eventually rain drove the mist away sufficiently to allow the second lift to take the air, and by 15.00 hours it was beginning to arrive at Arnhem. 'In addition to our American crew there were eighteen of us in my stick,' records Major R. T. H. Lonsdale, D.S.O., M.C., second-in-command of the 11th Battalion, whose tenacity at Primosole had been of such value, 'we were flying at eight hundred feet as we crossed the Suffolk coastline, and I remember looking down on the old town of

228

Aldeburgh and its quiet streets and wishing myself there. One's thoughts get a bit mixed at times. Some of the fellows read, some of them talked. My batman—Lance-Corporal "Nobby" Noble—was, as usual in a plane, sound asleep. I glanced outside at the rest of the Dakotas. Well, I reflected—we've plenty of company, and we're all going the same way.

'We were still at eight hundred feet when we made the Dutch coast, and we kept over our own lines as long as possible. The first warning that we were approaching the dropping zone came from the co-pilot. "You've half an hour," he announced tersely. Ten minutes later the red light by the exit door signalled the "Get ready". We stood up and made a last check. There was nothing much to say.

'By now we had skirted Nijmegen and were over enemy-held territory. The luck was holding—we'd had no interference yet. Suddenly, it seemed right from beneath our feet, a crackling noise was instantly followed by a whip-like explosion. The plane lurched violently, flung us sprawling, then righted again. No need to ask if we'd been hit—we knew it. The air-burst—I reckon that was what it was—tore a great rent in the fuselage and wounded two of my lads in the leg. The American crew chief standing by the door was only partly saved by some armour-plating. I looked at my right hand and was surprised to see it streaming blood.

'We had barely time to unhook our casualties and move them to the back of the plane—"no jump today, boys"—when we got the green light to drop. The crew chief, although wounded, stuck to his post and saw us off. I was glad to go.

'I suppose we could not have been in the air more than thirteen seconds, but that was enough. The Jerry tracer came streaking among us; I never felt more like a sitting pigeon than I did then. Obviously the enemy had brought up their mobile flak units after the events of the previous day, and they gave it us hot.

'I touched down in the centre of a field, with the entire brigade dropping around. The Americans had dropped us slap in the right place, and I give them full marks for that. They didn't all get back. As I slipped out of my harness I watched one of their Dakotas crash in flames. Noble—good old "Nobby"—came dashing up to me. I'd bled a lot, and a stiffener from my flask helped me as he hurriedly bandaged my hand.'

The drops and the glider landings of the second lift were as successful as those of the day before. Once more the R.A.F. and

American crews had performed their task with skill. On this occasion one of them shewed that type of resolution which makes a man faithful unto death. Over the dropping zone a Dakota with sixteen parachutists on board was hit and set on fire. 'Suddenly a little orange flame appeared on the port wing,' notes a witness. 'I watched the plane gradually lose height and counted the bodies baling out. They all came out, although the last two were too low for comfort. But the crew stayed in the plane and flew straight, the flames getting larger and larger till eventually it flew into the ground.'

The 4th Parachute Brigade were dropping through the air to 'the clack of bullets and the thump of mortars. There were fires burning all over the heath. Quite a wind was blowing, and many found themselves in the fir woods. The speed with which we dropped down out of the trees was fantastic, for we had heard stories about parachutists in trees in Normandy'.

Once on the ground, the individual battalions began to form up, and the 11th Battalion had collected some eighty prisoners before it reached the rendezvous. The 4th Parachute Brigade, under Hackett, was composed of the 156th, 10th and 11th Battalions, who were soon ready to fulfil their appointed task. Hackett was in high fettle, for 'two of the enemy gave themselves up to me about two minutes after I was out of my parachute harness, and I had a couple of prisoners even before I had a command post'. He was met by Lieutenant-Colonel C. B. Mackenzie, the G.S.O.1 of the division, who described the situation. The fierceness of the opposition in Arnhem had caused Brigadier Hicks to change his plans. The 156th and 10th Battalions were to carry out their original orders, seize and hold the high ground north of Arnhem which had proved too difficult a task for the 1st Battalion; but the 11th Battalion was to make with all speed for the bridge, together with the other two companies of the 2nd Battalion of the South Staffordshire Regiment which had now arrived.

This force, the South Staffordshires in the van, lost no time in setting out. They moved but slowly, but by the time darkness fell they had reached the western outskirts of Arnhem. Here they fell in with the harassed but indomitable Dobie, whose 1st Battalion had already lost four-fifths of its strength. About 20.00 hours the three commanding officers, Dobie, McCardie in command of the South Staffordshires, and Lea of the 11th Battalion, held a conference not far from the Elizabeth Hospital. It was decided that the advance should begin again at 04.00

hours on the morning of Tuesday, the 19th, that was in about six hours. The 1st Battalion was to move down to the river bank, turn left and make their way towards the bridge, followed by the 11th Battalion. The South Staffordshires were to move down the main road.

At the chosen hour the South Staffordshires began to advance, only to be held up at a spot called the Monastery in the main street of Arnhem. Here they lost heavily, being overrun by tanks after their Piat ammunition had been exhausted. Withdrawing westwards, they reorganised and then delivered an attack on the Den Brink position which had proved so troublesome to the 1st Battalion when on its way to the bridge. The object was to make it possible for the 11th Battalion to reach a road running north from Den Brink. For a little time the gallant South Staffordshires prevailed, but hardly had they appeared on the high ground when enemy tanks drove them off it, and at the same time attacked the 11th Battalion, which was deprived of any chance it might have had to deliver the assault planned a few hours before. Taken in front and on a flank, the battalion suffered heavily, though the left-hand and rear companies were able to extricate themselves. The German tactics were those of men well trained: their tanks remained out of range of Piats, and 'solemnly knocked houses down or burnt them by firing phosphorus shells at the roofs, and then waited till the defenders were forced to withdraw or be burnt to death. German infantry, covered by the tanks, infiltrated between houses and gardens and mopped up the defenders or forced them back'.

Meanwhile the 156th Battalion, followed by the 10th, was moving along the line of a railway towards the high ground, its chosen objective. By nightfall on the 18th the first of these had reached the railway station at Wolfhezen, and the second was about a mile away. Hackett decided that at dawn on the next day the 156th Battalion should capture the village of Koepel to the north of Arnhem, while the 10th should form a firm base a thousand yards in front of the little village of Johanna Hoeve.

The 156th Battalion's attack began at 05.00, and by 10.00 hours had petered out after an initial success. By then its casualties were on a par with those sustained by the other battalions in this operation, and 'A' Company had lost all its officers. Nor was the 10th Battalion more fortunate: in moving to its assigned position it soon encountered the inevitable barrage of anti-aircraft guns used as light artillery, self-propelled guns and tanks. The battalion dug in with speed and address on either side of the Arnhem-Utrecht road, the intention of Lieutenant-Colonel Smyth being to endure the enemy's fire while day lasted and then to deliver a night attack with the object of reaching the Hueve position. Through the long day the Battalion stood its ground, though mortar fire was added to its other tribulations. The behaviour of Captain L. E. Queripel, during these heavy hours, was especially noteworthy. Commanding a company to which men separated from two other battalions had attached themselves, he crossed and recrossed the road under heavy fire to encourage his men and put them in position. At one moment, finding a wounded sergeant, he picked him up and took him to the regimental aid post, receiving a wound in his face while doing so. His next feat was to lead a small local attack against a strongpoint composed of a captured British anti-tank gun and two machine-guns. He killed the crew of all three, and the anti-tank gun thus recovered proved of great service.

As the autumn day waned the 10th Battalion found itself unable to hold on any longer and began slowly to withdraw. Queripel, cut off with a small party of men, took cover in a ditch. In addition to the wound in his face, he had now been wounded in both arms. He and his men lined the ditch to cover the withdrawal of the remainder of the battalion. By then they were short both of weapons and ammunition, having but a few Mills bombs, rifles and their personal pistols. German infantry were very near and more than once their stick bombs landed in the ditch, only to be flung back in their faces by the vigilant Queripel. The position became more and more untenable, but he waited until the last moment before he ordered those of his men still alive to leave while he covered their withdrawal with the aid of such grenades as remained. 'That was the last occasion on which he was seen.' He gallantry earned him a posthumous Victoria Cross. Queripel's gallantry and the steady shooting of Sergeant Kincaid and Private Waters, both of the Intelligence section, who could claim among their victims the crew of a German self-propelled gun, enabled the battalion to dig in once more and to hold its position, though by now the enemy had brought up several tanks. 'These soon received a taste of the Piat and did not like it.'

Thus before 19th September was ended everything had gone awry. The utmost efforts of the 1st and 3rd Battalions, and later of the 11th, to cut their way through the town to the bridge, had failed; and the 156th and 10th Battalions, somewhere to the north, had been equally unfortunate. The day was marked by two further disasters. In the afternoon the first supplies from the air were flown in, but since the division had been unable to make any contact with Dempsey's 2nd Army, no message had been sent warning Nos. 38 and 46 Groups of the Royal Air Force that the supply dropping point chosen beforehand to the north of Warnsborn was a considerable distance from any ground held by the division. Despite the display 'of every kind of sign and indicator', the pilots flew through heavy anti-aircraft fire to deposit their loads on the agreed spot. They fell into the hands of the Germans, who, strangely enough, did not keep them for themselves, but issued them to the local Dutch population. Even had the pilots seen the desperate signals made to them—they do not appear to have done so—they would in all probability have regarded them as a *ruse de guerre* and ignored them.

Then the arrival of the gliders belonging to the Polish Parachute Brigade provoked the most violent reaction on the part of the enemy; much of it fell on the unhappy 4th Parachute Brigade, then endeavouring to conform to a new, and for Urquhart a most melancholy decision. By the afternoon of Tuesday, the 19th, he was forced to face the unpalatable fact that all attempts to reach the bridge by the reinforcements, whether parachute troops or glider-borne, had failed and would continue to fail; for the enemy was very strong, and, moreover, possessed armour and heavy weapons. Accordingly, with the utmost reluctance he decided that he must form a perimeter round the little suburb of Oosterbeek, in the midst of which were his headquarters at the Hartestein hotel, and there hold out until the 2nd Army, if it was coming, arrived. This decision meant that the bridge, to which Frost still clung, and of which the seizure had been the main objective of the operation, must be abandoned.

The necessary orders, issued with no little difficulty, were carried out that night and next day. In obeying them, further losses, inevitable with troops in close contact with the enemy seeking to disengage themselves, occurred. The 156th Battalion lost all but a quartermaster and six men of 'S' Company, half 'B' Company and all 'C' Company when moving to their places in the perimeter. And on the next day, the 20th, the two hundred officers and men left fought a series of fierce actions in an attempt to cover the withdrawal of the 10th Battalion towards the perimeter. Their numbers dwindled steadily and not more than four officers and seventy other ranks survived to share in the last defence. The 10th Battalion, whom they had sought so hard to aid, suffered equally and was virtually wiped out. 'We were given orders,' reported Sergeant Bentley afterwards, 'to leave the wood. It was every man for himself, for by then we were all split up. . . . Sergeant Sunley and Sergeant Houghton were terrific. We ran across a playing field and found several men shewing yellow triangles. We understood that they were Poles . . . we had by then lost about two-thirds, but the men were still in good heart.'

During these efforts to move back to Wolfhezen and then to the perimeter one of its non-commissioned officers, Corporal Garibaldi, did not belie the famous name he bore. At a point where the woods receded he charged the enemy in his Bren-gun carrier and silenced their fire, only to be killed later. Eventually Lieutenant-Colonel Smyth and Major Warne, the commanding officer and the second-in-command, with about sixty other ranks, were all that were left standing when the final position was reached.

The remnants of one other battalion belonging to the brigade, the 11th, also eventually took up a position in the perimeter. That battalion, it will be recalled, had been sent towards the bridge with the South Staffordshires in a last effort to reinforce Frost, and had been almost entirely destroyed. A few men under Lieutenant J. E. Blackwood of 'B' Company succeeded in withdrawing in accordance with Urquhart's plan.

In this heavy fighting the brigadier and those with him took their full share. 'My brigade headquarters,' wrote Hackett months later when he had returned from Holland, 'with its clerks, signallers, Intelligence section and batmen, was holding the centre of our line as a unit. They were a splendid lot. The signallers were mostly Cheshire yeomen . . . the clerks were also "foundation members" for the most part and in the close-quarter fighting in the woods on 19th and particularly 20th September did brilliantly under Staff Sergeant Pearson, the chief clerk, one of the bravest men at really hand-to-hand fighting and one of the soundest in the brigade . . . I found myself on 20th September as "a broken-down cavalryman" (Urquhart's phrase) leading little bayonet rushes in the very dirty stuff the brigade had to contend with before we made contact with the division, and I was impressed with the stout hearts and accurate grenade throwing of the brigade Intelligence section, particularly after the Intelligence officer (Captain Blundell) was shot and killed at about twenty yards range on the same morning.'

Thus did the remnants of the 4th Parachute Brigade make ready with the rest of Urquhart's force for the last round. To some extent the brigade's fortunes, or rather misfortunes, were even more remarkable than those of the 1st. Its three battalions, the 156th, the 10th and the 11th, in their attempt to carry out the original plan and form the outer perimeter round Arnhem, had immediately to face a situation which made the fulfilment of their task impossible however hard they tried—and their efforts were heroic. The reason is not far to seek. They arrived in the neighbourhood of Arnhem, but, be it remembered, eight miles away from the town, on the 18th September, and they formed the major part of the second lift. By then all chance of effecting surprise had vanished and they were at once face to face with an alert enemy determined to offer fierce resistance. 'We had gunshot casualties in the air,' records Hackett, 'and during the reorganisation period on the ground it was disconcerting to walk into scattered parties of Boches, usually pretty frightened, fortunately, for the most part lying close in the heath and sometimes only flushed when you nearly stepped on them.' Thus the brigade found itself committed to immediate battle almost before it had reached the ground. Moreover, the fighting from first to last was at close quarters and endured for eight days, of which the last four were spent manning a dwindling perimeter. In these circumstances it is possible, even probable, that the 4th Parachute Brigade's casualties in killed and wounded were even higher than those of the 1st. After the battle was over, so few remained that it was disbanded and never reformed.

Of the 1st Parachute Brigade in the perimeter there was no sign. Dobie, commanding the 1st Battalion, had received orders at 01.00 hours on Tuesday, the 19th, to withdraw to Oosterbeek, but these were later cancelled and he and his men moved in accordance with the plan concocted earlier to the river. Here they turned left-handed with a high bank rising steeply on their left, and here, meeting with German infantry, they fought with them hand to hand. Major Perrin-Brown led a bayonet charge of 'T' Company, and a little later Major Timothy, another of 'R' Company, and the morning air was filled with the battle cry of 'Waho Mohammed' springing from the throats of desperate but indomitable men. Soon after dawn the battalion was attacked by tanks, and by 06.00 hours 'our position was becoming desperate, as the enemy were on high ground and in houses above us, and tanks were firing at point-blank range'. The strength of the battalion at that moment was, 'R' Company, six men ; 'S' Company, fifteen ; 'T' Company, eight ; battalion head-quarters, ten. Dobie, making a personal reconnaissance, saw at once that any further move was out of the question. He ordered what was left of his command to enter the nearby houses. They were occupied by Germans, who flung grenades at them, one of which wounded him. With six men Dobie eventually forced an entry into a house and made for the cellars, which were full of civilians. Only two of his party were unwounded. Here they remained for about an hour until some S.S. troopers entered and took them prisoner.

The 3rd Battalion was a little better case. Precisely how many officers and men belonging to it reached the perimeter is not known. After the final withdrawal, when a roll-call was called at Nijimegen, one officer and thirty-six other ranks answered to their names.

The 21st Independent Parachute Company under Wilson, and the Sappers under Captain H. F. Brown, played their full part. Wilson's men, among whom were a number of anti-Nazi Germans, were particularly fierce. Meeting with snipers belong-ing to an S.S. Battalion near the dropping zone before the second lift came in, they attacked them fiercely, and presently 'the Germans, in their snipers' suits, crawled out of their slit trenches and grovelled on the ground begging for mercy. They were terri-fied to see men in red berets and had to be violently persuaded to their feet'. Somewhat later in the battle the Germans shouted to them to surrender. 'We shouted back', says Wilson, 'that we were too frightened to do so, and that they must come and get us. Sixty of them were fools enough to do so, and were wiped out with twelve Bren guns at a range of a hundred and fifty yards. They died screaming.'

The sappers fought as infantry with great effect.

Before recounting the last stand at Oosterbeek, what happened to Frost and the 2nd Battalion must first be recorded. That Monday night, the 18th, which began in flame and smoke from the burning houses, gradually grew quieter, until soon after midnight 'there was absolute silence, or so it seemed to me', said Frost, 'for some hours'. The commander of the defence was able at last to snatch some sleep. Up till then he had had but half an hour, and had sustained himself with cups of tea and an occasional nip of whisky. Before dawn he had had to issue an order bringing sniping to an end, for ammunition was running low and would have to be kept for warding off the attacks which the enemy was bound soon to launch with increasing severity. The bridge was still covered by the guns of the 1st Air Landing Light Regiment under Lieutenant-Colonel W. F. K. Thompson, Royal Artillery, but these were their only support. 'It became more and more difficult to move,' recounts Frost, 'for the Boche were tightening their grip, though they made no effort to close with us. By then the number of wounded was very great, but the number of killed small.'

The men at the bridge held on throughout that day, buoyed up by rumours, first that the 1st and 3rd Battalions were at hand, and then in the later afternoon by the news that the South Staffordshires and the 11th Battalion were fighting their way towards them. It was a day of heavy mortaring and shelling by tanks which had crept up to a position close to the river bank. Towards noon Captain A. Franks went out against them, and scored three hits with the last three Piat bombs. The German tanks clattered away out of range and did not return. At dusk, however, a Tiger tank appeared and shelled in turn each house still held by the parachutists. Among the casualties caused by this fire was Father Egan, M.C., who had served with the brigade from the outset, and Major A. D. Tatham-Warter. They were both hit, but both remained with those still fighting and refused to go below to the cellars.

During this day the conduct of Trooper Bolton of the 1st Air Landing Reconnaissance Squadron was particularly noteworthy for the calmness with which he manned his Bren gun and refused to be parted from it. 'He hated the thought of anyone using it but himself,' says Captain Bernard Briggs, the staff captain at brigade headquarters, who had been at the bridge from the beginning, 'and would wake from a cat-nap at any moment and leap to it ready to fire'. Lieutenant P. J. Barnett, of the brigade headquarters defence platoon, shewed much courage and ingenuity when he succeeded in destroying 'a troublesome tank single-handed with grenades'. He was to earn the Medaille Militaire Willemswoorde, the Dutch Victoria Cross.

Night fell and it seemed to Frost, looking uneasily over his shoulder, that the whole town of Arnhem was on fire, including two large churches. 'I never saw anything more beautiful than those burning buildings.'

By now the defenders of the bridge were being driven from the houses as they caught fire. Their method of moving from one to another was, whenever possible, to 'mousehole'[1] their way from house to house in conditions which grew steadily worse. During this tedious dusty method of moving from one position to another Lieutenant Simpson succeeded in disabling a tank close to the house in which he was posted. Its crew got out and 'crept along the wall till they came to a halt beneath the window where I was crouching. I dropped a grenade on them and that was that. I held it for two seconds before I let it drop'.

Two things were of particular concern: the lack of water, and the breakdown of the wireless sets, which made it impossible to keep in touch with the rest of the division except by means of the civilian telephone lines. These, manned by the Dutch resistance, continued to play a part to the end, the operators paying for their fortitude with their lives. Frost had no continuous means of communicating with the battalions who he still hoped were on their way to his relief, but could sometimes speak with divisional headquarters. Perhaps the reinforcements were not very distant. They might even be within earshot. 'During a lull we yelled "Waho Mohammed",' says Briggs, 'hoping there would be some reply. But none came. Then we tore down wallpaper to make a megaphone six feet long, through which we shouted words and epithets that could only be British.' But there was still no reply.

Dawn on Wednesday, the 20th, shone on Frost, still clinging with difficulty to the north-west end of the bridge, but able to prevent the Germans crossing it. But now his personal good fortune was to desert him. During the morning he was badly wounded in the leg, and Major C. H. F. Gough, M.C., Reconnaissance Squadron, assumed command, but still referred major decisions to Frost, while Tatham-Warter, 'whose conduct was exemplary even amid so much gallantry', took over what remained of the 2nd Battalion. In reporting these changes to the divisional commander at Hartestein, Gough referred to himself as 'the man who goes in for funny weapons', so that no German or collaborator listening in on the town exchange which he was using would be able to identify him.

The area occupied by the parachute troops grew smaller and smaller, though they continued to control the approaches to the bridge. Conspicuous among them at this stage was Lieutenant Grayburn of 'A' Company. Early in the action, in leading the unsuccessful attack on the south end of the bridge, he had been

[1] Knocking or blowing a hole in the dividing walls and thus moving from house to house under cover.

hit in the shoulder, but continued to lead his men and was the last to withdraw. He then established his platoon in a very exposed house whose position was vital to the defence. In this he held out until 19th September, when it was set on fire, having repelled all attacks, including those made by tanks and self-propelled guns. Re-forming his depleted force, he was still able to maintain the defence and on 20th September led a series of fighting patrols, whose activities so galled the enemy that tanks were brought up again. Only then did Grayburn retreat and, even so, was still able to strike back. At the head of another patrol he drove off the enemy, thus allowing others to remove the fuses from the demolition charges which the Germans had succeeded in placing under the bridge. In so doing he was again wounded, but still would not leave the fight. Eventually, that evening he was killed by the fire of a tank. In his conduct 'he shewed an example of devotion to duty which can seldom have been equalled', and was awarded a posthumous Victoria Cross.

By the evening of that day all the buildings near the bridge had been burnt down except the U-shaped school. This now caught fire and all attempts to put it out failed. Captain J. Logan, D.S.O., the medical officer, who with Captain D. Wright, M.C., had been tireless in tending the wounded, therefore informed Gough that he must surrender them if he wished to save them from being burnt or roasted alive in the cellars. Just after dark, under a flag of truce, the enemy picked up many of the wounded, including Frost, who had been expecting his fate and had thrown away his badges. A moment before, Wicks, his batman, had taken leave of him and gone back to the fight. He, too, was soon afterwards badly wounded.

Gough and those still unwounded continued to resist. Though ammunition was practically at an end, they nevertheless succeeded in delivering an attack at dawn on 21st September in an attempt to retake some of the houses. It failed and what remained of the 2nd Battalion scattered in small parties in an endeavour to find their way to the XXX Corps, which they had awaited so long and so vainly. At last the bridge was once more in German hands.

In this action the 2nd Battalion had been wiped out; but seldom can a fighting unit of any army in any age have had so glorious an end. For thrice the length of time laid down in its orders it had held a bridge against odds which were overwhelming from the beginning. Buoyed up by hope and by frequent messages that relief or support was on the way, either at the hands of the rest of the 1st Parachute Brigade and later the 4th Brigade, or from XXX Corps moving up from Nijmegen, when that hope was deferred, the hearts of its officers and men were not sick. They continued to fight, and only ceased to fire when their ammunition was gone and their wounded, now the great majority, faced with a fearful and unnecessary death. The conduct of the 2nd Battalion at the Bridge at Arnhem is more than an inspiration or an example ; it was the quintessence of all those qualities which the parachute soldier must possess and display if he is to justify his training and the trust reposed in him. So great a spirit in evidence every moment of those three September days and nights can be overcome only by weight of numbers. That, and that alone, was the cause of their glorious defeat.

The Perimeter

IN THE attacks delivered by the 11th Battalion, when attempting to reach the bridge, Major Lonsdale, its second-in-command, had, to his chagrin, taken no part. The wound in his hand was too severe. On the return of Urquhart to the battle from his enforced imprisonment in the house on the outskirts of Arnhem he at once called upon Lonsdale to assume the defence of part of the perimeter he was then beginning to form. Lonsdale accordingly eventually found himself in command of the remnants of the 1st, 3rd and 11th Battalions and of the 2nd South Staffordshires, all of which had lost their commanding officers, and had for a time been fighting under Lieutenant-Colonel Thompson, commanding the 1st Airborne Light Regiment, Royal Artillery. Accompanied by Major Robert Cain, who survived the action to win a Victoria Cross, Lonsdale moved half a mile down the road to the white church of Oosterbeek, a square edifice with 'a funeral inscription on the wall with some cherubs blowing trumpets round it', and then further on to where his new command, what was left of them, were holding a number of houses.

Their most immediate concern was the activities of German snipers, and they spent the afternoon of the 19th blasting them from their hide-outs with anti-tank guns. Then came the German answer. 'About 6 o'clock,' says Lonsdale, 'I was standing at the doorway of my headquarters, a house set back from a cross-roads, when I heard a shout "Look out, they're coming", and, sure enough, they were. A quick glance shewed me three German tanks edging out of a wood two hundred yards away, and immediately we let drive at them with every automatic we had. Sergeant Baskerfield of the South Staffordshires, our anti-tank gunner, at the cross-roads swung round his gun . . . his first shot knocked out the leading tank and his second stopped number two. The third tank stayed put, and the German infantry hidden among the trees broke cover and tried to cross the roadway. Not one of them made it. Our lads gave them hell and the attack broke down. Baskerfield, whose gun had been knocked out, took over another whose crew had been killed. He fought it single-handed until he fell, shot through the head. His bravery earned him a posthumous Victoria Cross. Our own casualties were light, but we knew what to expect from now on.'

The men of the 3rd Battalion were driven from the houses and the woods by flame-throwers, 'almost blinding us with dense smoke', and retreated to the church at Oosterbeek. There they joined what was left of the Glider Pilot Regiment, and Lonsdale's command, known as Lonsdale Force and numbering perhaps five hundred officers and men in all, was complete. Before darkness fell the 1st and 3rd Battalions were covering a patch of open ground to the south, facing the Rhine. The 11th Battalion was on the Oosterbeek-Arnhem road, and the South Staffordshires near the church. 'Fortunately,' records Lonsdale, 'the night passed quietly. The enemy moved up, but we were not troubled, and some vigorous trench-digging and a general strengthening of our defences found us, when dawn came, well dug in. No one, of course, had any doubts this time as to the seriousness of the position. All hope of breaking through to the bridge had been abandoned.'

The perimeter, of which Lonsdale Force formed the south-eastern defence, was composed on the west of the survivors of the reconnaissance squadron, of a detachment of glider pilots, the remnants of the King's Own Scottish Borderers of the Border Regiment, those who were left of the 21st Independent Company (the pathfinders) and a number of Royal Engineers, its commander being Brigadier Hicks. The eastern half was held by more glider pilots, and members of the Royal Army Service Corps who had flown in with the gliders to maintain the vehicles and were now fighting stoutly as infantry, and the few survivors of the 156th and 10th Battalions. This half of the perimeter was commanded by Brigadier Hackett, soon to be badly wounded, but to remain at his post until the 24th, when his duties were assumed by Lieutenant-Colonel I. Murray of the Glider Pilot Regiment. This regiment was throughout the war particularly distinguished by its gallantry. Not only was each man a trained pilot of gliders, but once he had landed his aircraft he fought in the ranks of the airborne troops. The Regiment did excellent service in Sicily, Normandy, Holland and finally on the other side of the Rhine.

So what remained of the 1st Airborne Division settled down to hold out until relieved, or until further resistance was impossible. The first day, the 20th, was notable for the beginning of that heavy bombardment by mortars and shells which was the principal means by which the Germans sought to subdue Urquhart and his men, and which, reaching as it did at times a density of fifty mortar bombs a minute, was an ever-present accompaniment to their other activities. It was this mortar fire which caused so many of the casualties. There was no safe cover from it anywhere, not even in a well-dug and well-sited slit trench, of which 'more than one', said a survivor, 'looked very like a grave'. So savage a bombardment, prolonged as it was for five days and nights, had its effect. To remain cheerful beneath it when desperately short of water, food and ammunition needed a constant effort of the will. The remedy was action, and whenever possible the men of the division took large doses of it. Snipers were at all times an obvious target, and since the standard of marksmanship was high, very few of the bullets remaining to the defence missed their mark. Sergeant Quinn of the reconnaissance squadron and his men constructed a dummy out of a pillow, a steel helmet and a broomstick. They exposed this at various places and at different times along their section of the perimeter, and it never failed to provoke a German sniper into giving away his position. By the skilful use they made of it, they killed seventeen or eighteen.

In this form of retaliation the members of Wilson's 21st Independent Parachute Company were also experts. They were wont to leave their lines 'to crawl round the neighbouring houses and pick the Germans off from the roof-tops', says their commander. 'We were extremely lucky,' he continues, 'because we got a supply drop and we always had ammunition. . . I was frightened the barrels of the Bren guns would wear out. We must have fired over three thousand rounds per gun without changing the barrel. We had a lot of trouble with dust, and had to clean the guns quite frequently to keep them firing. Sergeant Carter, the armourer sergeant, constantly went round putting the guns right . . . my snipers used to cut a notch on their rifle butts for all confirmed victims. One man had eighteen notches.'

There was an occasional respite from the otherwise unceasing mortar fire. 'The Germans always drew stumps at seven o'clock,' says Wilson. 'In the evening I would go to my trench,' records another, 'and smoke a pipe. I used to watch an apple tree which grew nearby, and had red apples on it, and then I watched the stars come up.' It was at Arnhem some three centuries and a half earlier that 'another poet, the gentle Philip Sidney, had watched those same stars as he lay dying of a mortal wound'.

Apart from the beginning of the mortar barrage the 20th was noteworthy for a determined and successful attempt by the Germans to seize the main dressing station on the road east of Hartestein, and for a supply drop at 17.00 hours, which was more successful than any of the previous and which brought the beseiged men much-needed ammunition. The dressing station was established in the Tafelberg Hotel, where the British medical staff were helped by Dr. Giesbert and Mr. Bauman, an electrician of Oosterbeek who rearranged all the lights so that an efficient operating theatre could be established. He then made splints out of pieces of scrap iron or wood. Throughout the fighting he passed continually to and fro between his house and the hospital, bringing food and water, and carrying a white flag, which both sides were careful to respect.

That the second of the two dressing stations was not overrun was due to Private Dixon, cook of the Independent Parachute Company. A German commander sent Wilson, who was holding the house next door to it, a message to say that if the parachutists did not immediately leave their position, he would destroy the house with his tanks. Wilson replied that he would comply with this request provided that the Germans promised not to enter the hospital thirty yards away. At the same moment he called on Dixon to slip out by the back door and try to engage the German tanks. Dixon knew more of pots and pans than of Piats, but his first shot hit the leading tank and exploded some ammunition inside it. The Germans withdrew, and the hospital remained in our hands.

Conditions in it were very bad, for, lacking equipment, Captain Martin, Royal Army Medical Corps, could do little more than give first aid to the patients soon numbering more than two hundred. The owner of the house in which it was established, a Dutch lady, Mevrouw De Horst, worked without rest or food, helped by a boy of seventeen, who did likewise. What water there was had to be brought from a pump close by, till it ran 'red with blood'. Every evening the lady moved from room to room, her Bible in her hand, and in the light of a torch read aloud the 91st Psalm, 'for', said she, 'it has comforted my children and may comfort you'. Lying on mattresses or straw amid the stench of wounds and death, the men heard 'her soft voice speaking most carefully the words of King David'. 'Thou shalt not be afraid for the terror by night, nor for the arrow that flieth by day, nor for the pestilence that walketh in darkness, nor for the destruction that wasteth at noonday.'

Throughout the 20th and until the withdrawal on the 25th the serving of the guns of the Light Regiment under Lieutenant-Colonel Thompson was beyond praise. Their steady shooting broke up many attacks before they could develop. Most of the guns were situated in the firing line itself, so small was the perimeter. The artillery of the 2nd Army on the other side of the Rhine also gave very valuable support from 21st September until the withdrawal. Their fire and that of the Light Regiment were under the general control of Urquhart's commander, Royal Artillery, Lieutenant-Colonel R. C. Loder-Symonds, afterwards killed in an air accident in Java.

The day of the 21st was enlivened by a vigorous attempt on the part of the enemy to break into the perimeter. It was defeated by a bayonet charge of the Borderers which cost them four officers killed. Again a supply drop was attempted, and a few of the canisters fell upon the position.

Why was it that the pilots and crews of Nos. 38 and 46 Groups of the Royal Air Force were unable to locate the division? The primary reason was the presence of heavy woods and copses which made it very hard, if not impossible, for the aircrews to see the ground signals shewing where the containers should fall. There was also another reason. As has been explained, the original zones on which the supplies were to be dropped had never been captured, and, despite a wireless message to this effect, the Air Force at first continued to fly to it, though to do so meant heavy casualties. Why this very important message was not received has never been explained, nor is it known why the telephone system belonging to a private company with lines radiating in every direction through the province of

Gelderland was not more used to maintain communication between Urquhart in Arnhem and Browning in Nijmegen. In all probability our intelligence services hesitated to make use of a telephone system much of which passed through enemy-occupied territory, and their hesitation to do so in the circumstances may perhaps be excused.

Be that as it may, the lack of communications caused, as has been said, heavy casualties among the aircraft of the Royal Air Force. 'My most poignant memory,' writes Lieutenant-Colonel M. St. J. Packe, commanding the Royal Army Service Corps elements in Oosterbeek, 'will always be the time I spent watching the supply aircraft coming over and dropping their containers on an area not under our control. . . . They were met by a screen of flak, and it was awe-inspiring to see them fly straight into it, straight into a flaming hell. We thought that some would not face it and would jettison their cargoes, in which case we should get them, for they would fall short and therefore in our lines; but they all stuck to their course and went on, nor did they hesitate.' On at least one, and possibly three, occasions a Stirling and a Dakota, both on fire, were seen to circle what they believed to be the correct dropping zone while the crews on board continued to throw out containers until the aircraft fell 'like two torches from the sky'. Such cold-blooded courage is the extreme of heroism. Their losses were very high: 6 per cent on 18th September, 8 per cent on the 19th, and 20 per cent on the 21st. Among the casualties was the leader of the supply group, Wing Commander Davis, D.S.O. Others included men of the Royal Army Service Corps, the dispatchers, who unflinchingly shared the danger and suffered the fate of the crews. The story of how the Royal Air Force sought to supply the division from the air is a melancholy, but glorious, page of its history. Despite their efforts and their sacrifice, only 7·4 per cent of the total tonnage dropped was collected by Urquhart and his men.

On the 21st, too, an effort was made to reinforce the division by dropping part of the 1st Polish Parachute Brigade opposite their lines on the other side of the river, just east of the village of Driel. Since neither boats nor rafts could be collected the Poles were unable to cross the Lower Rhine, and remained where they were, until the night of the 22nd-23rd September, when this situation had been partially remedied and about two hundred joined the division in time to take part in the final withdrawal.

So the 1st Airborne Division continued to hold out, the perimeter daily shrinking. On its west and centre there were woods interspersed with fields; on the north and east the streets and houses of the trim suburb of Oosterbeek, with here and there an outlying farm in one of which, incredible to relate, an old Dutch farmer was to be seen at intervals raking his hay, while his wife busied herself with household chores. To the assaults of the enemy were added those of hunger and thirst. Each officer and man of the division who had dropped or landed by glider had brought with him a twenty-four-hour ration. Most made this last for forty-eight, but after that food became very short. Some men went four days without food. Such vegetables as could be collected, potatoes, cabbages and a few tomatoes, were eagerly devoured, and there were also a number of apples, but not many. 'There just weren't any army rations after the first day,' runs the report of an officer, 'but there were some tame rabbits, one of which I fed . . . one day a parachutist on the scrounge walked off with it, but I made him hand it over, and laid it down between my batman's slit trench and mine. There it was blown to pieces by a mortar bomb. Chickens did not seem to mind the mortaring at all; they lost a few feathers, but went on pecking and scratching quite calmly,' until they eventually were eaten. The 21st Independent Parachute Company were more fortunate than most and contrived to eat two meals a day. 'Once a kid ran across the lawn of my headquarters and we killed and ate it'.

For drink there was a well, and one company filled a bath half full of water before the supply was cut, and used it for cooking purposes even after the ceiling, falling into it, had transformed it into 'thin, unpleasant porridge'. In a number of houses a few bottles of 'champagne, Graves, a light claret and Bols gin' were discovered.

So the days passed slowly in hunger and thirst, flame, smoke and fire. Sometimes a Tiger tank would approach near enough to be attacked, and Lance-Corporal Coster, of the 1st Battalion, who had landed on a haystack in Sicily, jumped twice on the side of such tanks and dropped grenades through their open hatches.

One other attempt was made to send reinforcements. On the night of 24th–25th September about two hundred and fifty men of the 4th Battalion, Dorset Regiment, led by Lieutenant-Colonel G. Tilly, made a determined, and in the circumstances peculiarly gallant, effort to cross the Lower Rhine. The swiftness of the current and the sustained fire of the enemy defeated their purpose, and those who were not killed were made prisoner. By then the situation had long been desperate. Casualties were mounting, ammunition dwindling; but the perimeter was still held, though German snipers would sometimes slip through it and thus make movement within very difficult. The few jeeps still serviceable could not move far in any direction, for the roads were blocked by fallen trees and branches. In due course the Germans added another weapon to mortars, artillery, tanks and machine-guns—a loudspeaker. It was received in general with cheers and catcalls as it droned out 'a long dissertation on our desperate position. A Panzer division was about to attack us and had already captured our general. If we surrendered we should be treated well'. One day it arrived opposite the 21st Independent Parachute Company, who immediately fired a Piat at it. 'There was a big bang, and it stopped.'

Beset as they were on all sides but one, the worst place of all was perhaps the right-hand or eastern sector of the perimeter where Hackett commanded. By the evening of 22nd September he calculated that his brigade had been reduced to four or five officers and some sixty men of the 156th Battalion, two or three officers and about a hundred men of the 11th and perhaps thirty men with no officers of the 10th. Among the killed were des Voeux, commanding 156th Battalion; Dawson, the brigade major; and Blundell and James of the brigade staff. On 20th September Smyth, commanding the 10th, was badly wounded and died later in the hands of the enemy. Hackett himself was to spend five months the wrong side of the Rhine hidden and nursed by the Dutch.

As the days wore on the only sign of anxiety displayed by the men was the increasing frequency with which they put the question to their officers: 'Any news of the 2nd Army?' There was none; or none as yet for publication. Reading between the lines of the divisional diary with its stark staccato record of the main events, the sense of strain and the determination to overcome it are both apparent:

'21st September

'03.40 hours. Patrol under Lieutenant Heap with ammunition for 1st Parachute Brigade did not get through.

'21.44 hours. Main nuisance self-propelled guns; our casualties heavy. Resources stretched to utmost. Relief within twenty-four hours vital.

247

'*22nd September*

'20.05 hours. Perimeter unchanged. . . . Minor attacks defeated. Some self-propelled guns knocked out.. . . Morale high.

'*23rd September*

'09.45 hours. Supply situation serious. Majority no rations last twenty-four hours.

'20.15 hours. After many alarms and excursions the divisional perimeter remains substantially unchanged although very thinly held. . . . Re-supply a flop. . . . Still no food and all ranks extremely dirty owing to shortage of water. Morale still adequate. . . . We shall hold out at the same time hope for a brighter twenty-four hours ahead.

'*24th September*

'19.00 hours. A day of heavy shelling and mortaring and desperate fighting on all sectors. Many attacks at first achieved some penetration, but the situation was almost always restored, and by nightfall the perimeter was substantially the same. Never was darkness more eagerly awaited. . . .'

On the South-east of the perimeter Lonsdale force had been steadily losing men, and the 1st and 3rd Battalions were now reduced to a hundred all ranks. Lonsdale himself was wounded again, standing beside 'a Methodist padre Watkins, a Leeds man, one of the best, and the oldest padre in service in the Parachute Regiment'. The wound was dressed at the regimental aid post, and Lonsdale gave orders for the two battalions to withdraw to less exposed positions. 'The luck hadn't been on our side, but suddenly it seemed about to change. I could have cheered when Lord Billy Buckhurst, our liaison officer with 4th Brigade headquarters, brought me the great news that armoured reconnaissance units of the 2nd Army had reached the far bank of the river.'

Lonsdale at once decided to assemble the survivors of the 1st and 3rd Battalions in the church and there give them the news. Standing below the pulpit he did so. Few churches can have heard a stranger or in its way a more heartening sermon. 'The scene as I spoke inside the shattered church,' he says, 'lives vividly in my memory. I can still see the tired upturned faces of my congregation, the strangest ever gathered there. None of them looked their Sunday best: dirty, haggard, tattered, unshaven. Yes, I thought, but they're still defiant, still unbroken.'

248

After telling them that the 2nd Army had reached the river, he urged them to be ready to fight to the last man and the last round. They could do so, and they would. 'This,' he said, 'is by no means the first time we have fought the Germans. We fought the cream of their Army in North Africa, in Sicily, and in Italy. Now we are up against them here. We defeated them in those earlier campaigns; they were not good enough for us then, and they are bloody well not good enough for us now. They are up against the finest soldiers in the world.

'In one hour's time you will take up defensive positions on the north side of the Oosterbeek-Arnhem road. Make certain you are well dug in. Make certain your weapons and your ammunition are in good order. Conserve your ammunition, we are getting short, so that when you shoot shoot to kill. My H.Q. will be in the area of the church. Good luck to you all.'

Unknown to Lonsdale, Urquhart had already taken steps to get into touch with the long-awaited land forces. It was obvious that, despite every reserve of courage and fortitude the division might possess—and they appeared inexhaustible—the position at Oosterbeek could not be held much longer. By the night of 22nd-23rd Urquhart felt that what was happening north of the Lower Rhine should be laid before Browning in Nijmegen in all its stark simplicity. He therefore ordered two of his officers, Lieutenant-Colonel C. B. Mackenzie, his G.S.O.1, and Lieutenant-Colonel E. C. W. Myers, to cross the river for that purpose. They did so, and Mackenzie returned on the next night. Not, however, until Myers, who crossing with the Dorsets, brought a letter from the commander of the 43rd Infantry Division explaining that it was no longer the intention of the 2nd Army to form a bridgehead at Arnhem, were plans for a withdrawal made. Why the bridgehead could not be constructed will be discussed in a moment. On receiving this message, Urquhart immediately made the necessary dispositions, and at 21.45 hours on the night of 25th-26th September the withdrawal began.

For once the weather was favourable, a dark night with an overcast sky, heavy rain and a strong wind. While these conditions would make the crossing of the Lower Rhine, a swiftly flowing stream, more difficult, they made an unobtrusive departure easier.

Every man was ordered to muffle his boots, and, covered by the steady shooting of the 64th Medium Regiment, Royal Artillery, part of the XXX Corps, on the other side of the river, they moved off. This bombardment by the guns of the 2nd Army was evidently mistaken by the Germans as the prelude, not to withdrawal, but to the passage across the river of strong bodies of reinforcements. They therefore ceased their mortar and shell fire, presumably reserving it for newcomers. So the division slipped away down to the bank of the dark river. The perimeter had contracted still further, and not more than eight hundred yards separated its eastern side from its western. Infantry assault boats capable of carrying fourteen or fifteen men had been provided by the Royal Engineers. There was not enough of them, but the strong swimmers plunged into the flood, both they and the boats being guided by the flash of red tracer shells fired at the rate of a round a minute alternately in pairs for seven hours by a battery of anti-aircraft guns. When a rainy dawn appeared some one thousand seven hundred all ranks of the division and about four hundred and twenty glider pilots had crossed the Lower Rhine.

The survivors were taken first to Driel and then on to Nijmegen, where they were received in a large red brick school situated in a quiet tree-bordered thoroughfare. Here a hot meal awaited them, accompanied by tea and rum. And here they met with the seaborne elements of the division whose duty it had been to prepare the billets. 'They started to arrive about 23.00 hours,' says Warrant-Officer J. Sharp, 'and I kept asking, "Has anyone seen the 2nd Battalion", but no one had.' Through the night he waited, while such as remained of the division stumbled in, weary beyond measure, but sustained by the knowledge that they had done all and more than their duty. At dawn the first of the 2nd Battalion, a medical corporal, arrived. And by the time the last man had reached Nijmegen Warrant-Officer Sharp found himself providing accommodation for seventeen men. 'I don't think I was the only one there with tears in my eyes.'

The Wrong Side of the Rhine

SOME three hundred men, many of them wounded, in Oosterbeek or Arnhem, in the woods or hiding in back streets and farms, had been left behind. What happened to them and to others, who had failed to reach the perimeter but were still uncaptured at the time of withdrawal, must now be told.

First, the wounded in the Queen Elizabeth Hospital. It was here that the 16th Parachute Field Ambulance under Lieutenant-Colonel E. Townsend, M.C., had established itself on the evening of the division's arrival. It had followed in the wake of the 2nd Battalion and had not long begun work when the Germans arrived in force and took the unit prisoner. Everyone was ordered to move at once, but Townsend took a strong line and refused to leave the wounded already lying there under his care and attention. After much argument the Germans agreed to leave two surgical teams under Major Longland and Captain Lipmann-Kessel. All others were marched off, prisoners. These two officers used great ingenuity and shewed much determination in preventing their own forcible removal. On several occasions during the battle the Germans arrived and told them to pack up, whereupon the surgeons immediately started another operation which even the enemy did not have the heart to disturb. They remained in the hospital for several weeks, and did not pass into captivity until every man they had been tending was fit to move.

During this time the Dutch did their best to help, and some of them aided a number of the wounded, including Brigadiers Lathbury and Hackett, to escape from the hospital, the first in uniform, the second in civilian clothes. Chief of this gallant band of helpers was Mr. P. C. Kruyff, head of the Dutch underground movement in Arnhem. There was also a Mr. Montfroy, who smuggled a number of walking wounded to the railway line which there runs through a steep cutting. Thence he took them to a hut situated in the trackless sandy jungle extending for miles to the north of Arnhem and there hid them.

The Air Landing Field Ambulance under Lieutenant-Colonel Marrable established itself in the municipal hospital. They, too, were taken prisoner and moved with their wounded to Apeldoorn. Here they continued to exercise their craft. By the end of September eight hundred and fifty cases were under their care, and by the 16th October more than two thousand, both British and German. The enemy rendered them every assistance. In due course Colonel Graham Warrack, Assistant Director of Medical Services, and Captain Lipmann-Kessel succeeded in escaping with Brigadier Hackett.

Well aware from messages constantly received from the Dutch underground that a considerable number of parachute soldiers were still on the wrong side of the Rhine, the staff of the Second Army was determined to effect their rescue if they could. They were, again through the Dutch, in intermittent contact with, among others, Lieutenant-Colonel Dobie and Majors Tatham-Warter and Tony Franks. The measure of success achieved was very largely due to Dutch common sense and courage. First the adventures of Dobie.

It will be remembered that, wounded in the eye and arm, he had been taken prisoner in the early morning of 19th September. He was brought to a hospital on the northern outskirts of Arnhem, where his wounds were dressed and where he was able surreptitiously to remove his badges of rank. A German guard took off his wrist-watch, and while he was displaying this trophy to a nurse Dobie slipped away and hid in the hospital grounds. There he remained till nightfall, when he crossed the road, and, entering a partially demolished house, found a bed in which he slept soundly. He was awakened by a Dutch doctor, who, perceiving at once who he was, dressed his wounds again and hid him for five days. He was then taken to some friends of the doctor, who lived fifty yards from the hospital, next door to a house in which German soldiers were billeted. Here he stayed for more than a fortnight, and it was during this period that most of the citizens of Arnhem were rounded up and driven from the town. Dobie found himself presently alone save for a Dutch boy named Jan, who had been left to look after him. Together they made their way westwards till they reached the dropping zone where Dobie had landed more than a month before and here they parted. Dobie went south towards the river, being under the impression that the XXX Corps had by then crossed it. After threading his way between the ghosts of wrecked gliders, he presently found himself near a house in and out of which German soldiers were passing. Their presence shewed him that his surmise had been wrong and that the 2nd Army was not across the Lower Rhine. Nevertheless he pressed on in the early darkness and presently took cover in a ditch some five hundred yards from the stream. On the way he had ignored a challenge and thus provoked a German machine-gun detachment which had opened fire with tracer. Two British mortars on the other side of the Lower Rhine at once engaged it, and since he thought it certain that he would be seen in the light of the now risen moon, Dobie retraced his steps. At dawn he abandoned all thought of crossing the river and set out along the road to Ede, soon to fall into the company of a young girl, who

252

talked to him volubly in Dutch, 'to which I could only reply "Ja" and "Nay".' German troops were much in evidence along the whole route, and Dobie feared that he would be seized at any moment. He confessed as much to the girl, who at once took him to her father's house, where on the next morning he received the visit of 'Bill', the local leader of the Dutch underground army. Bill took him at once to his house in the centre of Ede, and there, to his delighted surprise, Dobie encountered Brigadier Lathbury, who had been living there for some time.

The brigadier, it will be remembered, had been left in the St. Elizabeth Hospital badly wounded, and had remained there until 25th September, 'a noisy and frightening day', he records in his diary. 'The evacuation of casualties by the Germans continued, and I decided that I should have to get out that night'. He did so, having by that time recovered sufficiently to hobble. He spent the next ten days wandering in the woods, mostly in the company of a private soldier, and then reached Ede, where 'Bill', Captain 'K', a Belgian, and other members of the Dutch underground forces took charge of him.

To this refuge, too, came Major Tatham-Warter. Like the others, he had escaped from hospital, but not alone. Major Tony Franks was with him and 'they were both fairly battered'. Tatham-Warter had spent a week on a farm in disguise, and was then given a bicycle, upon which he rode to Ede, past hundreds of Germans. Here he got into touch with 'Bill' and began to organise the mass escape of as many as possible of those who had been left behind. Posing as the deaf and dumb son of a lawyer at the Hague, he was able to move about quite freely.

At first it was hoped that Dempsey would cross the river, and the Dutch underground organisation, with Tatham-Warter, Franks, and two or three other officers, planned an operation to assist Dempsey's advance. All roads leading to any bridgehead established by the 2nd Army were to be ambushed. Each party so employed would contain a proportion of airborne troops fully equipped with Bren guns, Piats, anti-tank mines and personal weapons. These they would procure from containers to be dropped at night on zones arranged by wireless signals from the headquarters of the airborne corps at Moor Park in England. This plan and many other schemes and projects were drawn up in the underground operations room of what had by now become a highly organised secret army, intent on the exhilarating, if dangerous, business of harrying the Germans. From this room, for example, would be issued exact descriptions of targets suitable for the guns of the 2nd Army, which fired upon them, to the consternation of the German troops in the neighbourhood, who could not understand how the British guns had been able to discover them. Targets, too, for the Typhoons of the 2nd Tactical Air Force would be suggested, the most successful result achieved being perhaps the destruction by these fighter-bombers of a train of thirty-five vehicles immobilised so as to form an easy target by the blowing up of the rails in front and behind it. All this information, and with it the proposed plan, was passed to the Second Army over the private telephone system of the Dutch Company already mentioned.

Presently, however, it became obvious that Dempsey was not going to advance, and an escape *en masse* of the parachutists and airborne troops left behind, and still in hiding, was, there-fore, planned. For success four requirements were necessary: a safe area of concentration; a safe means of reaching it; the discovery of a suitable gap in the Germans' defences of the Lower Rhine; and the support of the 2nd Army. To secure this, and to make all things plain, Lathbury ordered Dobie to go back to General Dempsey's headquarters and explain either the plan for ambushing the roads if Dempsey had after all decided to cross the Rhine, or the intention to stage a mass escape. Life was now becoming more difficult, for on 15th October the German S.S. police arrived in Ede. By that date there were above a hundred men of the Airborne Division in the town, fifty more in farms outside it, and another hundred somewhat further away in the direction of Arnhem. All had been successful in eluding capture and were being collected and tended by the members of the Dutch underground movement.

On 16th October Dobie set off about four in the afternoon, passing 'a frowsy, dispirited crowd of the Wehrmacht collecting horses and setting up a headquarters'. Following his guide, Dobie pedalled industriously over the country roads, till he reached the hut, a rendezvous in the woods. His journey had been quite uneventful, though at one moment he had had to dodge a German staff car. In the hut Dobie found a British officer of the Special Air Service in charge of 'a strange party, working away in the light of their little oil lamp. The wireless, the winding of the power handle and its monotonous noise, the tap-tap of the buzzer, the quiet voice of "B" (an attractive blonde) as she decoded, the litter of equipment and weapons, the evening meal—all went to heighten the atmosphere of melo-drama and unreality'. On the next day, following the attractive blonde, Dobie cycled for nearly two hours against half a gale, 'through fields, over tracks, past Germans, along canals, and between pine trees rustling in the wind'. In a forest glade he bade farewell to his charming blonde guide, whom he never saw again, for she was shortly afterwards caught by the enemy and shot, and was taken on by a new guide, one designated as 'P', and brought to a farmhouse, where he enjoyed 'a glorious lunch'. Much encouraged by this and by the beauty of the day, 'which was one of those balmy soft autumn days when white billowy clouds fly away over the deep, deep blue', they walked over the fields and presently came to the Rhine. 'With a sudden pang,' says Dobie, 'I remembered all those who had crossed it four weeks ago going north full of high hopes, and the bitter cost. In a cumbersome steel rowing boat we crossed, the sturdy "P" wielding the huge oars mightily. We were met on the other side and I said goodbye to "P", one more of those wonderful people. Their high courage, their discipline, their constant good humour, yet their seriousness—all my life I will remember it.

'So to a house with a strange, low-ceilinged bedroom, strange nooks and crannies, the most delightful inmates, and the most stupendous meals. An evening playing some strange game called "Jokes" at which I was extremely bad—much to the family's amusement. But no crossing of the Waal.'

It should be realised that, though XXX Corps held Nijmegen and some part of the road beyond leading to Arnhem, the country between the Waal and the Lower Rhine was still in German hands. Dobie's diary continues:

'I was distressed at the thought of having to stay, so much depended on getting over, not only myself now but all those chaps of ours. I said I would swim it. With a very worried and uncertain outlook I went to bed and slept hardly an hour.

'*Wednesday*, 18*th October*. Doubt, another card game called Casino, more meals filled the day until just after lunch, then the joyful news I was to go at five. I said goodbye to these simple folk and with my guides set out for Y.[1] More Germans, more head winds, but Y was reached at six in the evening. More doubts, plans astray, anxious moments in a shop, then off again with a ·45 in my pocket giving me great comfort, no one would stop me. Another house, squalling children, worried men, more doubts, and my ultimatum. Franz, the young boy, so brave, so eager, yet so frightened. Eight o'clock, the patrol down to the Waal—turbulent, swift and sullen, forbidding indeed. Goodbye

[1] The secret crossing place over the Waal.

to another two brave Dutchmen, into the boat, the crude, large and cumbersome oars. Franz and I pulling lustily, the Boche on the bank we left. Poor Franz, he lost his oar and we saw it go rushing downstream and we were only quarter of the way across—he got rid of most of his clothes before I realised what he was doing. "For swimming," he whispered. However, I had too many precious documents on me. Eventually, after drifting a long way, I managed to get one of the seats loose and use it as a very cumbersome oar. It seemed centuries before we made the crossing; I suppose it was barely an hour—and at last we were on the British side. How thankful I was—practically carefree. I felt I was home.'

On Thursday, 19th October, he reached Dempsey's headquarters, handed plans, photos and other information to the Intelligence Branch, 'who were quite delighted about them', and then told his story to Dempsey. The general decided that the airborne troops must be brought back, and Dobie concocted a plot with Lieutenant-General Horrocks, commanding XXX Corps. Two crossings were suggested, but on telephoning to Tatham-Warter far away in Ede, the number had to be reduced to one, for the Germans were becoming active and further delay was dangerous. The date of the escape was fixed for the night of 22nd-23rd October.

Meanwhile on the other side of the Rhine a great influx of German police and Gestapo, who were rounding up men for labour and searching houses, while it made concealment more difficult, made concentration easier. On the 22nd the officers and men taking part in the escape were concentrated, and all reached the rendezvous. Major Anthony Hibbert and some twenty men arrived there in a lorry, and while they were climbing out of it a patrol of German cyclists passed, ringing their bells and shouting at them to get out of the way. When dark fell the parachutists and airborne troops—among them were six members of the Dutch underground movement and a Russian airman—marched three miles down to the river. Their progress was by no means silent, but all, including about thirty parachutists coming from Velp, who were in full uniform and armed, reached the bank of the Lower Rhine. There they waited for what seemed an interminable period. 'Just when we were convinced,' says Lathbury, 'that something serious had gone wrong, we heard a cheerful confident American voice hailing us in the darkness.' The waiting boats were but a quarter of a mile away. The party moved down the bank, 'complete, but in cheerful disorder', and in half an hour every man was safely on the other side.

Among them was Regimental Sergeant-Major Grainger, who had been wounded in the third day's fighting. With two companions he had been picked up by the Dutch and taken to a mental hospital, where the three remained for four or five days until the inmates were evacuated. Grainger and his two companions decided to go with them, and, so that they should not be remarked, succeeded in obtaining a white hospital blanket apiece, of the kind issued to the patients. These were led into the woods, and 'we joined them, being in the centre of a group of mental patients, some being led, some with their hands tied, and all of them dancing'. The parachutists danced, too, grimacing and flinging their arms about, so that the German troops, past whom they were led, were deceived and took them for lunatics. On reaching the woods they wandered about for some time, and were eventually hidden in a hole dug in the side of a bank by a Dutchman, who kept them well fed and supplied with cigarettes. They eventually got into touch with Tatham-Warter, who used Grainger to help in organising the mass escape. The regimental sergeant-major 'promenaded round the town of Ede', with a good-looking Dutch girl called Geraldine, and more than once saw parties of parachutists being taken away to captivity. One of them recognised him, but seemed to be more interested in Geraldine than in the R.S.M. 'I have a very high regard for the Dutch resistance,' said Grainger when making his report, 'and particularly the individual members with whom I came in contact. I was struck by their singleness of purpose and their patriotism of which I have never seen the like anywhere. These Dutch boys and girls of eighteen and nineteen exuded a spirit which was heartening in the extreme.' It was that spirit and the stubborn skill with which the Dutch civilians organised this operation—for operation it was—that made its success possible.

There were still many, perhaps two hundred or more, left behind, but a second attempt, organised by Major Maguire, came to nothing. The chief reason why it failed was the widespread stories which appeared in the Press and in broadcasts recounting the success of the first escape. It was even stated that the Dutch civilian telephone system had been used when organising it. The immediate and inevitable consequence was the replacement within twenty-four hours of all Dutch telephone operators by German. How such a glaring indiscretion was permitted is not known. Such wide publicity given to the story was indirectly responsible for many deaths and for the despondency which for a time gripped the Dutch helpers.

Other causes for the failure were over-confidence on the part of 2nd Army, increased vigilance on the part of the enemy, the establishment of a prohibited zone on the north bank of the Rhine and the physical unfitness of men who had been for a long time in hiding on short rations. 'The trouble was,' wrote one left behind for many months, 'that so many people on both sides of the river would not believe that anything like a repetition of Lathbury's feat was quite out of the question.'

Small parties, however, among them Brigadier Hackett, still weak from wounds, did eventually reach our lines in canoes. Hackett had been hidden for nearly five months in a house next door to a German military police billet and during that time had helped the Dutch by becoming 'our military correspondent' for a clandestine newspaper. Frost, 'the Mad Colonel of Arnhem' as the enemy called him, did not escape. He was taken to hospital, where his wounds were seen to by a German surgeon, the German nursing sister making no effort to relieve his pain. He then departed into captivity.

Briggs, who had led a party from the bridge after the order to scatter had been given, survived at liberty with his men for twelve hours. The S.S. troops who then captured them 'behaved very correctly and gave the men (they had had nothing to drink for three days) some Lager beer from a wrecked Dutch café'. They were confined for the first night in a house on the edge of Arnhem, but their spirits were high, for it seemed to them that rescue would be a matter of a few hours or days. Presently however, they found themselves in a lorry, bound for Zutphen, all save Major A. J. Deane-Drummond, M.C., who as a signaller had dropped with the 1st Battalion. He, it will be remembered, was one of the party which attacked the Tragino Aqueduct on the first occasion when British parachutists went into action. Made prisoner then by the Italians, he had eventually succeeded in escaping and had returned to his own division. Now he was once more a prisoner, but not for long. During the last fight of the 1st Battalion he had taken up a position with his batman in a deserted house which was shortly after entered by a detachment of the enemy. The German commander posted snipers in the upper rooms, and to make sure that they would stay there locked the doors on them. Deane-Drummond and his batman went to ground in the W.C., where they remained for forty-eight hours.

They locked the door, and though the handle on its outside was frequently tried, no attempt was made to force an entrance. Occasionally the Germans lapse into good manners.

When the fighting finally died away they slipped out and made for the Lower Rhine, where they separated. Deane-Drummond stripped, swam the river, put on his clothes again, and was cautiously making his way south, Germans 'coughing and talking all round us', when he fell headlong into a slit trench, at the bottom of which was a German soldier. Deane-Drummond pistolled him, but another German whom he had not seen jumped on his back and made him prisoner. In due course he joined Briggs and his party, who, before they were moved, succeeded in hiding him in a large cupboard. Here, incredible though it may appear, he remained for twelve days undiscovered, with nothing but a piece of bread and the contents of his water bottle. The cupboard was flush with the wall and papered with the same wallpaper, and to this he probably owed his escape. On the twelfth evening he slipped away, but it was three weeks before, with the aid of the Dutch underground, he rejoined the British forces.

To return to Briggs and his party, among whom was Major Hibbert. On the way to Zutphen Hibbert and Major Dennis Mumford attempted to escape. Hibbert got away, but Mumford was recaptured. 'Their leap from the truck,' says Briggs, 'was seen by the crew of a lorry approaching from the opposite direction.' These men signalled to the driver and crew of the lorry containing the prisoners. Furious with rage or fear, the crew turned upon the helpless men and opened fire with Schmeisser sub-machine-guns. Eight fell dead or mortally wounded. The remainder were lined up against a wall, their hands behind their heads, and told that they would be shot. It was Major Gough who saved them. He played for time and argued with the Germans for nearly half an hour until a Volkswagen arrived and inside it a German Intelligence officer, who ordered the prisoners and their dead to be taken to Zutphen. Among those murdered that day was Anthony Cotterill, the novelist and war correspondent. The only man to give them aid at this grim moment was a Dutch doctor, attracted to the spot by the sound of the shots. As he leaned over the fatally wounded he whispered, 'Courage, courage!'

Why were the 1st Airborne Division, who were to be in Arnhem, according to plan, for at most forty-eight hours, not relieved? The American 101st Airborne Division had seized the bridge intact at Grave over the Maas; the 82nd, fighting with magnificent gallantry, were equally successful at Nijmegen. The road, therefore, from the spearheads of XXX Corps through to Arnhem was open; but open only in the sense that the bridges were in American and British hands. The stretches between them were not. There is but one road as far as Nijmegen: it then splits into two, but joins again close to Arnhem. These two roads run first through orchards of plum and apple, and then through flat marshy fields, across which they are carried on causeways some three or four feet above the level of the surrounding country. No tanks or armoured vehicles approaching from Nijmegen could quit either of these roads without instantly becoming bogged. Since large stretches of both were under observation from high ground, any attempt to use the roads was easily thwarted by the German guns. That, in brief, is why the Guards Armoured Division failed to go further than Nijmegen.

Even then, perhaps—though this must always be a matter for conjecture—all might still have been well had matters not gone awry in Arnhem itself. They went awry for the very simple reason that there were not enough aircraft to put the division down as one unit altogether on one afternoon. That was the main cause of failure. Another—though this is more open to argument—was the choice of landing and dropping zones which were situated too far away from the main objective. The assaulting troops had to move on their feet at least five, and in many cases eight, miles to the bridge through close country infested with the enemy. Such a march could not be accomplished in less than four hours, and this was ample time for the defence, containing as it did so many trained troops, to organise resistance. The fact that the information made available to the division before it landed was scanty and at fault has already been noted. Arnhem held a number of highly trained troops under the command of Sturmbandführer Sepp Krafft, who belonged to the S.S. Panzer Grenadiers. The battalion, No. 16, was a reserve unit comprising thirteen officers, seventy-three non-commissioned officers and three hundred and forty-nine other ranks, not a very large number perhaps, but enough, if well armed and resolutely led, to impose an initial check and thus upset a necessarily somewhat complicated plan. This was exactly what happened. Krafft was an energetic and resolute commander. 'The only way to draw the teeth of an airborne landing,' he said as soon as the presence of the airborne division was reported to him, 'is to drive straight into it.' He did so with all his resources and with every tank and self-propelled gun he could collect. During the first and most vital hours after the first lift had landed, the Krafft battalion fought with the greatest fury in country most favourable to defence. Even so, by sundown Krafft reported his position to be almost desperate. The German general officer in command at Arnhem had been killed an hour before and Krafft's own casualties had not been light, but he nonetheless continued to hold on, cheered by the promise of support by midnight. It duly arrived in the form of the Hohenstaufen Panzer Division—more armour, it will be perceived, and more trained men. By this small margin did we fail.

Krafft had the highest opinion of the British parachutists. 'The troops were about twenty-five years of age on the average, and the best type, mentally and physically,' he reported after the battle. 'They all had some five or six years' service and most of them were veterans of North Africa, Sicily, Italy and Normandy. They were well trained, particularly for independent fighting, and of good combat value.

'The officers, graded in rank according to age, were the finest of the whole British Army. Very well schooled, personally hard, persevering and brave, they made an outstanding impression.'

The German officer's opinion of their valour and worth in battle was more accurate than the estimate he made of their politics.

'Not much information on political convictions,' he wrote, 'has been gleaned ; but it is known that, in England, when truth conflicts with the military powers, the truth is withheld. In this respect, chalked inscriptions on the gliders are interesting:

> ' "We are the Al Capone gang."
> ' "Up with the Reds."
> ' "Up with the Fräulein's skirts."

'How far this is connected with the political convictions of the troops themselves, or whether it is due to Bolshevist or American influences, is not known.'

None save the dead, wounded and those taken prisoner of the airborne division suffered more than the inhabitants of Arnhem. There were about a hundred civilian casualties in the town itself, and several times that number in Oosterbeek. Every house and farm in or near the dropping zones or the perimeter was badly damaged or destroyed. Of the town itself only a hundred and fifty houses remained intact. A few days after the action was over every man, woman and child in the city, to the number of ninety-eight thousand, were compulsorily driven out. The Germans then looted the place, systematically removing the contents of most of the houses. Fifty members of the Dutch underground army were shot for helping the 1st Airborne Division.

The great *coup* had not succeeded. Two of the crossings over the river defences of Germany had been secured, but not the third. The failure of the 1st Airborne Division to hold on to what it had seized must in the last resort be attributed to hazard and uncertainty, two indefatigable attendants on war. In holding out for nine days—during the first three of which, had it been able to push forward, the 2nd Army could have passed the bridge—against an enemy who was weak only in the first few hours of the action, the division performed a very great service to the Americans at the bridges of Nijmegen and Grave. The stubborn resistance and continued determination to fight displayed at Arnhem attracted German reserves and reinforcements as the proverbial candle attracts the proverbial moth. Such, at least, was the opinion of Montgomery, and he did not hesitate to say so. For that reason, and it is a very good one, all who fought at Arnhem, among them not the least the officers, non-commissioned officers and men of the Parachute Regiment, have good cause for legitimate pride. They accomplished all and more than had been asked—three times more in fact. Nor did they flinch at the heavy payment in casualties demanded. 'We have no regrets,' said Urquhart afterwards in his official report, and Hackett was even more explicit. 'Thank you for the party,' he wrote while still a wounded fugitive, hidden near the scene of action. 'It didn't go quite as we hoped and got a bit rougher than we expected. But speaking for myself, I'd take it on again any time, and so, I am sure, would everybody else.' Those who fought in the ranks of the Parachute Regiment would certainly endorse those words. They took part in what will undoubtedly be hailed in the future, as it is now, as a magnificent feat of arms. Let the deeds of the 1st Airborne Division, of which the regiment formed so important a part, be recalled in the words of the official account:

'In the tranquil sunshine of an autumn afternoon its officers and men descended upon territory held in force by the enemy. Some were in action while still falling or gliding through the air, and all were heavily engaged within an hour of landing. From that moment onwards not a man, save the dead or desperately wounded, but was continuously fighting, both by day and by night. They fought in thick woods, tearing aside the undergrowth to come to grips with the enemy; they fought in well-ordered streets, in neat houses, in town halls, in taverns, in churches—anywhere where a German was to be found.

'With no weapon larger than a 75-mm. gun, and for the most part only with Brens, gammon bombs and Piats, which can be carried and handled by one man unaided, they attacked Tiger tanks weighing fifty-six tons, and self-propelled guns with a range of seven miles. Of these they destroyed or put out of action some sixty. With no reinforcements save the wounded, who, if their legs would still bear them, staggered back to the firing line, they fought on. With an enemy growing ever stronger, pressing against them on all sides but one—and that a wide, swiftly flowing river—they fought on. Without sleep, presently without food or water, at the end almost without ammunition, they fought on. In attack most daring, in defence most cunning, in endurance most steadfast, they performed a feat of arms which will be remembered and recounted as long as the virtues of courage and resolution have power to move the hearts of men.

'Now these things befell at Arnhem.'

The Exploits
of the 2nd Parachute Brigade

WHEN the 1st Airborne Division quitted Italy it left behind it the 2nd Independent Parachute Brigade, under the command of Brigadier C. H. V. Pritchard. The advantage of leaving General Alexander with a brigade of trained parachute troops was obvious, provided they could be used as such. But as the weary campaign of 1943-4 dragged on it became more and more evident that this would not be their role. Pritchard, their commander, was, moreover, greatly hampered by a total lack of reinforcements, save for a number of glider pilots. Though outside the control of the War Office he was also cut off from his parent unit, the 1st Airborne Division, 'and left in a tiny village in Italy to be the airborne formation of a vast army in case of necessity'. His men were well trained, but had seen almost no active service except for the bickerings round Taranto. They had, moreover, no transport except a number of jeeps and three-ton lorries. Pritchard and his men were presently attached to the famous 2nd New Zealand Division, commanded by General Freyburg, V.C., who shewed them the greatest kindness. 'You just cannot imagine the assistance these New Zealanders gave us,' wrote the brigadier long afterwards.

In one other thing they were also fortunate until late in 1944. Most of the aircraft which transported them came from No. 51 U.S. Troop Carrying Wing, commanded by General Manning. The relations between the men carried in the aircraft and those who flew them could not have been better. The American pilots were extremely skilled and for them 'time and distance' meant nothing. On one occasion when the brigade was at Salerno Pritchard conferred with General Patch at Bizerta at 12 noon, at 6 p.m. he was in Rome, discussing plans with one of General Alexander's Staff, and at 9 p.m. was back in his office at Salerno.

A training establishment and parachute school was set up under Captain B. Fuller, first at Gioio and then, after the fall of Rome, at Lido di Roma, and here all volunteers for the brigade were trained. Packing and maintenance of parachutes was in the capable charge of Flight-Lieutenant Blackford, R.A.F., whose 'little team of airmen and soldiers . . . worked entirely on a "factory" system with Blackford as "boss" '. The parachutists placed complete and justified reliance in their skill and devotion. Besides Pritchard, the mainstays of the brigade were Colonel V. W. Barlow and Lieutenant-Colonel H. B. Coxen. There was also Major W. Lawson, who became brigade major. Like Coxen, he was not a professional soldier at that time. He had endeared himself in the early days to the men 'by falling between two barges in Bartella harbour and coming up covered in seaweed and smiles'. With officers such as these the brigade was in goods hands and remained so till the end of the war.

The brigade was in action at the River Sangro in November on the left flank of the 8th Army. The river was in flood, 'the humans, guns, tanks, lorries, plunging on to victory through mud, water, and gravel'. Thereafter for four months the brigade fought on the Adriatic front, gaining much experience, but steadily losing men who could not be replaced. The 5th Battalion, for example, in the line filling the gap on the left between the New Zealand Division and the mountains, lost an appreciable number of men in the Salorola sector opposite the enemy's main defensive line which there ran along a ridge between Orsogna and Guariagrele. The battalion's position was most exposed, for it was holding a promontory of land approached by a road of which the greater part was in full view of the enemy. 'D' Company, under Major P. Dudgeon, were the most forward of all on a bare mount called 'Tank Hill', and it was here that the battalion's chaplain, the Reverend Robertson, was severely wounded when conducting a burial party.

The enemy, however, did not have matters all his own way, for the parachutists retaliated fiercely by means of aggressive patrols. In one of these Lieutenant Bruce of 'B' Company established himself in the very mouth of the enemy at Orsogna, and had in the end to fight his way out, being covered by the fire of Private Morris, who by so doing won the Military Medal, the first decoration awarded to the battalion.

The 5th were in due course relieved by the 4th Battalion, one of whose patrols, under Lieutenant G. L. Mortimer, also paid a visit to Orsogna and returned with 'a complete section' as prisoners. For this he was awarded the Military Cross. On the next day Lieutenant L. J. Deacon of 'A' Company won a similar decoration, fighting a very sharp action at a range of fifty yards on another part of the ridge. Here Corporal Walker, Royal Army Medical Corps, particularly distinguished himself and won the Military Medal for tending wounded under fire. It was, indeed, in this sector that the brigade first developed that fighting ability which made its reputation.

December had now come and with it frost and snow. This made a major move forward impossible, but the two battalions continued to hold the line, the 4th in various places, notably the Bianco ridge, dominated as usual by the enemy, who, since he was conducting a defensive campaign, always had time to choose his positions. Here the parachutists were helped, or hindered—it is hard to decide which—by an Indian mule company, which carried their heavy equipment to the forward positions up a very steep climb and through endless mud and slush. This was a very uncomfortable sector, and the battalion was glad to move to rest near Naples at the end of March.

The 5th Battalion went through a similar existence. Having shewn Wynford Vaughan-Thomas, of the British Broadcasting Corporation, how Glasgow keep Hogmanay in the front line, they moved to the Ariele sector across the River Moro. Here they took over from a battalion of the King's Own Yorkshire Light Infantry, and here they remained for six weeks 'in sand-bagged positions . . . calling to mind stories of the 1914-18 war'. The heavy shellfire to which they were frequently subjected was on occasion followed by visits from enemy fighter aircraft which dived out of the sun 'and followed a line of smoke shells neatly placed in our positions by the enemy artillery as guide marks'. The orders were to patrol vigorously and to capture prisoners, who were at this stage of greater importance than usual, for since the landing at Anzio Kesselring had regrouped his forces and his order of battle was not exactly known. Those taking part in patrols clad themselves in sheets, for the land was deep in snow, and, thus arrayed, Lieutenant Shepherd, M.C., the battalion intelligence officer, one night entered a house numbered 13 and removed the chicken which the Germans were about to eat for their dinner. Lieutenant Miller of 'C' Company, an artist, spent days in no man's land sketching the enemy's positions. Their own suffered from shellfire and from the nightly visits of an adventurous German known as 'Schmeisser Joe', who was full of desire to cause mischief. Sergeant Walker was determined to put an end to his activities, and with a small patrol entered the enemy's lines and eventually returned in triumph, having dealt with Joe, through the 6th Battalion which was in position on the left.

About this time 'a German prisoner proved very obliging when he assisted our gunner forward observation officer in shelling his own positions'. On another occasion the German prisoners captured talked so much that it was possible for the leader of one of the battalion's patrols to pin up a personal message addressed to the commander of an enemy outpost by name, calling upon him to surrender or be wiped out by gunfire ; the German chose the second alternative. In this sector, too, casualties were suffered, and it was with great relief that the battalion, together with the 6th, moved back at the end of March to rest near Naples.

The fighting had all been of the same pattern : a patrol would go out, seek to ambush a German patrol, or itself be ambushed.

All three battalions became extremely expert in this form of warfare. It was 'tricky and dangerous work, with mud, snow and mines to contend with'. And before long every officer and man could rightly consider himself a veteran. By the time the brigade took its rest at Guardia in the Benevento area near Naples, the three battalions had fought at Orsogna, Ariele, Poggio, Forito (where every building was accurately registered by an enemy only a thousand yards away, and where 'A' Company headquarters of the 6th Battalion received seventeen direct hits in one day), on the slopes of Monte Mare, and in Pennapiedemonte.

The week's rest at Guardia was much enjoyed. The village, said its mayor, was reluctant to billet more than six men; it nevertheless proved sufficiently elastic to lodge almost the whole brigade. In one house a parachutist carrying a pile of plates was heard to remark to one of his friends, as he passed its owner's daughter on the stairs, 'Nice bit of stuff!' to which the girl replied in perfect English: 'Never mind about the nice bit of stuff. You look after my mother's plates.'

At the end of March the brigade moved to the Cassino sector, which proved, strangely enough, less unhealthy than that of Ariele but far from pleasant because of the widespread mines which cost Lieutenant J. Pearson, of the 6th Battalion, his legs. The three battalions patrolled the Rapido river under the eyes of a watchful enemy entrenched on Monastery Hill, and a percentage were able to rest in back areas. Those of the 4th Battalion who held the railway station, with Major Calvert of 'A' Company as station master, lived under a pall of smoke by day; for the slightest movement could be seen. On one occasion Down, on a visit to the brigade, moved towards the railway station, accompanied by Pritchard, the brigadier, and was received by salvoes of phosphorus shells, which 'partially ignited the general, and wounded the brigadier in the head, fortunately not seriously'.

In due course the brigade moved to a sector in the mountains further north, where all food and ammunition had to be carried up by mules at night. 'Seldom,' runs the history of the 6th Battalion, 'was this achieved without incident, and, curiously enough, it was always the mule bearing the "attractive" stores—rum, sugar or N.A.A.F.I. goods—which was laid low by a direct hit, or was last heard of "going spare towards 'B' Company, sir".'

The shells which fell in the brigade's positions were not always high explosive: some on bursting shot out leaflets designed to undermine the valour of the troops. The Germans, however, had made a wrong guess, for the propaganda received by the 5th Battalion was all addressed to Indians, and urged them to go home and not to waste their time fighting for the wicked British. 'Words cannot adequately describe,' runs the history of that battalion, 'how weird the atmosphere was at Cassino at this time: dominated by the Monastery which would be suddenly illuminated by a star shell at night, or obliterated as far as possible with smoke by day,' this position seemed curiously unreal, almost of another world.

By the end of May 1944, when the brigade was withdrawn from the line for a short rest, they could truthfully claim that they were a small, compact, but formidable body of men, having learnt the art of war on precipitous hillsides, in mud and snow and in wild mountain country. They rested at a camp south of Salerno, 'amongst vineyards with lovely weather'. As usual, the rest consisted of a bout of hard training, but 'everyone was in the best of spirits'.

Their last exploit in Italy was Operation 'Hasty', in which three officers and fifty-seven other ranks from the 6th Battalion dropped one hour before last light on 1st June to prevent the Germans, then withdrawing to the Pisa-Rimini line, from carrying out large-scale demolitions.

They were taken to their destination by aircraft of the U.S. Troop Carrier Command, which dropped them perfectly, 'in precipitous country, and in daylight'. To disguise the small size of the force, Pritchard made extensive use of 'dummies'. The success achieved was considerable. The Germans were deceived, one of their brigades was moved to deal with what they thought to be a serious threat to their communications and one division remained where it was, and was not brought up to reinforce the troops then heavily engaged by the 8th Army. The usual mishaps of war occurred: one detachment of signallers were captured, the pigeon carried by the parachutists failed to home, and the last remaining wireless set presently became unserviceable. Pritchard solved the problem of how to send orders of recall by dropping a shower of pamphlets bearing the message, 'Proceed Awdry forthwith.' This cryptic sentence puzzled the Germans and prisoners subsequently captured made many enquiries as to the identity of the 'girl Awdry'. The parachutists, however, understood, for 'the girl' was John Awdry, an officer of the 6th Battalion. In twos and threes they slipped back to our lines.

Hard though the life of these three battalions had been throughout that winter, and though like all troops they could buy experience only at the price of casualties, life was not wholly and completely drab, as these extracts from the letters of an officer who wishes to remain anonymous shew:

'21st September. The batmen have produced some amazing dishes out of practically nothing; for instance, the other day we had a tin of sausages for breakfast, so they scraped all the fat off them, and in the evening they broke down some dog biscuits, mixed the crumbs with the fat, made a pastry out of the mixture, opened a tin of peaches, with the result—a first-class tart.

'6th October. One prize fool threw an overripe fig, which found contact with the end of my nose and spread over the whole of my face; this was followed by a shower of confetti, which hit me in the same area, and I spent the rest of the journey picking sticky bits of confetti out of my ears, nose and eyes.

'1st November. Last night we were working out the average age of the Brigade H.Q. Mess; it turned out to be twenty-four. The brigadier is thirty-seven and ten years older than anyone else; there are five of us under twenty-four—I am the youngest at twenty-two. I wonder how that compares with the last war.

13th December. . . . but war makes you laugh at things which you might cry about in peace. You know how much I was looking forward to getting my kit, which we had left behind when we left Africa. . . . Well, they decided to bring it over a few days ago, and the ship which was carrying it was just entering harbour, when it was hit by a bomb and sank immediately. All our kit has been lost, and when we heard it we all screamed with laughter.

'31st December. One thing I have learned out here is that whisky was never really meant to be drunk in a bar. As you must know, whisky—just a little nip—can become one's greatest friend if it appears when you are out in the cold, wet hills; it really is worth going through a certain amount of misery to enjoy the satisfaction which whisky brings at the end of it all.

'6th March. . . . it is almost worth dying in Italy—just for the sake of the funeral. First of all you are put into a beautiful coffin; this is only on loan, and is returned to the carpenter when you finally disappear. The coffin is put into a glass hearse adorned with brass angels and copper cherubs, and is drawn by four black horses, which in turn are preceded by a long procession of Methuselahs and very young children draped in white sheets and red waistcoats. They take no interest in the funeral, but walk in front to clear the way. Behind the hearse the village band plays a dirge and is followed by the relatives and the officiating priests; altogether it is a very grand procession. But the best part comes when the funeral is over. For some reason there is a great rush by the professional supporters to get back. The other day I met one of these funerals returning; I couldn't get out of the way quick enough. In a cloud of dust the hearse, minus the body, came careering down the road. Inside the glass case sat the older Methuselahs, while outside were the children screaming and shouting, clinging for dear life to the brass angels, their robes flowing in the wind. Sitting on the horses, the two trumpeters from the band were blowing something like the post-horn gallop, and the steeds responded accordingly. One hour later the same procession appeared in all its sombre glory, but this time there was a different body in the hearse.'

The early days of June 1944 found them at Salerno, 'still hoping that we would be employed in the role for which we had been trained'. Fortune was about to smile once more, for after some strenuous weeks of training to relearn old lessons, they received orders to drop in southern France in order to prevent German reinforcements from moving to the coast and seeking to interfere with the building-up of the main invading force coming by sea. The brigade was in fact to take part in Operation 'Anvil', a general attack on southern France launched with the object of capturing Marseilles and then moving in strength upon the Rhône Valley in order to join with the main Allied army sweeping towards Germany.

The objective of the 2nd Brigade was the village of Le Muy, where three roads met some fifteen miles inland from Fréjus. D-day was 15th August, and the three battalions were to be taken to Le Muy by the American Mediterranean Air Force from airfields at Ciampino and Galera.

For once there was no postponement and they took off on the appointed day and at the appointed hour, the only mishap being to one aircraft which ran into a jeep carelessly left on the runway. But the weather on the day proved cloudy and only seventy-three sticks landed on the dropping zone out of a hundred and twenty-six. Fortunately among them was their brigade commander, who, though compelled to jump from a height of fourteen hundred feet, landed within fifteen yards of the Eureka beacon. 'The whole experience was exceedingly interesting,' said Pritchard afterwards. 'We left Rome on a lovely night. You can imagine circling round, getting into formation, one airborne division (all American except for the 2nd Brigade). All the aircraft had their lights on, and Rome was twinkling below.' Forty per cent of the 4th and 60 per cent of the 6th Battalion landed on the correct zone.

It was the 5th Battalion which went astray. They were to be dropped on a signal from the leading aircraft, and when in the air its occupants 'noted with some curiosity that the crew chief was using a screwdriver on the lights. Eventually it transpired that these had failed, and the jump had to be signalled by flashlight.' Had the Germans in the south of France been of an aggressive turn of mind this electrical failure in the key aircraft might have led to serious consequences; for its pilot, for lack of electrical current, was unable to pick up the Rebecca Eureka beacon and therefore did not find the dropping zone which was situated in mountainous country. The inevitable consequence was that three-quarters of the battalion were scattered over a wide area some fifteen to twenty miles away from its destination and further inland. 'B' Company, more fortunate, landed on the dropping zone in relatively good order, except for Sergeant Tucker of No. 2 Platoon, who landed on the roof of a German billet. All efforts to dislodge him by rifle fire failed, and its occupants eventually tendered him their surrender. 'They included the field cashier with the unit's pay.' The parachute soldier dropped furthest away from the objective was the second-in-command, Major P. Dudgeon, who anon came into contact with the Germans and was badly wounded, and the battalion headquarters group had the interesting experience of seeing a German anti-parachute patrol drive past. 'It consisted of a staff car and two ambulances bristling with armed men.'

In mixed parties 'A', 'C' and 'D' Companies, having discovered their whereabouts, began the long march to Le Muy, doing much damage on the way to the enemy, who 'seemed to be retiring in some confusion'. The prisoners captured were made to carry the packs of the parachutists. Not everywhere did the Germans throw in, or rather up, their hands. In places they resisted stoutly and Lance-Corporal Warnock and Private Kadique of 'D' Company found themselves holding a farm for an hour and a half against 'a sizeable enemy force armed with machine-guns'.

On reaching Le Muy the battalion found the battle nearly over. Those who had dropped there had seen very little fighting, to the disgust of a newspaper correspondent who had dropped with them. This was the first time in his life that he had jumped and in so doing he lost his typewriter which fell from his leg on the way down and was never seen again.

The parachutists made great friends with the Maquis, who impressed them with their earnestness and resolution. 'Most of them had cut up our parachutes to drape round their heads. This gave them the appearance of pirates.' During its short stay in France the brigade, being without any form of transport, collected vehicles wherever they could find them. Before they embarked once more for Italy, one battalion was in possession of a 'five-ton truck driven by steam, a tractor, two hay-carts, a steam-roller, and a cart which looked exactly like a hearse'. The only time they had occasion to use these vehicles, 'all the motors passed out one by one, and eventually the steam-roller had to pull everything'.

Back in Italy, which the brigade reached at the beginning of September, it moved first to Rome, and then south to the neighbourhood of Bari, where it made preparations to carry out Operation 'Manna', an airborne landing in Greece.

It was known that the Germans were about to withdraw from the country and it was considered very important for British troops to occupy Athens as soon as possible after its evacuation to help in the distribution of food and to prevent Greek guerrillas from establishing themselves in the city and thus in all probability provoking civil war. The German withdrawal took place later than had been expected and in the circumstances the brigade had time to plan the operation which would put it in control of Athens while the approaches to the Piraeus were being swept clear of mines to make it possible for the main force to arrive by sea. During the planning Lieutenant Legge of the 2nd Parachute Field Squadron, Royal Engineers, was dropped in Greece and made his way, wearing plain clothes, into Athens in order to set up wireless communications with the brigade in Italy.

It fell to the 4th Battalion to secure a dropping zone for the rest of the brigade, and on 12th October headquarters, 'C' Company, and some mortar detachments, the whole force forming a combat under Lieutenant-Colonel H. B. Coxen, D.S.O., M.C., took off from Brindisi, and after a very bumpy flight dropped on the airfield of Megara near Athens. A strong wind was blowing, and in landing the medical officer and forty other ranks were injured. Among the casualties was Lieutenant D. C. Marsh, one of the most experienced officers in the battalion, who afterwards died, a melancholy example of the hazards inseparable from this method of reaching the battle-field, though this is hardly a correct description of Athens when the brigade first arrived. This it did over the next few days and entered the city. Its welcome from the Athenians was tumultuous. 'The women wanted to kiss us,' says an officer, 'and the men wanted to shake our hands or fling their arms around us. Soon the crowds became so thick that we could not tell which was road and which was pavement.'

Pritchard arrived in advance of Lieutenant-General Scobie, the British commander, and at once summoned the chief of police and the Greek general commanding in Athens to a con-ference. The streets of the city were still full of citizens 'march-ing up and down, cheering and shouting whenever a British soldier came in sight'. Pritchard urged that the crowds should be immediately dispersed, but the police chief demurred. The day was hot and thundery, and presently Pritchard observed with dismay that people in the crowd were beginning to stamp on each other's toes and then to hit each other. Once more he appealed to the chief of police, who implored him to go and stand on the balcony when, so he assured him, 'the crowd will cheer and storm and then stop'. Pritchard did so and was greeted by three deafening cheers which had hardly died away when the sound of shots shewed him that his worst fears were likely to prove justified. His battalions were hemmed in by the crowd and the situation seemed critical, when the weather came to the rescue. There was a providential cloudburst above the town and a deluge of rain soon drenched 'everybody and everything'. 'While this was going on I was able to get all my soldiers into the vulnerable places.'

The 2nd Parachute Brigade was soon joined by the 23rd Armoured Brigade and with it became responsible for the policing of the city and the guarding of the more vital points. Control of these immediately became a matter of dispute with the left-wing E.L.A.S. guerillas, 'long processions of whom filled the streets throughout the day, hindering the movement of our own troops and making it exceptionally difficult for the brigade to carry out its task. The followers of E.L.A.S. were the political rivals of those of E.A.M. and trouble soon developed. Rival processions came to blows in the streets and instructions had to be issued forbidding further demonstrations. Strict orders were given to the parachutists and the men of the 23rd Armoured Brigade not to become involved in any incidents and they were rigidly obeyed despite increasing tension. On 17th October patrols of the 4th Battalion, ordered to leave the brigade and pursue the Germans who were still withdrawing, left the city and made for Thebes. The battalion moved northwards, but as it pursued its march it became more and more obvious that the assistance of Greek partisans would not be forthcoming and that E.L.A.S. guerillas regarded the British as intruders. On 26th October 'C' Company, temporarily commanded by Colonel Lord Jellicoe, D.S.O., M.C., of the Special Boat Service, was ordered to occupy a mountain above the town of Cozani where the Germans were still holding out. A sharp fight secured the position and all attempts to retake it were heavily defeated. With evening the company withdrew according to orders, carrying their wounded with them.

In the meantime the 5th Battalion had been ordered to Salonika and sailed on 4th November in the company of Brigade Headquarters and No. 9 Commando. After being held up by mines at the harbour entrance, they landed and entered the town, to find it entirely controlled by E.L.A.S., who shewed little disposition to welcome British troops. The pipe band, however, of which the battalion was very proud, was paraded and marched up and down, being sent 'to the trouble spots to distract the population'. In this they were successful.

The confused state of Salonika can be judged by the composition and behaviour of the dinner party given by the commander of E.L.A.S. in honour of Pritchard. He arrived to find 'the hotel full of bearded warriors caked with mud, and carrying arms in the old "Hardwick style". The atmosphere was like a channel fog, the noise terrifying'. The brigadier found himself seated at a table with, as his fellow guests, the local bishop and a Colonel Markos, afterwards to be one of the leaders in a bloody civil war. 'Food was plentiful, unleavened bread, the largest boiled fish I have ever seen on a platter, flowing wine and fiery spirit. I talked fluent French by the middle of dinner . . . the bishop was hungry and paid little attention to me.'

Presently the battalion, now temporarily attached to the 7th Infantry Brigade of the 4th Indian Division, moved out northwards into eastern Macedonia and Thrace. Here peace was being precariously maintained between Greek nationalists and supporters of E.L.A.S. by a single troop of No. 9 Commando stationed at Drama. In the circumstances the town was well named, for 'the air was electric in this area with the two factions desperate to get at each other'. Brawls and disturbances were frequent, but tact, combined with marching the various companies and platoons of the battalions round the town and through its streets, proved effective, and there was no outbreak of fighting. The followers of E.L.A.S. were highly suspicious, and one morning stopped Regimental Sergeant-Major MacLennan and pointed with scowls to the crown on his sleeve, 'which they obviously connected with their enemies the Royalists'. The warrant officer wasted no time, snatched their rifles from them, and, 'after discharging the magazines, handed them back again, and they were quite well satisfied'.

So uneasy a situation could not endure, and it inevitably turned to tragedy. At the end of a month the whole area from Drama to the Bulgarian border was alight with civil war. The parachute troops did their best, but there were too few of them, and their patrols were unable to prevent Greek killing Greek. The battalions were recalled in haste to Athens, the 5th landing at the Piraeus, 'to the accompaniment of the odd rifle shot'. Then began a hideous week for the brigade. It was a week of street fighting against fanatics skilled in arms who fought with desperate ferocity.

The parachutists and the men of the 3rd Armoured Brigade together known as 'Arkforce', became close friends and supported each other to the hilt. Their commander, Brigadier Arkwright, decided to hold the Acropolis and other centres in the city as the best way of establishing and maintaining control. Unfortunately the only bakery was on the outskirts of the town and to reach it the 2nd Parachute Brigade had to make a daily run in lorries escorted by tanks through streets for the most part held by E.L.A.S. Encounters were frequent, and the position was further complicated by the attempts by the enemy, on whom war had been officially declared on 7th December, to pass men through the sewers in an attempt to blow up the British headquarters. These were defeated by Major D. Vernon, M.C., commanding the 2nd Parachute .Field Squadron, Royal Engineers. To add to the grimness of the situation many in the ranks of E.L.A.S. did not respect the Red Cross. Undeterred, however, Lieutenant-Colonel Parkinson, R.A.M.C., the senior medical officer, together with a surgical team and the Parachute Field Ambulance, established himself in the Museum, where the work of everyone 'was beyond all praise'. They were aided by some dozen Greek ladies, whose 'charm, patience and pluck was an inspiration to the wounded'.

Snipers were active and dangerous. One of their posts was discovered, strongly sandbagged on a housetop, was provisioned daily by means of a bucket. This was let down on a rope and filled by 'small innocent children'. The post was destroyed one morning by Piat fire just as the bucket was being lifted over the edge of the sandbags.

During the siege 'Arkforce' was visited by the Prime Minister, Mr. Churchill, with his medical adviser, Lord Moran, and by General Alexander, who, in compliment, much appreciated by the parachutists, wore a red beret. A final handicap was the Americans in the city. These allies were not at war with E.L.A.S. and their presence in the battle area was an inevitable source of embarrassment.

Fighting was severe and the 5th Battalion spent a whole day forcing their way from Constitution Square along the Phaleron road towards the Acropolis, and were successful only after they had rushed E.L.A.S. headquarters in the Square. In so doing they suffered heavy casualties, among them being Lieutenant Conway killed, and Major W. Hunter very badly wounded. Not until night had fallen did 'B' Company establish themselves upon the Acropolis, which they found unoccupied. Here amid the noble ruins of Athene's shrine, with two thousand years and more of history at their backs, the parachute soldiers set up their bivouacs, their red berets bright against the honey-coloured stone.

Meanwhile the 6th Battalion had reached Omonias Square, across which the 'fire orders of Major Lloyd Jones roared', for he controlled his strongpoints by means of an electric loud hailer. The 4th Battalion held out in the district of the gasworks. During these days of strenuous combat the civilian population within the area proved a considerable embarrassment, for the troops had to provide patrols for all kinds of purposes, which included fetching milk from the Zappion for babies, and rescuing the wife of a Russian diplomat in the midst of what she fondly thought were her political friends. On Boxing Day and the day after the 5th Battalion, supported by tanks of the 23rd Armoured Brigade, attacked the heart of the E.L.A.S. resistance and presently reached the Piraeus road, there joining the 6th Battalion, with the 4th close at hand. On 4th January the whole brigade advanced slowly along this road, and after three more days of heavy fighting the E.L.A.S. formations sullenly withdrew and quitted the city.

The casualties in the 5th Battalion alone were above a hundred, and the 6th lost all its company commanders killed or wounded, for the fighting had been very severe, and every weapon from Piats to pistols had been brought into play. The men were much incensed against foes who had resorted to 'every conceivable low trick' to win the fight and had not scrupled to advance behind a shield of women and children. They wore no uniform, were of both sexes and all ages, and neither asked nor gave quarter.

Altogether it was a most bloody business, and the temper of the parachute troops was sorely tried. Their cup ran over when they learned from sections of the English press that they, who had continued to feed the population throughout the battle and who had given their blood so that wounded, friendly or not, might have a chance of life, had been employed in butchering innocent workers for the benefit of rich Athenian business men. So great was the agitation on this matter in England that the Trades Union Congress sent Sir Walter Citrine at the head of a delegation to discover the truth. Pritchard got into immediate touch with the delegates and took Sir Walter to a meeting of between six and seven hundred parachutists whom he had urged to speak freely and fearlessly. If they disliked their officers, they should say so ; if they had been ordered to shoot Athenian women and children, they should not hesitate to disclose it. Sir Walter and his colleagues made a thorough enquiry and returned home wiser men with the facts in their possession to lay before the Congress.

The open-mindedness of Sir Walter was greatly appreciated by the men, who realised that they were confronted by a man free from all prejudice, and it was therefore no surprise but a source of great satisfaction to everyone when, on his return to England, he 'made a very bold press announcement, upholding all that the brigade had done and was doing in Greece'. Not until the better part of two divisions had arrived by sea and air from Italy did it prove possible to quell the E.L.A.S. army in the Athens area.

By the beginning of February 1945 the brigade was withdrawn and returned to Italy, Pritchard, its commander, having been admitted to the Distinguished Service Order. After a fortnight's rest planning began for General Alexander's spring offensive, of which the object was the crossing of the River Po and the destruction of all the enemy's forces in Italy. From 19th March to 8th May, VE Day, the brigade remained in a constant state of readiness to support the 8th Army. To its chagrin it was never called upon to do so. More than thirty operations were planned. The troops entered their aircraft five times, but all were cancelled. If the remedy for hope deferred be hard work, the brigade was given it in large quantities. Its labours included loading aircraft in the heat of the Italian summer, and it set up a record by reaching a figure of seven tons a man a day.

VE Day came and went, and in May the 2nd Parachute Brigade headed for England to join the 6th Airborne Division and to go with them to Palestine. Its commander bore a letter from Alexander, in which he expressed his immense pride in having had so 'distinguished a brigade' under his command. 'You have a wonderful record of successes,' said the Commander-in-Chief, 'and in every battle you have fought you have shewn all the true qualities of good soldiers—high morale, dash, and fighting efficiency.'

His words will be endorsed by all future historians of the British Army.

The Ardennes, Holland and The Rhine

A FEW days before Christmas 1944 Major R. A. Keene, of the 7th Battalion, was taking a drink in the ante-room before dinner, when he was told that a conference would be held as soon as the meal was over. 'This seemed,' he says, 'a little strange, but stranger things have been known to happen.' It was surely hardly necessary to plan for Operation 'Christmas Leave', which he and the rest of the battalion, and for that matter the rest of the division, hoped to carry out within the next forty-eight hours. The hope, like so many others, was vain and he was told at the conference that the 6th Airborne Division was to move almost immediately to southern Belgium to help in resisting Runstedt's fierce counter-attacks. The enemy was making a last desperate attempt to stave off what he knew would be not merely defeat but ruin, and he had launched a massive assault in the wooded hilly country of the Ardennes with two Panzer divisions of his 7th Army. His immediate objective was Namur.

After the 6th Airborne Division's return from Normandy in September it had been put through a course of severe training during which street fighting had been practised in the ruined areas of Southampton, Birmingham, and other towns. All knew what was in the wind and their hopes were confirmed by 'Exercise Eve' in which the River Thames was made to do duty for the Rhine. Then in a few hours all seemed changed. The division was taken to the Ardennes by sea, and it was in its new positions by Boxing Day.

Its movements were hindered at the outset by severe fog, but, encouraged by the reception accorded to it by the Belgians, who, whether owners of châteaux, bourgeois occupiers of neat brick houses in neat brick towns, or nuns who insisted on providing 'the soldiers with large cauldrons of soup before going to bed', were all equally anxious to give a welcome to men snatched from rest to go once more into battle. The weather was exceedingly cold, and there was snow on the ground.

The 3rd and 5th Parachute Brigades had left England at very short notice, to arrive by devious routes in the area between Dinant and Namur, where the division was concentrated in order to cover the crossings of the Meuse. By the time the two brigades were in position Von Runstedt's advance had been brought to a halt and the Allies had gone over to the offensive. Just before New Year's Day, 1945, the brigades were grouped and ordered to advance against the tip of the German salient. The 5th Brigade moved forward on the right of the division in the direction of Grupont, while the 3rd, on its left, occupied the area of Rochefort. Though the desperate attempt of the enemy to prevent or at least postpone the doom which then was approaching with inexorable tread had failed, the German army was still full of fight and was not disposed to withdraw tamely. It became necessary, therefore, to attack it, and on 3rd Jaunry the 13th Battalion advanced against the village of Bure, the possession of which would put them in a good position to seize Grupont.

'After an approach march of eight miles in the sun,' the assault began at 13.30 hours. Fierce fighting developed almost immediately. The Germans were on the alert, and maintained a heavy and accurate fire. So heavy indeed was it that it might have brought the attack to a halt had it not been for the gallantry of Major J. R. B. Watson, M.C., who rallied 'A'

Company and burst into the village at their head. To aid them, 'B' Company, under Major G. K. Grantham, carried out a flank attack on the hilly ground to the right of Bure. Here they encountered the heavy fire of German tanks and artillery, to which that of small arms from German infantry was soon added. The company lost heavily, Grantham and two of his platoon commanders, together with the company sergeant-major, being killed, and its total strength at the end of the day being reduced to one officer and twenty men. Nevertheless the Germans failed, for their counter-attack which promised at one moment to be very dangerous, was foiled in the nick of time by Lieutenant R. Lagergren, who, before he fell, did such execution with grenades that the enemy faltered and slowly withdrew. Meanwhile 'A' Company gained control of about half the village, and at 17.00 hours were joined by 'C' Company. Throughout the next day the battalion held grimly to its gains, sustaining in all fifteen counter-attacks delivered by infantry and tanks. Their own resolution and the timely effective support of a regiment of field and a battery of medium artillery enabled them to stand fast. That evening 'C' Company of the 2nd Battalion of the Oxford and Buckinghamshire Regiment, under Major J. Granville, reinforced them, and with these new troops the village was cleared and held until the order to withdraw was received.

During this grim battle at Bure Sergeant Scott, D.C.M., Royal Army Medical Corps, went forward with an ambulance to pick up wounded. A German Tiger tank rolled up and put itself alongside. Its commander opened the turret and called to Scott in good English to 'take the casualties away this time, but do not come forward again as it is not safe'. Scott, who was on one occasion seen to bandage a wounded man, with bullets cutting his hands as he did so, was later killed in Germany.

This savage battle lost the battalion seven officers and a hundred and eighty-two other ranks. Among the decorations won was a Military Cross bestowed on the Reverend W. Foy, who remained behind after the battalion withdrew, with two volunteers to succour the wounded and bury the dead.

While the 13th Battalion was thus engaged at Bure the 7th were ordered to attack the village of Wavreille. They moved to it from Celles-sur-Lesse and Veve, whose two great châteaux, 'both perched on the top of precipitous cliffs overlooking the Lesse, had excited the admiration of all ranks'. The attack was carried out by 'A' Company, followed by 'B', and by nightfall they had together overcome about a hundred Germans supported by tracked vehicles, including tanks and self-propelled guns. 'The Boche, a past master at setting booby-traps and other evil gadgets, had placed wire across the roads at three-yard intervals.' These cost several casualties, including Sergeant Bird and Private Oliffe. They were devilish contrivances, not easily discovered in the snow, and the whole division had always to move like Agag because of them.

From Wavreille Lieutenant P. Kearney and Sergeant Cox made a number of patrols, during one of which Kearney found himself isolated in the village of Fourriere, when he was suddenly confronted by 'two Boches who were standing outside their slit trench. As the situation demanded a pretty quick decision, he shouted "Hande hoch!" (almost the only words of German any parachute soldier was able to learn) and flourished his Sten gun. This caused the Boche to roar with laughter. One turned to the other and then they both said "Ja, ja, Amerikano", and continued to laugh. . . . At this point Kearney thought that some solid English would have better results, so he shouted "Put your bloody hands up" and gave one of them a dig in the ribs. The effect was devastating. Hands have rarely gone up so quickly'. Kearney grabbed their rifles, flung them as far away as he could, and then left the place hurriedly before the enemy was reinforced.

The action at Bure was the most severe of any fought by a unit of the division at that time ; but patrolling, which was constant, was peculiarly hazardous in a land covered with snow. A good example is furnished by a corporal and six men of the 22nd Independent Parachute Company. They entered a wood near Marloie between Namur and the Luxembourg Border, their object being to get into touch with the Germans so that their whereabouts could be discovered. The leading parachutist trod on a mine and fell wounded. After ordering his men to halt, the corporal in command went to his rescue, when he, too, struck a mine. He at once sent messages asking for medical help and mine detectors. Five medical orderlies arrived in due course, but two of them were blown up by mines before they could reach the wounded. Then Captain D. J. Tibbs, M.C., the medical officer of the 13th Battalion, reached the spot. He ordered everyone to move back and not to enter the minefield whatever happened until the arrival of the mine detectors. 'He then went straight in, reached the first man, and stopped the bleeding, and with miraculous luck did the same for the other men, staying with the farthest off until help arrived.' By then he was in shirtsleeves, having put his tunic round the worst of the wounded. The temperature at the time was well below freezing point. Two sergeants—one of them was Sergeant L. J. Carrier—soon afterwards arrived with mine detectors and with their aid found a path through the minefield, being followed by volunteer stretcher bearers. They had reached the medical officer, 'who had not moved an inch'. 'We found him supporting the man he was with in a sitting position. Sweeping the spot with the detector, we located a mine, where the man's shoulders would have been if he had been allowed to lie down, and two more within a foot of the medical officer's feet.'

By the last week of January the division had moved back to Holland. A day or two before they had been visited by Field-Marshal Montgomery, who had recently been appointed Colonel Commandant of the Regiment. Their new positions were on the Maas in the area of Venlo and Roermond. Here patrolling was active on both sides, and here the brigades also met with propaganda shells of a kind similar to those fired against the 2nd Independent Parachute Brigade in Italy. One of the leaflets thus discharged bore the picture of an enormous steel monster described as the new German tank, 'an amphibious job with at least twenty pieces of main armament and other smaller stuff sticking out of the sides'. Other pamphlets cast aspersions on the fiancées and girl friends of the men left behind in England. These were eagerly sought after and sent with much delight to the ladies in question.

The patrolling carried on at this time was hazardous in the extreme, for the patrols had to cross the River Maas, which, in that part of Holland, was the size of the Thames at Westminster and in full flood. It was crossed in small-size craft, but it was never possible to foresee the spot on the far bank at which the craft would touch, for the current was strong and swept the boats along with it. Thus it sometimes happened that a patrol, instead of striking the bank fifty or a hundred yards from the enemy, was driven by the rushing water almost into their arms. The inevitable mines were also thick along the bank. It says much for the high standard of training reached by the Parachute Regiment that these patrols were, on the whole, successful and inflicted damage on the enemy, the 7th German Parachute Division, at relatively small cost. This is all the more remarkable when it is recalled that the weather throughout was bitterly cold and that it was some time before the officers and men were issued with the full winter clothing as worn by the troops who had been fighting in that neighbourhood for some time. No doubt the Spartan habit whereby each officer and man removed his boots and socks every day and ran barefooted in the snow did much to harden frames already tautened by strenuous training and frequent battle. Such a practice made the feet so cold that 'a brisk towelling was the natural consequence'; the blood was kept circulating and there were no cases of frost-bite. Indeed the health of the troops at that period and in that frost-gripped country was described with justice as 'amazing'.

In the third week of February the 6th Airborne Division returned to Salisbury Plain to prepare once more for a great feat of arms, the leap across the Rhine. The battalions of the Parachute Regiment left behind the bulk of their transport in Belgium, it being intended that this should join them after the operation, which was given the code name of 'Varsity'. For reasons of 'security' the men who thus remained in Belgium discarded their red berets and removed formation signs from all vehicles. The 6th Airborne Division was to be part of the 18th United States Airborne Corps commanded by Lieutenant-General M. B. Ridgewây, an American, with Gale as his second-in-command. Gale had handed over the division shortly before Christmas to Major-General E. Bols, D.S.O., on taking Browning's place as Deputy Commander of the 1st Allied Airborne Army.

The plan for Operation 'Varsity' was based on the experience gained at Arnhem and elsewhere, and therefore differed in a marked degree from previous operations of the same type. First, and perhaps most important, the decision was taken to transport all the airborne troops, both those who would land by parachute and those carried in gliders, in a single lift. The bitter misfortunes and the heavy casualties of the 4th Parachute Brigade which had landed in a hornets' nest at Arnhem were fresh in the minds of the planners. Such an error, however inevitable it might have been at the time, would not be repeated. Secondly the whole force was to land, not near, but on top, of its objective. There would be no approach march during which the enemy might get wind of their presence, as had happened at Arnhem, and have time to put themselves in a state and posture of defence. This being the plan, it followed that the operation would have to take place in daylight so that every man would be able to see whither he was going and what he had to attack. By choosing daylight instead of darkness the division might run a fearful risk. Nevertheless it was eventually accepted, for the advantages far outweighed the disadvantages. Finally, and perhaps the most striking innovation of all, the airborne troops were to land not before but after land operations on the largest scale had begun. The Rhine, in the first instance, was to be crossed by Commando troops and others, notably elements of the 15th Scottish Division. They were to seize and hold the small town of Wesel, and only when they had done so would the airborne troops arrive at the scene of action.

Once across the Rhine, the objectives for the 3rd and 5th Parachute Brigades and the Air Landing Brigade were clear and simple. On landing, they were to occupy the high ground east of Bergen in the wooded area of the Diersfordter Wald, the village of Hamminkeln and certain bridges over the River Issel. By so doing the north flank of the 18th U.S. Corps would be protected. These tasks were divided between the three brigades of the division. The 3rd Parachute Brigade, under Hill, was to land on the north-west corner of the Diersfordter Wald to capture the feature known as 'Schneppenberg' and hold the western edge of the wood. The 5th Parachute Brigade, under Poett, was to land north-west of Hamminkeln and seize and hold the area on each side of the main road running from the dropping zone to that village. The 6th Air Landing Brigade, under Brigadier R. H. Bellamy, D.S.O., was to capture the bridges over the River Issel and contain the garrison of Hamminkeln. The parachute brigades were to land first, followed closely by the gliders of the Air Landing Brigade, with divisional headquarters and the artillery bringing up the rear. As has been explained, all landings were to be made either very close to the objectives or actually upon them. This was a daring decision, and could only have been contemplated, let alone taken, provided that the Allies had absolute mastery of the air. As that was precisely what they had, and as, moreover, by this late stage in the war the ability of the Tactical Air Forces to quell light anti-aircraft fire with rockets, seemed well established, the risk of landing in the heart of enemy territory was one which, though still considerable, might reasonably be accepted. The whole plan, of course, was based on the assumption that the highest possible degree of co-operation with the artillery on the ground and the Royal Air Force in the air would be secured. As a further precaution it was decided that the 6th Airborne Division should land in the shortest possible space of time, thus reducing as far as possible the risk that the *Luftwaffe* might be troublesome.

On the face of it long lines of tugs and gliders presented a target to an enterprising German fighter pilot beyond his wildest dream or craziest nightmare. Bols proposed to fly in his division in broad daylight to an objective situated several miles on the further side of the Rhine, that great river along which, as the Germans sang, a perpetual watch and guard was kept. A single fighter squadron of the *Luftwaffe* had only to swoop down upon the slow-flying Dakotas and the straining tugs, all moving together 'in ranks and squadrons and right form of war', to do irreparable damage before ever a man set foot on the sacred soil of the fatherland. In the event no squadron appeared, nor even a single aircraft. To such a degree had Goering's once all-powerful force been mastered.

Dawn on 24th March 1945 broke bright and clear with the spring sun shining upon the airfields of No. 38 and 46 Groups of the Royal Air Force, and upon those of the American 9th Troop Carrier Command. The aircraft and gliders assembled upon them would before noon be riding the air above the sullen earth and dark forests of Germany. In that great host were the 3rd Parachute Brigade under Hill, made up as usual of the 8th and 9th Battalions and the 1st Canadian Parachute Battalion, and the 5th Parachute Brigade under Poett composed of the 7th, 12th and 13th Battalions. They took the air, the 3rd in one hundred and twenty-two, the 5th in one hundred and twenty-one Dakotas.

By now and for a long time before, every officer and man had the greatest confidence in their American pilots and crews, and the most wholehearted admiration for their courage and skill. The 9th Troop Carrier Command had become veteran experts, or expert veterans. They were in close formation, 'in nine ship elements', a formation of three lanes of aircraft, composed each of four sections of three, flying in Vics one behind the other. These dispositions made it possible to drop every battalion simultaneously and thus to concentrate a large number of men in a small area in the minimum of time. Speed and surprise—that was the essence of the plan, for Bols calculated that there were two factors which would throw the enemy off his balance. First the landing of the whole division, not before, but at least three hours after the Rhine had been crossed by the land forces and, secondly, the arrival within a very short space of time of six battalions of trained and ferocious men—and that in truth describes the officers and men of the Parachute Regiment—in two very small areas all close together and in no more than ten minutes. At the risk of repetition it is necessary to make it very clear that Operation 'Varsity' was based on the sum total of previous experiences, especially those acquired at Arnhem.

The parachute soldiers were in the highest heart. They had had three weeks to train for the operation, and though they had been told only two days before it took place what it was to be, they had had a very good idea and had done their best to fit themselves for a decisive stroke, Darling, commanding the 12th Battalion, having recovered from wounds sustained in Normandy, records that on one occasion he was visiting the thirty-yards range, where a number of his men were trying out their personal weapons. He was surprised to see them 'rushing round madly in circles on a hot afternoon, and running up to the firing point where they fired a few rounds from their Stens or rifles, and then returned to their antics'. On enquiring the reason for this procedure, he was told that 'they were practising getting out of breath and shooting Germans'.

The Parachute Regiment had by then evolved a system of carrying parachutists which, it was hoped, would shorten the period of chaos inevitable when they first reached the ground, and were seeking to form up in their prearranged order. In brief the plan was to allot lanes of aircraft to the sub-units (platoons and sections of platoons) instead of carrying them in consecutively numbered aircraft. The effect of this was that troops landing together would all belong to the same company. The system proved a complete success, and would have been adopted universally in all cases of a mass simultaneous drop had the war continued. Men carrying the heaviest loads were dropped nearest to the rendezvous. This, too, proved effective, Major J. D. Went, the officer commanding headquarters company of the 7th Battalion, landing on the site of Battalion Headquarters. Unfortunately he got caught in some trees. Thus did men now highly trained both in theory and in practice use to the full the sum of their acquired knowledge for an operation all knew to be the culminating point of the Parachute Regiment's career.

For some weeks beforehand Bomber Command had been very active all over the area. Roads, railways, marshalling yards, bridges and other targets, of which the destruction was likely to delay the movement of troops, were very heavily attacked, the most noteworthy achievement, perhaps, being the destruction of the Bielefeld viaduct by a single tallboys bomb weighing twenty-two thousand pounds. While the British and American heavy bombers of the 8th American Army Air Force and Bomber Command fulfilled this grim programme of destruction, the 2nd

Tactical Air Force, under Air Vice-Marshal Coningham, assaulted targets of immediate importance in the area chosen for the landing. Barracks, military positions, gun-sites, all received concentrated attention, and the aerial bombardment reached a climax on 21st and 22nd March, when two thousand seven hundred tons of bombs fell on ten airfields of the *Luftwaffe* and put them out of action. The stricken German air force did what it could to retaliate and lost fifty-two aircraft shot down in combat and one hundred and sixteen destroyed on the ground. On the day of the operation itself a final assault was delivered against anti-aircraft positions in the area, twenty-three of them receiving eight hundred tons of bombs. On that day some seven thousand seven hundred sorties were flown by the air forces of Great Britain and the United States of America.

To this prolonged bombardment from the air was added that of the guns from the 21st Army Group. So fierce a battering from the air and from concentrated artillery might reasonably have been expected to obliterate the anti-aircraft defences. In point of fact it did not, and its failure to do so provided a melancholy example of the uncertainty attending upon such tactics, even though they were the best available and carried out to a degree unparalleled in the history of warfare. The bombs in many cases missed their mark, and the shells from the guns, though doing much damage to the German positions in the Diersfordter Wald, did not fall upon the batteries east and north of that wood which were precisely those covering the main landing area. The fire of these guns was the chief cause of the casualties inflicted during the landing.

Such were the preparations, and to these must be added the hard unspectacular but vital work of the ground crews of the various airfields in England, from which the force was to take its departure.

By 24th March 1945, all was ready, and at 07.00 hours, in perfect weather, the division took off for Operation 'Varsity'. As they drew near the Rhine the ground below was seen to be covered with haze. This was caused not by nature but by the heavy bombardment which had been maintained till the last possible moment, and by myriad particles of dust blown from the stricken town of Wesel, to the south-east of the dropping zones, which had been obliterated by Bomber Command. 'I could see the Rhine,' says one to be in action that day, 'a silver streak, and beyond it a thick black haze, for all the world like Manchester or Birmingham as seen from the air.'

The 3rd Parachute Brigade landed first, nine minutes early, and the drop on the most westerly of the chosen dropping zones just north-west of the Diersfordter Wald was most accurate. The arrival of the brigade before the planned moment made it impossible for the elaborate barrage fired by the guns to be completed. As soon as the brigade began to drop these had to cease fire, and this, together with inability of the fighter-bombers owing to the haze to see all their targets, undoubtedly contributed to the failure to paralyse the enemy's anti-aircraft defences. The parachutists were met with heavy fire from light anti-aircraft guns and small arms; it came from the woods surrounding the dropping zones and caused casualties, among them Lieutenant-Colonel J. S. Nickin, commanding the 1st Canadian Parachute Battalion, who was killed. He was one of a large number who fell on the edge of the zone and whose parachutes were caught in trees from which they hung suspended, an easy target for German snipers. Lieutenant-Colonel Nicklin had once before only just avoided this unhappy fate, for when landing in Normandy his parachute had caught on the edge of a building from which he had hung till rescued. Major Kippin and Lieutenant A. Cox of the 8th Battalion also lost their lives on the dropping zone, as did Lieutenant J. England, the intelligence officer, who, while talking to his commanding officer, was struck by a glider which came down through the smoke and haze, all on board it dead. The commanding officer, Lieutenant-Colonel G. Hewetson, sustained a severe concussion, but remained in action.

Prominent among those tending the casualties was Corporal F. G. Topham, a medical orderly of the 1st Canadian Parachute Battalion. Hearing a cry for help, he went to the aid of a wounded man lying at a point where two medical orderlies who had already tried to help him had been shot down before his eyes. While tending the casualty, Topham himself was wounded but never faltered in his task. He carried the wounded man into the shelter of the wood and went about his business for the next two hours, refusing all medical assistance. Later in the day he rescued three Canadians from a blazing carrier. For these deeds, performed over a period of six hours during most of which he was in intense pain, he was awarded the Victoria Cross.

By 11.00 hours the dropping zone had been secured by the 8th Battalion and opposition silenced. There is no doubt that their swift and gallant clearance of the zone hastened the victory and reduced its cost. They had had a hard fight, for they had had to go into action immediately on touching the ground as soon as they had flung off the parachutes. Of the total casualties of the brigade, about two hundred and seventy, some eighty were killed, and most of them belonged to the 8th Battalion.

The immediate objective secured, the 9th Battalion and the 1st Canadian Parachute Battalion then moved against the wooded feature called Schneppenberg, and in three hours secured all their objectives, the 9th ensconcing themselves on the feature itself, while the Canadians took up positions close beside it.

The 8th Battalion had meanwhile gone into reserve, and later that day cleared a wood near divisional headquarters. About 15.00 hours the first elements of the land forces which had crossed the Rhine earlier in the day, a battalion of the Royal Scots, made their appearance. Before night had fallen about seven hundred prisoners had been taken, a fairly large number considering that the total strength of the enemy's forces in the neighbourhood of the landings was not above four thousand.

The flight of the 5th Parachute Brigade, like that of the 3rd, was uneventful. As soon as the River Maas was passed the parachutists hooked up, for there was barely twenty minutes to go. 'It was at once clear,' records Lieutenant-Colonel Darling, 'that we were over enemy territory, for not only could we see the chutes of the 3rd Parachute Brigade on the ground and hear the fighting, but also we could hear the sharp clack of flak directed at our aircraft. It was now only a matter of minutes. Somehow, in spite of the tension, these seemed peaceful moments. All the hurry and scurry of planning, checking and inspecting was over, and all that could now be done was to jump when ordered.'

The parachutists left their aircraft at between one thousand and eight hundred feet and were therefore in the air for a longer time than usual. This made it possible for the German anti-aircraft batteries to burst shells among them as they drifted down, and these caused casualties. On the other hand, the longer time in the air made it easier to pick up bearings, a matter of no little difficulty when falling on to haze-shrouded country. The picture presented by the brigade as it descended from the air 'was amazing', records one who watched it: hundreds of men were drifting down through the haze and landing on fields, on fences and in trees. 'As fast as they disentangled themselves from their chutes more parachutists dropped among them from succeeding waves and added to the general confusion. Above all this was the roar of passing aircraft, the sharp crack of small

289

arms fire . . . and the deeper thumps of heavy and light flak . . . we received nothing but help from the American crews, who in spite of the considerable flak flew straight and level over the dropping zone.' Of the Dakotas carrying the 12th Battalion only two were hit and set on fire, but the pilots flew grimly on and by their heroism enabled the parachutists to jump unscathed. The 13th Battalion had only one casualty in the air, a man hit while still in the aircraft ; he jumped, nevertheless, with his knee-cap shattered.

Immediately on landing the 13th Battalion pulled off their steel helmets, put on their red berets and began to rally to the cries of 'Tallyho' and the hunting horns blown by their officers. The 12th Battalion found that its rendezvous was under fire at very close range. It was for a time a very unhealthy spot until one platoon, under Lieutenant P. Burkinshaw, captured the four guns responsible. These were 88-mm. and had escaped unscathed during the preliminary bombardment. They had therefore been able to engage those arriving on the dropping zone at pointblank range and had caused casualties, not only to parachutists, but also to gliders when they came in to land. The process of sorting out the parachutists as they reached the rendezvous was carried on by Majors Bucher and Freegard and Captain B. W. Metcalf, who remained in action though a piece of shell had removed a number of his teeth.

The 7th Battalion, rallying to the notes of a bugle, were more fortunate, their rendezvous not being under the same heavy fire. Private Gay of 'C' Company had a curious experience : he landed in a tree and was unable to climb down. His rifle was in his kitbag attached to him by a rope. As he was hauling it up a German officer approached the tree, climbed it, pulled Gay by his rigging lines towards the trunk, and then cut them 'with a long vicious-looking knife'. Thus freed, Gay was able to reach the ground, where the German officer was awaiting him with his rifle, which he handed to the astonished parachutist, remarking in good English, 'The war is over, and if there is anything I can do for you I am at your service.'

Like the 3rd Brigade, the 5th secured their objectives with speed and dash. The farms and houses allotted to the 12th and 13th Battalions were attacked with vigour, the operations being assisted by a number of stout American parachutists from the 513th Regiment who had dropped awry. The two gliders allotted to the 12th Battalion were both hit as they touched earth. The regimental quartermaster-sergeant travelling in one of them was killed with three others, the only survivor being a private. By 15.30 hours the brigade, which had lost about three hundred men on the dropping zone, was digging in, the 7th Battalion being held in reserve, and patrols from the 13th were getting in touch with the Air Landing Brigade west of Hamminkeln.

This brigade had reached its landing grounds in good order, and nine-tenths of the gliders touched down, but of the four hundred and sixteen which arrived at the battlefield only eighty-eight landed undamaged, and thirty-seven were completely burnt out. These high casualties were caused to a great extent by German anti-aircraft fire, especially that of the four 88-mm. guns eventually captured by Lieutenant Burkinshaw.

This and the inevitable shellfire and mortaring steadily diminished as the day went on, and the objectives given to the division were captured one by one until, towards evening, it was possible to walk around the area freely. Major-General Bols, the divisional commander, making his rounds, was entertained by Luard, commanding the 13th Battalion, to a meal of scrambled eggs, 'the first cooked east of the Rhine', in a kitchen festooned with smoked hams. Brigadier Poett was provided with milk by one of his staff, a jockey in private life, who milked the cows of the farm in which headquarters had been established. At dusk Major-General Gale, who had been a spectator of the airborne operation, arrived in a jeep to greet his old division and was received with enthusiasm.

Thus ended the last airborne operation of the war, the total casualties of the 6th Airborne Division being thirty-nine officers and three hundred and eight other ranks killed and forty-eight officers and six hundred and eighty-three other ranks wounded. Of the three hundred and nineteen officers and men reported missing by sundown, most subsequently rejoined.

But for the division fighting was not over. They were to be granted the privilege of being in the van of Montgomery's armies on the final advance which was to bring them to the Baltic.

It began on 27th March, the division being provided with a continuous aerial 'cab-rank',[1] which attacked twelve targets. The 5th Parachute Brigade was in the lead. The first town met with, Brunen, was found to be empty and level with the ground, for it had been the target of a concentrated bombing attack, and the

[1] Term used to describe a number of fighter aircraft flying in a certain area, to which targets of opportunity were signalled by radio telephone by a controller with the land forces.

enemy did not shew fight again until Erle was reached. In the evening the 6th Airborne Armoured Reconnaissance Regiment was held up by what was at first thought to be two or three self-propelled guns. The 7th Battalion was ordered to deal with them and the 13th to seize some high ground, after which the 12th Battalion was to pass through the 13th and capture Erle from the rear.

The 7th Battalion moved to a flank, leaving 'C' Company to deal with the self-propelled guns which were holding a cross-roads. The company reached a point a few hundred yards short of these, and their leading Platoon, No. 7, under Lieutenant Whitworth, made for some farm buildings. They had not gone very far when the enemy opened a furious fire 'and a very bloody battle started'. The platoon was at a disadvantage, for it could only return the fire with Bren guns and rifles, whereas the Germans were using light anti-aircraft and anti-tank guns. Night was falling rapidly, and Major Keene, the company commander, decided to make a flank attack with his other two platoons under cover of smoke. This manœuvre was not altogether successful, but eventually a spot was reached from which the final assault could be launched. Reconnoitring the ground, the company commander and two of his officers 'saw that in the failing light the objective was some two hundred yards away, and there were at least three cattle fences across the line which we had to take'. The assault was therefore postponed and the company was put into a position along the edge of a wood. When darkness had fallen, the Germans, wishing to see their enemies, fired tracer into the haystacks round the farm, and soon 'the whole place was as bright as day. Unfortunately the woods sloped up and away, and so they could see just where we were'. 'C' Company being pinned down, 'B' Company sent out a strong fighting patrol under Lieutenant Pape, which approached the cross-roads from the north and utterly surprised the enemy. 'C' Company was then able to advance, and just after midnight arrived at the cross-roads, 'where about sixty dejected-looking Boches gave themselves up'. They dug in, and when the morning of 28th March broke found that the enemy had been holding the position with eleven dual-purpose guns, one 75-mm. anti-tank gun and a quantity of Spandaus and Panzer-fausts. An outstanding feature of this small but fierce fight was the bravery of Corporal Christopher and Private Hilliard, who silenced one of the anti-aircraft guns with Bren-gun fire before they were both killed.

In the meantime the 13th Battalion, still wearing its red berets, had seized their objective, and the 12th then advanced to Erle. To do so it became necessary to move some two miles across country in pitch darkness, and this the battalion accomplished, marching by compass and arriving at a position half a mile from their objective just as day broke. At that moment a German lorry appeared moving fast down the road towards the town. A grenade was flung at it, and since its own cargo was a stock of hand grenades it at once burst into flames. The sight of the burning lorry and the wild fire of the enemy, who were beginning to bestir themselves, was incentive enough to the battalion. 'The company surged forward, the men shouting and firing from the hip as they advanced.' The picture is a vivid one—the bright light of dawn over woods and still green fields, the red glare of the lorry, the dark figures of the advancing parachute soldiers, flashes of steel at their rifle ends and in the background the red-tiled houses of Erle, the new sunshine winking on the window panes.

Within fifteen minutes the position was captured, and very soon Erle had been cleared. The battalion then spent some pleasant hours ambushing German vehicles and dispatch riders, 'who continued to motor to Erle from all directions'. At the same time 'all ranks dug like moles, and by the time the inevitable shelling started they were well underground with good head cover'. Casualties were, in consequence, very small, and the battalion had reason to be pleased with itself, for it had marched twenty miles, five of them in darkness, and put into practice three lessons which all troops must learn before they can be considered veterans, the value of cutting your enemy's communications, the importance of speed and dash at the moment when the enemy is aroused and is about to defend himself, and the necessity to dig in immediately once a position has been taken.

Nor was the 3rd Parachute Brigade idle. The 9th Battalion attacked a small hamlet, Klosterlütherheim, advancing through the early morning mist on 27th March, along tracks and across country. They presently halted, and 'B' Company 'pushed on through the thick mist to locate the village'. Emerging from the fog, they came to the first houses, whereupon Lieutenants Lee and Brown at the head of the two leading patrols charged immediately. 'Twenty minutes of shooting and shouting ended in the capture of the whole place', with the exception of a big barn, which caught fire and was evacuated by its garrison. 'Still inside were twenty head of cattle maddened by the fire and the shooting, and "B" Company had a lively time extricating them from the burning building.' The Germans lost twelve killed and a hundred and eighty prisoners, the losses of the 9th Battalion being but two men wounded.

It remained in the village for the rest of the day and the following night, the passing hours being occupied by digging in, patrolling and allaying the apprehensions of German wounded in an improvised hospital, who 'seemed to expect immediate death at the sight of the red berets'. Lance-Corporal Etches of 'B' Company, a noted sniper, crawled up ditches to kill two Germans with two shots. 'Most of his company could see the whole stalk, and the slow advance of Etches upon his prey was most exciting to watch.'

The 8th Battalion cleared the village of Rhades, and then moved till it reached the hill overlooking the town of Lembeck, of which the garrison was determined to make a fight for it. This they did, and all that day the 8th was heavily engaged, its leading company fighting a hand-to-hand battle with two companies of a Panzer Grenadier training battalion. By midnight they were in the town and the Germans were all killed or captured. About three hundred prisoners were taken and the mopping-up was completed by the Canadians. Meanwhile the 9th had moved to the flank and taken the enemy in the rear. 'This involved a ten-miles march in the twilight across unknown country. The first hundred yards lay straight across some open fields in full view . . . of the Germans, and walking through it in open order made people feel very naked.' Having covered four miles, 'A' Company in the lead topped a rise just north of Lembeck and immediately engaged four German 20-mm. guns no more than four hundred yards away. Each side saw the other simultaneously and, while the German gun crews were prevented from serving their guns by a stream of Bren fire, Lieutenant Harpley, his batman, and Sergeant Costello crawled along a road ditch to within three hundred yards of the guns. Not pausing to wait for the rest of the patrol moving up from behind, the three men firing their Sten guns, killed several of the crew and captured twenty-five prisoners. Two lorries nearby were set on fire, and, despite the 'frenzied efforts of battalion headquarters to salvage a handsome staff-car', it, too, was burnt.

By 21.30 hours Lembeck was passed and the Germans withdrew or surrendered. At Billerbeck battalion headquarters established themselves in the town hall, from which they evicted 'a large bust of Hitler and a stand of Nazi flags. . . . Many Germans on the pavement laughed, to the disgust of the men of the battalion'. The drivers of several jeeps attached large swastika flags to the rear of the vehicles, so that they dragged in the dust, and a set of flags was kept and laid down as a carpet before the door of battalion headquarters wherever it was set up. At first sight such gestures may seem undignified and not in accordance with tradition. This is a shortsighted view. Those who performed them were members of a victorious army hard on the heels of an enemy whose behaviour everywhere had long caused him to be hated for the beast he was, and had stifled any memories of the 'chivalrous wars of past centuries'. The men of the Parachute Regiment were moving among an arrogant people who had plunged Europe into war three times in seventy years, and who were now at last beginning to learn its consequences. There was no reason to spare the Germans any of the bitterness of defeat. When resistance finally died away the 3rd Parachute Brigade were left the victors in a battle which had lasted almost continuously for eighteen hours.

The battle of Lembeck may be said to be the end of the first phase which began with the landing near Hamminkeln. Thereafter the division played the part of a normal infantry division, and in five weeks, between 29th March and 2nd May, marched more than three hundred miles to Wismar on the shores of the Baltic. To aid it there were attached to it a tank battalion, the 4th (Tank) Battalion, Grenadier Guards in Churchills, who were relieved towards the end by the Royal Scots Greys in Shermans. Its artillery was the 6th and 25th Field Regiments; in addition it had a self-propelled anti-tank battery, a medium regiment of artillery and three platoons of troop-carrying transports. The parachute troops were particularly delighted to have for their encouragement and support the tank battalion of the 4th Grenadier Guards. Its squadrons were attached to various battalions as occasion demanded; the men of the red beret found kindred spirits among the tall Grenadiers, and soon 'a most fruitful and happy partnership was established, and the parachute soldiers went into battle on the top of the guardsmen's tanks'.

For several days the division had been encountering many columns of slave workers, mainly French, now marching at long last back to their homes. 'They cheered madly at the sight of the red beret.' Food was becoming more varied, especially after the order was given that any perishable goods might be consumed by the troops. 'This news was gladly received, not that it would have made much difference if the order had not come out.' Huge quantities of food were found in the cellars and larders of the farmhouses, and 'delicacies in the shape of ham, eggs, sugar and butter' appeared almost daily on the menu.

On 30th March the objective of the 3rd Parachute Brigade was the bridge across the Ems at Greven. By 21.30 hours the leading troops had reached a point about three miles short of the town, where they abandoned their lorries and went forward on foot. The 1st Canadian Parachute Battalion set off at a brisk pace to capture the bridge by *coup de main* in the dark if they could. 'As sentries were being posted a huge, blinding orange flash lit up the whole countryside, and was followed a moment later by a long earth-shaking roar of a colossal explosion.' A few seconds went by and there was a second large explosion, 'and thereafter a series occurred lasting some two hours', during which 'showers of red, white, and green signal lights appeared in the sky', above 'mushrooms of red and orange flame and smoke . . . it was a spectacle of tremendous power and beauty'.

At first the 9th Battalion feared that their Canadian comrades had fared ill; but soon after 23.00 hours a message came back that the bridge had been captured and was intact. The 9th Battalion was at once on the move, and its commanding officer advanced with its reconnaissance group through the main street of Greven, strewn with dead Germans, most of whom had been 'knifed by the Canadians in their silent advance upon the bridge'. A few yards further on the bridge loomed black against the darkness, but there was no river in the bare water-course beneath it. Further on still the gleam of water and the shadow of another bridge could be seen. By then the 9th Battalion had joined the Canadians in the main road of Greven. Realising what had happened, 'B' Company pressed forward and Lieutenant-Colonel Crookenden and Major Smith went in advance to reconnoitre the position and make a plan for the seizure of the bridge. Hardly had they done so when there was another loud explosion, and 'when the noise of falling bricks and rubble died away the commanding officer and Major Smith came back out of the dusty darkness and rather unnecessarily declared the bridge to be blown'. The 9th Battalion then withdrew a little and moved south-east along the bank of the Ems. At 03.45 hours it discovered a foot-bridge intact, and made ready to advance across it at first light. The sun was not yet up when two patrols of 'A' Company, followed by a third and the reconnaissance group, ran across the bridge under fire and spread out on either side. The enemy shewed some resistance, and the leading patrol commander of 'C' Company, Lieutenant McGuffie, was killed. During the fight which followed the Germans were overcome in an hour and the town in our hands before 07.30 hours. 'As soon as the positions were assured, as many of the men as possible went fast asleep.'

After a few hours' rest the brigade advanced once more, this time with the 8th Battalion in the lead. By the late afternoon it reached its immediate objective, the Dortmund-Ems Canal. This waterway was two-thirds empty, for it had been attacked by Bomber Command with great effect. A broken-down bridge, a church, and half a dozen houses were discovered, but it was now dark and no further move was made until the next morning, 1st April. Earlier in the evening German snipers had proved troublesome; but these were dealt with by the redoubtable Lance-Corporal Etches, who, in the morning, was pleased to find 'one German in the target area neatly drilled through the centre of his forehead'. The 8th Battalion were over the canal by 10.30 hours.

Meanwhile the 5th Parachute Brigade was also moving up, and in the next few days reached Osnabruck. During its advance it fought various actions in a manner which had then become typical. The advance would be held up and one or more battalions would deploy and attack from a flank, occasionally covered by smoke. The short sharp battle at Natrup, fought by 'A' Company of the 12th Battalion, is a good example. Night had fallen on 3rd April, when No. 1 Platoon, under Lieutenant Burkinshaw, encountered two German sentries and dispatched them. This roused the enemy, and they opened fire at a range of thirty yards. The company, led by its commander, Major Ritchie, rushed the village in the darkness with the bayonet, No. 2 Platoon going straight through, while Nos. 1 and 3 swung to the left and right. Some hand-to-hand fighting followed, in which Sergeant Torrie dispatched a German with his knife, and Private Westerman won the Military Medal for his proficient clearing of a number of houses. Whenever possible attacks were made in the hours of darkness, a procedure which nonplussed the enemy, who nevertheless continued to maintain his resistance almost to the end.

Considerable feats of marching were also accomplished. There was, for instance, the advance of the 3rd Parachute Brigade from Greven to Minden, which was captured after covering seventy miles in thirty-six hours. The 5th Parachute Brigade was equally forceful and determined. There was indeed nothing to choose between the two brigades. Having crossed the Weser, the 5th moved a distance of forty miles to the Leine, the object being to seize two bridges, one at Bordenau and the other at Neustadt. Two miles short of them was an airfield at Wunsdorf, and here a hard battle was fought in which some of the German troops opposing the parachutists were found to have wooden legs. The advanced group of the brigade was made up of the 12th Battalion, supported by a squadron of the tank battalion of the 4th Grenadier Guards and some artillery. As 'C' Company in the lead neared the bridge at Bordenau, it became involved with the Germans holding the Wunsdorf airfield. Sweeping straight past these—for the object was to secure the more important objective, the bridge at Bordenau—its men jumped on the backs of the tanks, which set off at their best speed. As the leading tank rounded the bend 'the bridge could be seen intact, but on it was a German lorry with a couple of men moving about'. Every gun that could be brought to bear was fired at the lorry, the tanks charged the bridge and the leads of the demolition charges were cut.

In the meantime the next battalion in the line of march, the 7th, cleared the airfield at Wunsdorf, and set off for the other bridge at Neustadt. Like that at Bordenau, it was seen to be intact, and 'B' Company, under Major D. R. Reid, ran across it, noticing as they went that it had been prepared for demolition. This was indeed so, and before they reached the further end it blew up, killing twenty-two of 'B' Company and wounding many men. Nevertheless a bridgehead was secured by the action of Captain E. G. Woodman, Lieutenant G. B. Gush and two other ranks, who were in front of Major Reid and had reached the other side before the bridge was blown. This gallant action of the 7th Battalion, though it was not entirely successful, is typical of the speed and dash shewn by the Parachute Regiment in those crowded, glorious days when the Third Reich was crumbling beneath their victorious feet.

When the evening of 7th April fell, the three battalions of the 5th Parachute Brigade had the satisfaction of learning that they had advanced further into Germany than any other troops of 21st Army Group. The commander of the tank squadron, Major Ivor Crosthwaite, was admitted to the Distinguished Service Order, and the bridge at Bordenau renamed the 'Yorkshire Grenadier Bridge'.

So the advance continued, and presently developed into a race between the leading troops of the Russian Armies and the 6th Airborne Division for Wismar, a large town on the shores of the Baltic Sea. On 30th April both parachute brigades crossed the River Elbe, through a bridgehead which had been secured by the 15th Scottish Division a few days before. Then came the last and final move forward. The objective was Wismar, and the brigades first advanced along separate roads towards Gadebusch, fifteen miles to the south. Whichever brigade could reach Gadebusch first would win the race and be in Wismar before the other. It was a point of honour in every battalion of the regiment that a parachute formation should be the first to reach that town. The march was slowed up, not so much by the enemy as by streams of vehicles, mostly horse-drawn, and crowds of refugees. Nevertheless, time was found to capture prisoners, and the 12th Battalion took four thousand, although the 13th could claim an even more remarkable capture, that of four German generals who were seen 'surrendering at once in battalion head-quarters'. The race for Wismar was won by the 3rd Parachute Brigade, which were the first British troops to join with the Russians, who reached the town within half an hour of their arrival on 1st May. Two days later the event was celebrated in true Muscovite fashion, and a brigadier, noted for his courage, his abstemiousness, and his gentle smile, was in due course found asleep in his car in a convenient but fortunately shallow ditch.

VE day, when it came, was marked in the morning by a special service of thanksgiving conducted by the chaplains of the various battalions who, on that May morning, while rendering thanks for the victory, recalled its cost and reminded those now standing on the shores of the Baltic of the many who had fallen before this, the ultimate goal, had been reached. In the afternoon and for some days following, like Xenophon's ten thousand at Trebizond, some twenty-three centuries before, the division held games, and in the evening concerts and sing-songs by the warm glare of bonfires, 'which could be seen burning all round the countryside, the symbols of light returning to the world after so many years of darkness'. Horse races were held by the 12th Battalion, and Sergeant Bailey arrived in a light American aircraft 'in the guise of a representative' of a well-known firm of bookies. He was received with cheers, which increased when he 'shewed his appreciation by distributing cigars to all and sundry'.

For the division the war in Europe was over. Long before that date its officers and men could with pride describe themselves as of the highest order. Trained to enter a battle by a novel method, there to perform a specific task requiring special qualities of dash and daring, they had shewn themselves to be equally ready and able to face long marches interrupted by frequent bouts of fighting. Not since Murat's horsemen had stormed through Prussia after Jena had troops moved faster, or to greater purpose. For the second time in a generation Germany was in the dust, and the Parachute Regiment could claim no small share in putting her there. Arnhem was avenged.

This Strange Eventful History

IN THE first week of May the 1st Airborne Division which had been carrying on training in Lincolnshire found itself divided. The 1st Parachute Brigade was ordered to Copenhagen, but 'B' Company of the 13th Battalion of 5th Parachute Brigade were the first to arrive. They reached the city from Wismar on 5th May 'accompanied', records their commanding officer, Major A. A. McLoughlin, 'by more war correspondents than I would have believed possible. . . . All the Danes tried to kiss us'. This company was presently relieved by the 1st Parachute Brigade. The remainder of the division were waiting on the airfields in England ready to fly to Norway. This they did on 9th May and received an ovation from a people who, when in subjection to the Germans, had borne themselves with the greatest fortitude. So for the survivors of Arnhem the war ended appropriately enough in flowers and wine and the cheers of a liberated people.

The 6th Airborne Division formed part of the British Liberation Army from the beginning; but hardly had it reached Wismar when the initials B.L.A. seemed to portend what lay before its tired battalions only too accurately. 'Burma Lies Ahead,' said the wits, and for many officers and men this seemed no more than the truth. Before May was out the 7th Battalion, with the 12th and the 13th, were back in the United Kingdom under orders to move into the sphere of South East Asia Command. There they would find, newly formed and vigorously training, the 15th and 16th Battalions, to which in due course was added the 17th, which came into being in England nine days after the first atomic bomb fell on Japan and which went in due course to Palestine.

Eventually the 5th Parachute Brigade sailed for India, where it arrived towards the beginning of August. Its sojourn there, and later on in Java, and that of the battalions which went to Palestine, will not be described in this book. For this is the story of the Parachute Regiment in the Second World War, which ended officially on 15th August 1945, when Nagasaki had joined Hiroshima in smoke and flame if not in oblivion. Those parachute soldiers who went to the Far East or to Palestine were given work of a kind repugnant to all soldiers, especially those who belonged to the Parachute Regiment and who—so many of them—were fresh from bestowing upon it a lustre and a fame which will never fade. With those days of war and battle when this was their pride and duty, and with those only is this record concerned.

'Marked individualist' is a phrase with which perhaps more than one parachute soldier will disagree, for it is his strange and peculiar pride to proclaim at all times that, to quote Warrant Officer John Sharp of the 2nd Battalion, he is 'just an ordinary soldier doing a job', but arriving at the place where he is to do it by an unusual means of transport. In theory no doubt this is true ; in practice it is not. Consider, to give but one instance in which the parachute soldier differed from the ordinary man in the ranks of an infantry battalion, how he was chosen. 'The selection of parachutists,' says Major D. M. Freegard of the 12th Battalion, who had eighteen months' experience of this duty, 'was . . . designed to find the best material from all arms for the regiment. What we looked for was an officer and a man who, whatever his background, was likely to make a superlative infantryman. . . . It was nothing unusual for thirty or forty per cent of an inferior course to be turned down. . . .' The accent is surely on the word 'superlative'. For that was what they had to be, not only because their duties but often because their existence required it.

A moment's reflection will shew that so high a standard was unavoidable. Parachute soldiers did not enter battle as did other troops in sections or platoons each man near his neighbour, each man a member of an intimate team marching, fighting together. This was the second stage in their career ; the first was very different. The parachute soldier leapt alone through a hole or a door in an aircraft which, throttled back though it was, was moving at a minimum speed of between ninety and a hundred miles an hour. True he dropped one of a stick of ten or twenty: but even if every man cleared the Dakota, the Albemarle, the Halifax or the Stirling in no more than eight seconds, a very fast time indeed, forty to fifty yards separated each of them by the time they hit the ground. And forty or fifty yards could be a long way when the night was dark and the dropping zone many miles behind the enemy's line.

'I landed alone in the corner of a field, bounded by tall, dark trees, throwing dense shadows over the point where I lay desperately struggling to free myself from the rigging lines. No use trying to contact my men. They would all be scattered. . . .' 'The next thing I knew was that I was sitting in a field of Brussels sprouts, completely alone. I could neither hear nor see a soul. . . . I cried, rather weakly, "Vive la France", and stumbled off into the mist.' The solitude of parachute soldiers during the first and most vital moments of their arrival on the field of battle is emphasised again and again in their letters and reminiscences. Only when they reached the rendezvous, the gully with trees at Bruneval, the church at Ranville, the south-west corner of the wood at Arnhem, or wherever it might be, did they find company—if they were lucky—and become an organised unit. Then indeed they shewed themselves to be superlative infantrymen, a conspicuous example being the feat of the 9th Battalion, which destroyed the highly-defended coastal battery at Merville with no more than a hundred and fifty out of the six hundred and thirty-five officers and men dropped for the purpose.

In two other respects the difference between the Parachute Regiment and those of the Line was marked. The simple fact that a parachute soldier had to use his parachute to reach the scene of action inevitably increased the hazards of his training. Though accidents at Ringway were few, if the total number of men who passed unscathed through the school is taken into account, yet there were more of these than there were at any infantry training centre even at the redoubtable Commando Depot at Achnacarry. The same was true of the exercises and rehearsals which were an integral part of training and operations. 'It was during "Exercise Bluebell",' runs the history of the 8th Battalion, 'in June 1943, that one stick received their signal to jump just as the plane passed over the Firth of Tay. This resulted in two officers . . . and five other ranks . . . being drowned.' The men of the 1st Battalion disliked 'demonstrations' because they added to the normal risks of training. An injury rate of five per cent of a battalion during the period of initial jumps was not considered high.

But first and last the main difference was that the parachute soldier, like the commando soldier, was a volunteer. The National Service Act might send him in company with the rest of his age group to the colours; it could not send him to Hardwick. If he went there, it was by his own deliberate choice. In this, as in some other respects, he resembled French's Old Contemptibles and Kitchener's First Hundred Thousand of the First World War.

Therefore, strive as they might and do, to pretend the contrary, the officers and other ranks of the Parachute Regiment were by the nature of their calling men apart. This fact made them all the more anxious to be normal in all other respects. In the beginning they acquired a reputation for undue pride in their toughness which was for the most part undeserved. 'There were always a few men,' says one who has known them from the beginning, 'particularly in the early stages, who thought that being tough meant being untidy, quarrelsome and getting drunk. These people formed a very small minority of the whole but they did the Parachute Regiment a great deal of harm and were, by their red berets, very conspicuous. It was extraordinarily difficult to convince such men that such behaviour could do the regiment so much harm. I used to find it difficult to understand how a unit, which could turn out on parade in the best possible order, could include men who consistently behaved badly in the local town. We managed to eradicate most of this trouble by the end of the war, but it always had to be carefully watched.' This fault in a few—and that it was a very few the bearing of the regiment on the battlefields of North Africa, Sicily, Italy, Normandy, Holland, and Germany affords ample proof—was again due to the fact that the individual character of each man had to be studied and developed, while at the same time the corporate spirit, as in all fighting services, had to be inspired and cherished. Since not a few had been attracted to the regiment consciously or unconsciously by a desire to prove to themselves and to their friends that they were of that happy breed which can conquer fear however strongly it may beset them, this was not entirely easy.

The great majority of persons, who have never been called upon to don a parachute and who never will be, must not forget that in doing so the parachutist had to master a double dread—the fear of death or injury through jumping, and the fear that attacks any normal soldier when he finds himself under fire. It is impossible to say what was the normal reaction to parachute jumping; but the opinion of Lieutenant-Colonel John Frost, who landed with his men in France, North Africa, Sicily and at Arnhem is certainly as good as another's and probably represents what the ordinary parachutist thought about the business. 'Personally,' he says, 'I think each man feels differently about it, and then again, I think one feels differently about each jump, until one comes to regard it as a fairly normal thing to do. In just the same way that the novice feels extremely nervous before riding in his first point-to-point, and fiddles anxiously with his girths and stirrup leathers, so does the newly trained parachutist wait anxiously for the flight to begin and, while waiting, will test and tug at his harness until his clammy hands grow tired of futile exercise. How differently the veteran approaches the matter. He is full of confidence and nonchalantly picks up the first 'chute which comes to hand; he has it fitted in a trice and he never has to pay that last visit to the lavatory which betokens nervous strain. In the aircraft he has his chewing gum or tobacco handy, and once the plane is airborne he sits down quietly to read the morning paper. However, to some men jumping was a continual strain and after a time they found it almost impossible to continue. In the beginning a good many men who joined the regiment were very highly strung and a fair percentage suffered from an inferiority complex. To them parachuting was a heaven-sent opportunity to justify their existence, and there is no doubt that the characters of many of them developed immeasurably as a direct result of their suppressing their fears.' This is a reasoned judgment and is probably as close to what most of them felt as it is possible to go.

Like the commandos, the Parachute Regiment suffered from the misplaced enthusiasm of a section of the press. Its officers and men were only too often depicted as persons without mercy or scruple, with whom Bill Sykes would have felt at home. This distortion deceived many otherwise well-informed citizens. 'Once when I was having tea with the wife of a retired Major-General,' writes an officer of the Parachute Regiment, 'the assembled company was horrified to hear that I was a parachutist and my hostess informed me that she knew on very good authority that a number of Dartmoor convicts had been released to join the Regiment.' This was bad enough: but what, perhaps, was worse was 'the reaction of the chauffeur of an aunt of mine . . . who said bluntly, "So you are one of them paratroops now, are you, sir? Well, I reckon that's the quickest way of being taken prisoner that has yet been invented".'

Such publicity did the Regiment harm, for it created an impression utterly false, which was only dispelled by its own deeds in North Africa, when the admirable dispatches of correspondents like Alan Moorehead and Christopher Buckley redressed the balance.

For, in truth, the members of the regiment were neither the thugs depicted by the less reputable organs of the press nor the *preux chevaliers* certain of their more ardent well-wishers maintained. They were hard and tough and blunt as was required by their calling, though more than one German officer paid tribute to the chivalry of 'the Red Devils'. Such qualities were necessary for survival in men who might, and very often did, find themselves fighting alone, or almost alone, far away behind the lines of the enemy or thrust out perilously as at Arnhem beyond those of the Allies.

That some, indeed many, of them believed that they belonged to a *Corps d'Elite* is certainly no discredit except when it leads, as it did on occasion, to boasting and braggadocio. From these defects no army, no corps, no regiment is ever wholly free ; but the men of the Parachute Regiment were certainly no worse than their comrades in the ranks of the Commandos, the Brigade of Guards, the Rifle Regiments, the Royal Marines, or, for that matter, in those of any regiment with a pride and a tradition to maintain. Indeed, for the parachutists *esprit de corps* was perhaps not altogether easy to acquire and cherish, for they were drawn from units in which it was more often than not taken for granted, and became members of an organisation very new and quite untried, the product of warfare in its most modern and most unusual form. The fact that their instructors and, later, their officers never ceased to proclaim that it was far more important to be a good soldier than a good parachutist, and that the silken canopy supporting them for a few brief moments was merely a somewhat novel means to an end, did much to counteract any tendency to arrogance.

One attribute, wholly admirable, was soon noticed. Relations between officers and men were exceptionally close and cordial. Each knew himself to be the complement of the other and behaved accordingly. When, for example, in July 1945 Hill left the 3rd Parachute Brigade for another appointment, he said farewell to, among other units, the 1st Canadian Parachute Battalion who were already aboard the train which was to take them on the first stage of their journey home. They would not allow the train to depart until every officer and man had shaken him by the hand. Lathbury, Pearson, Frost, Luard, Tatham-Warter and half a hundred more, some alive, some dead, were equally beloved or revered, and the latest example of Henry V's band of brothers at Agincourt was to be found in North Africa, in Italy, in Normandy, in Holland and across the Rhine, where-ever members of the regiment were met together in battle. The parachutists were also united in bonds of close friendship with the glider pilots and glider-borne regiments, the Devons, the South Staffordshires, and the rest who with them shared the privilege of wearing the red beret.

As to the value of the Parachute Regiment in the field there can be no two opinions. Used at the outset in minor though important roles, they first shewed their true potentialities at Primosole. Up till then some may have regarded them as an expensive luxury, though the campaign they fought in North Africa should have dispelled any such illusion. But after Sicily, where, had they been used with greater foresight, they might well have been able to shorten the campaign by at least a fortnight, they were seen to be indispensable. When Leigh-Mallory, in charge of all the air forces for the invasion of Europe, expressed the gravest fears for the fate of the American airborne troops detailed to land on the right flank of the sea-borne invaders, the Supreme Commander came to the conclusion that 'to cancel their operations would inevitably mean cancelling the landing on Utah (the westermost) Beach, or I would condemn the assaulting forces there to even greater probability of disaster than was predicted for the airborne divisions'. Nothing could be more definite than that.

The protection afforded by the 6th Airborne Division and the commando to the left flank of 21st Army Group could probably have been secured by no other means. Certainly the seizure of the vital area to the north-east of Caen by parachute and air-borne troops, and the stubborn manner in which they clung to it in the face of the most determined efforts to dislodge them, provided that firm pivot on which the Allied armies turned to achieve the victory of France. Montgomery's plan depended on the creation and maintenance of that pivot, and it was to the airborne forces and the commandos that these were entrusted. The drop beyond the Rhine made the swift advance of the 21st

Army Group all the swifter. These two instances are enough to shew the importance of parachute troops in the complicated business of modern war.

The greatest value of the Parachute Regiment and its glider-borne comrades lay in its very existence. Airborne troops, until the battle is joined, and they are committed as part of an enterprise designed to overthrow the enemy, are an ever-present menace which causes him to disperse his forces and to condemn large numbers of his men to a defensive and therefore to a passive role. When the parachute units are sent into the fight they are a grave threat because of their very high fighting qualities, and the fact, among others, that to be surrounded is to them of little consequence. They are trained to deal with just such a situation, and any resulting disorder is more often to be found in the ranks of their opposite than in their own.

Perhaps the greatest drawback to their use was the large number of casualties they were liable to suffer. It is on this note, melancholy though it be, that this record of their achievements must end. Of the fourteen battalions of the Parachute Regiment which saw service in North Africa or Europe six were wiped out. They were the 1st, 2nd, 3rd, the 10th, the 11th, and the 156th, and they met their fate, unflinching, at Arnhem. The 1st, 2nd and 3rd were reformed. Altogether one hundred and ninety-eight officers and two thousand one hundred and twenty-four other ranks belonging to the Regiment were killed, on all fronts. Among them were ten officers and one hundred and twenty other ranks of the 1st Canadian Parachute Battalion. The names of those who fell are inscribed on vellum in a book to be seen in St. Martin's in the Felds.

Heavy casualties in the ranks of picked troops were an un-happy feature of warfare long before Leonidas held Thermopylae and, as such, have always been accepted. Among the para-chutists, representing as they did an entirely new departure from existing forms and practice, losses were liable, perhaps inevitably, to be especially severe. For to the ordinary hazards of combat were added those inseparable from a novel mode of transport to the battlefield. Unarmoured aircraft, which the Parachute Regiment used from first to last, were a relatively easy mark for anti-aircraft guns, especially at the moment of the drop, when the pilot had to throttle back and to fly on a straight course. The parachutists in the air and on the ground were entirely vulnerable until they had formed up and begun to move to their allotted task. If, as at Arnhem, they were compelled to fulfil it not for forty-eight hours, generally considered the maximum period of time during which they could be left unsupported, but for nine days, the consequences could not but be of the gravest.

Yet when all is said and done, when the number of highly trained and gallant men put out of action on any one occasion is computed and set against the end achieved, it can be maintained with truth and justice that the losses were not too high. They only became so when as in North Africa and Italy battalions of The Parachute Regiment were used not for tasks for which they had been specially trained, but as infantry of the Line. To this use, unavoidable though it may have been, a proportion of their heavy casualties was due.

One thing is certain. There was never a complaint from the officers and men of the regiment. From first to last they were soldiers leading the life of soldiers with all that that implied— the smooth: good food and billets, long periods, broken by intervals of leave, when training was their only occupation, a sense of comradeship more strongly developed, perhaps, than in other branches of the Service, the right to wear the red beret and blue wings with the consequent prestige and repute, so heartening to the young soldier, or indeed to any man who puts himself in peril on the battlefield—the rough: the drop on the dark night into enemy-held territory with a far from even chance of landing at the chosen spot, the fight with light weapons against odds and a foe strong in tanks and heavy guns, the hope of relief more and more deferred as one by one the garrison, each a comrade of trust and proof, died hard at Primosole or the bridge at Arnhem. Rewards and hazards alike, they accepted them with a quiet mind, and their motto might have been that of the Roman legion, *utrinque paratus*, ready to face good or ill fortune. For were they not volunteers, every man of them, members of that select company of the brave whose high courage constrains them to go

> 'Always a little further; it may be
> Beyond that last blue mountain barred with snow,
> Across that angry or that glimmering sea'

to reach a kingdom of the spirit they alone can understand, for they alone are worthy to cross its borders?

Epilogue

On 19th July 1950 the 1st, 2nd and 3rd Battalions, The Parachute Regiment, were drawn up on the Queen's Parade at Aldershot. They were under their commanding officers Lieutenant-Colonels C. H. P. Harington, D.S.O., M.C., G. W. White, M.B.E. and W. D. Tighe-Wood, M.C., respectively. The officer commanding the parade was Colonel K. T. Darling, D.S.O., O.B.E., officer commanding Airborne Forces Depot. At 11.30 hours, to the sound of a royal salute, His Majesty King George VI, accompanied by his queen, Elizabeth, arrived to present the King's and the Regimental Colours to each battalion. These were first consecrated by the Reverend Canon F. Ll. Hughes, C.B.E., M.C., T.D., M.A., Chaplain-General to the Forces.

The ceremony took place in the presence of Field-Marshal The Viscount Montgomery of Alamein, K.G., G.C.B., D.S.O., Colonel Commandant of the Regiment, of Lieutenant-General Sir Frederick Browning, K.B.E., C.B., D.S.O., Lieutenant-General Sir Richard Gale, K.B.E., C.B., D.S.O., M.C., Lieutenant-General Sir Kenneth Crawford, K.C.B., M.C., and a large company of past and present members of the Regiment.

After the service of Consecration, the King presented the Colours in turn to the three battalions on parade and then spoke as follows:

"Colonel Darling, Officers, Warrant Officers, Non-Commissioned Officers and Men of the Parachute Regiment:

I am very glad to be here to-day to present you with your first Colours, and to inspect the Parachute Regiment for the first time.

I have been deeply impressed by what I have seen, and I congratulate you on your fine bearing and drill.

This has been no surprise to me, for I have watched the growth of your Regiment from its earliest days, and I recognize in this parade the keenness and spirit which have brought you through the perils of so many difficult operations. Yours has not been a long history. Only a short time separated your first raids on the Tragino Aqueduct and the Bruneval radar station from the fighting in North Africa and Sicily; very soon afterwards, in the Sixth Airborne Division you were adding your weight to those great blows which fell upon the enemy in Normandy, at Arnhem and on the Rhine, and which brought the European War to an end. There were other battles and much varied training, for you had to fight not only as parachutists, but often for months at a time as infantrymen. The volunteers who came from all arms of the Service to fill your ranks had much to learn: they learned it quickly and they learned it well.

These Colours which I have just presented to your three Battalions are the traditional symbol of a soldier's loyalty. The qualities which they represent and call forth are those which are common to and, indeed, essential to all good soldiers in all ages: they are qualities which you have shown that you possess alike in war and peace.

I am fully confident that you will maintain the high standard which you have already established, and that these Colours will always be safe in your hands."

The occasion was historic for, as far as is known, there is no record in the proud annals of the British Army of three battalions of the same Regiment receiving their first Colours on the same day from the same hands.

The summer sun burned, the bands played, the men with their red berets marched past to the tune of their regimental march, "The Ride of the Valkyries."

It may well be that they were not alone. Unseen but alive in the thoughts of many then present were those who had fought and died at Bruneval, at Oudna, at Djebel Mansour and the battlefields of North Africa, at the Primosole Bridge, and in the long peninsula of Italy, at Merville, Ranville, Bréville and the villages and towns of Normandy, at Arnhem and at Athens, in the Ardennes and, as the victory they had done so much to secure shone in the East, in the fields beyond the Rhine and along the triumphant road to the Baltic.

The drums rolled above the crisp rhythm of marching feet; the colours flamed in the sunshine. It was a fitting end to a glorious beginning.

APPENDIX I

VICTORIA CROSSES WON BY THE PARACHUTE REGIMENT

Lieutenant John Hellington Grayburn
2nd Battalion, The Parachute Regiment

For supreme courage, leadership, and devotion to duty.

Lieutenant Grayburn was a platoon commander of the Parachute Battalion which was dropped on 17th September 1944, with the task of seizing and holding the bridge over the Rhine at Arnhem.

The north end of the bridge was captured and, early in the night, Lieutenant Grayburn was ordered to assault and capture the southern end with his platoon. He led his platoon on to the bridge and began the attack with the utmost determination, but the platoon was met with a hail of fire from two 20-mm. quick-firing guns, and from the machine-guns of an armoured car. Almost at once Lieutenant Grayburn was shot through the shoulder. Although there was no cover on the bridge, and in spite of his wound, Lieutenant Grayburn continued to press forward with the greatest dash and bravery until casualties became so heavy that he was ordered to withdraw. He directed the withdrawal from the bridge personally and was himself the last man to come off the embankment into comparative cover.

Later, his platoon was ordered to occupy a house which was vital to the defence of the bridge and he personally organised the occupation of the house.

Throughout the next day and night the enemy made ceaseless attacks on the house, using not only infantry with mortars and machine-guns but also tanks and self-propelled guns. The house was very exposed and difficult to defend and the fact that it did not fall to the enemy must be attributed to Lieutenant Grayburn's great courage and inspiring leadership. He constantly exposed himself to the enemy's fire whilst moving among and encouraging his platoon, and seemed completely oblivious to danger.

On 19th September 1944 the enemy renewed his attacks, which

increased in intensity, as the house was vital to the defence of the bridge. All attacks were repulsed, due to Lieutenant Grayburn's valour and skill in organising and encouraging his men, until eventually the house was set on fire and had to be evacuated.

Lieutenant Grayburn then took command of elements of all arms, including the remainder of his own company, and re-formed them into a fighting force. He spent the night organising the defensive position to cover the approaches to the bridge.

On 20th September 1944 he extended his defence by a series of fighting patrols, which prevented the enemy getting access to the houses in the vicinity, the occupation of which would have prejudiced the defence of the bridge. This forced the enemy to bring up tanks, which brought Lieutenant Grayburn's position under such heavy fire that he was forced to withdraw to an area further north. The enemy now attempted to lay demolition charges under the bridge and the situation was now critical. Realising this, Lieutenant Grayburn organised and led a fighting patrol, which drove the enemy off temporarily, and gave time for the fuses to be removed. He was again wounded, this time in the back, but refused to be evacuated.

Finally an enemy tank, against which Lieutenant Grayburn had no defence, approached so close to his position that it became untenable. He then stood up in full view of the tank and personally directed the withdrawal of his men to the main defensive perimeter to which he had been ordered.

He was killed that night.

From the evening of 17th September until the night of 20th 1944, a period of over three days, Lieutenant Grayburn led his men with supreme gallantry and determination. Although in pain and weakened by his wounds, short of food and without sleep, his courage never flagged. There is no doubt that, had it not been for this officer's inspiring leadership and personal bravery, the Arnhem bridge could never have been held for this time.

Captain L. E. Queripel
10th Battalion, The Parachute Regiment

At Arnhem on 19th September 1944 Captain Queripel was acting as company commander of a composite company composed of men of three parachute battalions.

At 14.00 hours on that day his company were advancing along a main road which runs on an embankment towards Arnhem. The advance was conducted under continuous machine-gun fire, which at one period became so heavy that the company became split up on either side of the road and suffered considerable loss. Captain Queripel at once proceeded to reorganise his force, crossing and recrossing the road whilst doing so under extremely heavy and accurate fire. During this period he carried a wounded sergeant to the Regimental Aid Post under fire and was himself wounded in the face.

Having reorganised his force, Captain Queripel personally led a party of men against a strong point holding up the advance. This strong point consisted of a captured British anti-tank gun, and two machine-guns. Despite the extremely heavy fire directed at him, Captain Queripel succeeded in killing the crews of the machine-guns and recapturing the anti-tank gun. As a result of this the advance was able to continue.

Later in the same day Captain Queripel found himself cut off with a small party of men and took up a position in a ditch. By this time he had received further wounds in both arms. Regardless of his wounds and the very heavy mortar and Spandau fire, he continued to inspire his men to resist with hand grenades, pistols and the few remaining rifles. On at least one occasion he picked up and threw back at the enemy a stick grenade, which had landed in the ditch.

As, however, the enemy pressure increased, Captain Queripel decided that it was impossible to hold the position longer and ordered his men to withdraw. Despite their protests, he insisted on remaining behind to cover their withdrawal with his automatic pistol and a few remaining hand grenades. This is the last occasion on which he was seen.

During the whole of a period of nine hours of confused and bitter fighting Captain Queripel displayed the highest standard of gallantry under most difficult and trying circumstances. His courage, leadership and devotion to duty were an inspiration to all.

Corporal Frederick George Topham
1st Canadian Parachute Battalion

On 24th March 1945 Corporal Topham, a medical orderly, parachuted with his battalion on to a strongly defended area east of the Rhine. At about 11.00 hours, whilst treating casualties sustained in the drop, a cry for help came from a wounded man in the open. Two medical orderlies from a field ambulance went out to this man in succession, but both were killed as they knelt beside the casualty.

Without hesitation, and on his own initiative, Corporal Topham went forward through intense fire to replace the orderlies who had been killed before his eyes. As he worked on the wounded man, he was himself shot through the nose. In spite of severe bleeding and intense pain, he never faltered in his task. Having completed immediate first aid, he carried the wounded man steadily and slowly back though continuous fire to the shelter of a wood.

During the next two hours Corporal Topham refused all offers of medical help for his own wound. He worked most devotedly throughout this period to bring wounded in, showing complete disregard for the heavy and accurate enemy fire. It was only when all casualties had been cleared that he consented to his own wound being treated.

His immediate evacuation was ordered, but he interceded so earnestly on his own behalf that he was eventually allowed to return to duty.

On his way back to his company he came across a carrier which had received a direct hit. Enemy mortar bombs were still dropping around, the carrier itself was burning fiercely and its own mortar ammunition was exploding. An experienced officer on the spot had warned all not to approach the carrier.

Corporal Topham, however, immediately went out alone in spite of the blasting ammunition and enemy fire and rescued the three occupants of the carrier. He brought these men back across the open, and although one died almost immediately afterwards, he arranged for the evacuation of the other two, who undoubtedly owe their lives to him.

This N.C.O. showed gallantry of the highest order. For six hours, most of the time in great pain, he performed a series of acts of outstanding bravery, and his magnificent and selfless courage inspired all those who witnessed it.

APPENDIX II

The Red Devils

Towards the end of the campaign in North Africa, Brigadier Flavell received the following message from General Alexander:

To: 1 Para Bde
From: Main First Army   045   17   ...

Following message received from 18 Army Group. Quote. For Comd 1 Para Bde from GENERAL ALEXANDER. Now that it has been possible to relieve the Parachute Brigade who have for so long a time played a most valuable role in the north I should like to express my thanks to and admiration for every officer and N.C.O. and man for the conspicuously successful part they have taken in the recent fighting. They have proved their mastery over the enemy, who have a very wholesome respect for this famous brigade which is best described in their own words for them quote red devil unquote. Unquote.

NEL BESTSELLERS

NEL P.O. BOX 11, FALMOUTH, TR10 9EN, CORNWALL

For U.K. & Eire: customers should include to cover postage, 15p for the first book plus 5p per copy for each additional book ordered, up to a maximum charge of 50p.

For Overseas customers & B.F.P.O.: customers should include to cover postage, 20p for the first book and 10p per copy for each additional book.

Name..

Address ....

....

Title... (MAY)

THE GREEN BERET

by Hilary St. George Saunders

The blood and guts of Commandos at war.

'I hope some of you guys will return. You'll be useful for the next show.'

With these words the Commandos' officer sent his heroic, devil-may-care fighting men into the direct line of machine-gun fire on the beaches of Sicily.

For their raids and battles far behind enemy lines in the Mediterranean, North Africa and Burma the men in the Green Beret have become a legend.

This book tells the *truth* behind the legend!

THE NEW ENGLISH LIBRARY

COLDITZ
by Reinhold Eggers

Colditz. Easily the best-known of all the German P.O.W. prison camps. A fortress where only the most dangerous and habitual escapers were confined. The Germans thought it was an excellent idea to try and keep all of their habitual escapees in the one jail.

During the latter part of the war the author was in charge of security at the prison and he reveals for the first time the German side, just how surprising the result was of their plan. The book is both entertaining and exciting. It is one of the finest and most unusual stories to come out of the Second World War.

'By far the best account of this extraordinary camp.' –
Airey Neave, M.P., in the *Sunday Telegraph*

'A must for escapologists Crammed with the techniques of escaping. I was impressed by the consistent accuracy through the book.' –
P. R. Reid (author of 'Colditz Story') in the *Evening Standard*

'Reveals a profound, unexpected knowledge of British P.O.W. psychology. Will provide great entertainment. More amusing than I thought possible.' –
Douglas Bader in the *News of the World*

THE NEW ENGLISH LIBRARY

GESTAPO
by Edward Crankshaw

The mastery of the Gestapo extended from the Atlantic to the Volga, the North Cape to the Mediterranean and it held Europe in an iron grip.

The Gestapo, under its fanatical leader, Himmler, was moulded into a highly efficient, ruthless, professional corps whose task was to penetrate every aspect of private and public life. Its aim was to seek out resistance to the Nazi regime.

The power of the Gestapo lay in its inhumanity to its victims, a cruelty unparalleled in the history of modern Europe.

THE NEW ENGLISH LIBRARY